Genealogy Online

About the Author

Elizabeth Powell Crowe has been writing for more than 30 years. Her previous editions of *Genealogy Online* have sold a combined total of nearly 200,000 copies. Crowe has been a contributing editor for *Computer Currents* magazine and the author of numerous articles in both popular and technical publications. Her work has appeared in *Civil War Times*, *PC World*, *C|Net*, *Digital Genealogist*, and other publications and websites. She has been a guest on WashingtonPost.com's chat with Jacquelin D. Salmon, DearMYRYTLE's Family History Internet podcast, and other national news programs. Ms. Crowe often makes speeches and conducts workshops on online genealogy; she has been a presenter at the Institute of Genealogy and Historical Research at Samford University and at GENTECH, and she has edited genealogy publications. She lives in Navarre, Florida, with her husband, Mark, and Sirius the Dog Star.

Genealogy Online
Ninth Edition

Elizabeth Powell Crowe

New York   Chicago   San Francisco
Lisbon   London   Madrid   Mexico City
Milan   New Delhi   San Juan
Seoul   Singapore   Sydney   Toronto

The McGraw·Hill Companies

Library of Congress Cataloging-in-Publication Data

Crowe, Elizabeth Powell.
    Genealogy online / Elizabeth Powell Crowe. —9th ed.
        p.   cm.
    ISBN 978-0-07-174037-1 (alk. paper)
    1. Genealogy—Data processing.   2. Genealogy—Computer network
resources—Handbooks, manuals, etc.   3. Internet—Handbooks, manuals, etc.   I. Title.
    CS21.C67   2011
    025.06'9291—dc22   2010032502

McGraw-Hill books are available at special quantity discounts to use as premiums and sales promotions, or for use in corporate training programs. To contact a representative, please e-mail us at bulksalesmcgraw-hill.com.

Genealogy Online, Ninth Edition

1 2 3 4 5 6 7 8 9 0   WFR WFR   1 0 9 8 7 6 5 4 3 2 1 0
ISBN   978-0-07-174037-1
MHID   0-07-174037-6

Sponsoring Editor
  Roger Stewart
Editorial Supervisor
  Patty Mon
Project Manager
  Vipra Fauzdar, Glyph International
Acquisitions Coordinator
  Joya Anthony
Copy Editor
  Lisa McCoy
Proofreader
  Claire Splan

Indexer
  Karin Arrigoni
Production Supervisor
  George Anderson
Composition
  Glyph International
Illustration
  Glyph International
Art Director, Cover
  Jeff Weeks
Cover Designer
  William Voss

This book is dedicated to my mother, Frances Spencer Powell
1926–2007

Contents at a Glance

Contents

PART III
The Nitty Gritty: Places to Find Names, Dates, and Places

Acknowledgments

As with any book, this one was made possible by the efforts of many people besides the author. First, I would like to thank each and every person mentioned in this book, as I obviously could not have done it without all of you.

Special thanks go all my genealogy friends on Facebook, Amy Coffin, Bill Ammons, Carly Stapleton, Cheryl Rothwell, Dick Eastman, Jane Fraser, Jeanne Henry, Jeri Weber, Leland Meitzler, Linda Mullikin of the FHC in Navarre, Liz Kelley Kerstens, Myra Vanderpool Gormley, Pat Richley, Randy Hooser, Roger Stewart, Russ Worthington, and all the staff at McGraw-Hill/Professional. Immense gratitude is due to all my family and friends, who were more than patient with me while I was writing this book.

Most of all I want to thank my mother, Frances Spencer Powell, who died January 8, 2007.

Introduction

"I've gotten more genealogy done in one year on Prodigy than I did in 20 years on my own!" my mother exclaimed some 18 years ago. This quote, from a genealogy veteran, shows how technology has changed even this age-old and classic hobby. The mind-boggling mass of data needed to trace one's family tree has finally found a knife to whittle it down to size: the computer.

The early editions of this book assumed you knew how to do genealogy but not how to use the Internet. Since that time, commercial online services and the Internet have added, expanded, revised, and changed what they offer, as well as how and when they offer it. From having to use a dial-up connection over a modem in 1992 to cable and satellite connections to today's iPhone, we've come a long way. Social networking and text and multimedia messaging make sharing your data easy and almost irresistible. So in this edition, the author assumes you know most Internet technologies and programs, and that you want to know how to use them to do your genealogy. I've gone from a "what button to push" approach to a "why would you want to use that" one.

The potential for finding clues, data, and other researchers looking for your same family names has increased exponentially in the last decade. Since 2000, push technology, streaming video, blogs, podcasts, social networking, and indexed document scans have radically changed what can be found on the Internet and how we search for it. If you feel you need formal instruction in researching family history, online courses, from basic self-paced text to college-level instruction, can now make that happen.

In short, online genealogy has never been better and it's a good time to try your hand at it!

Bill Ammons' Story

How does online genealogy work? Let's look at a case study.

Bill Ammons is a friend of mine who used a few hints on online genealogy from me to break down a brick wall in his genealogy research. Here is what he wrote to me about his quest:

> "I started my genealogy research 16 months ago with the name of the only grandparent I knew from my childhood. The journey has taken me from knowing a very small family to discovering an enormously large family. I have learned a lot about history, our society, family secrets, and what not to say in e-mails, even jokingly to family. I have hit roadblocks and gotten through some, while others are still being researched."

> Some roadblocks will never be resolved, he noted, as you will discover that documents were destroyed in the Civil War or in mysterious fires at courthouses or newspaper offices. However, on your journey, you, too, will become a collector of websites, books on dead people, and American history.

> "Roadblocks are very interesting challenges, in that one must begin to be creative in their research to find clues to get them through the roadblocks," Bill said. "If the information on the Internet leads to roadblocks, then try going to the county historical society office and then to the county courthouse to look for wills, land documents, Bible records, newspaper articles, and even personal letters. I have found old Bible records at the historical societies that have provided clues to names I was uncertain of and even provided insights into cemetery records. I started my journey with a simple posting to the Horry County, South Carolina Historical Society home page (www.hchsonline.org) (see Figure I-1).

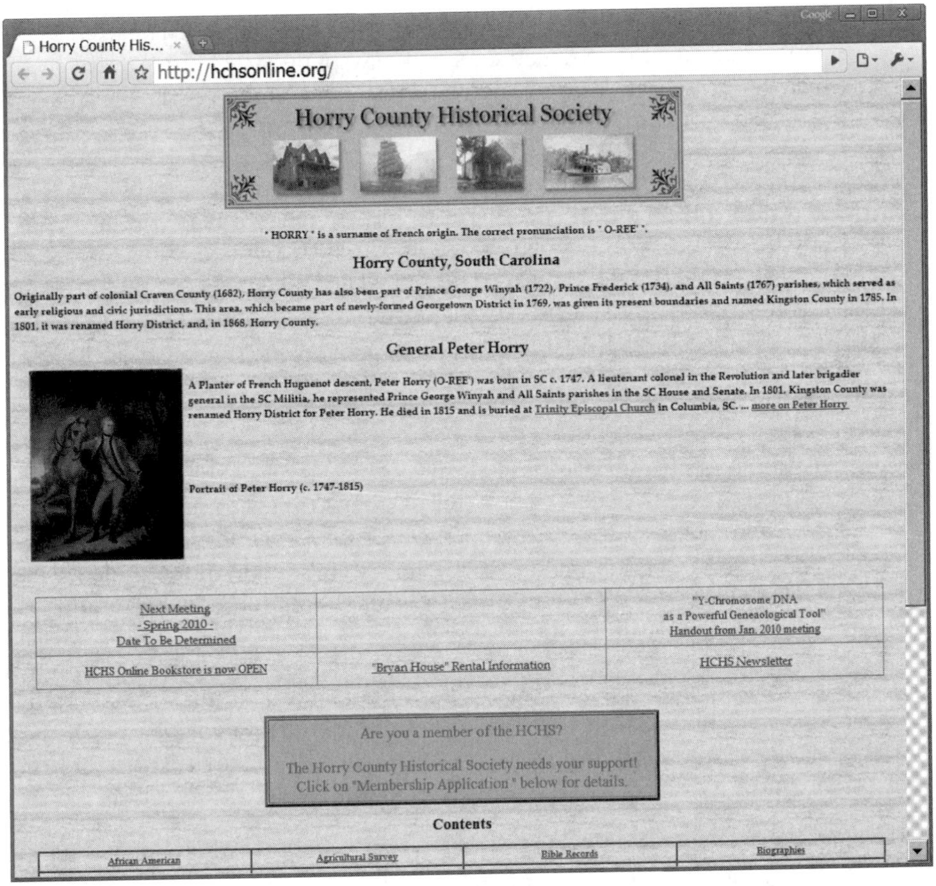

FIGURE I-1. *Local organizations, such as the Horry County South Carolina Historical Society, can be a big help in online genealogy research.*

"From a simple posting on the message board of the four family surnames (Ammons, Denton, Martin, and Tompkins), I received a response the next day that solved the Martin branch of my tree to 1810. My cousin is, in fact, one of the contributors of documents to the Horry Historic Society Site. Sometimes, one can find a new family member and find genealogy at the same time," Bill said.

"The next day brought another surprise when I received an e-mail from a gentleman in Atlanta and he provided the Denton branch of my family tree. His mother was my grandmother's sister. I never met my grandmother's sisters," he continued. "But this posting yielded another new family member and also information about the Denton family as a bonus. This family member pointed me to documents and newspaper articles that were available online that provided personal insight as to the possibilities that my grandmother and grandfather were Native Americans.

"Then I had to really get into the digging mindset to start finding information and documents on the other surnames. The Ammons surname has taken me from the coast of South Carolina to the Appalachian Mountains and back to Sampson County, North Carolina. I never had any idea that the Ammons family came from North Carolina, because I grew up with the understanding that the Ammons were 'Black Irish' that migrated to South Carolina. The real surprise has been in the documentation I have obtained that does not support this idea we were 'Black Irish.'"

Census reports from Ancestry.com (www.ancestry.com) were well worth the monthly cost for the subscription, Bill said. These census reports are searchable and easily accessed, even with a dial-up connection. The census reports provide a road map of where the family lived in different decades. Also, the census reports tell something about the family's living conditions, employment, education, and neighbors. From these documents, he was able to trace the family from 1780 to the 1920s. He found the Ammons family as early as 1780 in Sampson County, North Carolina. Next, they migrated to Marlboro County, South Carolina, after the American Revolution. In the next generation, the children migrated to Macon and Cherokee counties of North Carolina.

Bill found documents from the American Revolution at Wallace State College in Hanceville, Alabama. This community college has a tremendous records area on the American Revolution and the Civil War, as well as access to the 2.5 million microfilm reels from the Genealogical Society of Utah. The college also has courses in family and regional history. These records showed Bill that his Ammons family received a land grant in Marlboro County because they served in the American Revolution.

Using Cyndi's List (www.cyndislist.com) to help search the Native American connections, Bill found it a great help when researching roots that are connected to the federally recognized tribes. The issue of researching Native American heritage is a separate and interesting journey, which can involve discovering your genetic markers, such as Asian shovel teeth, anatomic knot, and genetically transmitted diseases.

Another helpful resource was the Melungeons page (www.melungeon.org), he said. "Some people are really confused about this group of folks that lived in North Carolina. The more I read about the forgotten Portuguese, the more interesting this hidden part of America's history became in tracking the family history," Bill said.

Bill's journey brought him to the Waccamaw Indian People of South Carolina and the Croatans of Sampson, County North Carolina. He is a tribal member of the Waccamaw Indian People of South Carolina. Among the helpful sites was the University of North Carolina at Chapel Hill Library's "Documenting the American South" page (http://docsouth .unc.edu) (see Figure I-2). This site has an HTML version of a book called *The Croatan Indians of Sampson County, North Carolina. Their Origin and Racial Status. A Plea for Separate Schools,* written in 1916 by George Edwin Butler.

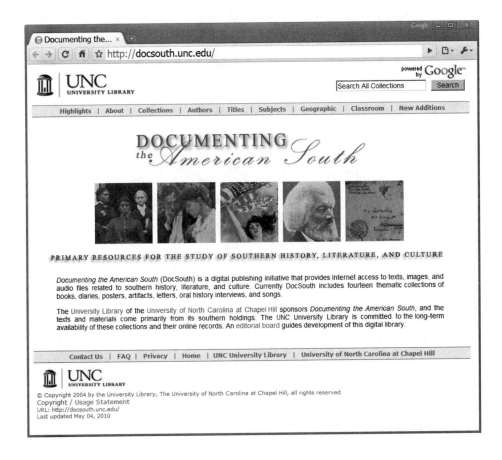

FIGURE I-2. *"Documenting the American South" has texts and materials primarily from the southern holdings of the University of North Carolina.*

The online book was a jewel of a find in this surname search. The book discusses the Croatans' possible connection with the lost colonists of Roanoke, which led Bill Ammons to research the census records again. The census places his family in the correct place at the correct time to strengthen this argument of where the family originated. Currently, Bill plans to continue the research focused on the county, state, and federal records of the time. A big plus was the photos in the book, with people who resemble family members who Bill knows today!

"In my research for records, I have been to the North Carolina Archives in Raleigh, North Carolina. (A word to the wise; don't take any ink pens and/or briefcases; you will not be allowed into the records area.) Believe me, it is a tremendous treat to see the historical records that remain. The information you can discover is well worth the frustration," he said.

As you can see, Bill Ammon's journey took him to many different online and offline resources:

- ♦ Search sites and search engines such as Cyndi's List to find online information about Native Americans (see Chapter 6)

- ♦ Local college resources for genealogy materials and knowledge (see Chapter 3)

- ♦ Online queries (see Chapters 7 through 11)

- ♦ Vital records from government archives (see Chapter 12)

- ♦ Online libraries (see Chapter 15)

- ♦ Ethnic resources online (see Chapter 17)

- ♦ Ancestry.com (see Chapter 19)

Bill took what he knew from his own immediate family, plus the family legends and gossip, to begin searching for the original records he needed. He went to some resources in person, such as the North Carolina Archives and Wallace State College Library, but only after online research told him that's where he needed to go. This is an excellent example of genealogy online.

Where Computers Come In

Databases, online services, online card catalogs, and bulletin boards are changing the brick wall syndrome, that frustrating phase of any lineage search where the information needed seems unavailable. Genealogists who have faced the challenges and triumphed are online, helping others.

State governments and the federal government have recently started to put data, such as death records, veterans' records, and so on, in machine computer-readable databases, which can then be accessible via the Internet. The Bureau of Land Management, the Library of Congress, and the National Archives and Records Administration are just a few examples of government sites that can help the family historian.

The United States alone has numerous genealogical societies that trace people's descendents. Some of these are national, but many more are local or regional, such as the Tennessee Valley Genealogical Society or the New England Historical Society. Others are specific to certain names. Many patriotic organizations, such as the Daughters of the Confederacy, limit membership to descendants of a particular historical group. Many of these groups offer courses in genealogy, which can help you with online and offline research.

There's no denying that the computer has changed nearly everything in our lives, and the avocation and vocation of genealogical research is no exception. Further, the Internet has added to the ways a genealogist can research, as with Bill Ammons' example, to find those elusive primary sources that are essential to any family history. This book explores many different networks, services, and websites that can help you in your pursuit of your ancestry.

Stories about how online communities have helped people in their genealogical research abound. Here are some examples.

DearMYRTLE Finds a Patriot

DearMYRTLE, a daily genealogy columnist on the Internet, was helping a friend move files, data, and programs from an old computer to a new one. In the course of the conversation, DearMYRTLE's friend wondered aloud what online genealogy could do for him but expressed doubt anything useful could turn up online.

Then the conversation turned to the new United States quarters celebrating the states in the order they joined the Union, specifically, the one with the Delaware patriot Ceasar Rodney on the reverse.

"Who was he?" asked DearMYRTLE's friend.

"All right," DearMYRTLE replied, "let's run a test. Your wife here will look up Ceasar Rodney in the *Encyclopedia Britannica*. You look him up on your old computer using Microsoft Encarta 97. I'll look him up on the Internet with your new computer."

Faster than the other two could use either a book or a CD-ROM, DearMYRTLE found a transcription of a letter from George Washington to Rodney, as shown in Figure I-3.

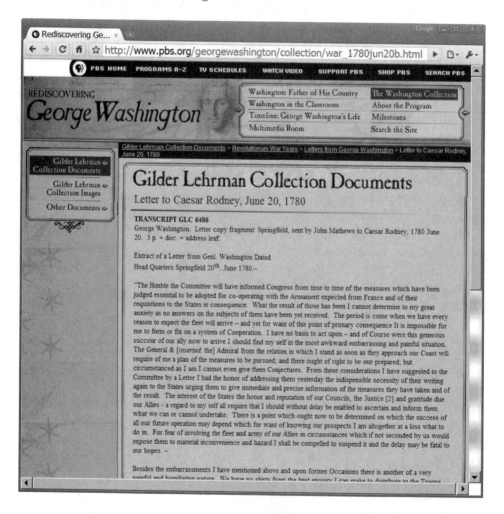

FIGURE I-3. *Online research leads to unexpected treasures, such as this letter from George Washington to Ceasar Rodney on the Historical Society of Delaware site.*

Nancy's Story

Nancy is a friend of mine from high school who knows more about computers and the Internet than I do, but not quite so much about genealogy. When her stepmother died recently, Nancy got a large box of her father's memorabilia and photos. She asked me about genealogy, and I showed her some good genealogy sites on the Internet on her laptop computer.

I didn't think much more about it until she called me a few weeks later in considerable excitement. She had not only found the USGenWeb (www.usgenweb.org) site for her father's home county in Texas, but also that the moderator of the site had known both her father and her grandfather. She was scanning the old photos and e-mailing them to the fellow, and he was identifying people in them left and right. One was of Nancy's grandfather as a child. Another showed her father as a teenager. Every day, the USGenWeb moderator was helping her fill in more holes in her family history.

A Quick Look at This Book

Part I: The Basics   This section of the book will be about general genealogy, in case you are starting from square one, or you have been doing it for a while and want to get better at it.

Chapter 1: Beginning a Genealogy Project   For those just becoming interested in how to research family history, this chapter will go over the steps you need to take. If you have been doing genealogy for a while, still glance at the chapter. Please be sure to take this one idea from the chapter, regardless of your experience level: BACK UP YOUR WORK REGULARLY.

Chapter 2: Software You'll Need   This chapter will help you learn about some of the software that can make genealogy both online and off easier to research and share.

Chapter 3: Genealogy Education   This chapter covers the online and offline ways to improve your level of genealogy expertise. From simple self-guided tours to formal accreditation, you can pursue genealogy education in many ways.

Chapter 4: Online Communities   This is a quick look at online etiquette. We all need to be reminded that on the Internet, common courtesy still applies.

Chapter 5: Ethics, Privacy, and Law in Genealogy   This is a subject that can get sticky as you pursue your family tree. When you find crime, illegitimacy, and surprise ancestors, you are faced with some interesting choices.

Part II: General Genealogy
Chapter 6: Revving Up Search Engines   Oh, those wonderful search engines and edited catalogs of links! Learn how to use them to find the sources you need, from scanned primary documents to uploaded genealogy databases.
Chapter 7: Talk to Me: Twitter, Skype, IM, and Chat   Real-time communication on the Internet, smart phones, and virtual worlds have really changed how genealogists connect to each other.
Chapter 8: Genealogy Mail Lists, Newsletters, and Mail Groups
Worldwide, continual discussions on any topic you can imagine is one more resource. And, of course, an electronic query can be your best tool online!
Chapter 9: Social Networking   Genealogists are using social networking tools to share and educate throughout the Internet. You can too!
Chapter 10: Social Bookmarking and Tagging   Sorting the Internet with bookmarks and tags can keep your research more organized and rewarding.
Chapter 11: Blogging Your Genealogy, Sites, Software, and More
Sooner or later, you will blog. Here's how to do it to further your research into your ancestry!

Part III: The Nitty Gritty: Places to Find Names, Dates, and Places
Chapter 12: Vital Records and Historical Documents   This chapter explores how and where to get those important government documents and certificates.
Chapter 13: The Church of Jesus Christ of Latter-day Saints   The Mormon church has one of the best online databases and library card catalogs on the Web. Learning to use it can save you a lot of time and effort!
Chapter 14: Ellis Island Online: The American Family Immigration History Center   Forty percent of Americans have an ancestor that passed through Ellis Island. This chapter explores how to find out if yours is one, and the best tools to use for the search. (Hint: they aren't on the official Ellis Island site!).
Chapter 15: Online Library Card Catalogs and Services   This is not your grandmother's library with paper cards in a physical catalog. You can search and use databases from your library or at home; libraries truly are information centers now.

Chapter 16: International Genealogy Resources   All our families come from somewhere. In the United States, when you get "back to the boat," you need to know how to search in the "old country."

Chapter 17: Ethnic Genealogy Resources   As you've seen in this Introduction, certain ethnic groups present special challenges in family history, but online resources can help you overcome them.

Chapter 18: The National Genealogical Society   This chapter explores one American resource that has education, data, networking, and more.

Chapter 19: Ancestry.com and RootsWeb   The oldest online genealogy community, RootsWeb, is part of the largest commercial genealogy company, The Ancestry.com Network. This company also runs Genealogy.com, MyFamily.com, and other sites full of resources for the family historian. This chapter will look at what is free, what is cheap, and what is expensive.

Chapter 20: Genealogical Publishing Houses and Their Sites   This chapter will show you the companies that publish genealogies and how you can do it yourself!

Chapter 21: A Potpourri of Genealogy   This chapter provides a quick tour of sites that you'll want to visit, and maybe bookmark!

Part IV: Appendixes
Appendix A: Genealogical Standards from the National Genealogical Society
Appendix B: Finding a Professional Genealogist
Glossary

I hope you'll find in this book the tools you need to get started—or continue—pursuing your genealogy with online resources, to share data with other genealogists online, and to participate in the online society in its many facets. Happy hunting!

Part **I**

The Basics

Chapter 1

Beginning a Genealogy Project

To paraphrase the ancient proverb, a journey of a thousand names begins with yourself. If you are just starting your genealogy, with or without the Internet, the process is simple and endlessly fascinating. This chapter will help you understand that process.

Organize from the Beginning

Friends often call and ask, "Okay, I want to start my genealogy. What do I do?" The process of genealogy has these basic steps: Look at what you already know, record it, decide what name to pursue next, research and query to track that information, analyze what you have to see what's needed next, and then do it all again. Experienced genealogists are more than willing to help the beginner. Pat Richley-Erickson, also known as DearMYRTLE, lists these important points for the beginner:

- Just take it one step at a time.

- Devise your own filing system.

- Don't let the experts overwhelm you.

- Use the Family History Library's Research Outline for the state/county where your ancestors came from. It will quickly orient you to what's available and what has survived that might help you out.

- Don't invent your own genealogy program. You can get a Personal Ancestral File (PAF) for free from www.familysearch.org/eng/default.asp?page = home/welcome/simplePAFRegistration.asp, or you can choose one of the commercially available ones.

- Only use a GEDCOM-compatible software program, because it is the generic way of storing genealogy data. This way, you can import and export to other researchers with common ancestors in the future.

That's the "what" to do, and soon we'll look at that more closely. "How" to do it includes these basic principles: document and back up. From the start, keep track of what you found, where you found it, and when. Even if it's as mundane as "My birth certificate, in the fireproof box, in my closet, 2010," record your data and sources. Sometimes genealogists forget to do that and find themselves retracing their steps like a hiker lost in the woods. Backing up your work regularly is as important as recording your sources is. Both of these topics will be covered in more detail in this chapter.

Your System

Software choices are covered in Chapter 2, where you will see how modern genealogy programs help you to do this. However, remember the good old index card (see Figure 1-1)? These can be useful to record data you find in a library, a friend's book, or even an interview with older relatives until you can get back to your computer.

A sample index card with page numbers indicated for the data collected is shown in Figure 1-1. The name of the book is written on the back. The handwritten index card also serves as a backup, which brings us to the second most important thing: Back up your data. For most of this book, I assume you are using a computer program to record and analyze your data, but even if you are sticking to good old paper, typewriter, and pencils, as my fourth cousin Jeanne Hand Henry, CG (certified genealogist), does, back that up with photocopies. Back up your

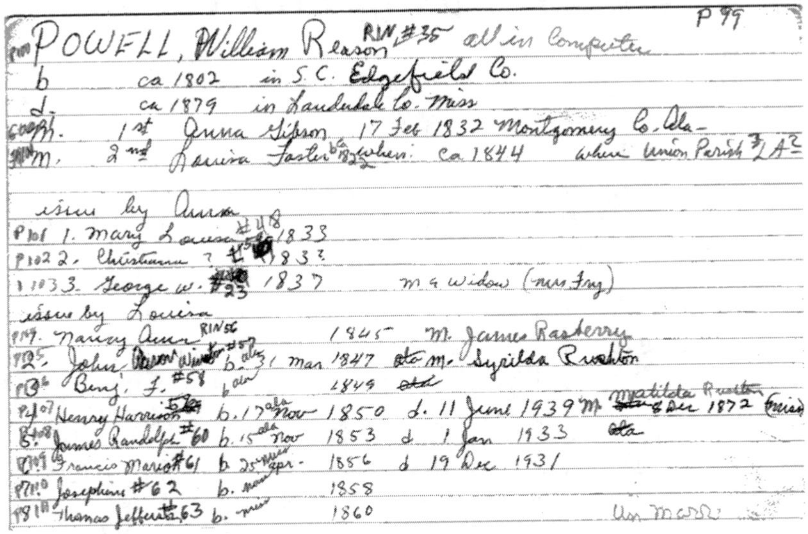
POWELL, William Reason RIN #35 all in Computer P 99
b ca 1802 in S.C. Edgefield Co.
d. ca 1879 in Lauderdale Co. Miss
m. 1st Anna Gibson 17 Feb 1832 Montgomery Co. Ala
m. 2nd Louisa Foster ca 1844 Union Parish LA
issue by Anna
1. Mary Louisa 1833
2. Christiana 1835
3. George W. #23 1837
issue by Louisa
Nancy Ann 1845 m. James Rasberry
John 31 Mar 1847 m. Syrilda Rushton
Benj. F. #58 1849
Henry Harrison b. 17 Nov 1850 d. 11 June 1939 m. Matilda Rushton Dec 1872
James Randolph #60 b. 15 Nov 1853 d. 1 Jan 1933
Francis Marion #61 b. 25 Apr. 1856 d. 19 Dec 1931
Josephine #62 b. 1858
Thomas Jefferson #63 b. 1860 Un marr

FIGURE 1-1. *Index cards are still a useful system.*

computerized data in some way: CD-ROMs, flash drives, or online storage sites (see the following box) are all options, but you must back up. Grace happens, but so does other stuff, like hurricanes, wildfires, and hard drive crashes.

Most people feel that finding a good genealogy program that enables them to record sources (as noted in Chapter 2) is the way to go. Paper sources can be scanned into digital form and/or stored in good old-fashioned filing cabinets. Remember to keep a record of all your research findings, even those pieces of information that seem unrelated to your family lines. Some day that data may indeed prove pertinent to your family; or you may be able to pass it on to someone else. Even if you decide to do the bulk of your research on a computer, you might still need some paper forms to keep your research organized.

The following box lists some Web sites where you can find forms to use as you research censuses and other records so that you can document your findings and sources. There's more about documentation later in this chapter.

A Baker's Dozen of Free Forms

You can find free, downloadable forms to record and track your research. Here are just a few places:

♦ A generous genealogist, Judith Haller, has developed templates for spreadsheets and word-processing programs, and offers them free for personal use at www.io.com/~jhaller/forms/forms.html.

♦ Ancestry.com has Portable Document Format (PDF) files of useful forms, such as a research calendar and source summary. You must have Adobe Acrobat to read and print them. Check out http://learn.ancestry.com/GetStarted/GetStartedLND.aspx.

♦ Canada GENWEB has a collection of forms useful for recording Canadian research at www.islandregister.com/forms.html.

♦ Family Tree Magazine has a page of forms in text and PDF formats for note-taking, checklists, and more (www.familytreemagazine.com/freeforms).

- Free-Genealogy-Forms (www.free-genealogy-forms.com) has forms to help you record data from North America and the United Kingdom.

- From the Family Search home page (www.familysearch.org), click Research Helps. Click Sorted By Document Type. Click Form. You'll find a list of forms, from charts to timelines to census worksheets. These files are in PDF format. You must have Adobe Acrobat to read and print them.

- Genealogy.com has a chart to keep track of your correspondence at www.genealogy.com/00000007.html? Welcome = 991338571 and a research log at www.genealogy .com/forms/f01-researchlog.pdf.

- Mary (Hagstrom) Bailey and Duane A. Bailey are two generous genealogists who have posted forms they developed for their own use at www.cs.williams.edu/ ~bailey/genealogy. They are free for nonprofit use.

- Microsoft Office Online (http://office.microsoft.com/en-us/ templates) has 14 different templates: sample letters requesting information, several family tree formats, and one book template for sharing your finds.

- RootsWeb members have posted their most useful forms at www.rootsweb .org/~ilfrankl/resources/forms.htm. For example, you'll find PDF files of family group sheets and a census summary chart.

- Search for Ancestors (www.searchforancestors.com/ genealogyfreebies.html) has a set of links to other sites with free genealogy forms.

- Search Genealogy has several downloadable forms for census information and pedigrees at http://searchgenealogy .net/ GenealogyForms.html.

- The Genealogical Society of Washtenaw County, Michigan, Inc., has a page at www.hvcn.org/info/gswc/links/toolforms .htm with links to forms and articles discussing how to use them.

Sources of Information Are Varied

Cite your sources is an important rule in genealogy. But what, exactly, is a source, and what are the different types of sources? Well, as you might expect, not all sources are created equal. Sources are sorted by their quality and their provenance. With respect to quality, we have two types. *Primary* sources are records created at or near the time of an event by a person who had reasonably close knowledge of the event. Usually, an official government record counts as a primary source: birth, marriage, and death certificates, for example. *Secondary* sources, on the other hand, are records created a significant amount of time after an event occurred or by a person who was not present at the event. This might be your grandmother's diary recording her niece's birth or my mother-in-law filling out a family tree from memory for me, for example. Sometimes a family Bible will be filled in with some events as they occur and others long after the fact. Now, both types of sources are important in genealogy research, but one gives a primary source more importance than a secondary one. Then we have the provenance, or inception, of the record. Here, we again have two types: *original* and *derivative*. Referring to the provenance of the record, original sources are those created by those involved or a government entity. A deed, a will, and a census record will all be created to record a specific event at the time it occurs. These are original records. A derivative source is one where the information was copied, abstracted, transcribed, or summarized from previously existing sources. Often you will find on the Internet that volunteers have indexed all the names in a marriage record book from a courthouse; this is an example of a derivative source. Original evidence takes precedence over derivative evidence.

So when you find an uploaded genealogy on the Internet, you are looking at a secondary, derivative source. Someone has looked at records and put together a set of facts. When you go to the Bureau of Land Records and order an original land grant, the information you get about the land itself and the owner is primary and original. But if it mentions the owner's birth date or place, that is secondary and derivative: The land agent has written down what he was given, but was not present at that place and time. The same is true of a death certificate: Name and death date would be original and primary. But the birth date and place may be secondary and derivative. So what do you do with all this? You start gathering sources, sorting, citing, and evaluating as you go.

> ## Note
>
> *A primary source is an original piece of information that documents an event: a death certificate, a birth certificate, a marriage license, etc. A secondary source is a source that may cite an original source but is not the source itself: a newspaper obituary or birth notice, a printed genealogy, a website genealogy, etc.*

Good Practices

To begin your genealogy, begin with yourself. Collect the information that you know for certain about yourself, your spouse, and your children. The data you want are birth, marriage, graduation, and other major life milestones. The documentation would ideally be the original certificates, as such documents are considered primary and original sources.

Photographs, with the people in them identified and the date on the back, can also be valuable, especially of those birth and marriage events. And don't forget some secondary and derivative sources: your wedding announcement in the paper, birth notices, and so forth. Family Bible entries can be scanned as well. You probably also have access to such information on your parents, and perhaps your spouse's as well. And poof, just like that, you have two generations and at least three surnames!

Pick a Line

The next step is picking a surname to pursue. As soon as you have a system for storing and comparing your research findings, you're ready to begin gathering data on that surname. A good place to begin is interviewing family members—parents, aunts, uncles, cousins, and in-laws. Ask them for stories, names, dates, and places of the people. Write down some of your own memories as well (see the journaling software in Chapter 2).

If at all possible, find out where the original and primary sources are: the birth and marriage certificates, the deed to land once owned, even divorce decrees. Record that for future use. When possible, get copies of those documents to back up what you're told. Family Bibles, newspapers, diaries, wills, and letters can help here.

A good question to ask at this point is whether any genealogy of the family has been published. Understand that such a work is still a secondary source, not a primary source. If published sources have good documentation included, you might find them a great help. Visit a Family History Center (FHC) and the FamilySearch site (www.familysearch .org), which has indexes to The Church of Jesus Christ of Latter-day

Saints' (LDS) genealogy information (see Chapter 13). This includes the International Genealogical Index and the Ancestral File.

Adventures in Genealogy

Family legend can be a good starting place, but be prepared for adventures! I'll give you an example from my own experience.

When my husband and I were dating, his family's stories fascinated me. One is that his mother is descended from Patrick Henry's sister, who settled in Kentucky soon after the American Revolution. Her Logsdon line was also said to be descended from a Revolutionary War hero. T. W. Crowe, Mark's paternal grandfather, said his (T. W.'s) grandmother was full-blooded Cherokee. My husband's maternal line was researched and proven by Mark's mother as part of a Daughters of the American Revolution project. Documentation galore helped provide the proof. But the paternal line was more problematic. While T. W. Crowe had some physical characteristics of Native Americans, as does my husband, no documentation of marriage or birth is available to prove the connection. Had I been able to prove it, our children might have been eligible for scholarships and special education in Native American history.

After we married and had children, I asked T. W. for the details on the Cherokee ancestor, but he would not discuss it with me. Indeed, the more I pressed for information, the more reticent T. W. became, and he died in 1994 without my finding the evidence. Finally, a relative told me that T. W., in effect, had been testing me: The Native American grandmother was something not talked about in his generation or the one before him. By telling me what was considered a "family scandal," T. W. was trying to find out if I would be scared off from dating his grandson. The poor man had no idea he had chosen to test me with something that would get my genealogy groove on!

So this is my point: While all family history is fascinating to those of us who have been bitten by that genealogy bug, to others, some family history is, at best, a source of mixed emotions and, at worst, a source of shame and fear. You must be prepared for some disagreeable surprises and even unpleasant reactions. You will find out more about this in Chapter 5.

International Genealogical Index (IGI)

The event-based International Genealogical Index is the largest single database in the world. Use it with care, though, because sometimes mistakes are included.

Ancestral File (AF)

This is a patron-submitted pedigree format genealogy. It includes the Old Parochial Register (OPR), which contains indexed and microfilmed vital records for Scotland before 1855. They are far from complete, as registering with a local parish was not required, and cost money, but they are still a valuable resource.

All the previous databases are made up of research done by LDS members, but they might include data on people who aren't members.

Record all you find in your system of choice. This is tedious, but necessary. Get someone to proof your entries (typing 1939 when you meant to type 1993 can easily happen).

References to Have at Hand

As you post queries, send and receive messages, read documents online, and look at library card catalogs, you will need some reference books at your fingertips to help you understand what you have found and what you are searching for. Besides a good atlas and perhaps a few state or province gazetteers (a geographic dictionary or index), having these books at hand will save you a lot of time in your pursuit of family history.

- ◆ *The Handybook for Genealogists: United States of America* (9th edition) by George B. Everton, editor (Everton Publishers, 1999): DearMYRTLE says she uses this reference book about 20 times a week. This book has information such as when counties were formed; what court had jurisdiction where and when; listings of genealogical archives, libraries, societies, and publications; dates for each available census index; and more.

- ◆ *The Source: A Guidebook of American Genealogy* by Sandra H. Luebking (editor) and Loretto D. Szucs (Ancestry Publishing, 2006) or *The Researcher's Guide to American Genealogy* by Val D. Greenwood (Genealogical Publishing Company, 2000): These are comprehensive, how-to genealogy books. Greenwood's is a little more accessible to the amateur, whereas Luebking's is aimed at the professional, certified genealogist, full of invaluable information on family history research.

♦ *Cite Your Sources: A Manual for Documenting Family Histories and Genealogical Records* by Richard S. Lackey (University Press of Mississippi, 1986) or *Evidence! Citation & Analysis for the Family Historian* by Elizabeth Shown Mills (Genealogical Publishing Company, 1997): These books help you document what you found, where you found it, and why you believe it. The two books approach the subject differently: The first is more amateur-friendly, whereas the second is more professional in approach, but is rapidly becoming the standard reference. Also, Mills' two worksheets, *Citing Online Historical Resources* and *Citing Ancestry.com Databases and Images* are always at my right hand as I do online research. They give excellent templates and guidance for putting the correct citations in your research.

Analyze and Repeat

When you find facts that seem to fit your genealogy, you must analyze them, as noted in the section "How to Judge," later in this chapter. When you are satisfied that you have a good fit, record the information and start the process again.

Success Story: A Beginner Tries the Shotgun Approach

My mother shared some old obits (obituaries) with me that intrigued me enough to send me on a search for my family's roots. I started at the RootsWeb site with a metasearch, and then I sent e-mails to anyone who had posted the name I was pursuing in the state of origin cited in the obit. This constituted more than 50 messages—a real shotgun approach. I received countless replies indicating there was no family connection. Then, one day, I got a response from a man who turned out to be my mother's cousin. He had been researching his family line for the last two years. He sent me census and marriage records, even a will from 1843 that gave new direction to my search. In pursuing information on my father, whom my mother divorced when I was two months old (I never saw him again), I was able to identify his parents' names from an SS 5 application and, subsequently, track down state census listings containing not only their birth dates, but also the birth dates of their parents—all of which has aided me invaluably in the search for my family's roots. Having been researching only a short while, I have found the online genealogy community to be very helpful and more than willing to share information with newbies like myself. The amount of information online has blown me away.

—Sue Crumpton

Know Your Terms

As soon as you find information, you are going to come across terms and acronyms that will make you scratch your head. Sure, it's easy to figure out what a deed is, but what's a cadastre? What do DSP and LDS mean? Is a yeoman a sailor or a farmer?

A *cadastre* is a survey, a map, or some other public record showing ownership and value of land for tax purposes. *DSP* is an abbreviation for a phrase that means "died without children." *LDS* is shorthand for the Church of Jesus Christ of Latter-day Saints, or the Mormons. And finally, a *yeoman* can designate a farmer, an attendant/guard, or a clerk in the Navy, depending on the time and place. Most of this is second nature to people who have done genealogy for more than a couple of years, but beginners often find they are completely baffled.

And then there are the calendars—Julian, Gregorian, and French Revolutionary—which means that some records have double dates. No, wait, don't run screaming into the street! Just try to get a handle on the jargon. I have included a glossary at the end of this book with many expressions. As the book progresses, many words are defined in context. But here are a few terms you need to know:

- ♦ **About** (or circa, in Latin) Often used in front of uncertain dates.

- ♦ **ahnentafel** An "ancestor table" that organizes information along a strict numbering scheme. An alternative to the pedigree chart.

- ♦ **BCG** Board for Certification of Genealogists.

- **CG** Certified Genealogist by BCG

- **CGI** Certified Genealogical Instructor by BCG.

- **CGL** Certified Genealogical Lecturer by BCG.

- **CGRS** Certified Genealogical Record Specialist by BCG.

- **family group sheet** A one-page collection of facts about one family unit—husband, wife, and children—with birth and death dates and places.

- **French Revolutionary calendar** The French Revolutionary calendar (or the Republican calendar) was introduced in France on November 24, 1793, and abolished on January 1, 1806. It was used again briefly during the Paris Commune in 1871. The months have "nature" names, the week is replaced with a 10-day cycle, and the year begins on September 22 of the old calendar, or the first day of autumn.

- **GEDCOM** The standard for computerized genealogical information. It's a combination of tags for data and pointers to related data.

- **Gregorian calendar** The Gregorian calendar was introduced by Pope Gregory XIII in 1582 and was adopted by England and the colonies in 1752, by which time it was 11 days behind the solar year. So it was adjusted in September 1752, moving George Washington's birthday from February 11 to February 22 when he was 21 years old. This is just one example of what confusion it caused!

- **Julian calendar** The Julian calendar was replaced by the Gregorian calendar when it had also fallen behind the solar year.

- **NGS** The National Genealogical Society, U.S.

- **pedigree chart** The traditional way to display a genealogy—the familiar "family tree," where one person's ancestors are outlined. Other formats are the fan chart, the decendency chart (starts with the ancestor and comes down to the present), and the timeline.

- **Soundex** A filing system, usually for recording surnames, using one letter followed by three numbers. The Soundex system keeps together names of the same and/or similar sounds, but of variant spellings. This allows you to search for Powell, Powel, and other variants of the name, for example.

- **SSDI** The Social Security Death Index. Details from the SSDI often can be used to further genealogical research by enabling you to locate a death certificate, find an obituary, discover cemetery records, and track down probate records. Several sites offer online searching of this resource for free.

If It's on the Internet, Is It True?

Most genealogists who discuss online sources, whether hobbyist or professional, want to know if they can "trust" what they find on the Internet. Many professional genealogists I know simply don't accept what's found on the Internet as proof of genealogy, period. Their attitude is this: A source isn't a primary or original source unless you've held that very document in your hand. Furthermore, in this view, a primary source isn't proof unless it's supported by at least one other original document you've held in your hand. In short, these genealogists insist that seeing a picture of a scanned original on the Internet isn't "proof."

For example, Caleb Johnson's site, MayflowerHistory.com (www .mayflowerhistory.com), has extensive information on the original colony, with some scans of original documents. In the view of these genealogists, this is all good secondary information, but not proof of any of the data there.

In Figure 1-2, you can see an image of a census page from Pilot Family Search (http://pilot.familysearch.org). In this image, on line 5, is my ancestor Reason Powell. My mother used a microfilm reader to find this information in the 1970s. Now I can look at it online. This is derivative because it is an image of the original, not the actual physical document. Still, I consider it good proof that Reason and his family were in Lauderdale County in 1870, just as family lore holds.

Some genealogists get annoyed with those who publish their genealogy data on the Internet without citing each source in detail. Once, when I was teaching a class on how to publish genealogy on the Internet at

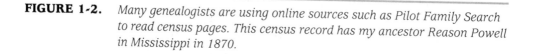

FIGURE 1-2. *Many genealogists are using online sources such as Pilot Family Search to read census pages. This census record has my ancestor Reason Powell in Mississippi in 1870.*

a conference, a respected genealogist took me to task over dinner. "Webpages without supporting documentation are lies!" she insisted. "You're telling people to publish lies, because if it's not proven by genealogical standards, it might not be true!"

I have to admit I don't see it that way. In my opinion, you must evaluate what you find on the Internet, just as you evaluate what you find in a library, courthouse, or archive. Many a genealogy book has been published with errors, and the same is true of online genealogies. On the Web, no real editors exist. You can find all kinds of information and sources on the Internet—from casual references in messages to documented genealogy to original records transcribed into Hypertext Markup Language (HTML). The range is astounding. But the same can be true of vanity-published genealogies found in libraries.

You can find some primary materials online, even if they are derivative because they are images, not the actual documents. People and institutions are scanning and transcribing original documents onto the Internet, such as the Library of Virginia and the National Park Service. Volunteers are indexing census records and marriage records at http://indexing.familysearch.org. You can also find online a growing treasure trove of indexes of public vital records, scanned images of Government Land Office (GLO) land patents (www.glorecords.blm.gov), and more (see Figure 1-3).

These are examples of how the Internet is helping genealogists put together a family history, that is, the story of our ancestors' lives, beyond the names, dates, and places. I can send to the GLO for a certified copy

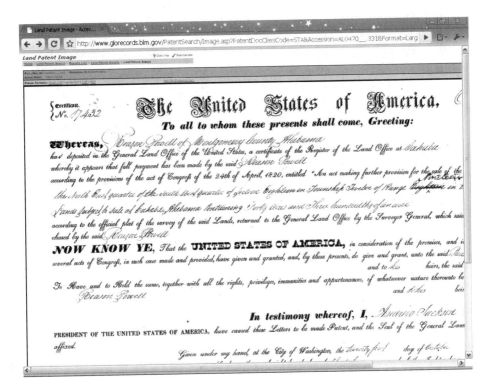

FIGURE 1-3.   *At the Government Land Office site, you can view an image of an original land grant. This is Reason Powell's land grant for a parcel in Cahaba, Alabama.*

of the land patent, but for now it is enough for me to know that Reason was in Alabama in 1820.

So my philosophy is that we cannot sneer at the Internet, saying nothing of genuine value can be found there for the genealogist. This might have been true only a few years ago, but not today. Now you can find scanned images of census records at many locations, including the U.S. Census Bureau site (www.census.gov) and volunteer projects, such as the USGenWeb Digital Census Project (www.rootsweb.com/census). Looking at these records on a webpage is as good as looking at them in microfilm or microfiche, in my opinion, and often much cheaper, even if you have to pay a subscription to a site such as Ancestry.com to find them. I say this as a hobbyist, mind you, not someone trying to impress anyone with my family history, and no important issue hangs on whether I have managed to handle the documents myself. If I wanted to register with the College of Arms, then the original documents would be necessary. If I just want to know what my husband's great-grandfather did for a living, reading a census taker's handwriting on the Internet will do.

That said, you should know that derivative and secondary sources are much easier to find than primary sources. The main value of these sources on the Internet is finding other genealogists who are researching the same lines. In addition, you might uncover leads to finding primary and secondary sources offline and, in rare cases, get a glance at an actual data source, perhaps even a primary source. Simply knowing that a source such as a diary, a will, or a tax document exists can be a breakthrough.

How to Judge

The first thing the online genealogist finds is that millions of people are putting their family trees online. You'll find, however, that varying degrees of care and scholarship go into these online genealogies. You must study and weigh the data and the evidence to decide if you are going to accept these data as fact.

Although many of these websites don't have the disk space available to include complete documentation, most people who publish online are willing to provide pertinent details to anyone who has data to exchange with them. Therefore, I still believe in publishing and exchanging data over the Internet as long as you remember to use good judgment. The criteria for the evaluation of resources on the Web must be the same criteria you would use for any other source of information.

Be aware that just because something is on a computer, this doesn't make it infallible. Garbage in, garbage out.

With this in mind, ask yourself the following questions when evaluating an online genealogy site.

Who Created It?

You can find all kinds of resources on the Internet—from libraries, research institutions, and organizations such as the National Genealogical Society (NGS), to government and university resources. Sources such as these give you more confidence in their data than, say, resources from a hobbyist.

Publications and software companies also publish genealogical information, but you must read the site carefully to determine whether the site owners actually have researched this information or simply accepted whatever their customers threw at them.

Finally, you can find tons of "family traditions" online. And although traditions usually have a grain of truth to them, they're also usually not unvarnished.

How Long Ago Was It Created?

The more often an HTML page is updated, the better you can feel about the data it holds. Of course, a page listing the census for a certain county in 1850 needn't be updated every week, but a pedigree put online should be updated as the author finds more data.

Where Does the Information Come From?

If the page in question doesn't give any sources, you'll want to contact the page author to acquire the necessary information. If sources do exist, of course, you must decide if you can trust them—many a genealogical error has been printed in books, magazines, and online.

In What Form Is the Information?

A simple GEDCOM published as a webpage can be useful for the beginner, but ideally, you want an index to any genealogical resource, regardless of form. If a site has no search function, no table of contents, or not even a document map (a page of links leading you to different parts of the site), it is much less useful than it could be.

How Well Does the Author Use and Define Genealogical Terms?

Does the author clearly know the difference between a yeoman farmer and a yeoman sailor? Does the author seem to be knowledgeable about genealogy? Another problem with online pages is whether the author understands the problems of dates—both badly recorded dates and the 1752 calendar change. Certain sites can help you with calendar problems.

Does the Information Make Sense Compared to What You Already Know?

If you have documentary evidence that contradicts what you see on a webpage, treat it as you would a mistake in a printed genealogy or magazine: Tell the author about your data and see whether the two versions can be reconciled. This sort of exchange, after all, is what online genealogy is all about! For example, many online genealogies have a mistake about one of my ancestors because they didn't stop to analyze the data and made erroneous assumptions.

In Figure 1-4, you can see an image of the 1850 Census of Lake County, Indiana. The column labeled HN is for household numbered in order of visitation; the column labeled FN is for families numbered in order of visitation. You can see Abraham Spencer (age 58) and his wife Diadama (age 56, her name is misspelled on the census form) have children Stephen through Elisabeth, and underneath are Amanda, age 27, and then three children under the age of 5. Some genealogies I have found on the Web assume that Amanda and the following children are also offspring of Abraham and Diadama, but if you look at the ages and how the families are listed—with Amanda and the younger children under the youngest of Abraham and Diadama's children—you see this doesn't make sense.

Now, if you were to look at the mortality schedule for the county for that year, you would see that Orsemus Spencer (Amanda's husband and Abraham's son) died in February before the census taker arrived in October. Amanda and her children moved in with her in-laws after her husband's death. The three youngest ones are part of the household, but they aren't Abraham Spencer's children; they are his grandchildren.

With this in mind, becoming familiar with the National Genealogical Society's Standards for Sharing Information with Others, as shown in Appendix A, would help. Judge what you find on the Internet by these standards. Hold yourself to them as you exchange information, and help keep the data on the Internet as accurate as possible. After you

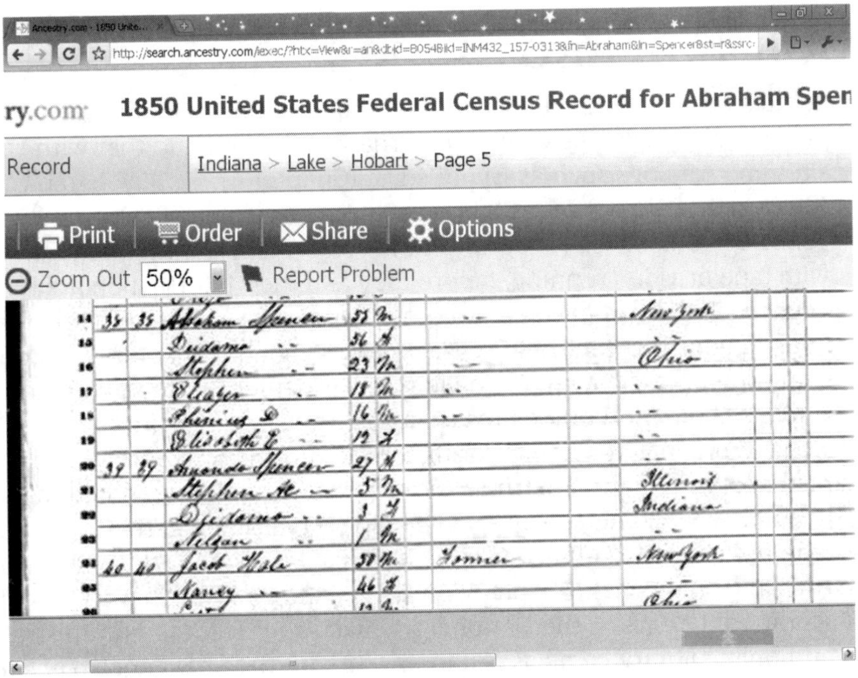

FIGURE 1-4. *Census records need careful study. Examine information for logical conclusions.*

have these standards firmly in mind, a good system to help you track what you know, how you know it, and what you don't know, as well as the surnames you need, is simply a matter of searching for the facts regarding each individual as you go along.

> *Note*
>
> *A mortality schedule contains data collected during a census about those who died before June in the year of the census. For each person, the following information is listed: name, age, sex, marital status (married or widowed), state or country of birth, month of death, occupation, cause of death, and the length of the final illness. In 1918 and 1919, many of these records were returned to the states; others were given to the Daughters of the American Revolution. Many volunteer-run genealogy websites have posted transcribed mortality schedules for specific counties.*

Look Far and Wide

Some steps you might consider to gather the information: Find published genealogies with your surnames. You can do that with search sites and catalogs such as Cyndi's List (Chapter 6), FamilySearch.com (Chapter 13), RootsWeb (Chapter 19), Ancestry.com (Chapter 19), and genealogy databases (Chapter 6). Interview older family members now, with tape or video running, before they and their information are beyond your reach. Communicate with other people searching the same family lines as you. You can do that with search engines (Chapter 6), through chat programs (Chapter 7), mailing lists (Chapter 8), RootsWeb and Ancestry.com, and other sites (Chapter 21).

Find original documents or historical information. Sometimes, historical information (such as the fact that mortality schedules are included with some censuses) will help you decide where to look next, whether online or offline. You can do that with the World Wide Web; certain vital records (Chapter 12); Ellis Island Online (Chapter 14); the Library of Congress, the National Archives and Records Administration, and online library catalogs (Chapter 12); international genealogy sites (Chapter 16); ethnic genealogy sites (Chapter 17); and many other sites, such as state archives (Chapter 12). Learn more about genealogy techniques and practices. Chapters 3 and 4 will give you pointers.

Standards of Genealogical Research

Genealogy is a hobby for most of us, and we do it for fun. The average genealogist is not doing this for fame and fortune, but because of an insatiable curiosity about the people who came before us. Given that, this little section may seem a bit too serious, even "taking all the fun out of it." Still, I believe that if you approach this hobby with the right attitude and care, it will be more rewarding than if you just dive in without a thought to the best practices and ethics of this rewarding pastime. Despite the fact that there are no official "rules" to this when you are a hobbyist, following guidelines and standards can, in the end, make your experience easier and more enjoyable.

As mentioned previously, in the appendixes to this book you will find the latest standards and guidelines from the National Genealogical Society (www.ngsgenealogy.org), and I suggest you study them. Though you can (and should) take many excellent courses in genealogy, if you review and understand these documents first, you will be better prepared to proceed on your family history quest in the best manner.

To summarize them briefly, these NGS standards and guidelines emphasize the following: Taking care not to assume too much from any piece of information and to know the differences between primary and secondary sources.

Sources That Can Help a Genealogical Researcher

- **Vital records**   Birth, death, marriage records, and the Social Security Death Index. Several states did not require these before the 20th century.

- **Court records**   Wills, adoptions, land and property bills of sale, tax rolls, deeds, naturalization, and even lawsuits often have clues to family relationships. And don't forget criminal records as well!

- **Church records**   Baptisms, marriages, burials, and so on are recorded by many churches.

- **Newspapers and magazines**   Not only obituaries, marriage, and birth notices, but also social news; perhaps parents, siblings, or cousins are mentioned. These are good data, even if secondary and derivative.

- **Military records**   Enlistment, commission, muster rolls, and veterans' documentation. Sometimes an age is given, but remember that some World War I and World War II soldiers lied to sign up before they were of legal age.

- **Fraternal organizations**   Organizations such as sororities, fraternities, civic groups, and associations can sometimes help pin down an ancestor at a certain time and place.

- ◆ **Ships' passenger lists**   Not only for immigrants to your country, but travel within. For example, a ship going from New York to New Orleans might have an ancestor on it. Also, some rivers, such as the Tennessee, were the site of many a pioneer marriage.

- ◆ **Family History Centers** have resources such as the International Genealogical Index, Ancestral File, and Old Parochial Register. More about these in Chapter 13!

- ◆ **State archives and libraries** (many online!).

- ◆ **Census records,** not only federal, but also local and state.

- ◆ **Published genealogies.**

- ◆ **Relatives older than you are**   Aunts, uncles, cousins, grandparents, and folks who knew them before you were born.

Keep Careful Records

- ◆ Give credit to all sources and other researchers when appropriate.

- ◆ Treat original records and their repositories with respect.

- ◆ Treat other researchers, the objects of your research, and especially living relatives with respect.

- ◆ Avail yourself of all the training, periodicals, literature, and organizations you can afford in time and money. Joining the NGS is a good first step!

- ◆ And finally, take the time and effort to mentor other researchers as you learn more yourself.

Another good outline to the best way to practice genealogy is the Board for Certification of Genealogists Code of Ethics and Conduct on their website at www.bcgcertification.org/aboutbcg/code.html. This is also a guide to choosing a professional, should you decide to get some help on your genealogy along the way!

How to Write a Query

Genealogy is a popular hobby, and lots of people have been pursuing it for a long time. When you realize that, it makes sense to see whether someone else has found what you need and is willing to share it. Your best tool for this is the query.

A query, in genealogy terms, is a request for data or at least for a clue where to find data on a specific person. Queries may be sent to one person in a letter or in an e-mail to the whole world (in effect). You can also send queries to an online site, a magazine, a mailing list, or another forum that reaches many people at once.

Writing a good query is not hard, but you do have to stick to certain conventions for it to be effective. Make the query short and to the point. Don't try to solve all your genealogical puzzles in one query; zero in on one task at a time. You must always list at least one name, at least one date or time period, and at least one location to go with the name.

Do not bother sending a query that does not have all three of these elements, because no one will be able to help you without a name, date, and place. If you are not certain about one of the elements, follow it with a question mark in parentheses, and be clear about what you know for sure as opposed to what you are trying to prove. Here are some points to keep in mind:

- Use all capital letters to spell every surname, including the maiden name and previous married names of female ancestors.

- Include all known relatives' names—children, siblings, and so on.

- Use complete names, including any middle names, if known.

- Finally, proofread all the names.

- Give complete dates whenever possible. Follow the format DD Month YYYY, as in 20 May 1865. If the date is uncertain, use "after," "before," or "about" as appropriate, such as "Born circa 1792" or "Died before October 1850."

- Proofread all the dates for typos; this is where transpositions can really get you!

- Give town, county, and state (or province) for North American locations; town, parish (if known), and county for United Kingdom locations, and so on. In other words, start with the specific and go to the general, including all divisions possible.

- If you are posting your query to an online message board, it is helpful to include the name, the date, and if possible, migration route using > to show the family's progress in the subject line. For example: Powell 1802 > SC > GA > AL > MS > .

- Finally, include how you wish to be contacted. For a letter query or one sent to a print magazine, you will want to include your full mailing address. For online queries, you want to include at least an e-mail address.

Here's a sample query for online publication:

```
Query: Crippen, 1794, CT>MA>VT>Canada
I need proof of the parents of Diadama CRIPPEN born 11 Sept
1794 in (?), NY. I believe her father was Darius CRIPPEN, son
of Samuel CRIPPEN, and her mother was Abigail STEVENS CRIPPEN,
daughter of Roger STEVENS, both from CT. They lived in
Egremont, Berkshire County, MA and Pittsfield, Rutland County,
VT before moving to Bastard Township, Ontario, Canada. I will
exchange information and copying costs. [Here you would put
your regular mail address, e-mail address, or other contact
information.]
```

Note

Do not ever send a letter or query that says, "Send me everything you have on the Jones family" or words to that effect. This is not a game of Go Fish. It is rude and unfair to ask for someone to just hand over years of research. When you ask for information, have some data to exchange and a specific genealogy goal to fill. Also, always offer to pay copying and/or postage costs.

This query meets the criteria in the bulleted list above. It is aimed at one specific goal: the parents of Diadama. The spelling matches the death notice that gave the date of birth—a secondary source—but because it is close to the actual event, it's acceptable to post this with the caveat "I believe." It has one date, several names, several places, and because this one is going online, a migration trail in the subject line (CT > MA > VT > Canada). If the author knew Diadama's siblings for certain, they would be in there, too. When you have posted queries, especially on discussion boards and other online venues, check back frequently for answers. If the site has a way to alert you by e-mail when your posting receives an answer, be sure to use it. Also, read the queries from whatever source you have chosen to use, and search query sites for your surnames.

As you can see from the previous information, queries themselves can be excellent clues to family history data!

Documentation

Document everything you find. When you enter data into your system, enter where and when you found it. Like backups of your work, this will save you countless hours in the long run.

A true story: At the beginning of her genealogy research in the late 1960s, my mother came across a volume of biographies for a town in Kansas. This sort of book was common in the 1800s. Everyone who was "someone" in a small town would contribute toward a book of history of the town. Contributors were included in the book, sometimes with a picture, and the biography would be a timeline of their lives up to the publication of the book, emphasizing when the family moved to town and their importance to the local economy.

One of these biographies was of a man named Spencer and included a picture of him. He looked much like her own grandfather, but the date was clearly too early to be him. Still, she photocopied it, just in case. However, she didn't photocopy the title page or make a note of where she had seen the book, which library, which town, and so forth.

Fast-forward 15 years to the 1980s. At this point, my mother is in possession of much more data, and in organizing things, came across the photocopy. Sure enough, that biography she had found years before is of her grandfather's grandfather; she had come across enough primary sources (birth certificates, church records, and so on) to prove it. And now, she knew this secondary source had valuable information about that man's early life, who his parents were, and who his in-laws were.

However, all she had was the page, with no idea of how to find the book again to document it as a source! It took days to reconstruct her research and make a guess as to which library had it. She did finally find it again and documented the source, but it was quite tedious. Just taking an extra two minutes, years before, would have saved a lot of time!

Backup

Back up your data.

I'm going to repeat that in this book as often as I say "Document your sources." Documentation and backup are essential. On these two principles depend all your effort and investment in genealogy.

Why bother with backups? Because hurricanes happen. Fire and earthquakes do, too. Software and hard drives fail for mysterious reasons. To have years of work gone with the wind is not a good feeling.

Pick at Least One System

If you are sticking to a paper system, make photocopies and keep them offsite—perhaps at your cousin's house or a rental storage unit. If you are using a computer, as most of us are these days, then back up on whatever you have: floppies, CDs, thumb drives, whatever. Or print it all out on paper as a backup to the digital files. Then be sure to keep a copy offsite, and update your backup often.

An alternative is online backup—that is, using someone else's computer to hold your data files. Again, you may have family at a distance that can do that for you, but you may also consider one of several free online storage services.

Free Online Storage Services

Online storage services are a convenient way to store offsite backup copies of critical information. Some services that are free until you reach some level of use are Google Docs, Dropbox, HP Upline, SOS Online Backup, Carbonite Online PCBackup, IDrive, Mozy Home Online Backup, and Wuala. Simply use your favorite search engine to find one.

If you need more than the basic free space, they all offer additional storage, costing from $5 to $30 a month, depending on how much room you need. Several of these services will let you make certain files available to other people while keeping other files secret and secure. Although all of them will work with both Macintosh and PC computers, some of them are picky about the web browser you use. Experiment with several of the free services and find the one with the right fit for you. Then use it often!

I loved the Xdrive service that AOL used to offer, but they discontinued it in 2009. Now I use both Google Docs and Dropbox.

Publishing Your Findings

Sooner or later, you're going to want to share what you have found, perhaps by publishing it on the Internet. To do this, you need space on a server of some sort. Fortunately, your choices here are wide open. You can publish your genealogy on the Internet in many places.

Most Internet service providers (ISPs) allot some disk space on their servers for their users. Check with your ISP to see how much you have. Dozens of sites are out there, offering up to 10 megabytes (MB) of space for free, including RootsWeb, ATT.net, Yahoo!, Xoom, and more.

Most of these are free, as long as you allow them to display an ad on the visitor's screen. Some software programs, as noted in Chapter 2, will put your genealogy database on the software publishers' website, where it can be searched by others. Some websites, such as WorldConnect, let you post the GEDCOM of your data for searching in database form instead of in HTML.

In short, publishing on the Internet is doable, as well as enjoyable.

By publishing at least some of your genealogy on the Internet, you can help others looking for the same lines. But don't get carried away—not everyone may be thrilled to be part of your project. Some people get upset at finding their names published online without their written permission. Some genealogists consider anything published, whether it's online or in hard copy, to be false unless the documentation proving it as true is included in the publication. Still others feel that sharing their hard work without getting data and/or payment in return is a bad idea.

For these and other reasons, you want to publish data only on deceased people, and publish only enough data to encourage people to write you with their own data.

So, be careful about what you post on the Web and how you post it. The National Genealogical Society recently adopted a set of standards for publishing genealogy on the Internet. With their permission, I included these standards in Appendix A.

Almost every good genealogy program now includes a way to publish on the Web. Ultimate Family Tree, Family Origins, Family Tree Maker, The Master Genealogist, Generations Family Tree, and Ancestral Quest are only a few of the programs that can turn your genealogical database into HTML. Most of them simply create a standard tree-branching chart with links to the individuals' data. Others may create a set of family group sheets. Many of them let you have "still living" replace the vital statistics for certain people. In many of these programs, the process is as uncomplicated as creating a printed report, and you just choose HTML as the format.

Some of the programs, however, don't give you a choice of where you post your data. Family Tree Maker (FTM), for example, publishes your data on its site. Once there, your data becomes part of the FTM database, which is periodically burned to CD-ROMs and sold in stores.

By posting your data on the site, you give them permission to do this. Quite a bit of discussion and debate is ongoing about this privatization of publicly available data. Some say this will be the end of amateur genealogy, whereas others feel this is a way to preserve data that might be lost to disaster or neglect. Still others say it takes money to store and maintain this data. It's up to you whether you want to post to a site that reuses your data for its own profit.

Success Story: Finding Cousins Across the Ocean

After ten years of getting my genealogy onto computer, I finally got the nerve to "browse the Web," and to this day I don't know how I got there, where I was, or how to get back there—but I landed on a website for French genealogists. I can neither read nor speak French. I bravely wrote a query in English: "I don't read or speak French, but I am looking for living cousins descended from my ancestors ORDENER." I included a short "tree" with some dates and my e-mail address.

Well, within a couple of hours I heard from an ORDENER cousin living in Paris, France. She did not know she had kin in America and had spent years hunting in genealogy and cemetery records for her great-great-grandfather's siblings! She had no idea they had come to America in the 1700s and settled in Texas before it was a state of the Union. So, while I traded her hundreds of names of our American family, she gave me her research back to about 1570 France when the name was ORTNER!

About four months later, another French cousin found me from that query on the Web. He did not know his cousin in Paris, so I was able to "introduce" him via e-mail. One of them has already come to Florida to meet us! What keeps me going? Well, when I reach a brick wall in one family, I turn to another surname. Looking for living cousins is a little more successful than looking for ancestors, but you have to find the ancestors to know how to go "down the line" to the living distant cousins!

Genealogy is somewhat like a giant crossword puzzle—each time you solve a name, you have at least two more to hunt! You never run out of avenues of adventure—ever!

—Patijé Weber Mills Styers, Sarasota, Florida

Caveats

In discussing how to begin your genealogy project, we must consider the pitfalls. This chapter has touched briefly on your part in ethics and etiquette, and Chapters 4 and 5 will expand on that. We must also consider the ethics of others, however, and be careful.

In the 21st century, genealogy is an industry. In fact, a November 4, 2009, article in *U.S. News and World Report* said that, after pornography, genealogy is perhaps the most popular use of the Internet. Entire companies are centered on family history research and resources. Not surprisingly, you will find people willing to take your money and give you little or nothing in return in genealogy, just as in any industry. Many of them started long before online genealogy became popular, and they simply followed when genealogists went online.

"Halberts of Ohio" is one notorious example. Dick Eastman covered this in a March 2001 article that is still worth looking up at www.ancestry .com/library/view/columns/eastman/3538.asp. Other scams abound as well. Books with titles such as *The World Book of [YOUR SURNAME]* and *Three Centuries of [YOUR SURNAME]*, sold via junk mail flyers as well as online, often turn out to be no more than what you would find in a telephone book. You have to read such pitches carefully, and before you send any money, ask on the e-mail lists, chat rooms, and blog sites whether anyone has had experience with the company.

Your Family's Coat of Arms

Until you have researched your family back to nobility and proven your genealogy, don't believe anyone who tells you the College of Arms has a coat of arms or a crest for your surname. These are assigned to specific individuals, not general surnames. Indeed, several members of the same family may have different coats of arms, and some in the family may have none. (Although a crest may be assigned to an entire clan in Ireland—the crest is the part above the shield.) Today, as always, coats of arms come only from letters patent from the senior heralds. Other European countries also have authorities who grant armorial achievements.

In the United Kingdom, a right to arms can only be established by registering in the official records of the proper authority. This entails a pedigree showing direct male line descent from an ancestor who was granted a letter patent or by making an application through the College of Arms for a grant of arms for yourself. Grants are made to corporations as well as to individuals. For more details, go to www.college-of-arms.gov.uk.

Other heraldic organizations:

- Royal Heraldry Society of Canada: www.heraldry.ca

- Bureau of Heraldry of South Africa The State Herald
  Postal address: Private Bag X236, PRETORIA 0001
  Street address: 24 Hamilton Street, Arcadia, PRETORIA
  Tel: (012) 441 3200 Fax: (012) 323 5287
  Fax : 086 529 6407
  E-mail: heraldrydac.gov.za

- The Court of the Lord Lyon (Scotland): www.lyon-court.com/lordlyon

- Office of the Chief Herald of Ireland: www.nli.ie/en/heraldry-introduction.aspx

- The Flemish Heraldic Council: www.onroerenderfgoed.be/nl/heraldiek

- The Herald's Site of the Court of Spain: http://fmunozaltea.cronistas.info

Some sites to help with fraud, scams, and myths:

♦ Cyndi's List Myths, Hoaxes, and Scams (www.cyndislist.com/myths.htm) Cyndi Howells keeps on top of myths, lies, and scams in genealogy on this page, and has a good set of links to consumer protection sites, should you fall prey to one of them.

♦ Kimberly Powell's Genealogy Hoaxes page (http://genealogy.about .com/cs/genealogyscams) This site lists some current and historical cases of people losing good money for bad genealogy.

♦ If you feel you have been scammed, report it to the Federal Trade Commission (FTC) at www.ftccomplaintassistant.gov.

♦ For information on consumer protection in many countries, try this site: www.consumerworld.org/pages/agencies.htm. Consumer World is a public service site with 2,000 links to consumer resources in Europe, Australia, and Asia.

Wrapping Up

A genealogy project involves specific steps. Here are the most important points:

♦ Record your data faithfully. Back it up faithfully. These two things will save you a world of grief some day.

♦ To begin your genealogy project, start with yourself and your immediate family, documenting what you know. Look for records for the next generation back by writing for vital records, searching for online records, posting queries, and researching in libraries and courthouses. Gather the information with documentation on where, when, and how you found it. Organize what you have, and look for what's needed next. Repeat the cycle.

♦ Beware of scams!

Chapter 2

Software You'll Need

Online genealogy is simply using new tools to do the same research always required of genealogists. When pursuing genealogy with online tools, instead of using a photocopier, you make copies using your printer. Instead of sending queries in an envelope, you send them by e-mail. Instead of reading an article in a magazine, you read it in a browser. And instead of (or before!) going to the library in person, you can search the card catalog and even the text of whole books from home. In other words, you are doing the same tasks with additional tools.

Please understand—I don't mean to imply that you won't ever do things the old-fashioned way again. Of course you will! But you'll use these online techniques much more frequently, and often before you set out to research the traditional way.

Look Ma, No Wires!

You'll need to learn about the Internet, software, and techniques for online information exchange to get the most out of the experience. This chapter covers such considerations and the software you might want to use. Of course, it is assumed you have a computer with some connection to the Internet. High-speed connections are best, as so many genealogy resources are now available as online images that take up a lot of bandwidth. Some people use dial-up service at home just for checking e-mail, and surf the Web at a local library using their high-speed connection. The disadvantages to that are obvious: In such a setup, you can only work on your genealogy when the library is open, and you certainly can't work in your pajamas at the library, which is part of the fun of online genealogy!

Still, there will be days when you do go to the library, and then a laptop and a wireless card are useful. For example, at the Family History Library in Salt Lake City (and many other libraries), you can now use your laptop computer, smart phone (such as a Blackberry or iPhone) or handheld personal digital assistant (PDA) with Wi-Fi wireless networking to check your e-mail, visit genealogy sites, or otherwise surf the Web. You can do all this without connecting any network cables; the wireless networking card in your device will connect via low-power radio waves to the building's network.

This benefits you and the library in several ways. Often, you will find all a library's computers are reserved on a busy day, but you can pull out your laptop and use that instead when the library has Wi-Fi network capabilities. The library saves money because it does not need to purchase so many computers, and they don't have to worry about what you might be downloading because it stays on your computer. And, in many local libraries, the card catalog is all online; with a laptop and Wi-Fi, you can even search for the book you need.

An all-in-one printer or fax modem could be useful when asking for vital records from a courthouse miles away, so you may still use your phone line for some genealogy chores. A good color inkjet printer, especially an all-in-one that can scan and copy, can help you preserve images of your original documents and primary sources. And there are other choices in hardware.

Note

Have you backed up today? This week? This month?

Back Up Your Data

A CD burner is good for storing and backing up your data, which you must do on a regular basis. If you don't use CD-ROMs, thumb drives and portable hard drives are available. Use an online storage service (see Chapter 1). Whatever you have, use it to back up your data. Don't put this off for later. When you are making a lot of progress, back up at least once a month. Once a week is better, because if you lose more than a month's work to a lightning strike or natural disaster, you may be too discouraged to start again.

Software

Once you have your hardware in place and you know how you're going to connect, you need to look at your software. Many Internet service providers (ISPs) include software as part of the package: the communications software, browser, file transfer program (FTP), e-mail, and other programs you need. The programs you use to access the Web are often called browsers or clients. These programs send commands to other computers, called servers, instructing them to display files and information to you or to run programs for you. The resulting display might be e-mail, a Web page, or a GEDCOM you want to study.

Which Browser Should I Use?

I'm often asked, "Which is the best browser?" In my opinion, this is like asking, "Which is the best car?" It all depends on your taste, habits, and needs. The current leaders in the browser wars are still Microsoft Internet Explorer and Netscape's progeny, Mozilla Firefox. Apple's Safari is catching up, however.

Microsoft Internet Explorer: Entire books are devoted to helping you get the most out of this browser. The major online services and ISPs have lined up with one or the other for their customers to use and install automatically with their software, so you don't have to do any extra work to use it. Internet Explorer is free, and you get it (whether you like it or not) when you buy a Windows system. It works well with Outlook, Microsoft's calendar, contacts, and e-mail program.

Firefox can also be obtained free of charge, has a nice user interface, and is easy to use. It now has a companion e-mail program called Thunderbird, which is covered in the section "RSS Readers." Some sites, you will find, do not look as "clean" in Firefox as they do in Internet Explorer, especially if the site was created with a Microsoft product.

Google's Chrome browser is based on Firefox, with some tweaks to make it easier to use to access Google's products such as e-mail, calendar, document storage, photo storage, and, of course, Web search. Tabs and windows work much the same way.

Apple's Safari is the default browser for iPhone, iTouch, and Macintosh. Safari's presentation is much like that of Firefox and Chrome except that the tabs are placed below the navigation bar, not above it. The status bar and menu bar are hidden by default; you have to click on the options to show them. You can make toolbar changes and customizations by clicking on the gear icon—another similarity to Chrome. Safari boasts fast performance, a simple user interface, easy bookmarks, pop-up blocking, inline find, tabbed browsing, automatic form filling, built-in RSS (Really Simple Syndication), resizable text fields, private browsing, and security.

If you have disability issues, such as macular degeneration or arthritis, there are browsers that magnify the type on a Web page, read the words out loud to you, accept spoken rather than typed commands, and more. Check out www.e-bility.com/links/software.php for a list of pointers to information and some demonstration versions of alternative browsing methods.

My advice is to test-drive a few different browsers and see which one suits you best if you don't like the one that comes with your Internet service provider.

Genealogy Programs

Your most important software will be your genealogy program, which is basically a database program for recording, maintaining, and sharing your data. In shopping around for the right genealogy program for you, consider these factors:

♦ First and foremost, check the program's ability to record your sources. If it doesn't have a way for you to track where and when you found a fact, reject it out of hand. You'll wind up retracing your steps a thousand times without the ability to instantly retrieve the sources you've already used.

♦ Second in importance, but only slightly second, is the appearance. This may seem trivial, but it's not. Most genealogy programs have some sort of metaphor: When you open the program, the screen looks as if you are working on a scrapbook, 3 × 5 cards, or a genealogical chart. Finding one that presents the data in a way that suits your methods is important.

♦ Third, consider how you output your data. Don't use anything that can't output to GEDCOM the standard for all programs. A GEDCOM is a text-only file with the data formatted so that any other program can use it. This is important for comparing your research to others', but that's not the only output form for your work.

For hard-copy output, think about what you want to create. The output can be simply data, whole books with pictures, or wall charts, a website, iron-on transfers, even a giant mural for the next reunion. Look for a program that fits your output needs.

Note

Importing and exporting data between programs is often problematic, despite the standard of GEDCOM 5.5. Each software engineer implements that standard slightly differently. For that reason, backing up your data just before importing any other data is critically important!

♦ Fourth, look at the software package's support, and ask friends what their experience was when they needed support. Read the manual to see how much support is included with the purchase price and for how long. Understand that within a year, the software (any software) will be upgraded. Find out whether upgrades are free or available for a minimal charge. A really good program may cost from $25 to $50 a year to keep it current; some shareware gives you upgrades for $5 or less. Also, ask at the next meeting of your local genealogy club whether anyone has the program you are interested in and is willing to help you with the learning curve.

♦ Which brings us to the final consideration, the cost. When you find the program you want, can you afford it? If not, see whether the program comes in different versions—some less powerful but also less expensive than others. Sometimes the cost includes CD-ROMs of secondary or primary material, but perhaps some of this material is available at your local library, and you need not buy it.

The following sections provide a quick roundup of some popular programs that you can at least try for free.

Brother's Keeper

Brother's Keeper (www.bkwin.org) is a good program with excellent choices in printing out reports of your data. It has a learning curve, too, because it does not have a lot of on-screen cues, but it is a good, basic program.

Success Story:
The Newest BK Version

"The 6.3 version has all the features and reports from previous versions, plus there is a new Individual Timeline report and a new All Relatives report," John Steed, the author of the program told me. "The Individual Timeline will show a timeline of major events of your close relatives in the order that they happened. So you can see when your relatives were born, married, and died in the order that those events happened. The second new report is the All Relatives report. It will show all of your relatives on all sides of the family, including spouses, and even relatives of the spouses, and how they are related to you. Most users like the ease of use, and the large variety of charts and reports that can be printed, displayed, or sent to a file."

—John Steed

Source recording is a strength of this program. With Brother's Keeper 6.3 (BK), you can attach sources to any event, person, or family; access a source to view it or modify it separately from data; and print a list of all sources (separate from data). In Figure 2-1 you can see the screen for sources.

Brother's Keeper 6.3 can be used with Windows Vista and Windows 7. There is no Macintosh version of Brother's Keeper, but a Macintosh computer that can run Windows programs can use BK in Windows mode. A trial version is free. You may order the registered program with the manual for $45 (or less for current registered users) if you decide you like it.

Output can be a GEDCOM, a list of people with any fields you want to include, and you can output that list as a text file or as a comma-delimited file. You can send certain types of reports to a disk file and include photographs and other pictures with most of them. In the descendant report, group sheets, and custom lists, you set up the report and then choose File | Create Text File. In the Register Book, Indented Book, and Ahnentafel Book, you set up the report and choose File | Create RTF File.

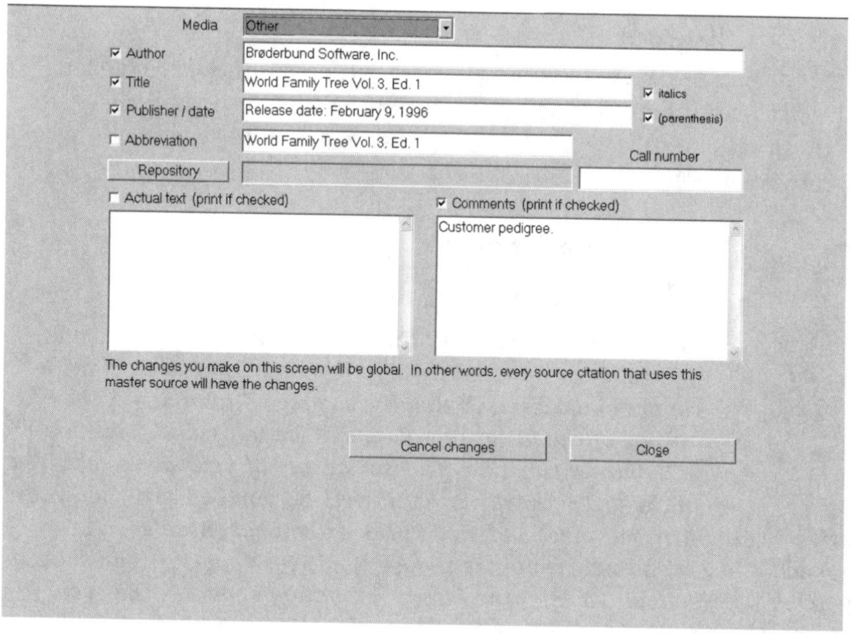

FIGURE 2-1. *The source screen of Brother's Keeper allows you to deal with sources separately from data or concurrently with it.*

Then you load the rich-text format (RTF) file into Word or WordPerfect. On the Group Sheet screen, you can also choose File | Create HTML Files.

Brother's Keeper 6.3 is easy to use and has more than 30 different chart and report formats. This program has been around for a long time (longer even than Family Tree Maker). Also, the author is open to suggestions from users and will answer requests for help.

Personal Ancestral File

Personal Ancestral File (PAF, www.familysearch.org/eng/default.asp?page = home/welcome/simplePAFRegistration.asp) is the program from the Church of Jesus Christ of Latter-Day Saints (LDS). You can get it in English, Chinese, German, Japanese, Korean, and Swedish. Personal Ancestral File is free on the Internet at www.familysearch.org; click on the link from the FamilySearch opening page. PAF 5.2 is available on

CD-ROM as well for a small fee. For less than $7, you can also download PAF Companion for more choices in printer output, including color.

English-language, step-by-step lessons for using PAF v5.2 are also on the site. You can access them when you select Lessons from the PAF v5.2 Help menu or go to www.familysearch.org/eng/paf/lessons/paf5.html.

PAF 5.2 can output, either onscreen or on paper, family histories, pedigree charts, family group records, and other reports to help users in their search for missing ancestors. An individual record adjusts to naming conventions from throughout the world. It can convert PAF 3.0 and 4.0 data files to its improved file format. One view of PAF is in Figure 2-2.

PAF has fields that are used to submit family members for Temple records that non-Mormons will not need. However, it is designed to be simple, to output in GEDCOM and other formats so you can share your data, and is supported by several forums on the Web.

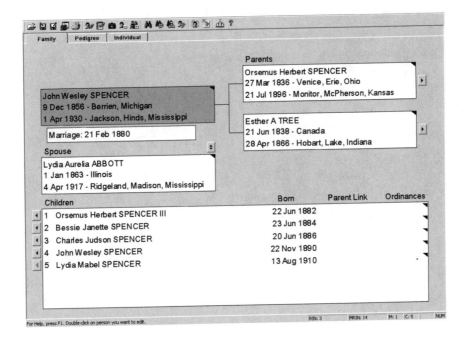

FIGURE 2-2. *PAF is simple to use and free.*

RootsMagic

This $30 program has many features of BK and PAF, plus more: It has a function to create CDs to share with your family, to run the software and data directly from a portable flash drive, and to integrate a feature called WebSearch to help you pursue your genealogy online.

RootsMagic has five main views, plus a sidebar for easier navigation. You switch between the views by clicking on the tab for the desired view. You can navigate using either the mouse or arrow keys. Double-clicking on a person's name brings up the data entry screen for that person. You can even open multiple databases side by side.

The RootsMagic edit screen lets you add an unlimited number of facts for every person (such as birth, death, marriage, occupation, religion, description, etc). The edit screen is shown in Figure 2-3. If you want to add a fact type that isn't in RootsMagic's predefined list, you

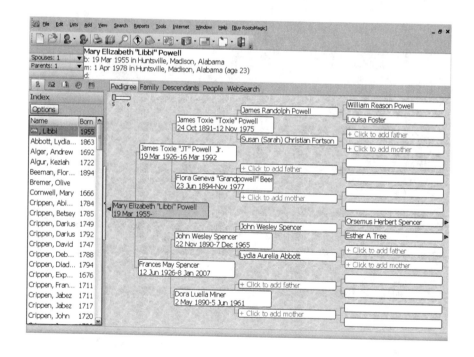

FIGURE 2-3. *RootsMagic's edit screen lets you see facts about one person, and even open two databases side by side for comparison.*

create your own fact types. RootsMagic also allows notes and unlimited source citations for every fact, and you can attach more than one person to a source and more than one source to a fact. You can add, edit, delete, merge, and print the sources of your information.

Every piece of information on a person is available from the main screen: name, parent and spouse info, personal and family facts, DNA test results, alternate names, or LDS information. You can directly access the notes, sources, media, and more for every item.

Output includes pedigree charts, family group sheets, four types of box charts, six styles of books, 27 different lists, mailing labels, calendars, hourglass trees, graphical timelines, relationship charts, letter-writing templates, individual summaries, five types of photo charts, and seven types of blank charts. Your database can be output into a pedigree chart with Hypertext Markup Language (HTML) links among the individuals in the genealogy.

Family Tree Maker

Family Tree Maker (www.familytreemaker.com) is Ancestry.com's product now, and it is closely integrated with the website. You can use Ancestry.com and Family Tree Maker together to get the most out of both by importing your family tree and attached images from the website to the program or vice versa. From the Family Tree Maker program, you can search Ancestry.com and merge what you find into your tree. It also uses the Ancestry.com hints feature to suggest records that might match your data.

You can scan documents and photographs, and then organize your photos, document images, and other graphics into slideshows, books, and other formats as well (such as sound and movies). The source function has standard source templates to help you save the right information about a source and rate each source on how useful you found it.

Once you have your data in, you can view relationships within the context of your entire family tree, with timelines and interactive maps highlighting events and places in the lives of your family.

The user interface lets you quickly switch between important features, and import data from any program that can produce a GEDCOM. It has tools for merging duplicate individuals, calculating dates, creating to-do lists, and more. It retails for $39.95 and requires at least Windows XP or Vista to run.

The Master Genealogist

The Master Genealogist (TMG) does everything the previously mentioned programs will do, but more—it helps you organize your search. Cheryl Rothwell, who writes three genealogy blogs, said, "I have used TMG since before it was officially released. I don't know how to do everything and I never will. There are some features I will just never need. But it is flexible enough to do what you want the way you want." A screenshot is in Figure 2-4.

You can tie many more facts and historical context to your ancestors with TMG, as it is affectionately known, as well as output in almost any format you like. Mind you, it has a learning curve, and the program is written with professional genealogical standards in mind. That should not deter you, however. It comes with a tutorial and has much more flexibility than its easy-to-use competitors. It is designed to let the novice get started quickly and grow into the more advanced features. Wizards, "cue cards," data-entry templates, ditto keys, macros, and other features make TMG easy to learn and use.

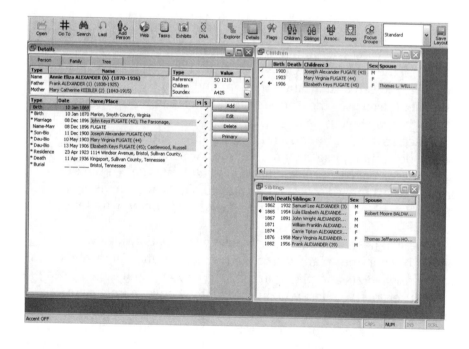

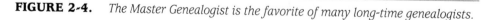

FIGURE 2-4. *The Master Genealogist is the favorite of many long-time genealogists.*

It is this flexibility that makes people feel The Master Genealogist is worth the effort to use. The program allows for an unlimited number of people, events per person, names per person, relationships, user-defined events, freeform text, photographs, citations, and repositories. You control the data. It also has features to help you track what you need to find and a to-do list of genealogy chores.

Referencing source data is TMG's strongest point for the serious genealogist. Each entry provides space for documenting an unlimited number of citations, including a rating scale for their reliability, which is an important point. Newspaper articles, family bibles, and interviews with your relatives all have different reliability, which can be recorded with TMG.

For $40 for the Silver edition and $80 for the Gold, The Master Genealogist is the favorite of many long-time genealogists.

Consider the Surface Scratched

The short list presented thus far merely scratches the surface of available genealogy programs by presenting those that are arguably the most popular. Go to Cyndi's List (www.cyndislist.com/software.htm) and poke around a few websites. Go to local meetings of your genealogy club and ask for recommendations. Go through the checklist of programs I gave you and test-drive a few that are shareware. Then you'll be ready to choose.

Smartphone and PDA Applications

Handheld Web-enabled devices, webbook computers, and cell phones with e-mail access are becoming the standard. They all can offer you convenience when traveling, but cost will be a big factor. Sometimes you might have issues with connectivity, depending on your data plan, and for those with far-sightedness, those tiny screens can be hard to see. Still, you might find some of these useful.

Personal Digital Assistants

The personal digital assistant (especially those models with an Internet connection) has become popular with genealogists. In addition to its usefulness in note-taking, retrieving e-mail, and, if it has the proper port, uploading and downloading information to desktop or laptop computers, some surprisingly functional software for these devices is available.

A list of Palm programs is maintained at Cyndi's List (www.cyndislist.com/software.htm#Palm).

Here are some examples:

♦ **1850-1930 U.S. Census Questions for HanDBase** 1.0 databases for each U.S. Census between 1850 and 1930 to help you determine what information is available in each of them.

Note

HanDBase (HDB) is a database program for the Palm operating system. You can get a program to convert data from Microsoft Access or any Open Database Connectivity (ODBC)–enabled database to the HandDBase format.

♦ **BirthCalc 1.0** A Palm operating system utility for determining birthdates when only the date of death and age are known, as is often the case on tombstones. The full version allows data to be exported to MemoPad for printing, beaming, or importing into the desktop, and it uses both real month lengths and a 30-day fixed month. This shareware program costs about $5.

♦ **Cemetery v2.0** This Palm OS program is a database application designed to collect records from cemeteries. You could use this either onsite at a cemetery or to enter information you find in a cemetery transcription in a library or online. For $10, it is a useful little program.

♦ **Chapman Code for HanDBase** A database of the three-letter Chapman County codes for the counties in the UK. This freeware program runs on the Palm OS.

♦ **Etat Civil 1.3** Etat Civil is an application that helps you conduct genealogy-related research in the French archives on your Palm device. It is free.

♦ **GedStar** This program lets you browse a GEDCOM (see the Glossary) and could be useful for trips to the library. The program even has its own discussion list (http://groups.yahoo.com/group/genpalm). The GedStar Pro version ($24.95) works on smart phones as well as

PDAs. The basic version ($15.95) works on the Palm OS. The data conversion and processing is one-way only; data cannot be modified on the handheld device and directly synced back to your PC, but you can put your latest PC data onto your Palm OS device before you head out to the library.

- **GedWise 6.2**   This is a $19.99 GEDCOM viewer to access your data when you take a research trip. It works on any Palm OS or Pocket PC handheld device.

- **Gen2Do 2.0**   (Genealogy To Do database) This $6 app runs on Palm OS. Items on the checklist include Look For (person, place, item), Microfilm, Microfiche, City Directory, CD (check which to look in), Year to look at, Location (place, microfilm #, microfiche #, etc.), Book (title, location, number, etc.), and Information Found (enter all of the information you find.)

- **Gen2Do for HanDBase 1.0**   This simple-to-use HanDBase applet is designed to assist genealogists in keeping a to-do list of research items for the next trip to the library. It is free.

- **GenRes 3.0**   Keep track of genealogy resources with this free Palm OS applet. It is also available for HanDBase.

- **LDSFilm for HanDBase 1.0**   This can be used to keep track of microforms ordered through a Family History Center of the LDS. It runs on Palm OS and is free.

- **Middlesex Census for HanDBase 1.0**   A list of all of the Public Records Office references for Middlesex (England) census districts for 1841 to 1891. It runs on Windows Mobile, Pocket PC, Palm OS, Symbian, and Windows, and is free.

- **MIGen for HanDBase 1.1**   Monumental Inscriptions (MI) HDB is a nifty little system for recording inscriptions found on tombstones while visiting cemeteries. It runs on Windows Mobile Pocket PC and is free.

- **My Roots 4.05**   This genealogy software for is designed for Palm OS handheld computers, but there is also a version for Windows Mobile. My Roots comes with a free conversion utility (for Windows or Macintosh) for importing data from GEDCOM files created by all the best-selling desktop genealogy applications, including Family Tree Maker, Legacy, PAF, and Reunion. The MyRoots (www.tapperware.com/MyRoots) full version is $24.95, and you can use a trial version for free.

- **Personal Ancestral File (PAF) 5.1** Available from FamilySearch .org, this program has Palm capability, which is handy for storing work until you can upload it to your computer. After you download this free software from www.familysearch.org, go back to the PAF page, and scroll down until you see PAF Data Viewer For Palm Handhelds. Then download that, too.

- **Pocket Ancestry 1.10.1** A freeware program for the Pocket PC 2002 operating system that shows GEDCOMs in various layouts, including, a list of all the persons in a data file, a list of "patriarchs" (persons with great-grandchildren), information about one person selected from the list, ancestry and descendant charts, and family groups.

- **Pocket Genealogist Advanced 3.11** At a cost of $35, Pocket Genealogist is now smart phone-compatible and can be run on PDAs. It has a relationship calculator, a new Individual View, multimedia, research to-do lists, GPS support, a redesigned desktop interface, better support for Windows Mobile 5 and 6 devices, and a variety of other features and fixes. The latest version reads data directly from The Master Genealogist (v4 or later), so you do not have to deal with a GEDCOM at all if you don't want to. Pocket Genealogist offers data support for events, facts, notes, sources, images, repositories, addresses, to-do lists, alternate names, and LDS ordinances. Pocket Genealogist Basic 3.11 for $20 has fewer features, but is still quite usable.

Smart Phones

Connection to the Internet through a cell phone used to be slow, expensive, and hard on the eyes. The latest generations of smart phones, which are more like PDAs with voice capabilities, have changed that.

- **AGeneDB** A simple, freeware genealogy program for Android, it allows you to view the contents of GEDCOM files. It shows the individuals, families, and family tree, and allows you to navigate to children of an entry. It takes up 610KB of the phone's memory.

iPhone/iTouch Software

- **FamCam**   This free iPhone/iPod Touch application that genealogists might find useful is a photo-sharing application by FamilyLink.

- **FamViewer**   A $14.99 stand-alone GEDCOM viewer, FamViewer accepts GEDCOM imports from your desktop genealogy software, as well as from Ancestry.com. It is not tied to any specific genealogy software, and you can view the data in several formats, and with your iPhone or iTouch held either vertically or horizontally. It is only available in English.

- **GedView**   This $3.99 stand-alone GEDCOM viewer for the iPhone by David Knight offers individual and family views, as well as sources and notes. You can view a surname index or a family index, and you can edit, create, change, or delete individuals in the GEDCOM on the iPhone, and then export to your desktop. In iPhone OS 3.0 and later versions, you can also save the location of any fact or event to the iPhone Maps application.

- **MobileFamilyTree**   This $4.99 application has a Virtual Tree view format, and allows you to edit data on the device and upload the changes to the desktop. You must have Synium's MacFamilyTree software on your Macintosh desktop to use this mobile application for the iPhone and iPod. When you sync the device with your computer, it adds the changes to the MacFamilyTree program.

- **Reunion for iPhone**   To use this application, you must have Reunion 9.0 on a Macintosh computer and a wireless connection. Take your family data with you to a research site, and you can add, view, search, and navigate your genealogy on the iPhone and then upload them to your Mac. It is compatible with iPhone OS 3.0 and is available in English, Dutch, French, and Swedish. It costs $14.99.

- **Shrubs**   Unlike many of the genealogy apps available for the iPhone, Shrubs is a stand-alone program and can import a GEDCOM file from your desktop genealogy program of choice. At $9.99, it is a viewer only and does not support editing or files greater than 4MB.

Additional Programs

There are other programs that are not, strictly speaking, genealogy programs. These include databases, journaling programs, and other, more mundane software, such as word-processing programs, that can be used to make your quest for family history easier. You may want to consider any combination of these.

Organization Programs

Some programs help you collect, organize, and/or analyze what you have, what you need, and what to do next.

GenSmarts

GenSmarts (www.gensmarts.com/index.html) analyzes the data you have and develops a profile of your ancestors based on where and when they lived. GenSmarts reads popular genealogy software file formats directly; no need to create a GEDCOM. The profile is matched with a database of known records to predict records your ancestors may have left behind, prioritizing and highlighting the sources you need to check. The logic behind each suggestion is fully explained.

GenSmarts comes with a known records inventory that supports research for the United States, Canada, and the UK. There is also a little content for Australia. You can add your own known records inventory definitions for any country. This program costs $24.95, and updates to the version you purchase are free. It runs on Windows 98, 98 SE, NT, 2000, XP, Vista, and Windows 7, but not on Macs or on VirtualPC's emulation of Windows 2000 and XP.

The full edition of GenSmarts v2 includes support for:

- RootsMagic (including RootsMagic 4)
- Family Tree Maker (including FTM 2008, 2009, and 2010)
- PAF 5
- The Master Genealogist
- Legacy
- Ancestral Quest
- Ancestry Family Tree
- Brother's Keeper (v6)
- Ultimate Family Tree
- Family Trees Quick and Easy
- Heritage Family Tree Deluxe
- GEDCOM

Evernote

One of my friend's favorite "genealogy" programs is Evernote. It allows her to take notes by typing or in handwriting, scan pictures, clip or take a screenshot of pages of online research, and so on in one place. The data is stored in the "cloud," that is, on the Evernote servers, as well as on her computer. She can turn on any computer or her smart phone anywhere, see the notes, and add to them.

You can carry the program on a flash drive so you don't have to install it on a borrowed computer. And Evernote automatically indexes your data and makes it searchable, including handwriting and those pages in the book you photographed. You can find the software at www.evernote.com.

Clooz

Clooz is not another genealogy program, but instead a database designed for Microsoft Access. You use it to systematically organize and store all the documents and clues to your ancestry that you have collected over the years. It is an electronic filing cabinet that assists you with searching and retrieving important facts you have found during the ancestor hunt, showing you a complete picture of what you have and what you lack. It has 35 templates for entering genealogical data from a myriad of document types, and your data can be sorted in dozens of ways. Once you have imported the individual family members from your genealogy program, you can start to assign documents to each person. Then, a report on a person will show you all the wills, deeds, birth and death certificates, diary entries, or other documents that mention him or her.

Clooz can also help you organize your genealogy to-do list and help you track what needs to be done.

Database CD-ROMs

You'll find that many records have been indexed and transcribed or scanned onto CD-ROMs. Some of these you can access at a local library; some you can order with software or by themselves; some are available from the Family History Centers. Census records available on CD-ROM include the U.S. federal census, various census records from Canada and the UK, Cherokee and African American census records, and a few local censuses. Cemetery records and death records from all over North

America and the UK are available on CD-ROMs; so are parish records. Check out www.cyndislist.com/cd-roms.htm#Vendors for sources of these CD-ROMs.

Word-Processing Programs

Don't overlook the lowly word processor as one of your genealogy tools. You can use it for journaling your genealogy quest, creating custom write-ups of your results, and even creating a book. You can use a word processor to create and track your to-do lists, write letters for vital records, and more.

As with your genealogy program, you need a word processor that can handle all of your chores, yet isn't more trouble to use than it's worth.

Maps

Sooner or later in tracing your genealogy, you're going to need maps, and not just your handy 2011 road atlas. The boundary lines of cities, counties, states, and even countries have changed over the years; Kentucky used to be part of Virginia after all! A dictionary or index of place names is called a gazetteer. As I mentioned in Chapter 1, a hard copy is a handy thing to have, but you can use software and Internet versions, too. I list several good map and gazetteer sites in Chapter 21. You may also want to have on hand a program such as U.S. Cities Galore, Microsoft Streets, or Pocket Streets to find current places. Check out Cyndi's List at www.cyndislist.com/maps.htm#Software for the latest in such software.

E-mail

Reading mail is the biggest part of online life. Some of the best information, and even friendships, come through e-mail. If you have an account with an ISP, a mail reader makes your life much easier. The mail readers in browsers tend to have fewer features than the stand-alone mail clients. To get the most out of electronic mail, you need to get a few things under your belt.

Filters

A filter is an action you want the mail program to take when a message matches certain conditions. For example, you can have an e-mail program reply to, copy, move, or destroy a message based on such things as the sender, the subject line, or the words found in the text. You can have the e-mail program do all that before you read your mail or even before the e-mail gets downloaded from the ISP's mail server. If you've never dealt with e-mail, this might seem like a lot of bells and whistles, but believe me, when you start getting involved in active mail lists (see Chapter 8), you'll want to sort your mail by geography, surname, and time period, at least! Furthermore, there'll be some people who you don't want to hear from. You can have your mail filters set up to delete mail from those people.

Most e-mail programs also come with built-in detectors for the unsolicited advertising e-mail and scams that circulate regularly. If you ever get an e-mail promising you riches or touting an "unknown stock," forward it to your ISP's customer service department so they can block that sender.

RSS Readers

One way to avoid the unsolicited advertising e-mail is to subscribe to your favorite blogs, genealogy columnists, and lists via RSS, Atom, or other "push" technology. RSS stands for Really Simple Syndication. Atom is the same thing using a different set of commands. They are both ways for a site to send you information, but it is much harder for a spammer to send you things you don't want. RSS feeds are a safe, reliable, and fun way to get the latest news, techniques, releases, and information, as well as to keep up with changes to your favorite websites. While you can use RSS feeds to get regular updates from CNN about news or the National Weather Service about your local tides and water temperature, using RSS feeds for genealogy is just a dream come true.

In the old days, someone surfing the Web would have to bookmark and remember to visit a favorite site to find updates. To get information from columnists such as DearMYRTLE and Dick Eastman, the person would subscribe to an e-mail newsletter, risking unsolicited e-mail as well. Other information came to him or her via an e-mail newsletter or, back in the dark ages of the Internet, a Usenet newsfeed. Problems arose with each of these methods: viruses, unauthorized posts, and sheer volume, to name a few. While the volume problem may still apply to RSS feeds, the benefits include better organization of your information and protection from viruses, unsolicited bulk e-mail, and other ills of e-mail and newsfeeds. In addition, RSS formats for iPods, smart phones, and PDAs mean you don't have to be in front of your desktop computer to use them!

You can get a simple program, such as RSS Reader, to gather your desired information, or use a Web-based program that also retrieves feeds, such as Google Reader, making it as simple as reading e-mail to catch a feed. As with e-mail, you can get overwhelmed with the volume of entries, so be choosy!

Audio Resources

The Internet has become a broadcast medium, and radio shows originating thousands of miles from you can stream right down to your computer over the Internet. To listen, you need a good media player, whether it is Microsoft's Windows Media Player, RealAudio, iTunes, or some other program. Most such programs have a free version and are usually easy to set up and use. Furthermore, most chat programs now allow voice and sound as well as text. AOL Instant Messenger, Skype, and others have functions that let you speak into a microphone attached to your sound card, sending your voice to your buddy using the same program.

Viruses and Worms

No journey is without risk. Whenever you enter the jungle of cyberspace, that dreaded microorganism, the computer virus, might be lurking about. Not only that, but your activities could attract Trojan horses and worms, too, so keep a sharp eye out.

A virus is a program hidden on a disk or within a file that can damage your data or computer in some way. Some viruses simply display a message or a joke, while others can wipe out all the information you saved to the hard drive. Therefore, I strongly recommend that you inoculate your computer before using any mode of electronic travel. One breed of computer virus is the Trojan horse. This is a program that seems to be useful and harmless when it first arrives, but secretly might be destroying data or breaking down the security on your system. The Trojan horse differs from a virus only because it doesn't propagate itself as a virus does.

A worm is a program that causes your computer to freeze or crash as it sucks up all of your available resources, such as system memory. A worm can make copies of itself and spread through connected systems. Programs to detect and remove these exotic virtual creatures are available from your local computer store or various online services. Some are shareware, while others are more costly. But if the program manages to delete a virus before it harms your system, it's worth the price. The two major virus-protection suites are Norton AntiVirus and McAfee VirusScan, which include one free year of virus updates, available to you once or twice a month. Whatever program you buy, however, be sure to keep it updated.

Even if you have virus-protection software, you need to take precautions. Make a backup of everything that is important to you—data, letters, or e-mails—and resave it no less than once a month. The virus-protection software may offer the ability to make a recovery disk; do so. This can save you much time and trouble later on down the line if your system needs to be restored.

Generally, when you download a file, look for an indication that it has been checked for viruses. If it's not there, reconsider downloading from that site. Any time you get data from someone else, always run a virus check on the disk before you do anything else. Once a virus is copied to your hard disk, removing it can be a major headache. In addition, make sure that you run a virus check on your hard drive at least twice a month, just to be certain. This should be part of your computer's regular tune-up and maintenance.

Virus protection is good, but if you opt for a high-speed, continuous connection, such as DSL or cable Internet, you also need a firewall to help protect you from hackers, Trojan horses, and worms. A firewall is a piece of software, hardware, or combination of both that forms an electronic boundary, preventing unauthorized access to a computer or network. It can also be a computer whose sole purpose is to act as a buffer between your main computer and the Internet. A firewall controls what goes out and what comes in according to how the user has it set up.

Examples of firewall programs are ZoneAlarm by Zone Labs, BlackICE Defender from NetworkICE, and Internet Security 2000 by Symantec Corp. A detailed description of how firewalls work can be found on Shields Up, a website devoted to broadband security created by programmer Steve Gibson, head of Gibson Research Corp. (www.grc.com) of Laguna Hills, California. Run the tests. You'll be surprised.

Publishing on the Internet

You can use several free sites to publish as well as search your genealogy, sites that let you post your facts in HTML, and sites that let you create any sort of page you want. As far as genealogy goes, there are other options as well.

Turning a GEDCOM into HTML

Several methods can help you turn your information into a static webpage: Translators, HTML editors, and websites allow you to place your information in their predesigned pages.

Translators

Some programs are available that take a GEDCOM from any program on the market and turn it into HTML. An inexpensive program ($10), such as GedPage (www.gedpage.com), turns GEDCOM files into attractive HTML files.

You can choose a version for Macintosh or Windows (versions 3.1 and later). The output is formatted as family group sheets. First, create a GEDCOM. Then change the files Header.htm and Footer.htm to say what you want—generally, this is your contact information. (You can do this in any text editor. Simply replace the text and leave anything within the < and > brackets alone.) Start GedPage, and fill in the blanks for the URL and the e-mail address; then choose colors if you like. Click Create Page. Then you use an FTP program to upload the files to your site. This program is only one example; others are out there. Check out Cyndi's List for a current list of programs (www.cyndislist.com/software.htm).

HTML Editors

For the real do-it-yourselfer, HTML editors can help you create your own site from the ground up. Most modern HTML editors work just like word processors; in fact, many word processors can save any document file in HTML format, complete with links and graphics.

Websites

Ancestry.com, RootsWeb.com, Genealogy.com, FamilyTree.com—the sites where you can upload your genealogy for free or nearly free are numberless. You'll learn how to use these sites in later chapters.

Blogging

Another way to publish is to keep a "web log" or "blog." You don't have to learn HTML, FTP, or any other arcane computer language. You simply log on to a site such as Facebook or Blogger.com and follow several, easy onscreen prompts within your browser to create your blog. These sites provide for easy typing or copying and pasting your data from then on. You add bold, italics, and underline in the same way you do in e-mail or using your word-processing program. As soon as you click the Publish button, the item is added to www. < yourtitle > .blogspot.com. Record your family history, anecdotes, and recipes, or just keep a journal of your progress. In fact, DearMYRTLE is using hers to preserve stories she told her daughters when they were children (www.dearmyrtle.com).

Wrapping Up

Software is an important part of Genealogy Online; to get online, you need the following:

♦ A computer (with lots of hard disk space!)

♦ An Internet service provider

♦ A browser

♦ A genealogy program

♦ A program that can play podcasts, sound files, etc.

♦ A way to post your results on the Web

Chapter 3

Genealogy Education

A lot of genealogy is learning by doing, but that's no reason to reinvent the wheel. Workshops, seminars, reading, and courses can help you start climbing that family tree efficiently and effectively. "I always stress education, especially for those who are new to genealogy and think that everything is on the Internet," said Liz Kelley Kerstens, CG, CGL. She is the creator of the software program Clooz, the electronic filing cabinet for genealogical records; is managing editor of *NGS Magazine*; and authored the books *Plymouth's First Century: Innovators and Industry*, a photo history of Plymouth, Michigan, and *Plymouth in Vintage Postcards*, a postcard history of 20th-century Plymouth. She is the executive director of the Plymouth Historical Museum and retired from the U.S. Marines as a major.

"I'm always telling people about the NGS courses and conferences because it's hard to learn in a vacuum. The courses and conferences fill your head with so many ideas that you have to take something away from them." Kerstens said that she herself, a genealogist of note, is currently pursuing a master's degree in history, pacing her studies around pursuing her own genealogy and her work. She recommends the system of melding work, study, and research.

"Even one course can be overwhelming with my life's pace, but I finish them because I made a commitment," she said. "And when I'm taking a course, I try to give it as much attention as I can because, first, I'm paying a lot for graduate tuition, but also the whole point of taking the courses is to learn. It's so much more fun to learn when you're doing it for fun and not worrying about getting a fabulous job or the next promotion. I already have a fabulous job and can't think of anything I'd rather be doing (other than sleeping)!"

Teach Yourself, Be Taught, or Do Both

You have many options when it comes to learning about genealogy, and none are mutually exclusive. You can read books like this one, take college-level courses, read genealogy blogs and RSS feeds, or read "how-to" articles on websites. You can learn about one aspect such as wills or land grants, or study to become a Certified Genealogist. You can go to a class or have a class come to you over the Internet. If you decide to go to a class, you can still sign up for it online, usually. Find what suits you best!

Books, magazines, and online articles, such as in blogs and RSS feeds, are ways to teach yourself about genealogy. The advantage of this method is that you can choose to learn at your own pace and choose the topics according to your needs at the moment.

However, if you want to learn from someone else, you can find resources for that, too. Online courses allow you to learn at your own pace, create your own experience, and keep the rest of your life going. There are courses that you simply read; in other online courses, you interact with the instructor and/or other students. This chapter will show you several online courses that are free; others may involve fees, but will also confer education credits of one sort or another.

"Offline" classes, seminars, and conferences are also worthwhile. Amateurs and professionals, beginners and experts, all benefit from them. Most conferences and seminars have tracks for the beginning, intermediate, and advanced levels. Plus, there is an indescribable joy in meeting new friends who share your passion (which many family members may not yet understand!).

Most of the time, if someone else is teaching you, fees are involved—sometimes modest and sometimes more substantial—but if you share travel and lodging with a genealogy buddy, it need not be prohibitively expensive. And, often with a little research, you can find good conferences and classes right in your own backyard!

Teaching Yourself:
Columns, Podcasts, and Blogs

Here are some resources to help you continually hone your genealogy skills and knowledge. In general, these are some form of periodical, though the distribution method changes.

Roots Television

Roots Television (www.rootstelevision.com) is a site where you can learn genealogy by watching videos produced by and for avid genealogists and family history lovers of all stripes. Some of it is pay-per-view, but a lot of it is free. The difference between this and your regular television is time: You can watch the show in three- to eight-minute chunks or all at once, and you watch when you choose, not when a network has scheduled it. This excellent site has information on archives and libraries, scrapbooking, genealogy travel, Civil War reenactments, DNA genealogy, reunions, sepia-toned photos, Internet sites, different aspects of history and old country traditions, story-telling, multicultural food, flea markets, nostalgia, and mystery solving. You'll find interviews, lectures, presentations, and their delightful "Who Do You Think You Are?" series. Do not miss the clip "A Psychic Roots Tale!"

Note

Institutes are week-long courses of study on a specific area, usually held at the same site every year, with class size ranging from 15 to 30 students, allowing more personalized instruction. Conference formats are usually speakers and panel discussions over a few days, where attendance for each session can be in the hundreds, and the site usually changes every year. Seminars are somewhere in between with regard to duration and group size.

DearMYRTLE

Pat Richley-Erickson has been helping folks do genealogy online and offline for nearly two decades. Her screen name, DearMYRTLE, comes from one of her great-grandmothers, and was her ID on AOL's genealogy forum.

DearMYRTLE's daily genealogy blog has free news and tips, problem-solving and other discussions, and much more. It's a must-read for any beginner. You can visit her site www.DearMYRTLE.com to subscribe by RSS feed and have her writing come to you.

Dear MYRTLE also has a library of podcasts. On her site, you can find older columns, especially her Beginning Genealogy Lessons. DearMYRTLE's Lessons, at www.dearmyrtle.com/lessons.htm, are 12 how-to articles on specific topics, such as keeping dates straight and using government resources.

Note

For several years, DearMYRTLE (http://podcasts.DearMYRTLE.com) hosted a weekly Tuesday Internet radio show (and later podcasts) on genealogy, with tips, interviews, and her special "mighty mouse" tours of interesting websites. In late 2008, obligations forced her to suspend the regular shows, but you can still download older shows.

Finally Get Organized is her series of columns on how to keep your work from getting lost in the shuffle. If you've been at genealogy for more than a year, you are probably feeling a little overwhelmed by all you've collected, what's still on your to-do list, and how to integrate it all. This list takes you through a checklist for each month of the year, with goals for each week and tasks to reach each goal. By the time you have gone through the checklist, you will be on top of your genealogy game!

The site also has links to other sites, such as Kid's Genealogy, a list of links to help you find lesson plans, mailing lists, and school projects to teach young people about genealogy.

Success Story: Using Message Boards Solves a Mystery

Betty Krohn took one of DearMYRTLE's classes on Internet genealogy research, where it was recommended that the students go to www.rootsweb.com and check out the message boards. Betty decided that her first task was to find information on Robert Suiters, Sr., an uncle of Betty's who had left Ohio in 1929 and lost touch with his family.

"The very first message to pop up when I entered the name of Suiters (my maiden name) was from a person who was looking for any family of Robert Suiters. Until that time I had been unable to locate any trace of Robert Suiters. We knew he existed, but didn't know if he was still alive or where in the world he would be living. So you can imagine my excitement when I read

that message," Betty said. "We learned that Robert had gone to Oklahoma, married, and had a son, Robert, Jr., but that marriage ended in divorce, and Robert, Sr. left again, leaving the son and never contacting him again."

Robert was alive, and he was soon on the phone with Betty's father. Through the message board, Betty was able to reunite much of the family.

Eastman's Online Genealogy Newsletter

Eastman's Online Genealogy Newsletter is one of the oldest and best sources of information for the amateur and professional genealogist alike. Dick Eastman has these RSS feeds available:

- ♦ Eastman's Online Genealogy Newsletter (EOGN): http://blog.eogn.com

- ♦ EOGN's Other News: http://othernews.eogn.com/index.rdf

- ♦ EOGN's Genealogy Announcements: http://announcements.eogn .com/index.rdf

The daily blog will have interesting articles on new products, sites, and online resources, as well as discussions on techniques. Like DearMYRTLE's blog, the site allows comments by readers, which are sometimes even more interesting than the original article. The free blog will often have news updates, such as Ancestry.com's newest databases or the National Archives and Records Administration's (NARA) newest workshop. The main value of the daily blog is that Dick is so good at keeping up with the latest news and releases. The "Plus Edition" has more detailed articles, most of all his thoughtful and honest reviews of sites and software. The "Plus Edition" is about $20 a year, or you can try it for three months for about $6.

Crowe's Nest

Crowe's Nest, at http://blog.epcrowe.com, is my blog. I post most weekdays, usually press releases, news, and snippets about my own genealogy. Sometimes I will opine on current events in the genealogical world as well. I often do a roundup of news on the DNA genealogy front, and I also participate in some genealogy blog cues as "Tombstone Tuesday," "Wordless Wednesday," and "Treasures Thursday."

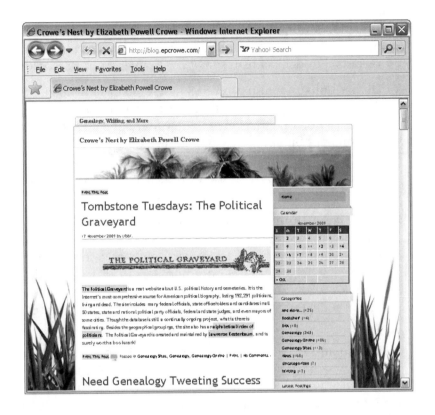

FIGURE 3-1. *My blog is at http://blog.epcrowe.com.*

Other Blogs and Feeds

It is completely possible to spend your entire day reading interesting, informative, and entertaining genealogy blogs. But if you did that, when would you do your genealogy? So, out of the hundreds of blogs and feeds out there, I'll point out the ones you should start with, and let you explore further to discover others that fit your schedule and needs:

♦ **We Tree** (http://wetree.blogspot.com) by Amy Coffin is subtitled "Adventures in Genealogy." Coffin says she is the fruit of a storied family tree. She has a Master of Library Science degree and a persistent streak. "Both have come in handy as I find more pieces to my family puzzle," she said. You can subscribe by RSS feed.

- **Del.icio.us Genealogy Sites** has an RSS feed of new and changed pages with "genealogy" in their tags that have been submitted by readers. Put del.icio.us/rss/tag/genealogy in your RSS reader.

- **DistantCousin.com** has an RSS newsfeed of new documents on this online archive of genealogy records and scanned images of historical documents from a wide variety of sources, such as newspaper obituaries, city directories, census records, ship lists, school yearbooks, military records, and more. Use of all the records at DistantCousin is free. Add http://distantcousin.com/RSS/rss.xml to your reader.

- **Eats Like A Human** (http://eatslikeahuman.blogspot.com) is the blog of a programmer who has worked with the LDS Church and pursues genealogy with a software engineer's perspective. "Taking Genealogy to the Common Person" is the subtitle of his blog. He recently used Twitter to pose a genealogy question (how to find a death certificate in Kansas prior to 1911) and recorded all the responses, and how quickly they came in, on the blog.

- **Leland and Patty Meitzler's Genealogy Blog** is at www.genealogyblog.com. The original founder of Heritage Quest, Leland edited Everton Publishers' *The Genealogical Helper* until February 2009, and later that year, he became a contributor to *Family Chronicle* magazine. Besides GenealogyBlog.com, Leland and Patty also have a small publishing company called Family Roots Publishing, which specializes in genealogy guidebooks.

- **FamilySearch Labs** at http://labs.familysearch.org/blog chronicles the newest software for FamilySearch.org (see Chapter 13). Great for the geeky genealogist!

- **Random Genealogy** (www.randomgenealogy.com) picks up news stories involving genealogy that other blogs haven't seemed to mention.

- **Renee's Genealogy Blog** (http://rzamor1.blogspot.com) started in September 2005 and uses AtomFeed to syndicate it to readers. Renee started doing genealogy at 15, and is now the secretary for the Utah Valley PAF Users Group and a Family History Consultant at the Alpine Family History Center. Renee is an old hand at genealogy and generously shares her insights and news. Her blogs are thoughtful and eclectic. A good read!

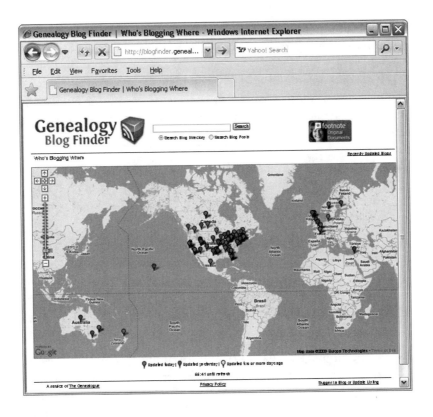

FIGURE 3-2. *BlogFinder helps you find blogs by topic.*

◆ **BlogFinder** at http://blogfinder.genealogue.com is a good way to keep on top of the newest blogs, but again, be careful not to let blogs substitute for genealogy! See Figure 3-2 for the "Who's Blogging Where" page of this site. If you want to find a French Genealogy blog, this is the place to go!

Podcasts and Streaming Audio

Podcasts are like radio shows that you can play whenever you want. You can listen to them live as they happen with any program that plays sound files: Microsoft Media Player, QuickTime, RealPlayer, iTunes, etc.

With the same program, you can download the file and listen to it at your convenience, either while sitting at your computer or on your MP3 or WMA player (e.g., iPod).

Here is a quick list of some of the best genealogy podcasts out there. Most of these programs can be sent to your computer via RSS or similar "push" feed, or you can get them from the sites listed, either live or archive versions:

- **Eastman's Online Genealogy**   Dick Eastman offers interviews with many of the world's leading genealogy experts on an occasional basis. Download them at http://blog.eogn.com/eastmans_online_genealogy/podcasts/index.html.

- **Genealogy Gems**   Lisa Louise Cook provides inspiration and techniques to help family researchers get the most out of their research time. You can download the podcast at http://genealogygemspodcast.libsyn.com (see Figure 3-3); the shows are posted about six times a month. These are always interesting and fun!

- **Genealogy ON DEMAND**   Shamele Jordon offers quick weekly tips to motivate you in your ancestral search. Johnson is a e-searcher, lecturer, and writer; she is a researcher for the PBS series *African American Lives*; a family reunion expert on *Ebony* magazine's Black Family Reunion Tour; an advisory board member of the Family Reunion Institute of Temple University; the former president of the African American Genealogy Group in Philadelphia, Pennsylvania; and a lecturer at the Institute of Genealogy and Historical Research at Samford University in Birmingham, Alabama. Her site, http://genealogyondemand.wordpress.com, also has a list of resources for each show, and all past shows are available.

- **Irish Roots Cafe**   Michael C. O'Laughlin hosts a Monday podcast on Irish genealogy and family heritage at www.irishroots.com/podcast/rss.xml.

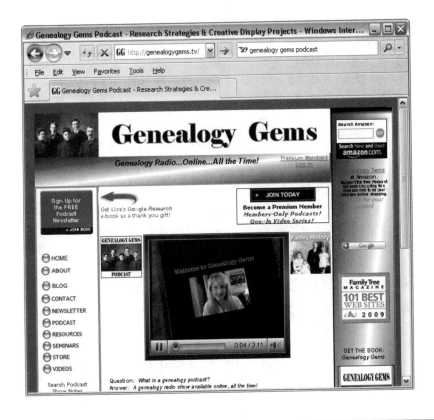

FIGURE 3-3. *Genealogy Gems podcast is one of the most popular on the Web.*

- **The Genealogy Guys Podcast** George G. Morgan and Drew Smith discuss genealogy each week and answer e-mail questions from readers. You can subscribe to and download the podcasts at www.genealogyguys.com. The show is posted at their website most Sundays, occasionally on Monday.

- **The Seeker Magazine Radio Hour** This airs at 11:00 a.m. Eastern Time on Saturdays as streaming media over the Internet. Linda Hammer, a former private investigator and process server, talks about finding missing friends and relatives live on the air from WTMY in Sarasota, Florida. Tune in over the Internet at www.the-seeker.com/radio.htm.

> **Note**
>
> *Streaming media differs from podcasts in that it is more like radio and television: You have to either catch it as it happens or set up a system to record it for later playback.*

Online Courses

In some cases, you can have the education come to you—that is, learn by independent study. Genealogy societies and even universities have such courses, and in some cases, you can take the class over the Internet.

Family History Live Online

Tex and Lynne Crawford offer lectures, classes, and even seminars, live over the Internet, with software called ReGL. The classes, with topics such as Hispanic Research and Indexing, are presented by experts and Certified Genealogists. Some are fee-based, but many are free. With the software, the lecturer's voice is transmitted live over the Internet, as are charts, pictures, and whiteboard displays. You type in your questions and follow along. It's as exciting as being at an "onsite" class, with the added advantage that you are at your own computer and can try out the techniques, websites, etc., right away.

One of the most enjoyable things about the site is the occasional "fair." This is a free, day-long series of interactive lectures on varied topics, usually on a Saturday. DearMYRTLE explained blogging, and Justin Schroepfer explained FOOTNOTE in just two of the eight sessions of a recent fair. The fairs are free. Check out www.familyhistoryliveonline .com for the current schedule.

> **Note**
>
> *A good listing of both resources and education in genealogy, and a site that was quite up-to-date as of this writing, is at www.academic-genealogy.com; look for the topics and regions you need.*

Genealogy.com

Genealogy.com has several free, self-paced courses to help you get started in genealogy. Click Learning Center on the home page navigation bar to find them. The Learning Center has the following articles:

- Begin Your Research at Home
- What's in a Name?
- Collaborating with Others
- Finding Existing Research
- Outfitting Your Genealogy Toolkit

Brigham Young University

Brigham Young University (http://ce.byu.edu/is/site/courses/free.cfm) has a series of free, self-paced online tutorials on family history research. Among the courses are

- Introduction to Family History Research
- Writing Family History
- Family Records
- Vital Records
- Military Records
- Courses on researching in France, Scandinavia, and Germany

National Institute for Genealogical Studies/University of Toronto

At www.genealogicalstudies.com, you can find The National Institute for Genealogical Studies, which has joined forces with the Professional Learning Centre, Faculty of Information Studies, University of Toronto, to provide Web-based courses for both family historians and professional genealogists. Countries included are the United States, Canada, England, Germany, Ireland, and Scotland. There are also certificates in librarianship and general methodology.

Search College Sites for Other Courses

Use any major search engine to search "genealogy courses independent study" or "genealogy courses distance learning," and you will come up with many smaller colleges and institutions that offer at least a course or two, and sometimes continuing education units. Also, go to the site of the nearest community college, junior college, or other higher-learning site and simply search for "genealogy." Often, library science and information science majors will include a course or two in genealogy.

Offline

Getting your genealogy education online is fun, but perhaps you would like some face-to-face (or F2F) time with others who are learning, too. In that case, you might investigate the following ideas for some educational opportunities in the real world.

Professional Organizations

Several institutions accredit the services of professional genealogists and researchers around the world. One of their primary goals is to establish a set of standards and a code of ethics for the members. Often, the accrediting body will offer courses, instruction, and testing. You don't have to be accredited to do family history research for hire, but it does offer clients assurance of a level of standards and professionalism that is accepted within the profession. Genealogy Pro (http://genealogypro .com/articles/organizations.html) has a list of several such organizations in English-speaking countries.

Genealogy Conferences and Cruises

The publishers of Wholly Genes software came up with the idea of a late-year, educational cruise of the Eastern Caribbean with a series of speakers and workshops on genealogical research methods, tools, and technologies from some of the most popular speakers and authorities in those fields. Several genealogy companies jumped on the bandwagon, so to speak, and now conferences at sea are a regular event. Put "genealogy cruise" in your favorite search engine to find one.

NGS

At www.ngsgenealogy.org, you can find many resources for online and offline learning. Courses they offer are shown at www.ngsgenealogy .org/cs/educational_courses.

American Genealogy For many years, NGS has offered a home-study correspondence course entitled "American Genealogy: A Basic Course." The NGS recommends that you take the online introductory course first and then move on to the home-study course, which covers some of the same topics in more depth and includes many more besides. Those who successfully complete the online introductory course will receive a discount coupon that can be applied toward the home-study course. Check the NGS website for the current fees.

The 16 lessons are "hands on" and require trips to libraries, courthouses, and other sites, as well as the ability to write well about your research. The NGS website, however, has online resources to help you with this. Most people take 18 months to complete the course, although extensions are granted.

BYU Center for Family History and Genealogy

The Center for Family History and Genealogy supports the Family History (Genealogy) students at Brigham Young University. At http://familyhistory .byu.edu, you can find information on:

♦ Family History (Genealogy) Major

♦ Family History (Genealogy) Minor

♦ Family History Certificate

♦ Map for Majors

♦ Family History Internships

University of Washington Genealogy and Family History Certificate

A nine-month evening certificate program for teachers, librarians, amateur researchers, and others interested in researching their families, this on-campus program is described at www.extension.washington.edu/ext/certificates/gfh/gfh_gen.asp. Participants develop a completed family history project as part of classes that meet one evening per week on the UW campus in Seattle.

Through lectures, discussions, readings, and field trips, students learn how to use the resources and methods necessary to develop a family history and to examine such topics as the migration of ethnic groups, population shifts, and the differences in urban and rural lifestyles. Students have access to the resources of the University of Washington libraries while enrolled. Participants receive nine Continuing Education Units (CEUs) and a certificate when they complete the program. Check the website for fees.

Genealogy Events

Finally, you can learn about genealogy at events such as seminars, workshops, and even ocean cruises! You can search for them on the following websites:

- About.com Genealogy Conferences (http://genealogy.about.com/cs/conferences)

- Cyndi's List (www.cyndislist.com/events.htm)

- Genealogy Events Web Ring (http://k.webring.com/hub?ring = gencon)

FGS Conferences

The Federation of Genealogical Societies (www.fgs.org/conferences/index.php) holds a national conference each year for genealogists of all levels of experience. The conferences spotlight management workshops for genealogy organizations, genealogical lectures by nationally recognized speakers and regional experts, and exhibitors with genealogical materials and supplies. Check the website for fees, which historically have been under $200.

National Institute on Genealogical Research

Information on this venerable genealogy institute can be found at www.rootsweb.com/~natgenin. The National Institute on Genealogical Research started in 1950 and is sponsored by the American University, the American Society of Genealogists, the National Archives, and the Maryland Hall of Records. The National Archives provides strong support, including meeting space. The cost for this week-long event is usually around $350.

The institute's program takes an in-depth look at federal records of genealogical value located primarily in the Washington, D.C. area. The program is for experienced researchers (genealogists, historians, librarians, and archivists) and is not an introductory course in genealogy. For example, sessions for 2003 included "Advanced Census Research Methodology," "Federal Land Records," and "Cartographic Records."

Institute on Genealogy and Historical Research

Held at Samford University (Birmingham, Alabama) every June, this five-day event is for intermediate to advanced genealogists. It is academically and professionally oriented, and is cosponsored by the Board for Certification of Genealogists. Small classes are held during the day. Each evening of the institute features a dinner with a speaker as well. Details and registration information can be found at www4.samford .edu/schools/ighr. Check the website (see Figure 3-4) for fees, which historically have been under $400.

The Salt Lake Institute of Genealogy

Held at the Family History Library in Salt Lake City, Utah, by the Utah Genealogical Society, this is a week-long, hands-on event, usually held early in the year. Check the Utah Genealogical Association website at www.infouga.org for fees, which historically have been under $400. In 2010, attendees could choose from 12 different courses of lectures, including topics on American, Canadian, and German research.

FIGURE 3-4.   *The IGHR in Birmingham, Alabama, is an intensive five-day event.*

Regional and Local Workshops and Seminars

Many state historical societies hold seminars. An example is the Wisconsin State Genealogical Society, which has two events each year—one in conjunction with the annual meeting in the spring and one in conjunction with the fall meeting. Events are open to the public for a nominal registration fee. Each one features a nationally known expert, speaking on a facet of genealogical research of particular interest to

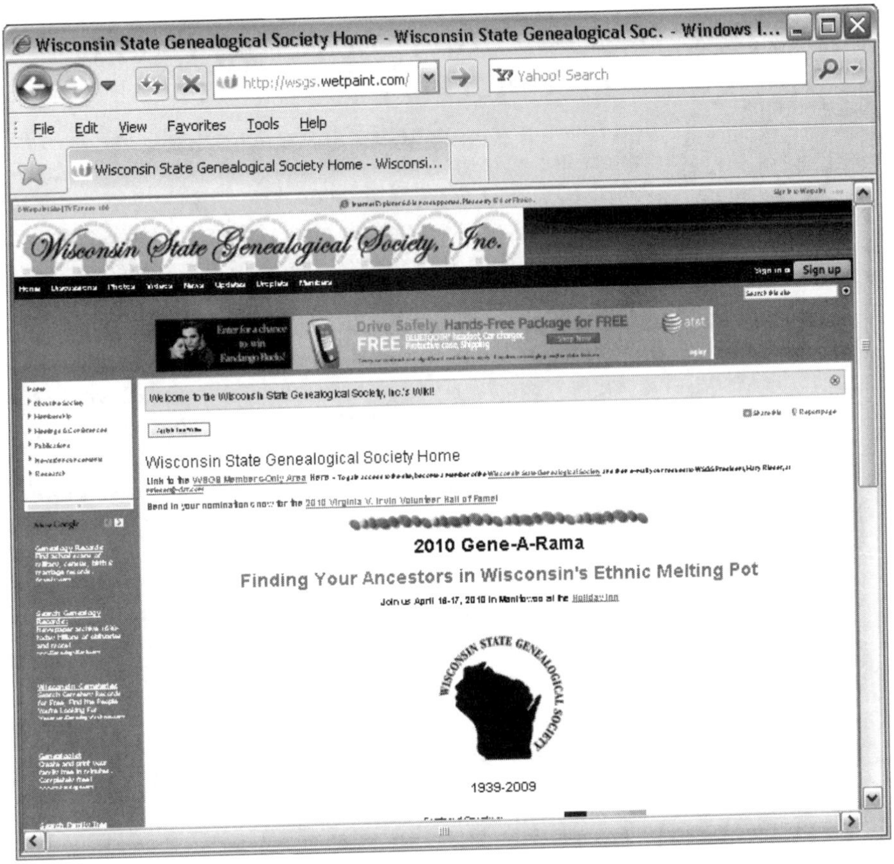

FIGURE 3-5. *Learn about upcoming Wisconsin and national genealogy events at http://wsgs.wetpaint.com.*

Wisconsin researchers. The Spring Gene-A-Ramas are held at various locations around the state, whereas the fall seminars generally alternate between the Madison and Milwaukee areas. Details and registration forms can be found at http://wsgs.wetpaint.com (see Figure 3-5).

Success Story: Learning to Plat at a Conference

Ann Lusk, attending a beginning genealogy course in her hometown of Huntsville, Alabama, learned about platting deeds. To plat a deed, you draw a picture of a piece of land from the description on the deed. Taking what she learned from the class, Ann worked with two Tennessee deeds, described in meets and bounds, a method that notes adjoining land. By platting two deeds for land owned by men with her husband's surname, cutting them out, and laying them on the table together, she saw the two pieces fit together "like hand and glove." This helped her show that the two men were father and son, and from that she could look for the original family plat. This information not only helped her Daughters of the American Revolution (DAR) application, it also qualified her for the First Families of Tennessee (www.east-tennessee-history.org/ index.cfm/m/52).

Finding a local class, seminar, workshop, or other event near you is the best way to start. Query a search engine for "genealogy" and the name of the town you live in or will be visiting. Also, check Cyndi's List page (www.cyndislist.com/events.htm), Dick Eastman's weekly newsletter, and DearMYRTLE's sites often for announcements.

Wrapping Up

- ◆ To summarize, you can learn about genealogy at all levels, online and offline, and both venues are enjoyable.

- ◆ Taking beginners' courses can save you some time and effort in your research.

- ◆ Seminars, conferences, institutes, and courses are a good way to meet other genealogists and expand your skills.

- ◆ Local, regional, and national programs give you a wide choice of how to learn about genealogy.

Chapter 4

Online Communities

My mother once said that the online friends she made in researching her genealogy were among the nicest people she knew. She found her Crippen line back to the boat from corresponding with someone on a Prodigy group. She also helped many people she never met with the data she had gathered on Spencers and Powells.

The online community can become more "real" to you than your physical community. From Facebook to YouTube, from Blogspot to Yahoo!, people are exchanging their knee-jerk reactions and deepest thoughts.

In the earliest days of the Internet, people felt anonymous when they posted messages, data, and pictures on the World Wide Web. So few people were using it, and mainstream media paid it little mind. A common adage went, "On the Internet, no one knows you're a dog." Times have changed. Here we are in the second decade of the online century, and the Internet has become the mainstream. Further, we all realize that what goes online stays online.

Perhaps, forever.

RootsWeb (see Chapter 19) has mail list messages dating back to 1987; employers routinely "Google" applicants; people have been fired for what they write in their blogs. And as some former executives have learned, "erasing" an e-mail does not mean it is really gone.

Manners Matter

by Kevin Kelly

Sit up straight, folks—Miss Manners is here. She has mastered her voice mail, got control of her cell phone, and now she's logged on to the Net.

In real life, Miss Manners' true name is Judith Martin. For years she's written about excruciatingly correct behavior for all those moments when the modem is not on; now she has a few interesting things to say about the wired life. For example, people who don't give a hoot about sending thank-you notes are suddenly bent out of shape when they get an e-mail message typed in ALL CAPS. *Wired* spoke to Miss Manners and asked her, very politely, how etiquette is bringing civility to the online frontier.

Wired: What is it about cyberspace that has rekindled interest in etiquette?

Miss Manners: Freedom without rules doesn't work. And communities do not work unless they are regulated by etiquette. It took about three minutes before some of the brighter people discovered this online. We have just as many ways, if not more, to be obnoxious in cyberspace and fewer ways to regulate them. So posting etiquette rules and looking for ways to ban people who violate them is the way sensible people are attempting to deal with this.

Wired: Do you find online etiquette rules parallel the rules of etiquette offline?

Miss Manners: Yes. Spamming is the equivalent of boring people or mixing in business. Flaming is the equivalent of being insulting. You may not realize how annoying it is when you ask an obvious question to a group that has been meeting for a while. So etiquette refers you to an FAQ file. I'm delighted people are doing a good job on the Net.

Wired: To sort out the correct behavior when corresponding through technology, you suggest the body is more important than any disembodied communication. Somebody sitting in front of you should take precedence over just a voice—like a phone conversation. And a voice takes precedence over a further disembodied e-mail. The more disembodied the communication is, the less precedence it has. Is that fair?

Miss Manners: Yes. And it is disobeyed flagrantly. The interesting thing is why people think that someone who is not present (a phone ringing) is more important than someone who is. Generally, it has taken a person a lot more effort to come to see you than to call you on the telephone.

Wired: Let's see. I need some advice. E-mail has an alarming proclivity to be copied. What are the rules for passing on private e-mail?

(Continued)

Miss Manners: Even if you have been online for years, I strongly recommend that you read *Netiquette* by Virginia Shea, an online book of proper online behavior. You can find it at www.albion.com/netiquette/book/index.html (see Figure 4-1). In my opinion, it should be required reading, similar to the driver's education handbook you had to read to get your license. For e-mail, the old postcard rule applies. Nobody else is supposed to read your postcards, but you'd be a fool if you wrote anything private on one.

Wired: Most people are not writing their e-mail that way.

Miss Manners: That's their mistake. We're now seeing e-mail that people thought they had deleted showing up as evidence in court. You can't erase e-mail. As that becomes more commonly realized, people will be a little wiser about what they type.

Wired: You're very much of a stickler for keeping one's business life from intruding upon one's social life. That distinction online is coming more blurred all the time. There seems to be a deliberate attempt to mix these two up—working at home, for example. Is this the end of civilization as we know it?

Miss Manners: Blurring the two is not conducive to a pleasant life, because it means that the joys of being loved for yourself and not for how high-ranking you are or what you can do for other people quickly disappear. People who are downsized, for instance, find they've been dropped by everyone they know because they don't have real friends. They only had business acquaintances. One of the big no-nos in cyberspace is that you do not go into a social activity, a chat group, or something like that and start advertising or selling things. This etiquette rule is an attempt to separate one's social life, which should be pure enjoyment and relaxation, from the pressures of work.

Reprinted with permission from *Wired* magazine, November 1997 issue.

FIGURE 4-1. Netiquette *by Virginia Shea is available online as a free e-book.*

Civil Discourse

Always remember that you cannot hide behind your modem. If you would not say something at a party or in church, you probably should not say it online, because it will be there forever. Besides, you catch so many more flies with honey!

Flames

A flame is a message on a mail list, bulletin board, social networking site, or chat room with an insult or rude contradiction. A flame war is a series of such messages in which people type insults and angry messages back and forth; an electronic argument, in other words. Often, these arguments are the result of a misunderstanding, where one person misinterprets another, who, in turn, takes offense. And then they're off on a flame war.

No matter how you converse online—social networking, e-mail, chat, or instant messages—things can sometimes get tense; that's human nature. Shea's book *Netiquette* posits that flames are sometime necessary to prevent rudeness from running amok: In other words it's a self-regulating mechanism for releasing tension. That may be, but I still do my best to avoid flaming.

Flame wars do happen. Part of it is human nature, part of it is the difficulty in expressing ourselves without body language, and part of it is simply a lack of patience. Always be as patient as you would like someone to be with you. Help the newcomer, and try not to click Send until you have read your text—twice.

Flame wars accomplish nothing. They never change any minds, and they hurt feelings. If someone flames you, the best course of action is to: a) inform the moderator if there is one, or in the case of social networking, alert the management and b) don't respond to the flamer. Indeed, you might even want to set up your social networking page, e-mail program, chat program, or RSS reader to filter out all messages from the flamer. Most social networking sites have a way to block someone who is offending you with a simple click and to report someone for inappropriate behavior or spam. If it happens on a message board, simply stop opening messages from that sender.

Read the Rules

No, we're not talking about dating, but rather about conversations online. Sometimes you get flamed because you broke a rule—a rule you were probably unaware even existed. The best way to avoid this is to keep informed of the standards and traditions of the group. You can do this in two ways: One way is to lurk until you get the lay of the land, so to speak. To lurk is to read the messages without responding to or posting any messages yourself. This isn't considered rude.

Most message systems and social networking sites won't alert others to your presence until you post something, although there are exceptions. Regardless, lurking before you leap is completely acceptable in online genealogy.

Name a topic, and someone who has dealt with it for years has written a file of frequently asked questions (FAQs) on it, which has become the de facto rulebook. These FAQs are available easily, so another way to become familiar with online rules is to read the rulebook.

You can find many of these handy guides at www.faqs.org. The home page of this site has a Search box. Type **Genealogy** in the Search box, click Search, and you get a list of FAQ files for various groups, as shown in Figure 4-2. You might also want to search the FAQ archive for adoption, family history, and ancestry FAQs for related groups.

Mail lists often store their FAQ files on a website and also send it to you as your first message after you subscribe to the list. Save the message as a text or document file for future reference.

Getting Along

Try to stick to the topic being discussed in any online conversation. Again, the FAQ should list the acceptable topics. Ads are usually verboten. A product announcement is typically okay, but an outright sales pitch isn't. Straying off the topic commonly leads to flames. Generally, whether you are posting a comment to a blog or answering a query on a message board, you need to stick to the topic at hand.

Remember: What you send is posted exactly as you send it, unless the site, group, or mail list (such as soc.genealogy.surnames) has a moderator who edits all incoming messages. On chat and instant messaging, when you press

ENTER

it is sent off—mistakes and all.

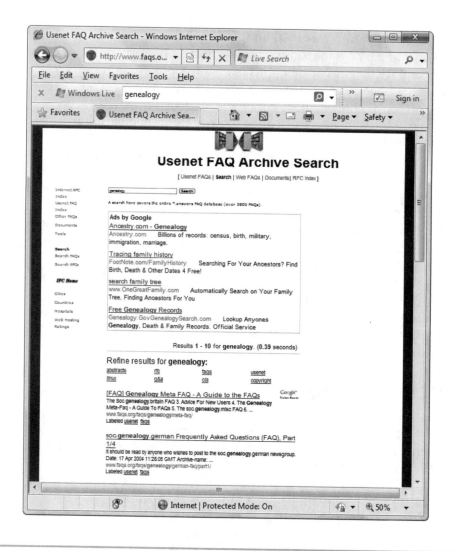

FIGURE 4-2. *Search for genealogy FAQs at www.faqs.org.*

Participants in genealogy groups want the topics of discussion to relate directly to genealogy or family history. In some groups, however, the tacit agreement is that anything a subscriber thinks is appropriate, is appropriate, as long as it relates to genealogy. To discern these tacit rules at a particular site, lurk for a while to discover if it tends to be more lax about off-topic posting.

Assume an attitude of courtesy among subscribers and readers. Remember, your postings and comments might be seen by as many as 20,000 readers on different networks throughout the world. Read carefully what you receive to make certain that you understand the message before replying. Read what you've written carefully to ensure that your message won't be misunderstood. As a matter of fact, routinely let a reply sit overnight and then read it again before sending. This can prevent that sinking feeling of regret when you realize that what you posted wasn't what you meant to say.

Avoid sarcasm. If humor seems appropriate, clearly label it as such. A smiley face like this: :D can be used to indicate humor. It is easy to misunderstand what's being said when no tone of voice, facial expression, or body language can guide you. A corollary: Give others the benefit of the doubt. Perhaps what you understood to be rude was meant to be funny. Communicating online is a fine art!

Know your audience and double-check addresses. Make sure the person or list of people you're sending your message to is the appropriate one.

Be tolerant of newcomers, as you expect others to be tolerant of you. No one was born knowing all about the Internet or any program or client thereon. Don't abuse new users of computer networks for their lack of knowledge. As you become more expert, be patient as others first learn to paddle, swim, and then surf the Net, just like you. Be an active participant in teaching newcomers.

Avoid cluttering your messages with excessive emphasis (**, !!, > > > >, and so on). This can make the message hard to follow. Also, know how your mail program answers messages. Many mail programs default to copying the entire message over again into the reply. When you respond to a message, either delete all but the relevant part of the original message or explicitly refer to the original's contents, but delete the unimportant parts of the original message. People commonly read your reply to the message before they read the original, because usually messages are presented "newest first."

When you're responding to another message, your subject line should be the same, with RE: at the beginning.

Always include a precise subject line, with a surname, in your message. Your subject line is like a headline: It should be something that attracts attention, and the only way to do this is to make sure that the subject line describes the main point of your message. Don't put "Looking for..." as the subject line with no surname. People will scroll right past your message and never read it. If you're seeking information about a family, include the surname in uppercase letters in the message's subject line. Many readers don't have time to read the contents of all messages. Here's an example of a bad subject line:

```
Wondering if anyone is looking for JONES
```

And here are some examples of good subject lines:

```
Researching surname ENGLE 1700s
SPENCER: England>MA>NY>OH>IN>MS
Delaware BLIZZARDs pre-1845
? Civil War Records
```

In the good examples, note these conventions: Surnames are in all caps, but nothing else is. A greater-than sign (>) is used as an arrow to denote migration from one place to another. A date is always helpful. If your message is a question, indicate this in the subject line. Although passages in all uppercase are considered shouting, the exception to this rule in genealogy is that surnames should be in uppercase, just as in any query.

Limit a message to one subject. This allows readers to quickly decide whether they need to read the message in full. Second subjects within a single message are often missed.

Questions are often the exception to this rule. You might need to post a message that's full of questions on a subject. When you ask a question within such a message, end it with a question mark (?) and press ENTER. This should be the end of that line. Be specific, especially when you ask questions. If you ask about a person, identify when and where the person might have lived. In questions concerning specific genealogical software, make clear what sort of computer system (Linux, PC/Windows, Apple Macintosh, and so forth) is involved. The folks reading message boards are helpful but busy, and are more likely to answer if they don't have to ask what you mean.

A good idea is to put your name in the text of your message, along with your best e-mail address for a reply. You might want to disguise your e-mail address, though, to prevent its being harvested for unsolicited bulk e-mail. A good convention is:

```
Please reply to libbic "at" aol "dot" com.
```

The end of the message is a good place for your name and e-mail address.

Sometimes, the message systems get absolutely clogged with messages, for example, if rotten weather, an earthquake, and a national holiday all converge on a certain Monday and many people are at home online because they were unable or not required to go to work. In this case, you must choose what to read based on the subject line or sender because it is impossible to read everything posted to the group that day. This is when an RSS reader and e-mail program that lets you filter the messages for the subject headings are invaluable.

Message Etiquette

Twitter, Facebook, and other new communication techniques may not have an FAQ at the Usenet archive mentioned previously, but we can still examine some accepted practices.

Generally, you will find helpful, polite people in genealogy discussions. Often, especially if you have one of the instant message programs such as AOL Instant Messenger, you'll be chatting with people you've at least contacted before, if not close friends and family. And, of course, if you're taking an online course, specific rules are going to be in force as to who can "talk" and when.

Nevertheless, in all these scenarios, you must meet certain etiquette standards in these situations.

All of the etiquette rules covered earlier in this chapter apply to chat, social network updates, and microblogs such as Twitter. Using all capital letters, except to mention the surnames you're researching, is considered shouting. Flames are useless and annoying; you should show respect for everyone. And make certain that you aren't taking offense when none was intended.

Stay on topic or, if you get sidetracked, create a separate message thread to follow your tangent.

Lurk before you leap into sending messages: Check out the message stream and see if the topic is what you're looking for.

- You can send your e-mail address by private message, but don't post it in the message system, because if you do, the spammers will flood your mailbox. If someone refuses to give you an address, don't be insulted—it is probably just a security measure.

Many social networking sites and most of the instant message programs enable you to send sound files, pictures, and even programs. Be wary of this feature for two reasons: First, it represents a security risk to receive files from someone you don't know well; second, this adds to the traffic on the server and slows down everyone's interaction, not only that of the sender and the receiver.

Chat, social networking, and instant message programs have some limit in the number of characters that can be sent in one chunk. If your thoughts run longer, type the message in parts, each ending in an ellipsis (...) until you finish. Don't be surprised to find that, as you do this, other messages are popping up between your lines. Those paying attention can follow your train of thought better if you take advantage of a feature many programs have: the capability to send your text in a specific color and/or typeface.

Note

A handle, screen name, or display name is simply the identification for you that appears to other users when you are using chat or instant messaging. It is often best to use something other than your real, full name.

Don't Pass It On!

For some reason, people delight in spreading myths, legends, and hoaxes through every medium in existence, online, offline, and everywhere in between. Your mailbox will often be clogged with these, from text to video to carefully edited pictures.

The proper online etiquette here: First, do not respond to messages that seem fishy (as in winning a lottery you did not enter or inheriting money from someone you never heard of). They are often scams and hoaxes, and responding only encourages the scoundrels. Second, when you receive e-mail chain letters, virus warnings, and "true stories," don't send them on. That just clogs the bandwidth.

Always check out such "forwards" at The Urban Legends page, www.snopes.com (see Figure 4-3), which keeps daily tabs on the various urban legends going around.

Ideally, please just delete them! You'll be doing a lot to make the online world a better place!

Viruses and Other Electronic Wildlife

As noted in Chapter 2, it is important to have some sort of virus-checking software as well as a firewall on your system. This is also part of making a happy online community: If you are careful, you can avoid infecting your own computer and others.

Be certain your e-mail program is set up to check both incoming and outgoing messages for viruses, Trojan horses, worms (malicious programs that replicate until filling all of the storage space on a drive or network), and spyware.

If you suddenly find your e-mail program sending out many messages without your telling it to, you've been infected, and you are spreading the infection to everyone in your address book. Immediately go to safe mode, and use your virus protection program to find and remove the virus.

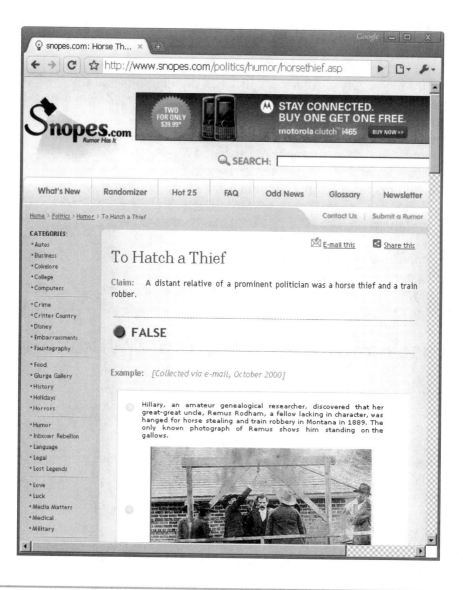

FIGURE 4-3. *Always check out warnings, chain letters, and "inspirational story" e-mails, and resist the urge to pass them on.*

Be Safe and Polite on the Internet

Friends don't give friends viruses. Remember these rules:

◆ Back up your files regularly.

◆ Do not accept files from anyone you don't know, whether in social networking sites, chat, instant messaging, or e-mails.

◆ Do not click on links from someone you do not know in chat, instant messaging, social networking sites (e.g., Facebook), or e-mails.

◆ Install a virus protection program. Your ISP may provide one free of charge.

◆ Set up a regular time to update and run virus scans of your whole computer, and do it, automatically if possible. If you don't keep your computer up-to-date on protection, then you are leaving yourself vulnerable. More than 200 new viruses are reported each month.

◆ Some viruses will send e-mail (and the infection) to *everyone* listed in a user's e-mail address book, making it look as if it is from that person. Afterwards, the virus will delete itself and the victim has no idea what happened. Creepy, isn't it? So do not run or even look at files in an e-mail if you didn't ask for it or if it is from someone you don't know.

◆ When you download a file, even a GEDCOM, be sure it's from a reputable site or someone you know. Run it through your virus checker, even then.

Wrapping Up

Let's sum up the rules of online life this way:

◆ To be polite, stay on topic.

◆ Read the FAQ files for any group you participate in.

- Use filters and commands to track the conversations and e-mails that interest you, and ignore those that don't.

- Use the right formats: Don't use all capital letters except for surnames; do use symbols and acronyms to keep things brief.

- Don't clog up everyone's mailboxes and news feeds with the latest urban legends, "true stories," and "warnings."

- Never open an e-mail from someone you don't know.

- Never open an attachment or file from someone you don't know.

- Keep your virus protection up-to-date.

- Back up. Back up. Back up.

Chapter 5

Ethics, Privacy, and Law in Genealogy

Genealogy has a long history of legal and ethical concerns. From the settling of estates, to the eligibility of soccer players for national teams, to the very course of a nation's destiny, genealogy has had a role to play. The validation of genealogical information and the publishing of that information, online and otherwise, will also have legal and ethical ramifications. Therefore, ethics, privacy, and copyright are important to consider when you practice your genealogy.

Note

Disclaimer: I am not an attorney, and this chapter is not meant to be legal advice but merely information.

Say, for example, you find an illegitimate birth, an ethnic surprise, or a convicted criminal in your family history. If the information is only one or two generations back, you perhaps would deal with these facts differently than if the events happened more than 100 years ago.

You will have three basic issues to confront in genealogy: accuracy, privacy, and copyright. These issues are just as important in the "real world" as they are online. Happily, it isn't hard to be on the right side of all of these issues!

Note

Keep these three principles in mind:

1. *Do not publish vital statistics about living persons because the data can be used in identity theft.*
2. *Do not use anything you find in a book, a magazine, GEDCOM, or online without proper attribution and permission. Facts are not copyrightable. The presentation and formatting of facts are copyrightable.*
3. *Be aware that not everyone in the family will be thrilled to see family skeletons published. In fact, you may find that some relatives have emotional reactions to what you find; be prepared.*

Privacy

Many professional genealogists agree that simply publishing everything you find is not a good idea. What you find might not be accurate; it may be accurate but damaging; it may be accurate and not damaging, but surprising. Discretion, consideration, and tact can go a long way in avoiding trouble.

Gormley's View

"Genealogists are sharing, caring people, and most of us think nothing of handing over all of our genealogical data to distant cousins, even strangers," says Myra Vanderpool Gormley, Certified Genealogist (CG), editor of *RootsWeb Review*, and author of the Ancestry Insider blog (see Figure 5-1). "However, we should start thinking about the ramifications of our actions. The idea of sharing genealogical information is good, and technology has made it easy. However, technology is not exclusively a tool for *honest* people. If detailed personal information about you and your living relatives is on the Internet, crooks can and do find it, and some scam artist might use it to hoodwink your grandmother into giving out the secrets that will open her bank account. It has happened. If your bank or financial institution still uses your mother's maiden name for a password, change it," Gormley said.

Remember that your living relatives have the same rights to privacy that you do, and among these rights are:

♦ The right to be free of unreasonable and highly offensive intrusions into one's seclusion, including the right to be free of highly objectionable disclosure of private information in which the public has no legitimate interest

♦ Use of one's name or likeness by another only by consent

♦ Not being in false light in the public eye—the right to avoid false attributions of authorship or association

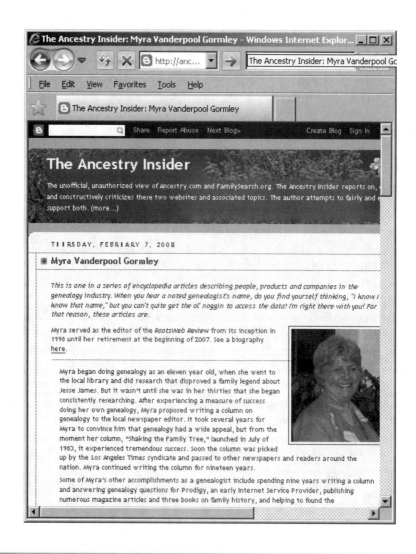

FIGURE 5-1. *Myra Vanderpool Gormley, CG, advises caution in privacy issues.*

Publishing private genealogical information—and the important word here is *private*—about a living person without consent might involve any or all three aspects of their right to privacy. Publishing is more than just printed material or a traditional book. Publication includes websites, GEDCOMs, message boards, mailing lists, and even family group sheets or material that you might share with others via e-mail or traditional mail. They might be able to seek legal relief through a civil lawsuit. It is okay to collect genealogical information about your living relatives, but do not publish it in any form without written permission, Gormley said.

"We should exercise good manners and respect the privacy of our families—those generous relatives who have shared personal information with us or who shared with a cousin of a cousin," Gormley added. "Additionally, there is another and growing problem—identity theft. Why make it easy for cyberthieves to steal your or a loved one's identity? But, identity theft involves much more than just your name, address, or phone number. This idea that one's name, address, phone number, and vitals fall into the area of privacy laws is a common misconception by many people. In reality, the facts of your existence are a matter of public record in most instances. However, personal information, such as health issues, a child born out of wedlock, spouse abuse, how much money you have in the bank, etc.—those are things that are not general public knowledge, and these are personal things that if you publish them about your living relatives, there could be an invasion of privacy involved (but I'm not a lawyer)," Gormley says.

DearMYRTLE's View

DearMYRTLE (Pat Richley-Erickson), the daily genealogy columnist, says, "Fortunately, I know of only one person who has stated she is unwilling to share her compiled genealogy data and documentation with others because she plans to print a book. I suspect, though, that the individual in question most certainly benefited from previously compiled research in books, websites, and CD databases. It would be impossible to avoid the use of these items as clues leading to the discovery of original documents. For example, one would even have to consider a clerk of the court's marriage indexes as previously compiled research. Such an index is indeed one step removed from the original creation of marriage licenses and marriage returns."

In other words, all the data has been used before, or you would not be able to collect it in the first place. Still, Richley-Erickson said, one must always be sensitive to the feelings of others who might be affected by the data you publish.

Eastman's View

"The concept is simple, although it is far more complicated in execution. In short, ask yourself repeatedly: 'Is there anyone who will mind if I publish this information?' There are legal issues as well with living individuals and with publishing info about people within the past 72 years in the [United States], 100 years in Canada and the UK," says Dick Eastman, editor and publisher of one of the most popular genealogy columns online. Eastman's genealogy tips have helped thousands of online genealogists over the last 15 years. His blog, Eastman's Genealogy Newsletter, has been a treasure trove of news and tips for years, and is profiled in Chapter 3 (see Figure 5-2).

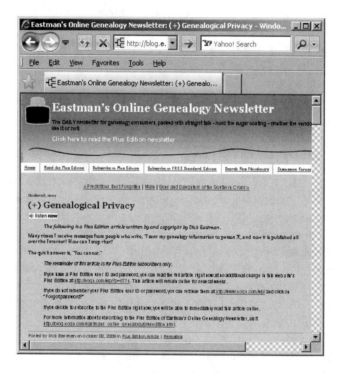

FIGURE 5-2.   *Dick Eastman often deals with privacy in his blog.*

> **Note**
>
> *"When you post public messages (on message boards and mailing lists, for example) about your research, it is sufficient to say you are researching a Jones or a Cynthia Jones line. You don't have to reveal relationship by saying she is your mother or maternal grandmother. In the pursuit of our ancestors, let's not inadvertently hurt our living family members or ourselves. Think twice before you post or share any data about the living."*
>
> —*Myra Vanderpool Gormley, CG*

"Protecting the privacy of living individuals and the issue of whether or not to publish sensitive family information (such as a great-great-aunt's child born out of wedlock) are big concerns," Eastman says. "Those can become legal issues if a distant (or not-so-distant) relative takes exception to your publishing such information. Lawsuits have been launched because of these things."

A Contrarian View

In his webpage, "Genealogical Privacy - A Contrarian's View," http://leverton-genealogy.com/PRIVACY.htm, genealogist Paul Lareau of Minnesota states, "If you send me information, it will be shared with anyone who wishes it, and no attempt will be made to hide it. If you do not feel comfortable with this attitude or want to hide family secrets, do not share them with me!" In his view, more people complain when their families are left out of a genealogy than complain of being included, and furthermore, if you have a secret, it's always best not to tell *anyone*.

On the other hand, it is worth noting that Lareau distributes information *voluntarily* sent to him, with this public and clear caution that he publishes information on the living and the dead equally. Whether this protects him legally is an open question; my point is that he is up-front, honest, and obvious about his objective to use information he receives. He does not deal in nasty surprises or ambushing people, and anyone sending him data is informed of his intended use of it. This is a good policy to follow, in my view, if you are determined to share data you collect.

Copyright

A sad fact of Internet life is that some have come to believe that the entire Internet is "public domain"—that is, free for the taking. It just isn't so. Copyright applies equally to online material and offline material. The fact that any material is online changes nothing about its copyright or lack thereof. Copyright laws are not, however, the same all around the world, and that's where online copyright becomes complicated.

As a genealogist, you should educate yourself about copyright laws (not just U.S. copyright laws) and understand what "fair use" of another's work is and what is copyrightable in the first place. A good start is the publication "Copyright Basics" from the Library of Congress, available online at www.copyright.gov/circs/circ1.pdf and in hard copy (see Figure 5-3). Be aware that if you take copyrightable material

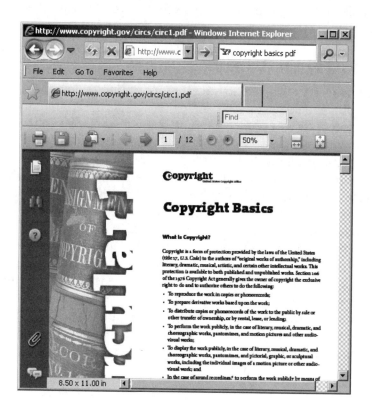

FIGURE 5-3.   *"Copyright Basics" is a good starting place to learn about U. S. copyright laws.*

without permission, you may be plagiarizing. In most instances, however, genealogists will share some or all of their material with you, if you ask first.

Copyright laws vary by country, but for most countries, the basic premises are the same:

- Facts and data cannot be copyrighted.

- Narration, compilations (that includes a genealogy database), and creative works can be copyrighted.

Some International Copyright Information Sites

- **Australian Copyright Council**   www.copyright.org.au

- **Canadian Intellectual Property site**   www.cipo.ic.gc.ca

- **European Commission page on copyright**
  http://ec.europa.eu/internal_market/copyright/ index_en.htm

- **United Kingdom page on intellectual property**
  www.ipo.gov.uk/home.htm

- **World Intellectual Property Organization site**
  www.wipo.int/clea/en

- **Nolo.com (www.nolo.com)**   Click the Patents, Copyright & Art tab.

Protecting Yourself

The other side of the coin, of course, is to decide how you want to protect yourself from plagiarism. The presentation of facts can be protected by copyright, but not the facts themselves. When you present data in your own distinctive format, such as a book, then that presentation of the material is protected by copyright, even though the facts are not. Still, when you put your work out there, expect others to use it.

Gormley says, "If you do not want to share your genealogical research, that is fine, but you cannot claim copyright to facts, and a great deal of 'online genealogy' is nothing more than compiled facts—although seldom verified or even referenced as to the actual source of the information. If you don't want to be 'ripped off'—and if you mean by that that you do not want others to use genealogical facts you have compiled—then don't share your genealogy with anyone: Put it in a vault."

Note

Just as bad as stealing another's work is posting your data with certain facts changed, such as a date, to "protect" your information. Posting what you know is not true does not advance the art and science of genealogy in any way. Don't ever do it.

"I wish I knew!" says Dick Eastman when asked how to protect data you have carefully collected. "There is no foolproof method [to avoid] being ripped off. Of course, you should always add copyright claims. But that only stops the honest people and maybe a few unknowledgeable ones who never thought about copyrights until they read your claim.

"I used to recommend technical solutions: I recommended Adobe Acrobat PDF files. However, a free program appeared that does a great job of converting PDF files back to useable text, so now even that recommendation has been weakened. I do not know of any other way." Eastman says there are no easy answers, only guidelines. "The person who is to publish the information needs to ask himself: 'Am I sure that I have a legal right to use this information?' If you have any doubts, don't publish! However, determining whether or not you do have a legal right to publish a piece of information can become very complex. I spent a lot of time discussing this with a lawyer who works for a Boston legal firm that specializes in intellectual properties issues. She is also an experienced genealogist and a member of the advisory board for a prestigious society. The more she talked, the more confused I became. At the end of our conversation, she said, 'Well, there really is no easy way,'" Eastman concluded.

However, complicated as it is, there are still steps you can take. You can (a) ask for permission to use data when you find it on someone else's site and (b) copyright your own formatting and presentation of that data. Use the previously mentioned "Copyright Basics" to find out how to do both.

Note

"In a perfect world (online or off), everyone would cite their sources properly and give credit to all who have shared research and information with them. Alas, there is no such place—never has been. Even basic good manners—such as saying 'thank you'—are rare. But the genealogist with good manners is far more likely to be rewarded with a wealth of material and help than those without."

—*Myra Vanderpool Gormley, CG*

Other Matters

Be prepared for relatives to be sensitive about certain family history, as my husband's grandfather was (see Chapter 1). A long thread on the Ancestry.com ethics discussion board described one researcher's problems in tracing her husband's line. Her in-laws became angry and insulting when asked a simple question about her husband's grandfather. She then researched discreetly, without asking her in-laws any more questions. When she came across a fact that may have been what upset her in-laws, she resolved to keep the data private.

In such a case, you may even want to put the information aside in something to be opened with your will, and ask your descendants to add it to the family tree after everyone involved is gone.

Success Story: DearMYRTLE Helps Analyze Data

Tracy St. Claire of BibleRecords.com, recently came across a potentially delicate problem: Her transcribing of a set of diaries and letters from a mid-19th-century man. The writings could possibly be interpreted as circumspect homosexual love letters and diary entries. Or not, as her mother-in-law did not get the same feeling from reading the materials. Perhaps the man was simply purple in his prose. Still, the question occurred to her: Is she "outing" not only the author, but also the correspondent, who was not a relative?

She posed the question to DearMYRTLE, who pointed out that if the materials are transcribed, not abstracted, then full context allows not only honesty, but also tools for objective analysis. Family historians are not judges, but conveyors of facts. As the materials are more than 100 years old and the family did not file extension of copyright at the end of 75 years, copyright does not apply. So in being both transparent and accurate, the transcription of the materials and posting them on the Internet do meet the criteria for ethical genealogy, and the age of the material means copyright does not apply.

"Traditionally, genealogists have been a kindly, sharing group of individuals," says Pat Richley-Erickson, also known online as DearMYRTLE. "After all, no single researcher has every piece of the ancestral puzzle. We need to share research back and forth among those with common ancestors. Successful genealogy research does not exist in a vacuum where one works totally alone. It is then only a matter of common sense to cite the source of each piece of the puzzle, to leave a wide audit trail for those that follow, and to give credit where credit is due.

"That wide audit trail is essential for others to be able to evaluate the reliability of our research in our absence. Given such source citations (author, title, call number, microfilm number, publication date, etc.), it would be possible for a great-great-grandchild to obtain photocopies (or whatever they'll be using) of original documents relating to his family tree. Should additional documentation come to light in the meantime, that distant great-great-grandchild should compare it with our old compiled genealogy to see if the new information supports or refutes the lineage assumptions we've made.

"Genealogies will improve over time, as one generation takes what others have compiled before and gathers additional documentation—perhaps distinguishing between two John Smiths in an area where it was previously thought there was only one individual by that name. In such a case, it isn't

necessary to denigrate the work of the previous researcher. Merely point out the expanded list of documents proving the distinctions and bring the family puzzle into a new light. But in doing so, cite all sources!

"There is also a need for individuals who merely photocopy 25 pages of their personal recollections at the local office supply store and send them in manila envelopes to their distant family members. Wouldn't we each give our eyeteeth to have such a write-up from our Civil War or Revolutionary War ancestor? But, as always, family lore must be proved before incorporating it into our pedigree charts. Looking at documents created at the time our ancestors lived are eyewitness accounts of life as they knew it," she concluded.

For further reading, DearMYRTLE recommends Evidence! Source Citation & Analysis for the Family Historian *by Elizabeth Shown Mills (Genealogical Publishing Company, 1997) available at www.genealogical.com.*

Give Back

Finally, it is at least as good to give as to receive, and it is more ethical to give back to the genealogy community than to just take everything you find. Once you have some experience, you should consider contributing to the amount of good, accurate information available online. For example, on www.familysearchindexing.org, you can volunteer to be part of their indexing project. In the first quarter of 2007 alone, volunteers indexed nearly 30 million names by simply reading scanned documents and typing the names and page numbers. This was done by thousands of volunteers, some of whom can only spare one hour a month. But in that hour, you can probably index 50 or so names. Multiply that by the hundreds of thousands of people who use www.familysearch.org, and you can see what an impact that can make!

Similarly, most of the USGenWeb and international GenWeb sites are thrilled to have volunteers help them index and transcribe wills, deeds, letters, tax rolls, or any other primary source you can get your hand on. Again, give an hour a month, and you can be of great help to many other researchers! Check out www.usgenweb.org, drill down to the states and counties for which you have data, and contribute. Join a local historical or genealogical organization, and share your findings with the membership in their publications and online sites.

As an example of giving and receiving good genealogy karma, for years my mother edited LeDespencer, the Spencer Historical and Genealogical Society (www.spencersociety.org) newsletter, which ran articles such as transcribed original materials from letters and diaries and narratives about ancestors of the members. She indexed each volume herself, too. She learned a lot about our branch of Spencer ancestors as well as lots of other branches in the process while disseminating invaluable data.

NGS Standards

In the back of this book you will find the standards for genealogy published by the National Genealogical Society. These genealogical standards and guidelines are aimed at making the practice of genealogy clearer, better, and more understandable. While NGS is neither an accrediting nor an enforcement agency and will not keep track of whether you as an individual are following these standards, nevertheless, if you use the standards and guidelines in your personal pursuit of family history, then they have served their purpose. The current standards are

- Guidelines for Genealogical Self-Improvement and Growth
- Guidelines for Publishing Web Pages on the Internet
- Guidelines for Using Records Repositories and Libraries
- Standards for Sharing Information with Others
- Standards for Sound Genealogical Research
- Standards for Use of Technology in Genealogical Research

Further Reading

The following are some good online articles on these topics:

- 10 Myths about Copyright Explained by Brad Templeton (http://www .templetons.com/brad/copymyths.html)
- Association of Professional Genealogists' Code of Ethics (http://www .apgen.org/ethics/index.html)
- Board for Certification of Genealogists' Code of Ethics (http://www .bcgcertification.org/aboutbcg/ code.html)

- Can You Copyright Your Family Tree? by Kimberly Powell (http://genealogy.about.com/od/writing_family_history/a/copyright .htm)

- Copyright Fundamentals for Genealogy by Mike Goad (http://www .pddoc.com/copyright/genealogy_copyright_fundamentals.htm)

- Genealogist's Code of Ethics (http://www.rootsweb.com/ ~gasaga/ ethics.html)

- Horror on the Web by Myra Vanderpool Gormley (http://www .ancestry.com/columns/myra/Shaking_Family_Tree10-29-98.htm)

Wrapping Up

- Ethics, privacy, and copyright are the three concerns with genealogy legalities.

- Do not publish anything about living people, on the Web or otherwise. This helps prevent someone from getting a name, birth date, and birth place to create a false identification or to steal an identity. On the other hand, do not try to protect privacy by publishing anything you know to be untrue. Doing so will result in bad data becoming part of the Internet forever.

- Be sensitive about publishing information on those who have passed on. You may find it fascinating that your great-great-grandfather was illegitimate and a pirate; perhaps your cousins won't be so enthralled.

- Cite your sources, both to protect intellectual property rights and to leave a wide audit trail for future genealogists.

- Do your best to follow the standards and guidelines of the National Genealogical Society, and familiarize yourself with the codes of ethics professional genealogists use.

- Contribute to the collection of good, accurate data on the Internet by becoming involved with indexing, transcribing, and discussing original sources.

Part II

General Genealogy

Chapter 6

Revving Up Search Engines

As I write this book, pointing you to the best genealogy resources on the Internet as I know them at the time I am writing, I am aware that you may find some of the links are broken. By the time you read this, untold numbers of sites may have been created, or deleted, or changed from wonderful to not-so-much, and vice versa. Keeping track of all of this is made much easier by search engines and portals. Search engines and portals offer ways to send changes and news stories that match certain keywords to you via e-mail or push technology, and I will show you how to take advantage of that.

Certainly, as a genealogist, you've experienced the thrill of discovering things for yourself—it can be quite a kick to find a website or blog none of your friends know about. To do this, you need a way to find genealogical resources on the Internet on your own. That's where search sites come in.

Defining Terms

Search engine is an all-purpose label used to describe anything that will let you search for terms within a group of data. That data could be on a single site or on billions of pages on the Internet, or on some subset in between the two. Just about anything that lets you search gets called a search engine, but some other terms are more accurate for specific sites.

A *spider* is a program that looks for information on the Internet, creates a database of what it finds, and lets you use a Web browser to run a search engine on that database for specific information. As noted, this can mean billions of pages or only the pages on one site.

Note

If you are interested in search engines, how they work, and how they compare to one another, check out Search Engine Watch (http://searchenginewatch.com) and Search Engines.com (http://www.searchengines.com).

A search site might have one or more search engines and can claim to use spiders to search "the whole Web," but, in reality, most probably cover about 15 percent of the Web at any given time. This is because pages quickly appear and disappear on the Web. That's why you might want to use several different search sites when you are searching for specific information or for general types of sites. Or, you might want to try one of the many meta-search engines that try several search sites at once.

A search site called a *directory* or a *catalog* uses a search engine to let you hunt through an edited list of Internet sites for specific information. The value of these sites is that in a directory or catalog, websites are sorted, categorized, and sometimes rated. Most often, the directory is included in a portal, which pulls together searches of news, information, text, pictures, and whatever into one page, which you can modify to your liking. And this is what an online genealogist needs.

Yahoo! (www.yahoo.com), shown in Figure 6-1, was one of the first catalogs or directories established online; it is also a good example of a portal that offers other services, such as chat, news, forums, RSS readers, and more.

A *portal* is a little bit of everything: a search engine for the Web at large, a catalog of sites the owners recommend, and usually a group of other features, including stock prices, Web-based e-mail, shopping, and so on. In the figure, you can see that I have personalized My Yahoo! page to pull genealogy information onto the portal for me. To do this is simple.

First, establish a Yahoo! account and password. Then click the Add Content button. On the Add Content page, search for "genealogy," and add the modules that interest you. Save the changes. Then, choose Add Content again, and browse the News section. You can create news clippers that post or e-mail you a notice when a story appears on any topic from "genealogy" to "Kentucky basketball." I added the modules to the portal page; you may choose to have it e-mailed to you or picked up by an RSS reader.

You can add additional pages and access them by tabs, so you could have one for general genealogy, one for surnames, and so on. Google, MSN, AOL, Excite, and even my Internet service provider (ISP), Bellsouth.net, all offer similar capabilities. Once you have the portal set up the way you like it, you can make it your home page.

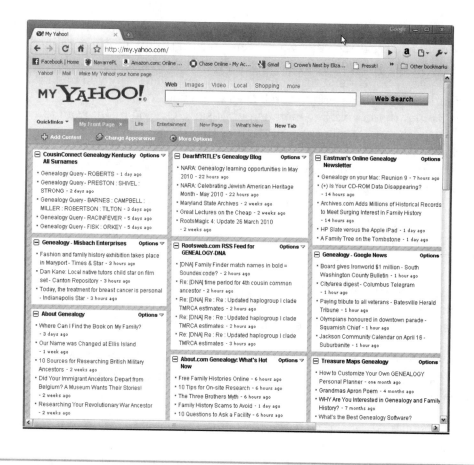

FIGURE 6-1. *Yahoo! is an example of a portal that lets you track news, blogs, and sites according to topic. This page is set up for genealogy.*

A *meta-search engine* submits your query to several different search sites, portals, and catalogs at the same time. You might get more results, and you will usually be able to compare how each one responded to the query. These searches may take longer, however, and getting millions of results is almost more trouble than getting one. There are genealogy-specific meta-search engines, and you will find information on some of them later in this chapter. Examples of general meta-search sites are Dogpile, Mamma, Profusion, and others. You can also check out the page www.dmoz.org/Computers/Internet/Searching/Multi-Search (see Figure 6-2) for a list of many different meta-search engines.

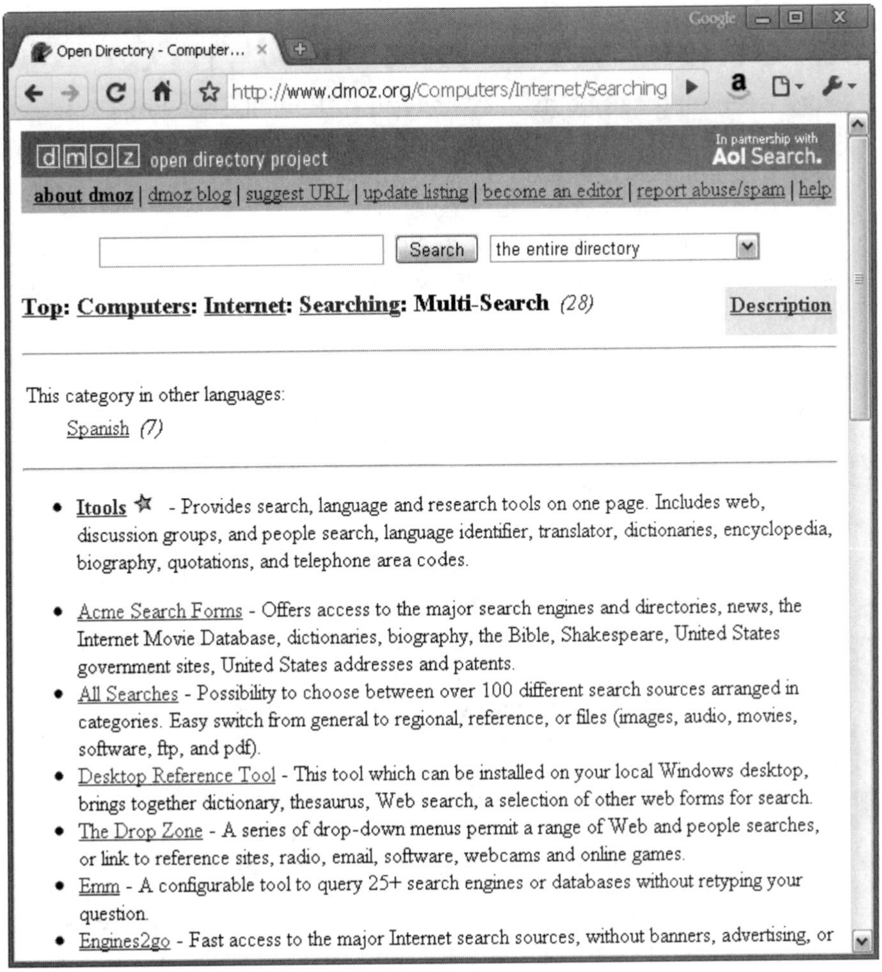

FIGURE 6-2. *DMOZ, The Open Directory Project, has an edited list of meta-search engines.*

Searching with Savoir Faire

Now, searching can be as easy as typing "Powell Genealogy" and clicking the search button. Be warned, though, that might also get you so many hits that you feel you are drinking from a fire hose. It doesn't have to be that way. You can make the spiders boogie if you just speak their language. Thankfully, search algorithms (the language of the spiders) have come a long way since the days when search engines could not tell the difference between a blind Venetian and a Venetian blind!

Here are some general search tips:

♦ Use phrases instead of single words in your searches. Type several words that are relevant to your search. Typing Spencer genealogy Ohio will narrow a search well.

♦ Enclose phrases in quotes. Searching on the phrase Spencer family history without quotation marks will match all pages that have any of those three words included somewhere on the page, in any order, and not necessarily adjacent to each other. Searching with the phrase "Spencer family history" (with quotation marks) will return only those pages that have those three words together.

♦ The more specific you are, the better. Searching for Irish genealogy databases will give you fewer, but closer, matches than searching for Irish genealogy.

♦ Use plus and minus signs in your searches. A word preceded by a plus sign (+) must appear on the page to be considered a match. A word preceded by a minus sign (–) must not appear on the page to be considered a match. No spaces can be between the plus and minus signs and the words they apply to. For example, entering

```
+Spencer -royal genealogy
```

would ask the search engine to find pages that contain the word "Spencer" but not the word "royal," with the word "genealogy" preferred, but optional. Most search engines would get some Spencer genealogy pages but leave out those that include Lady Diana, Princess of Wales. More about this type of search can be found in the following section about Boolean searches.

Every now and then, search for "geneology" instead of "genealogy." You will be amazed at how many pages out there use this misspelling in their titles and body text!

> ## Note
>
> *Narrow your search if you get too many matches. Sometimes, the page with your search results will have an input box to allow you to search for new terms specifically among the first results. This might mean adding terms or deleting terms and then running the search again just on the results from the first search.*

Using Boolean Terms

Searching the Internet is no simple matter. With literally billions of sites, some of them with millions of documents, and more words than you can imagine, finding exactly the right needle in all that hay can be daunting. The key, of course, is crafting a precise query.

Boolean operators are handy tools for honing your searches. Named after George Boole, the 19th-century mathematician who dreamed up symbolic logic, Boolean operators represent the relationships among items using terms such as OR, AND, and NOT. When applied to information retrieval, they can expand or narrow a search to uncover as many citations, or hits, as you want.

The Boolean OR

When you search for two or more terms joined with an OR operator, you receive hits that contain any one of your terms. Therefore, the query

```
Powell OR genealogy
```

will retrieve documents containing "Powell" or "genealogy," but not necessarily both. Note that nearly all search pages default to OR—that is, they assume you want any page with any one or more of your terms in it.

You can see it makes good sense to use OR when you search for synonyms or closely related terms. For example, if you're looking for variations on a name, search for

`SPENCER SPENCE SPENSER`

The average search engine will assume the OR operator and find any page with any one or more of those terms. However, the average search engine will also sort the results such that the pages with the most relevance appear at the top, using all your search terms to score that relevance.

The Boolean AND

In the Boolean boogie, joining search terms with AND means that all terms must be found in a document, but not necessarily together. The query

`George AND Washington`

will result in a list of documents that have both the names "George" and "Washington" somewhere within them. Use AND when you have dissimilar terms and need to narrow a search. Usually, to use AND in a search, you type a plus sign (+) or put the term AND between the words and enclose everything within parentheses, like so:

`(Spencer AND genealogy)`

The Boolean NOT

When you use NOT, search results must exclude certain terms. Many search engines don't have this functionality. Often, when you can use it, the syntax is to put a minus sign (–) in front of the unwanted term. The query

`Powell NOT Colin`

will return all citations containing the name "Powell," but none including "Colin," regardless of whether "Powell" is there. Use NOT when you want to exclude possible second meanings. "Banks" can be found on genealogy surname pages as well as on pages associated with finance or with rivers. Searching for

```
banks AND genealogy NOT river
```

or

```
banks +genealogy -river
```

increases the chance of finding documents relating to the surname Banks (the people, not riversides). In some search engines, the minus sign often takes the place of NOT.

Note

Remember, a simple AND doesn't guarantee that the words will be next to each other. Your search for George AND Washington could turn up documents about George Benson and Grover Washington!

The fun part is combining Boolean operators to create a precise search. Let's say you want to find documents about the city of Dallas, Texas. If you simply search for "Dallas," you could get copious hits about Dallas County in Alabama (county seat: Selma), which might not be the Dallas you want. To avoid that, you would use AND, NOT, and OR in this fashion:

```
(Dallas AND Texas) NOT (Selma OR Alabama)
(Powell AND genealogy) NOT (Colin AND "SECRETARY OF STATE")
```

Note that parentheses group the search terms together.

Beyond AND/OR/NOT

Some search engines enable you to fine-tune a search further. The WITH operator, for example, searches for terms that are much nearer to each other. How "near" is defined depends on the engine.

Some search engines would look at "George WITH Washington" and deliver documents only containing the words "George Washington" next to each other. Others might consider words in the same sentence or paragraph to be near enough. This makes a difference if there might be an intervening (middle) name involved in your search.

You can also sometimes use a question mark or an asterisk to find many different variants of a word. Check the search engine's Help files to see if it uses wildcards or word stemming (for finding all variations of a word, such as ancestry, ancestral, ancestor, and ancestors).

Using these techniques, you can search the Web much more efficiently, finding just the right document on George Washington Carver or a genealogy site on the right set of Powells. Learn the steps to the Boolean boogie, and you'll soon be Web dancing wherever you please!

Search Sites

The Web has an embarrassment of riches, some of which are more useful to genealogists than others. The following is a representative list of genealogy-related catalogs, portals, and search engines, in alphabetical order.

Access Genealogy

At this site, www.accessgenealogy.com, you can read and search free of charge for many different types of records for genealogy research, including newspapers and periodicals; emigration and immigration forms; census reports; voting records; and archives from libraries, cemeteries, churches, and courts (see Figure 6-3). The site is also widely known for Native American data, and for ten years has been one of the best genealogy search sites.

Ancestor Hunt

This site is an edited catalog, and it is wonderful. With this meta-search site at www.ancestorhunt.com, you can search for ancestors and locate surnames in some of the best and largest databases of genealogy records online. The site has unique searches, such as the Surname Search Portal and the Obituary Search Portal, both of which search several sites at once.

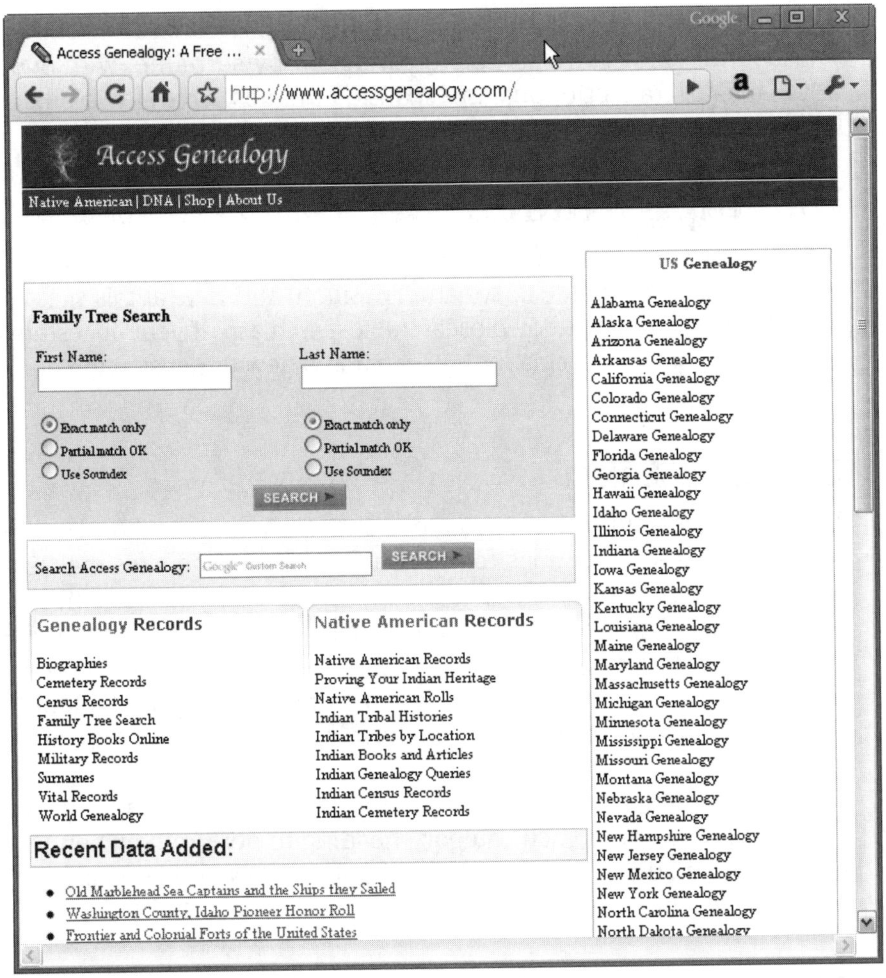

FIGURE 6-3. *Access Genealogy is a family history meta-search site with quite a bit of Native American data.*

Two of the exceptional pages are Genealogical Prison Records and Past Sheriffs of the United States. You will find these, along with many other search engines and free genealogy resources, in the Genealogy Search Engines And Contents menu, which is located on each page.

One of the most popular sections is the Bible Records Transcriptions. These family Bibles are completely indexed by surname, with over 200 pages of transcriptions and scanned images. This site is one to bookmark!

Biography Guide

Was any ancestor of yours a member of Congress? Search for biographies of members by last name, first name, position, and state at this site: http://bioguide.congress.gov/biosearch/biosearch.asp. If your ancestors are in the database, this fascinating site can add a new dimension to your family history.

Cyndi's List

The site www.cyndislist.com catalogs about a quarter-million genealogy websites. You will find links to the genealogy sites and sites that simply would help a genealogist. This is the first place many new online genealogists visit. The links are categorized and organized, and there's also a search box for finding the subjects you want quickly. Cyndi Howells works on the list every day, updating, deleting, and adding sites. Each new or updated link will have a small "new" or "updated" graphic next to it for 30 days.

The main index is updated each time activity occurs on Cyndi's List. Check the date under each category heading to determine when the last update was made for that category. The date is also updated at the bottom of each category page.

Free Genealogy Search Help for Google

This free genealogy site is designed to help you use Google for genealogy-specific searches. It will create a series of different searches using Google's advanced features that will likely improve your results.

The site has a small family tree as a form for you to fill in with an ancestor, and this site will set up the best searches for you, based on what you enter. Now, if you don't know an ancestor's parents but know one of the ancestor's children, use the child's name for the First Name and Last Name (and spouse, birth, and death) and then enter the ancestor as the Father or Mother. This gives more information for building a search.

It's quick and easy and gives good results.

Genealogy Pages

A collected catalog of genealogy sites, the website www.genealogypages .com also offers you a free e-mail inbox and a browser-based chat site, so it qualifies as a portal.

You can browse the collection of links by category or search the entire collection. Because it's all about genealogy, you don't have to put that term in the search box. For example, a search for "South Carolina Powell" in the regular search box turned up nothing, even though in the advanced search box I could choose between AND (the default) and OR. And even if it was recognized as a phrase, I couldn't get a match on all three. Searching on "South Carolina" got good results, however, as did searching on "Powell."

Genealogy Research Resources

At www.misbach.org/resources.html, you can find input boxes for some of the most popular search engines on the Internet for doing genealogical research. When you enter your search criteria in any of the fields, it will take you to the labeled website and show you the results of your query. You have to navigate back to Genealogy Research Resources to do the next search, however, so you may want to bookmark this page.

GeneaSearch.com

This portal at www.geneasearch.com, is along the lines of Genealogy Pages. Several search options exist, but searching by surname is your best bet. GeneaSearch gives results similar to those of Genealogy Pages. They will both return submitted GEDCOMs from users that will be secondary sources for genealogy.

The site's services include free genealogy lookups, free genealogy sites, family surname newsletters, data, books from genealogy societies and individuals, surname queries, female ancestors, new site announcements, a beginner's genealogy guide, and free clip art. Other genealogy resources include tools, links, and lists of societies. Also, there are free genealogy databases and genealogy resources for each state.

GenGateway

Another version of a catalog of websites organized into categories for genealogists is www.gengateway.com, by Steve Lacy. It indexes thousands of webpages and sources. Choose the category you want to search, such as surname or obituary, and you'll get well-sorted results.

To navigate the site, use one of the many useful gateways listed in the navigation bar on the left of the home page. If you're new to the site, first try the Beginners Gateway or the Search Pages.

GenServ

This is one of my favorite genealogy sites. GenServ has been online since 1991 and on the Web since 1994. GenServ, at www.genserv.com, is a collection of donated GEDCOMs with a sophisticated set of search commands. The database has over 25,000,000 individuals in more than 19,000 databases. All this family history data is online and available by search and reports to subscribers. You can search a limited amount of the data in a free trial (see Figure 6-4).

To access the system, you have to at least submit your own GEDCOM. If you pay the optional yearly fees, you can perform many more searches per day than the free access allows.

Note

GenServ is a huge database of submitted GEDCOMS. Therefore, it is all secondary source material. When you seem to have a match, you need to contact the submitter to determine what primary source material he or she might have and offer to exchange what data you have.

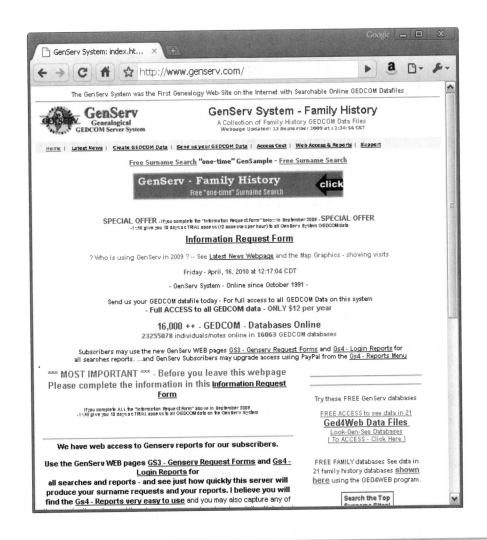

FIGURE 6-4. *GenServ is bare bones in presentation, but sophisticated in programming.*

The capability to do complex searches on the databases means you will have a real learning curve. Only the "surname count" search can be done from the Web; all the the other searches are done via e-mail messages. This has the advantage of letting you input your terms and then surf on to other sites. The results, meanwhile, come back by e-mail (and quickly, too!).

Uploading your data and learning how to query this set of databases is worth your time.

GenSource

The specialized genealogy directory site www.gensource.com provides the online genealogist with three databases to assist with research online.

The first database is called Search Common Threads, which will help you find other genealogists researching your family name. If you're at a "brick wall" in finding information on an ancestor, add an entry to Common Threads so other family members can find you.

Search the second database, I Found It!, to locate genealogy sites on the Internet. You can use the I Found It! search engine to locate pages on surnames, one-name studies, ship passenger lists, genealogical societies and associations, researchers, software, books, family mailing lists, online records of churches, census data, cemeteries, and more.

Search the third database, the IFI (I Found It!) Archives, for sites containing actual historical records. Many people have taken the time to transcribe records and place them on the Net for your use, all of which are indexed for research purposes.

NedGen

Trace your roots in Europe with this genealogy and ancestry search engine dedicated to indexing family history and roots on personal home pages with online family trees in Europe.

This is one example of a beyond-the-U.S. search engine aimed at genealogists. At www.nedgen.com, you can search more than 60,000 genealogy websites in the United States, Canada, Europe, France, Germany, Italy, Ireland, Netherlands/Belgium, Scandinavia, the United Kingdom and other European countries, Australia and New Zealand, Asia, and African and Jewish genealogy. You can also use the page navigation bar to search ship and passenger lists, adoption records, census records, online databases, vital records, and Ellis Island records. Search migration, military, personal home pages, genealogy software, Origins.net, Ancestry.com, and Classmates.com from here, too!

RootsWeb Search Thingy

This is one of the first genealogy search sites I ever used on the Web, and I still go to it often. Go to www.rootsweb.com, click Searches, and click Search Thingy. Then put in your search terms. The meta-search goes through all RootsWeb pages and databases. The disadvantage to Search Thingy is that OR is the only Boolean operator you can use, so a search for James Reason Powell will return any page with any one of those terms.

Surname Web

Located at www.surnameweb.org, Surname Web has a database of names submitted by users, as well as pages from other websites. Simply input the surname you are looking for.

WorldConnect

WorldConnect (http://worldconnect.rootsweb.com) is a division of RootsWeb. RootsWeb's motto is "Connecting the world, one GEDCOM at a time." People can upload to and search this collection of GEDCOM databases for free. All you need to do is fill out the form with name, place of birth and death, and dates of birth and death. You can choose an exact search if you're sure of your facts, or a range of 2 to 20 years for dates, and Soundex searches for names and places.

It's fast, but the results depend entirely on the uploaded GEDCOMs. If you have no hits, consider uploading your information for others. If you have uploaded your information, you can exclude your own database from future searches.

Like GenServ, WorldConnect is all-volunteer, amateur information, secondary material, and only as reliable as the person submitting it. You must contact the submitter of a database to find out the primary sources for the data. However, unlike with GenServ, you can do the searches via the Web.

General Search Sites

Many Web-wide search engines and portals can help you find genealogy resources. Using the search techniques previously mentioned, you'll probably have good results trying these general search engines. Some of them have catalogs of genealogy sites. For those that do, information on how to browse them is provided in the following list. On all of them, though, searches as described in the beginning of this chapter will work:

♦ Search (www.search.com) is a mega-search engine.

♦ Dogpile (www.dogpile.com) is a mega-search engine. One search will query several other search engines. It has an Advanced Search that allows Boolean searches. Don't bother with the Dogpile "Web directory," because it's simply a listing of their paid advertisers. The search function, however, is fast and gives good results.

♦ Yahoo! has been mentioned previously, and is worth using.

♦ Google (www.google.com) provides the obvious search of your surnames and ancestors' hometowns, as well as many tools to help the genealogist.

One of the exciting things added to Google recently is the Timeline feature. Begin by entering your surname plus the term `family history`. Then, in the upper-left quadrant, find the link to Show Options. Select Timeline, and you will be presented with a timeline of history of that surname. Figure 6-5 shows what I got when searching `Powell Family History`. Within the timeline, you can zoom in to specific date ranges, for example, 1800–1820, to see pages that mention Powell family history in that time period.

Another cool Google feature is using the tilde (∼) to see synonyms. For example, to find death records, add a tilde to the front of the word (∼death) and the results will have synonyms for the death in the results. Google has a news search, as shown in the previous Yahoo! example, and can send an RSS feed, an e-mail, or post it on your personalized Google site when your keywords are found in a news story. I keep a "genealogy" one going, and often use it to read newspapers' genealogy columnists from around the world.

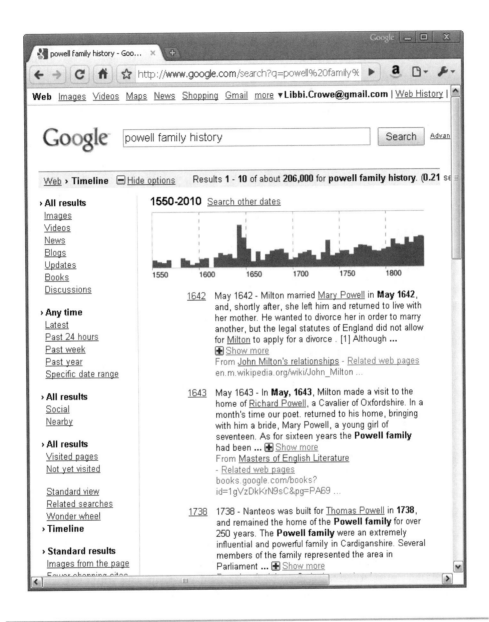

FIGURE 6-5. *Google's Timeline can help you search for pages about your family's history and present to you the timeline of the citations.*

Another important feature is page translations. Click Language Tools on the main Google page. You have a choice of putting in a page you already found or simply pasting in a block of text to be translated. Also, if a regular Google search turns up non-English pages, one of your choices will be Translate This Page—great for when you get beyond the boat to the "old country!"

Google Book Search can make you feel like a kid in a toy store. On the Google page, click More and then click Books. Now type the genealogy information you're looking for, such as a surname or a location, or just "genealogy." The Google Book Search looks in the full text of thousands of books, and within seconds returns hits based on relevance. The fun doesn't stop there. Click a book title, and you'll see basic information about the book similar to a card catalog. You might also see a few sentences with your search term in context. If a publisher or author has granted permission, you'll see a full page and be able to browse within the book to see more pages. If the book is out of copyright, you'll see a full page, and you can move forward and backward to see the full book.

Clicking Search Within This Book allows you to perform more searches within the book you've selected. Clicking Buy This Book connects you to an online bookstore where you can make an online purchase of it. For some books, you will see a Find This Book In A Library link: this goes to a local library where you can borrow it.

Bing is Microsoft's competition to Google. (A common joke is Bing stands for "But it's not Google!"). Bing's initial results on Powell Genealogy are weighted toward sites with the most recent changes or creation date. Bing also gives you suggested alternative searches (see Figure 6-6) in a panel to the left, such as "Powell Family Tree" or "Powell Family Crest" (see Chapter 2). Move your cursor to one of the results, and a bubble pops up with a preview of the site.

Also, note that Bing can treat a phrase as a Boolean WITH if you use quotation marks around it. When searching for a specific name, `"William Reason Powell"` again, it turns up the most recent first. In the first ten results, all the pages are either my own or pages where I am quoted about Reason—not a lot of help.

Bing does not have a Book Search capability, the Google-style date range search, or a synonym search. Bing doesn't appear to find results when searching for surnames with foreign letters such as umlauts and accents. It will, however, give you the latest-dated results, which can be a boon when looking for living relatives or for people currently working on your surnames.

FIGURE 6-6. *Bing suggests alternatives to your search terms and returns more recent pages first.*

Obituary Search Pages

Several pages enable you to search recent and older obituaries:

♦ Free Obituary Searches (www.obituary-searches.com) lists several different pages for death notice searches, around the world, mostly contemporary.

♦ Legacy.com (www.legacy.com/Obituaries.asp) has a page called ObitFinder that searches recent obituaries by name, keyword, and location.

♦ Obituary Links (www.obitlinkspage.com) searches cemetery records, obituaries, and other pages from sites such as Ancestry.com, RootsWeb, and so on. This is a meta-search engine that focuses on death records.

♦ Origins.net (www.origins.net) is a fee-based genealogy search site; you can try a sample search for free. Users pay a license fee for use of the Origin Search software at $5 for 24 hours or $15 for 14 days. Origins.net provides access to databases of genealogical data for online family history research in the United Kingdom, Canada, Australia, New Zealand, and the United States.

White Page Directories

So far, you've looked at search engines and directories for finding a website. But what if you need to find lost living relatives? Or what if you want to write to people with the same surnames you're researching? In that case, you need people search engines, called White Page directories. Like the White Pages of your phone book, these directories specialize in finding people, not pages. In fact, all the search engine sites mentioned previously have White Page directories.

The AT&T site (www.att.com/directory) has an excellent set of directories for people and businesses, with a reverse phone number lookup (put in the phone number; get the name). It's basically a White Pages for the whole United States.

Switchboard (www.switchboard.com) is one of many White Pages services on the Web. It's free, and it lists the e-mail addresses and telephone numbers of millions of people and businesses, taken from public records. It's also a website catalog. If you register as a user (it's free), you can ensure that your listing is not only accurate, but also has only the information you want it to reveal.

Wrapping Up

- ♦ Learn to use Boolean search terms to target your Web searches.
- ♦ Use genealogy-specific sites to search for surnames and localities.
- ♦ Use general search sites and catalogs that gather news and links about genealogy.
- ♦ Use White Pages search sites to find living people.

Chapter 7

Talk to Me: Twitter, Skype, IM, and Chat

Sometimes you might want to talk to a fellow genealogist to resolve problems you're encountering in your research. The online world can help you there, too, with more ways than you can shake a stick at. Voice over Internet Protocol (VOIP), Twitter, instant messaging, and even good "old-fashioned" chat can all help you make personal connections with other genealogists.

Twitter

Twitter has become a phenomenon as well as an Internet application. Twitter is free, and it combines social networking (see Chapter 9) with blogging on a very small scale (see Chapter 2). With it you can send and receive messages, links, and more.

When you send something on Twitter, it is called a tweet. A tweet is a text message of no more than 140 characters displayed on your Twitter profile page and delivered to your followers, who are people who have subscribed to your tweets. You can determine that only those you choose can receive your tweets, or open it up to the world (the latter is the default). You can send and receive tweets via the Twitter website Short Message Service (SMS) on your smart phone or external applications.

Note

Although Twitter itself costs nothing to use, accessing it through your smart phone's SMS could rack up fees from your phone service provider, as each tweet will be a text message.

That 140-character limit also spurred usage of URL-shortening services such as tinyurl, bit.ly, and tr.im, where you can shorten a long address to just a few characters.

Since Jack Dorsey created it in 2006, Twitter has seen an increase in use by many millions of people. Alexa web traffic analysis ranks Twitter as one of the 50 most popular websites in the world. And, of course, genealogists are among them (see Figure 7-1).

FIGURE 7-1.   *Genealogy tweeting is very popular.*

An example:

```
ACoffin  @epcrowe I use Twitter to share  #genealogy news,
hi-lite blog posts and ask reference-type questions.
ACoffin  @epcrowe I also use Twitter as a  #genealogy news feed
of sorts. If it happens, someone will post it here, asap.
```

Notice the conventions of Twitter messages: If you want a term in your tweet to be searchable, put an octothorpe (#) in front of it. If you want a certain person to be sure to see it, put an at sign (@) in front of that person's handle.

Your eyes are glazing over. I can see it. Okay, let's unpack this.

Replies and Mentions

Once you sign up for Twitter (a simple process, but it requires a valid e-mail address), you can have the program search your AOL, Google, or Yahoo! address books under "Find People." Everyone has a "handle," or user name, often some short version of a real name or a company.

An @reply is a message sent from one person to another, although everyone who follows them can see it. You should put the "@username" at the beginning of the message. When a message begins with @username, the Twitter software considers it a public reply. You do not have to be following someone to reply to that person, and all your replies and mentions are shown in the @username tab in your home page sidebar.

Note

A tweet that begins with username is a reply, and a tweet with @username anywhere else in the message is considered a mention. *Both kinds of messages will be collected to your sidebar and are public. A tweet that starts with the single letter D will be sent directly and privately.*

Also, you can send a private reply by starting the message with a D and a space, then the username. *Direct messages* (see Figure 7-2) are private messages sent from one Twitterer to another. You can only send a direct message to a person who follows you. When you receive a direct message, it goes to your direct message inbox, which you access from the Direct Message tab in the sidebar in your home page. You can set your e-mail preferences to receive an e-mail from Twitter when you receive a direct message.

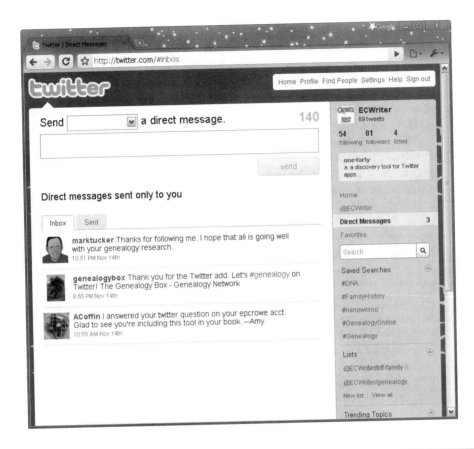

FIGURE 7-2. *Direct messages are private, but still limited to 140 characters.*

Success Story: Amy Coffin Uses Twitter for Genealogy

Amy Coffin, MLIS, is a genealogy and records research librarian, blogger, and researcher (http://amycoffin.com) who uses Twitter daily.

"I use Twitter mainly as a news aggregator," she said. "I seek out the genealogy-related people and vendors I want to follow and they are the only ones who show up in my Twitter stream. Twitter gets a bad rap from those who have never used it or don't see its value. I tell people Twitter is like television. There's a lot of junk on Twitter, just like there's a lot of junk on television. The key is

finding what you want to see and blocking out everything else. There is useful genealogy information to be had on Twitter; you just need to set your account up so it comes to you."

She also uses it for live reporting just as people in many fields do. For example, conference attendees send live tweets right from the conference, allowing discussion about the event between those who are attending and those who are not.

"Usually before a conference, a dedicated 'hashtag' is established and everyone attending or talking about the conference uses that hashtag in their tweets. This makes them more searchable and distributes the information better. For example, I'm attending the Southern California Genealogy Jamboree in June 2010, where the hashtag will be #scgs10. If you search Twitter using '#scgs10' during that time, you will see all the tweets about the conference," she said.

It also serves as her "mini-reference desk." Amy uses her Twitter account to ask questions of other genealogists and librarians that she follows.

"Once, I had a distant cousin tell me that our great-great grandfather was given acknowledgement in a book of an award-winning author. Could this be true? I sent a request to all my librarian Twitter followers and had my answer in minutes," Amy said.

Other uses Amy has found: publicity for her blog entries and friendship.

"I've become friends with many of my Twitter followers. It's always exciting to meet them for the first time at genealogy events," she said.

Hash Tags

With all those millions of users tweeting 24 hours a day, seven days a week, how on earth do you find the messages that might interest you? Hash tags: using an octothorpe (#) to tag a message's topic.

The Twitter community created hash tags because the Twitter software had no easy way to sort out the tweets by category or add extra data with that 140-character limit. So, the Twitter community came up with this solution. Hash tags have the octothorpe "hash" or "pound" symbol (#) preceding the tag, for example, #genealogy, #FamilyHistory, #DNA, or #ancestry. Although the hash tags can occur anywhere in the tweet, often you will find them at the end of a tweet.

These hash tags are not an official element of Twitter, but they have become standard practice. You can see in Twitter Search that hash tag terms are often in trending topics, the list of keywords seen most often in the current postings.

Using Hash Tags

If you add a hash tag to your tweet and you have a public account, anyone who does a search for that hash tag can find your tweet. There are no formal rules for hash tags, except never use one for spamming. Nevertheless, even though any word with a # in front could be considered a hash tag keyword, some are more commonly used.

It is a good idea to use them sparingly and always relevantly. A maximum of three hash tags to a message is considered good form.

As they have become more accepted, you can now search for hash tags, as well as any other keyword, by using the search box on the sidebar of the home page. If you search for #FamilyHistory and come up with good results, you can click "Save This Search" and receive a link to all recent tweets with that hash tag. Figure 7-3 shows a recent

FIGURE 7-3.   *Use hash tags to search for recent tweets on topics that interest you.*

search for that hash tag. You can also create an RSS feed of your favorite searches, again with a single click.

But notice the phrase I used earlier: "any other keyword." If you search on anything: your surname, a noun, even a verb, you're likely to find tweets that match. The hash tag is to help you filter out messages from someone *named* Powell from messages *about* a Powell.

Twitter Commands

- ◆ *@username* + message directs a twitter at another person and causes your twitter to be saved to that person's Replies tab. Example: @ECWriter when does the book come out?

- ◆ D *username* + message sends a person a private message that goes to a device, and is saved in that person's web archive. Example: d ECWriter I have some Powell genealogy data

- ◆ SET LOCATION *place name* updates the location field in your profile. Example: set location Salt Lake City

- ◆ WHOIS *username* retrieves the profile information for any public user on Twitter. Example: whois ECWriter

- ◆ GET *username* retrieves the latest Twitter update posted by the person. Example: get ECWriter

- ◆ NUDGE *username* reminds a friend to update on Twitter. Example: nudge ECWriter

- ◆ FAV *username* marks a person's last twitter as a favorite (hint: reply to any update with FAV to mark it as a favorite if you're receiving it in real time). Example: fav ECWriter

- ◆ STATS command returns your number of followers, how many people you're following, and your bio information.

- ◆ INVITE *phone number* will send an SMS invite (text message) to a friend's mobile phone. Example: Invite 555 555 1212

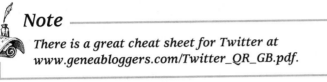

Note
There is a great cheat sheet for Twitter at
www.geneabloggers.com/Twitter_QR_GB.pdf.

You can also create lists of Twitter users to follow, another way to quickly categorize the tweet feed. Twitter lists are groups of people whose tweets you want to stay current on. Note if you want to see the tweets of someone without adding that person to your follow inventory, lists let you to do that.

The Twitter software allows you to build lists in several ways. Usually, you start one by clicking New List on the Twitter sidebar and entering your list name in the pop-up box. You can also make the list public (everyone can see it) or private (only you can see it). At this writing, you are limited to 20 lists per account. If a list is public, you can follow it even if you didn't create it. Some public lists are useful, and you don't have to reinvent the wheel. Check out the following lists:

- ◆ @TamuraJones/geneawavers

- ◆ @hikari17/genealogysocieties

- ◆ @BBPetura/genealogy

- ◆ @GenFreelancers/internationalgenealogists

- ◆ @southerngraves/genealogy-history

With public lists like these, you can start following them with a click and avoid building a list of 166 different accounts all by yourself.

You can add people to a list (including yourself!) from most places on Twitter. Look next to any profile and find and click the Lists button. This includes:

- ◆ "Find people" searches

- ◆ Profile pages (including your own)

- ◆ Public lists pages, both yours and others'

Removing someone from a list is just as easy; simply uncheck the box.

On your Twitter home page, clicking on the "listed" number (which is next to your "followers" number) will bring up your lists page (see Figure 7-4). The first tab on this page shows the lists of other people, which includes you. The first column of numbers represents the number of members of this list. The second column displays the number of subscribers to that particular list. The second tab shows your lists, with the same information you find in the first tab.

On this lists page, you can do list maintenance, such as editing the list name and deleting the list from your profile.

FIGURE 7-4. *You can be on someone's list, and create your own lists of people to follow closely.*

Following a list is just like following any other Twitter user. Go to the list page and click on Follow underneath the name of the list you want to read. You can quickly view your lists that other people have decided to follow and look at the lists you follow on the sidebar. You can always remove yourself from a list by blocking the creator of it.

You can @mention any Twitter list as you would any Twitter user; just add a forward slash (/) followed by the list name to the list owner's user name:

```
@<username>/<listname>
```

Tweeting on Your Smart Phone

As of this writing, some 30 applications are available for the iPhone 3G that let you use Twitter from your phone without using your SMS (texting). Blackberry users also have quite a few applications to choose from.

Currently your lists can only appear on the Twitter web application, not these third-party ones for smart phones and iTouch. That will probably change as the software programs are updated to recognize them.

These programs range in price from free to about $20, but my favorite at the moment is the free application called Twitterrific. It allows you to use the commands, searches, and filters. The free version also has ads, but they are not intrusive.

Skype and Other VoIPs

Skype and its many competitors are audio/video/text programs for communication over the Internet using Voice over Internet Protocol (VoIP), Person to Person (P2P). Skype is quite popular, and the other VoIP players (Yahoo!, Jajah, Google, and Lycos have all released no-cost or low-cost VoIP P2P solutions) work pretty much the same, so let's look at Skype.

Skype is available for systems running Linux, Linux-based Maemo, Mac OS X, iPhone OS (iPhone and iPod Touch), Microsoft Windows (2000, XP, Vista, Windows Mobile), and even Sony's PSP. There is a pay version that lets you call any phone number, whether on Skype or not, but most people use the free version, even though you can only use it to communicate with other Skype users.

How can a genealogist use Skype? Well, talking to distant relatives for free (if they have Skype) or under $10 a month (if they don't) is one way.

Another is to videoconference. In Figure 7-5, I am conferencing with Russ Worthington, a genealogist who lives in New Jersey. Beau Sharbrough, of Footnote.com, recently offered virtual lectures to distant genealogy societies on using Footnote.com, online search assistants, genealogy in 2020, and other topics, using the Skype videoconference interface.

An additional use: instant messaging. Skype can communicate in text, send files, and do all the other tasks an instant messaging program such as AIM or Windows Messenger can do.

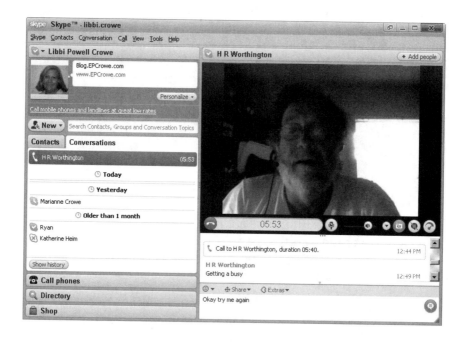

FIGURE 7-5. *Skype can be used for text, video, and sound.*

Instant Messaging

The most popular form of chat today is instant messaging, thanks in large part to America Online's Instant Messenger program, known to users as AIM, and MSN Messenger. In this form of chat, a select, invited list of people (from two to a whole "room") exchange typed messages in real time. This feature has become so popular that instant messaging is used 200 million times a day, according to AOL PR people. Another example is ICQ (I-seek-you).

The other most common chat program is a Java-based chat that shows in your Web browser. As long as you have the latest version of Java on your computer, nothing else is needed to participate. Different programs enable you to have one-on-one and multiperson conversations with people. Some require you to sign on to a chat server, where the program you use doesn't matter. Others only let you chat with people using the same program and who have allowed you to put them on their "buddy list." The former lets you connect with more people; the latter gives you more security. A few will let you do both.

AOL Instant Messenger

AOL Instant Messenger (AIM) is now available as a web app, so you do not have to download it to your computer as in the old days. In Figure 7-6, you can see that it tells you which AIM buddies are online, lets you post a one-line status, and lets you choose a picture to represent you. In an expanded view of the window, you can have a second tab, Lifestream, which lets you set up a connection between AIM and other social networking sites so that your AIM status is reflected in sites such as Facebook, Twitter, and YouTube.

On the iPhone, AIM is available as a free program with ads, or a more powerful one for about $3 that allows you to use your phone's text messaging, GPS locator, and camera to send pictures.

Windows Live Messenger

This program comes already installed on many computers running Windows, and it works very much like AIM. You register as a user for free, choosing a screen name and a password. If you already have a Passport account, you can use that login information.

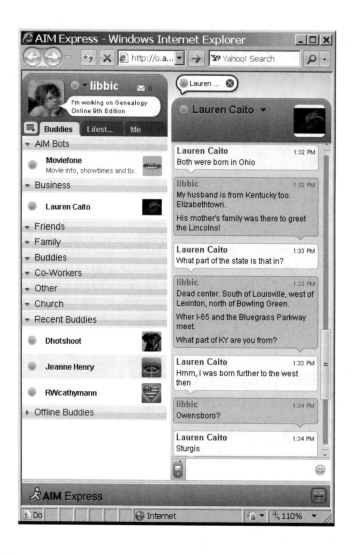

FIGURE 7-6. *AIM (as AOL Instant Messenger is known) works from the Web, so no separate software program is needed to use it.*

Success Story: GenPals Solves a Mystery

Charlene Hazzard, CharAH1@aol.com (NY "G" families), and Mary Martha Von Ville McGrath, marymarthavonville@ hotmail.com (Ohio "G" families), solved a mystery through GenPals (a site now defunct).

"When new to the Internet, I found a message on Guenther/Ginther/Gunter/Gunther (from Charlene Hazzard), and when I finally figured out how to write a message, got an answer from her. She had my line into what is now a different country in Europe and had it back two generations from there!" Mary Martha had a town name of Herstom in Germany. Charlene knew that this was the common nickname for Herbitzheim, which is now in France. Charlene had communicated directly with the Herbitzheim (aka Herstom) town historian until he died in 2000. "I had only a nickname for the town of origin, and Charlene explained the real name of the town. By the way, her message was from 1999, and she is the only one who had info from Europe," said Mary Martha. "What an answer to a 30-year-old prayer. Thank you, God!"

Mary Martha and Charlene became the coordinators on GenPals for the descendants of this family who settled in New York and Ohio (many are still in both states). Mary Martha found Charlene's message four years after it was saved, truly a miracle in their book.

Yahoo! Messenger

Yahoo! Messenger works just like MSN and AIM. Go to www.yahoo.com, click Chat, click Genealogy, and pick a room for web-based chats, or you can download Yahoo! Messenger to set up your own private chat room. Join the Yahoo! group Genealogy Chat Friends (http://groups.yahoo .com/group/genealogychatfriends) to view the calendar of chats and transcripts of past chats.

ICQ

ICQ ("I seek you") started out as a stand-alone application but has morphed into a social networking suite/website/message/smart phone program. On the site, www.icq.com, the developers suggest these ways to use ICQ for genealogy:

- ◆ Develop genealogy and search sites.
- ◆ Add ICQ status indicators to listings of members so your site visitors know when they're online.

- Add an ICQ search panel to enable Web and people searches from your site.

- Add an ICQ Webcast panel to launch announcements directly onto your site.

- Create an ICQ user list for an online directory of ICQ users, categorized by topic, location, and more.

- Create and add a guestbook to collect feedback and suggestions from site visitors.

- Join an ICQ ring to link your site to other people's search engines and sites.

ICQ for iPhone supports ICQ sounds and allows you to communicate with friends on mobile phones via SMS (ICQ to SMS is not available in all countries). With the iPhone version, you can send and receive messages over Wi-Fi, EDGE, or 3G; add "friendly names" for your contacts; hold multiple IM conversations and "swipe" to view other conversations; and connect to anyone on the AIM network worldwide, whether they're on AOL, AIM, Mac, or MobileMe.

Several genealogy sites use ICQ for communications. One such site, Kentuckiana Genealogy (www.kentuckianagenealogy.org/icq), covers the Indiana counties Clark, Crawford, Dubois, Floyd, Harrison, Jefferson, Lawrence, Orange, Perry, Scott, and Washington; and Kentucky counties Breckinridge, Bullitt, Hardin, Jefferson, and Meade. They have an ICQ list so that genealogists and family historians can chat whenever they like and share ideas, discuss similar interests, or anything else. The webmaster of Kentuckiana Genealogy lists the ICQ numbers of willing members, allowing quick contact with members for anyone who may visit this page and allowing them to send files (GEDCOMS!) to each other.

The Genealogy List at www.thistlekeep.com/ashabon/icqlist.html is another site that has chosen ICQ for chat, files, and other communication. All Genealogy List members are included in the list default, and each member lists the surnames he or she is pursuing.

Internet Relay Chat

Internet Relay Chat (IRC) is still around, but hardly anyone cares, and it has fallen into disuse. The increasing attractiveness of instant messaging programs, text messaging on phones, and microblogs combined with spammers' bad habit of using contact info in chat rooms to blast the online world with spam have left IRC looking like an old downtown pub that lost its clientele to a pre-fab chain restaurant down the road. Only the die-hard addicts remain.

Some genealogy chats continue, mostly in web-based form, and generally as a moderated format where a leader answers typed questions with either text or VoIP. For the most part, chat rooms are now Java-based and do not require a separate chat program. Many genealogists also use instant messaging programs for scheduled or impromptu one-on-one communication on brick walls, recent finds, and new resources. The modern chat is useful for education: chat as online classroom. With sound capabilities, that metaphor becomes much closer to reality. In addition, some chat rooms are still just a fun place to hang out and discuss the weather, your health, and computer problems when you take a break from genealogy.

> *Note*
>
> *As with any online genealogy topic, search your favorite portal (Google, Yahoo!, MSN, Excite, etc.) for "genealogy chat" (or "geneology chat") and see what comes up!*

Reach Out and Touch the World!

To me, what is exciting about all these different programs and formats is that they are all becoming interconnected. Your entry into AIM can be mirrored to your Twitter account; your Twitter tweets can show up on your Facebook page, and on and on.

As Amy Coffin pointed out, you can spend all day shooting questions, links, observations, and files to other genealogists, and getting them back. You start typing messages with your buddy in Omaha on Twitter, and then your son at college calls you on Skype, and then your sister-in-law shares a link on AIM, and suddenly you discover the day has slipped by. All forms of chat are this addictive. Beware!

Wrapping Up

- ◆ Internet messaging can take many forms and helps you connect with other genealogists.

- ◆ Twitter is a form of "microblogging" that can help you keep up-to-date with the news in genealogy.

- ◆ Skype and VoIP take instant messaging into audio and video as well as text formats.

- ◆ Instant messaging (e.g., AIM, ICQ, and Windows Live) is the most common form of chat, and the simplest to use.

- ◆ IRC is fading from use, but you can still find this form of chatting.

- ◆ All these forms are becoming more and more connected, with the exception of IRC.

- ◆ All chat forms can be addictive—handle with care!

Chapter 8

Genealogy Mail Lists, Newsletters, and Mail Groups

Electronic mail (e-mail) lists are discussion groups based on e-mail messages. All subscribers can send and receive e-mail from the list. Messages sent to the mailing list are forwarded to everyone who subscribes to it; no message is private when posted to the list, even though you will receive them with your e-mail program just as you do private messages. Replies to messages from the list are sent as well, where they are forwarded to all participants. These are often mirrored to sites like RootsWeb or Ancestry, where forums of messages still reside.

Mailing lists can be completely automated, with a program taking care of subscribing people to the list, forwarding messages, and removing people from the list, sending your chosen lists to your e-mail inbox. Or, real people can get into the loop, handling any and all of the mailing list functions that programs can do. Either way, if it is a mirrored list, to read the messages on sites such as RootsWeb or Ancestry.com, you have to log in with your user name and password and then go to the forum of interest.

Such "moderated" mailing lists can take two forms: They might have restricted membership, where you need to be approved to subscribe; or a moderator (or moderators) might let anyone join but would review each incoming message before it is distributed, preventing inappropriate material from getting on to the list.

Forums are message-based systems where the messages are held on a website, waiting for you to come read them. Most forums are divided into topics, which are general categories of messages. Topics are usually locations, surnames, and general genealogy issues. Within the topics are more specific messages called threads.

Forums may have an option to e-mail you a notice when a message is posted. Others may have the option to e-mail you all new messages one by one or in a collection called a digest, which makes them like a mailing list to the user. Certain forums are moderated; most genealogy ones are moderated.

Many mailing lists and forums focus specifically on genealogy. In addition, many more lists and forums, although not specifically for genealogists, cover topics of interest to genealogists, such as ethnic groups and historic events.

Mailing Lists

With a decent mail program, participating in mailing lists is easy. You simply have to figure out how to subscribe, manage, and unsubscribe to a list. Often, the instructions are included in the mailing list's home page.

Subscribe to Mailing Lists

Say you want to know more about genealogy in the Mobile, Alabama, area. Sure enough, mail lists exist for that. Searching for the Mobile Genealogy Mail List in Google, you find the RootsWeb page with nine different mails lists for that area. The following listing has the details for just one:

Topic: A mailing list, sponsored by the Mobile Genealogical Society for anyone with a genealogical interest in the Mobile Bay, Alabama, area — specifically Mobile and Baldwin Counties in Alabama plus the bordering counties in Mississippi (George, Greene, Jackson), Alabama (Clarke, Escambia, Monroe, Washington), and Florida (Escambia). Topics for the list include genealogical queries and discussions of resources having to do with the above counties and various time periods in the area's history such as the Louisiana Purchase (Mobile was the first capital of Louisiana), Spanish West Florida, the Confederate period, the Mississippi Territory, etc. In addition, "press releases" from genealogical societies and libraries in the aforementioned counties are welcome.
There is a Web page for the **AL-MOBILEBAY** mailing list at http://www.siteone.com/clubs/mgs/.
For questions about this list, contact the list administrator at AL-MOBILEBAY-adminrootsweb.com.
Subscribing. Clicking on one of the shortcut links below should work, but if your browser doesn't understand them, try these manual instructions: to join **AL-MOBILEBAY-L**, send mail to AL-MOBILEBAY-L-requestrootsweb.com with the single word *subscribe* in the message subject and body. To join **AL-MOBILEBAY-D,** do the same thing with AL-MOBILEBAY-D-requestrootsweb.com.
Subscribe to AL-MOBILEBAY-L
Subscribe to AL-MOBILEBAY-D (digest)

Now you know how to subscribe. Because you are sending this message as a command to a mailing list program, it's best to put "END" on the line below "subscribe" (see Figure 8-1). That way, should your automatic signature slip in, it will be ignored by the list program. If you do not do this, it's very likely that you will get a message back describing all the different ways the program does not understand what you sent.

You will receive a welcome message, which you should save to a text or document file. It will tell you how to manage your subscription to get off the list, suspend it temporarily, and prevent your own messages to the list from coming to you from the server.

An important point to note in the previous listing: Most mailing lists have two e-mail addresses. You use one address to subscribe or change how you use the mailing list and another to post messages to the other people on the mailing list. Some mailing lists might have a third address to use for certain administrative chores, such as reporting some violation of the list's rules to the moderator. One of the most common and annoying mistakes one sees on mail lists is when someone posts "unsubscribe" to the address for posting messages instead of to the same address used to subscribe. Some folks simply refuse to look at the directions and continue to post "unsubscribe" messages to the message address over and over until someone flames them. Don't be one of these people.

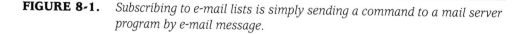

FIGURE 8-1. *Subscribing to e-mail lists is simply sending a command to a mail server program by e-mail message.*

Note that in some mailing list programs, you can send a command—who or `reveal`—to find out who is subscribed to a certain list. To prevent your address from being listed in the who command, you often have to send a specific command to the list server. The welcome message will tell you how, but it's usually the command `conceal`.

Success Story: Board Leads to Reunion

The most meaningful success I have had was because of posting to boards. I found an aunt I never knew I had. Got to go meet her. She lives about 40 miles from me. I was adopted, so finding a biological relative was great. It was from an old posting, so keep posting everywhere. You never know when you will see results!

—G.F.S. Tupper, host of Maine Genealogy chat, Beginners Chat, and Beyond Beginners Chat on AOL

The Granddaddy of Genealogy Mail Lists

Imagine a discussion group where novices and experts exchange help, information, ideas, and gossip. Now imagine this conversation is conducted by e-mail, so you needn't worry about missing anything. You've just imagined ROOTS-L, the granddaddy of genealogy mailing lists on the Internet.

ROOTS-L has spawned entire generations of newer genealogy mailing lists—some large, some small—but this is the original. The mailing list page at http://lists.rootsweb.com hosts more than 30,000 mailing lists about genealogy and history (see Figure 8-2).

To subscribe, you need to do two things:

♦ Make sure your e-mail inbox is large enough to hold the volume of messages you'll receive. If you have limited space, use digest mode, if available, and check your inbox more than once a day.

♦ Send an e-mail message to roots-l-request@rootsweb.org, with the message "Subscribe." You don't need to include anything else in the message—no signature block, no name or address.

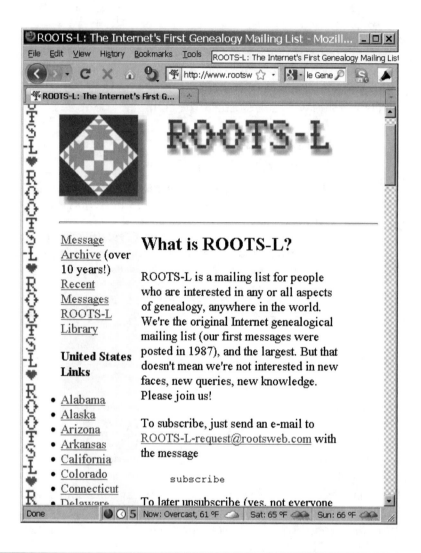

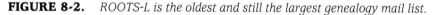

FIGURE 8-2. *ROOTS-L is the oldest and still the largest genealogy mail list.*

Some ROOTS-L Rules

ROOTS-L clearly states its rules in its welcome message. It would be wise to apply these rules to every mailing list you join, whether or not they're explicitly stated: The list isn't a place to bring up wars of the past or to discuss religion or politics. Advertising or selling a product is not, in general, acceptable. You can, however, post a new-product announcement, as in "I have a new genealogy software product" or

"I have just published my genealogy." Make sure that you spell the word "genealogy" correctly in all your messages. Don't post messages longer than about 150 lines, unless you're sure they'll be of general interest. Don't include a "surname signature" in your messages. These are lists of surnames that appear at the end of every message some people send. The surnames play havoc with the list's archive searches, so don't use them. Don't post copyrighted material, such as newspaper articles or e-mail messages sent to you by other people. Quote only enough of previous messages to be clear about what the discussion is about. Never quote previous messages in their entirety because this bogs down the list. You should search all the archives of the ROOTS-L mailing list for keywords, such as your surnames and places. Sometimes, you'll find someone posted years ago something that you wanted to know.

Success Story: The Web Helps a Mobility-Challenged Genealogist

Being mobility-challenged and on a very limited income, I have to depend mostly on the Internet at this time for my genealogy work, and I've had some success. I had a query on an Irsch surname board for my great-grandfather and the fact he had married a PITTS in Noxubee, Mississippi, in 1860. I just happened to decide to go to the PITTS surname board and posted the same query for a Lucretia Emmaline PITTS, who had married a Frank IRSCH. I received a tentative confirmation from someone whose great-grandfather had a sister who had married an IRSCH about that time. A few back-and-forths later, we thought we might have a connection; I asked if she had ever heard the names Aunt Em and Uncle Henry HILL. I had heard my grandmother speak of them, but didn't know if they were blood relatives. We both knew we had established the connection. "Aunt Em" was the sister of her great-great-great-grandfather, Lafayette Newton PITTS, and another sister, Lucretia, had married Frank IRSCH. Their father's name was James W. PITTS and their mother's name was Mary. We still haven't discovered her maiden name. She had a picture of some of the IRSCH family that Lizzie EATON/BENNETT had identified for them as her brother and family and Grandma PITTS. She wasn't sure if the older woman was her Grandma PITTS, but she didn't think so. Lizzie EATON/BENNETT was my grandmother, and if she identified the older woman as Grandma PITTS, it would have been her grandmother, Mary ?-? PITTS. I remember my mother telling me of Aunt Annie IRSCH and Grandma PITTS sending

Christmas gifts when she was little. Now we proudly know we have a picture of our shared great-great-great-grandmother. We are working on other shared lines, but I would call this a wonderful tale of success from the Internet!

—Louise McDonald

Losing Contact with a Mailing List

It's possible you'll stop receiving messages from a mailing list, even though you didn't unsubscribe. If this happens, it may be because:

♦ Your Internet service provider (ISP) could be having trouble with their e-mail service. Any service can have intermittent problems.

♦ Sometimes, a whole section of the Internet might be out of order for a few minutes or even for hours. If all your e-mail stops coming in—not just mail from a mailing list—this could be the cause. Your mailing list may be sharing an IP address with a known spammer, through no fault of the list owner. Contact your ISP to tell them to let your mailing list through as legitimate mail.

♦ You're using a different e-mail address than the one you used to subscribe to the mailing list. Most e-mail server programs will only send to the return address of the subscribe message. If all else fails, subscribe to the mailing list again. That should get the messages flowing for you.

Forums You Might Explore

Forums are message exchanges on a website or portal. They are in effect mail lists, where the messages stay on one site instead of being delivered to your e-mail box. However, there are exceptions: Some forums do have an e-mail option so that messages on topics you choose are e-mailed to you. In that case, a forum will look just like an e-mail list to you. You can visit the forum often to see if there are new messages, but people just take advantage of the notification option.

You can specify that you want to know when someone posts to the "SPENCER" board, for example, and an e-mail message will be sent to you when that happens. Sometimes the actual message will also be delivered to you.

Genealogy forums abound on the Internet. Genealogy.com has 14,000; ROOTSWEB/Ancestry.com has 161,000 message boards. The best way to find what you want is to use a search engine for the topics.

For example, I would like to discuss Powells in South Carolina. In Google, I could search for "Powell Genealogy Forum" and get the result in Figure 8-3. That gets about 116,000 hits, the top ones from GenForum.com, Genealogy.com, Genealogy.About.com, etc. Now I can narrow that by clicking Advanced Search in Google and adding "South Carolina" to the terms. That cuts the results to 15,900.

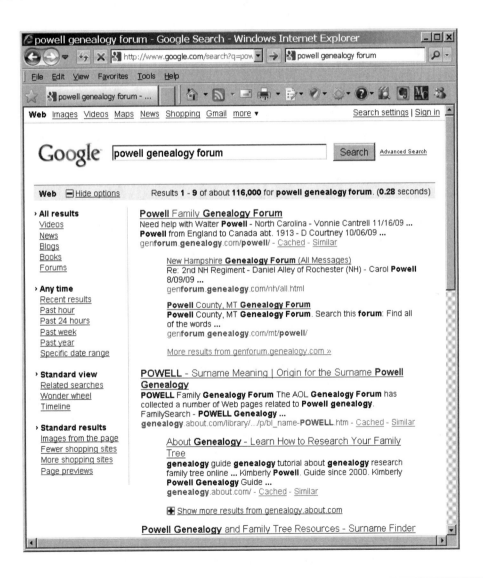

FIGURE 8-3. *Use a search engine to find forums on topics that interest you.*

Another good technique is to use a search engine to search for the name, date, and place you are looking for. This will result in hits from both forum and mailing list archives. Or visit some of the top sites listed in Chapter 21 and search those forums. Finally, search the portals mentioned in previous chapters. A short sampling includes:

◆ **JewishGen (www.jewishgen.org/JewishGen/DiscussionGroup .htm)** The Jewish Genealogy site hosts two or three dozen groups based on geography, projects of the site, and other interests.

◆ **Yahoo! (http://groups.yahoo.com)** Yahoo! has thousands of discussion groups based on surnames, geography, and ethnicity. Some are public, which means anyone can post to them, and some require you to sign up before you can post to them. Go to the Yahoo! Groups page, and search for "genealogy" and/or the surnames you need.

◆ **GenForum (http://genforum.genealogy.com)** Genealogy.com's discussion groups are lively and searchable by keyword.

◆ **Genealogy Register (www.genealogyregister.com)** This site lists links to personal family histories, and features message boards for discussion.

◆ **Family Tree Circles (www.familytreecircles.com)** Here you can post your research information and connect with other family tree researchers.

Finding More Mailing Lists

Even though it may seem like we've covered more mailing lists than you can shake a stick at, many more exist. To find more, first check out the RootsWeb website for their ever-growing list. If you point your Web browser to www.rootsweb.org/~maillist, you'll have access to the hundreds of mailing lists hosted by RootsWeb.

Another site that keeps a list of discussion boards is Genealogy Today. To find some forums, lists, and boards go to www.genealogytoday .com/genealogy/city/genforum.html.

For years, the best categorized and detailed list has been the one maintained by John P. Fuller. He died in 2009, and Linda Lambert and Megan Zurawicz are carrying on the list in his memory at www.rootsweb .com/~jfuller/gen_mail.html (see Figure 8-4).

Cyndi's List (www.CyndisList.com/magazine.htm) is a good site to visit to keep up on the latest in mailing lists and newsletters.

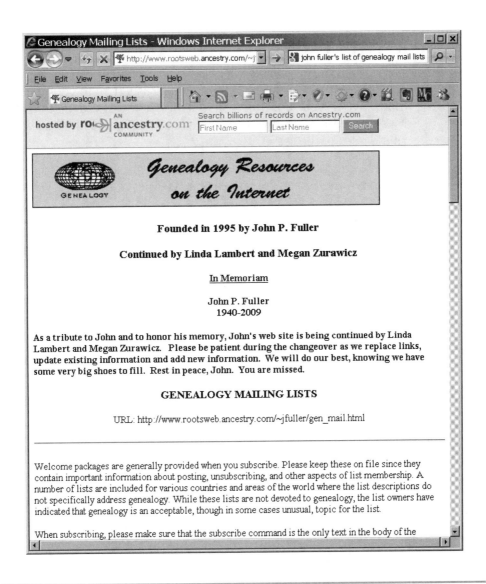

FIGURE 8-4. *Linda Lambert and Megan Zurawicz are maintaining John P. Fuller's catalog of genealogy-related mailing lists.*

Wrapping Up

♦ E-mail discussion lists bring other genealogists right to your e-mail inbox. When you subscribe to a mailing list, always save the reply message, which usually has the "unsubscribe" instructions as well as the rules of the list.

♦ Forums are usually associated with websites. You can go to the site to read the latest messages or have them e-mailed to you so that it is as easy as an e-mail list.

Chapter 9

Social Networking

Social networks are the most popular way to contact other folks on the Web these days. You can keep up with genealogists all over the world with social network services. Using these tools, you can have conversations, read up on the latest news, make new friends, and have fun generally. Oh, and by the way, get some genealogy done!

"Social networks have expanded in all directions and it's often difficult to wrap your head around the size and the scope of all these possibilities," said Amy Coffin, a professional genealogist, librarian, and blogger. "Genealogists who are just beginning to discover all that is available online should pick one or two social networking tools and learn to use them for the benefit of family history research."

A Few Definitions

Some academics define social networking sites as having three common elements: a member profile on a web-accessible page, a user-defined list of contacts, and interaction between members of different contact lists with greater and lesser degrees of access. As you can see, this definition would have fit Prodigy, AOL, MSN Network, and CompuServe in their first iterations, except for the web access part. CompuServe and Prodigy are long gone; AOL and MSN have morphed into portals, so these new and interesting "social networking sites" have popped up.

While social networking sites vary in the tools and functionality they provide, usually where the old "online services" had forums, the newer social networking sites have a way for you to search based on common interest, connect with people, and exchange public or private messages. However, it is not as easy as it was to sign on to CompuServe, input the GO word "genealogy," and wind up someplace where that is all that's going on. You have to work at it, but you can build your own filters to keep things manageable. This chapter will show you how.

So let's look at how to use these tools for genealogy.

Social Networking 101

At this writing, Wikipedia listed some 170 popular social networking sites worldwide. Some are very general; some are very topic-specific. Most hobbyist genealogists belong to one or more of the very general ones, like Facebook (FB). As that is the one I use most often, I'll take you through using Facebook to contact other genealogists. Once you know how to use one of them, the rest are fairly easy to figure out.

Signing up for FB can be very simple: your real name (or company name) and a valid e-mail address. Once on, you'll be asked to fill out your profile. You can fill out much more information (if you want) than is probably wise; to begin with, be sure to add your activities and interests, because these will be keywords by which others can search for you (see Figure 9-1).

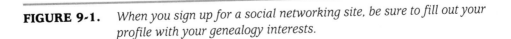

FIGURE 9-1. *When you sign up for a social networking site, be sure to fill out your profile with your genealogy interests.*

Now that you have yourself set up, you can begin to search for friends, blogs, and applications to make FB useful for your genealogy. FB has pages for people, as well as pages for groups, companies, and organizations. At the top right of the FB page is the search box. Type in **genealogy**. You will see a page similar to the one in Figure 9-2.

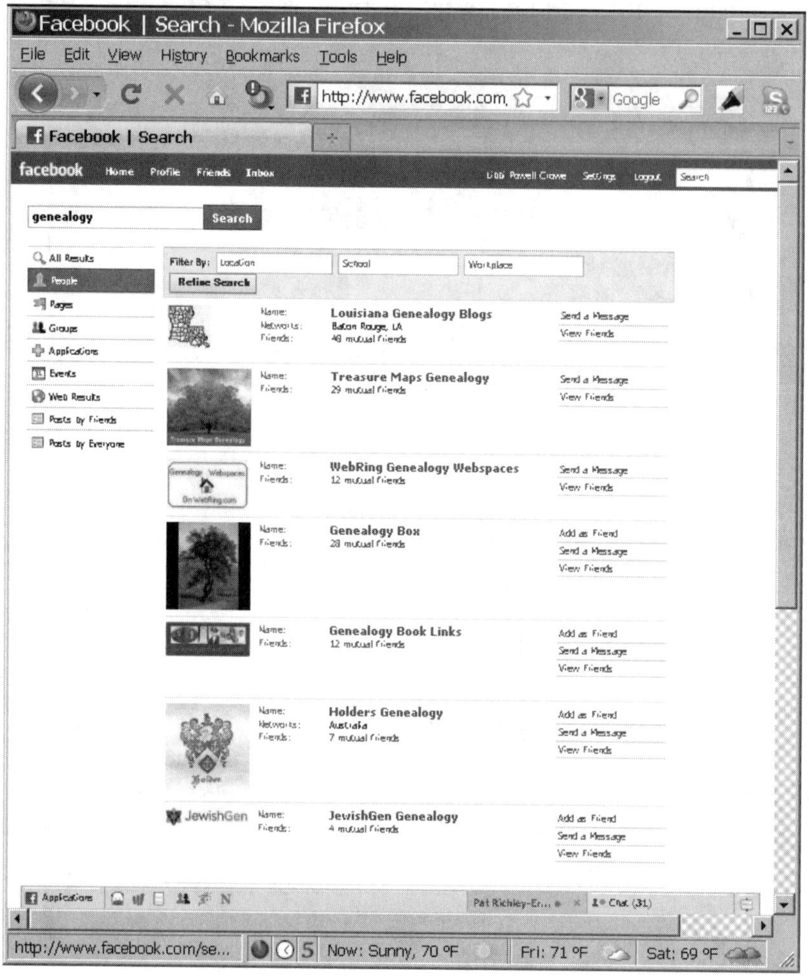

FIGURE 9-2. *Search for "genealogy" on your social network service of choice to find groups and people in genealogy.*

On this page you can filter the results by people, pages, groups, and applications by using the buttons on the left. I have recommendations for getting started in choosing from these results when you are on this results page.

- Click groups, and find a group searching your surnames or a geographical area you are pursuing.

- Click on "people" and send out some friend invitations. Be sure to include a short message about what lines you are searching or the geographic area or genealogy organization.

- Click on Applications, and try the Family Tree application, which helps you build your ancestry tree for others to link to. Also, the Networked Blogs application, which has many genealogy bloggers attached to it.

- Check out the Events tab in the genealogy search results for lectures, meetings, and online events, such as Carnival of Genealogy Web Pages.

- Click Posts By Everyone and look at what FB users are posting about genealogy today (see Figure 9-3).

- Do a new search for genealogy blogs, and follow the ones that interest you.

You will very soon find yourself with many social network service friends, many of whom you haven't met physically yet. The way to get a handle on this embarrassment of riches is to use the FB Lists feature. Click Friends | All Friends. At the top of this page are three buttons: Create New List, Edit List, and Delete List. In Figure 9-4, you can see a portion of my Genealogy Buds list. Create a list, and then use the drop-down button on the right of each friend to assign that person to a list. When you go back to the Home button, you will be able to filter the feed by list, looking at only Genealogy Friends, for example. Notice how like Twitter this is; you can also set up Twitter to mirror your tweets to your social network service status.

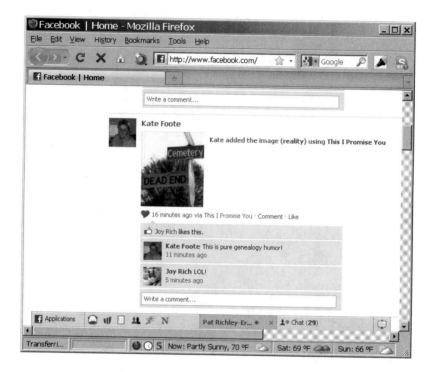

FIGURE 9-3. *Genealogy posts on social networking can be fun and useful.*

Success Story: Facebook Connections Become Face to Face

"Facebook used to be for college students, but that's no longer the case. Now it's a mainstream social networking tool, and can be used effectively for family history purposes. Users can join groups based on common interests, provide short updates about any topic, and link to 'friends' to form networks. Often, users' extended family members are also on Facebook, and you can use the site as a way to collect family history information. Beginners may want to ask a friend or family member to help set up an account and learn the ropes. Facebook can be overwhelming until new users learn how to set up filters and limit the amount of information coming in at the same time. The result is worth it, however, as many friends can be made with this highly popular social networking tool.

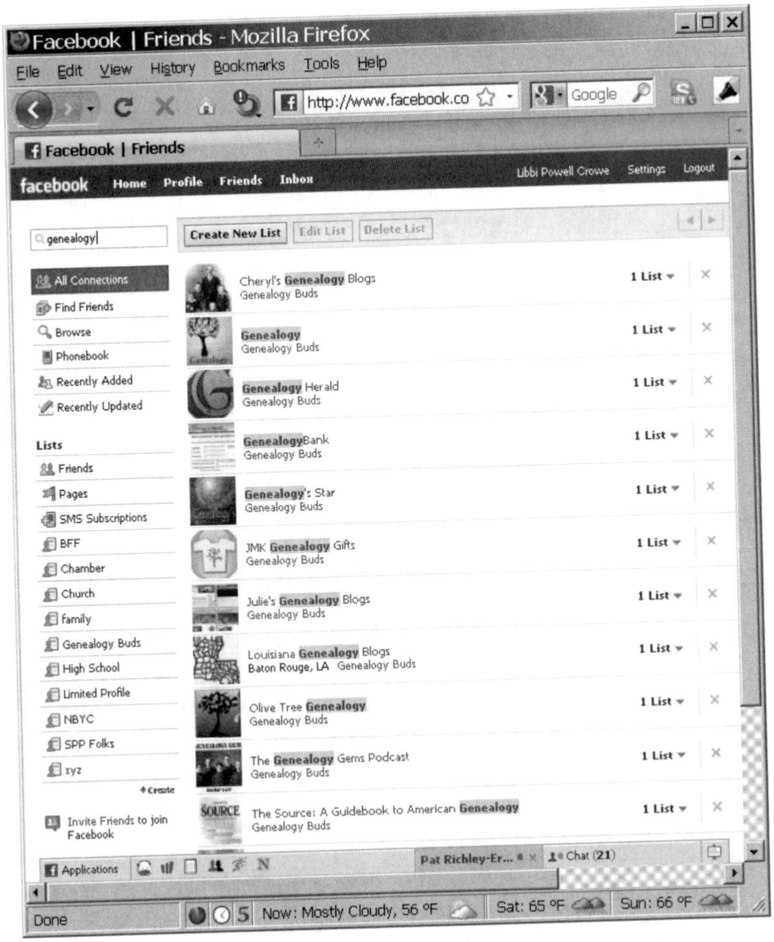

FIGURE 9-4. *Organize your friends by lists. Then you can filter the news feed by lists.*

"I've had a Facebook account for a while, but never used it as a way to connect with genealogists until 2008. Using Facebook's message feature, I started contacting other Texas genealogists asking if they would be my friend. Many agreed and we got to know each other online. Fast-forward several months and I made plans to attend a genealogy meeting three hours away. Since I was new to the group, I expected to sit in the back watching everyone else chat. Imagine my surprise when I arrived and realized that I already knew six people from our interactions on Facebook. I didn't sit in

the back of the room. In fact, I sat right in the middle and talked with all my friends like we'd always known each other."

—*Amy Coffin, MLIS, APG, amycoffin.com*

Another good site for genealogy social networking is GenealogyWise .com, which calls itself "the genealogy social network." The site is free and easy to join, making it a good starting point for social networking beginners. Here your lists can be based on surnames or research interests. The site has live chat and message board posts, where you can ask questions, post queries, or just shoot the breeze with other genealogists (see Figure 9-5).

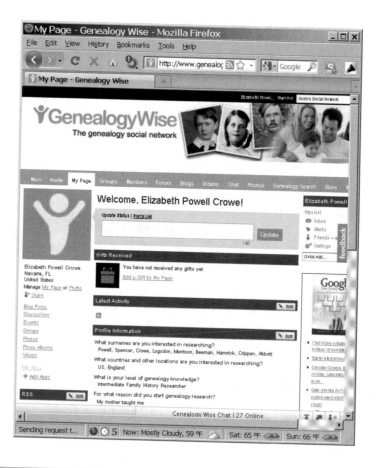

FIGURE 9-5. *GenealogyWise.com is an all-genealogy social network service.*

If you have completed the previous steps for Facebook, GenealogyWise will feel familiar. It has the same features, and though I do not find it as friendly a place as Facebook, you may find it useful.

Social Networking Services with Avatars: Second Life

Long ago in the early days of online services (circa 1985), one could visit virtual "rooms" and meet for conversations, play games, and "travel" to magic realms. It was all text, so you really had to use your imagination.

Just a few years back, many chat programs added avatars so you had a visual component to all of the aforementioned. Now, games, meetings, conversations, and more are possible with sound, animation, music, joint web browsing, and more. Once such service is Second Life (SL). The software is free, and most of the use of Second Life is, too. You can, if you want, spend real money on virtual goods and a premium account, but you don't have to.

Note

Second Life is feature-rich and resource-greedy. Go to SecondLife.com and read the system requirements. Second Life is not compatible with dial-up Internet, satellite Internet, and some wireless Internet services. It may not run on graphics cards other than the ones listed on the webpage. You should have an earphone/microphone headset to fully enjoy the voice chat. When traffic gets heavy, say over two million connections, you may find yourself losing your connection repeatedly.

Go to www.SecondLife.com and download the free software. Signing up is as simple as creating a fictitious name, entering a real e-mail address, and confirming the e-mail address. Once registered, you can fill out a profile that has some details of your life in the real world. As in Facebook, this SL profile is most useful if you include your genealogy interests so that others will see your entry when they search for "genealogy."

Then the software guides you through some training videos to help you over the SL learning curve. Your avatar can walk, talk, touch and carry things, change clothing (the genealogists do have costume parties from time to time), as well as sit, fly, and teleport. The software shows you the steps for modifying hairstyles and adding clothing to your preference. This is all great fun, but you can skip all that, take your avatar as created by the software, and go find others to talk to and interact with: others who share your love for climbing family trees.

Genealogists from all over the world have discovered Second Life could be a useful way to collaborate and congregate with other like-minded folks. DearMYRTLE, Pat Richley-Erickson, recommends genealogists join in on Second Life's genealogy discussions in real time and mingle with family historians at all levels of expertise.

To find any genealogy-related area, use the Search button (see Figure 9-6). Click on an entry in the list, and after reading about it, you can click the Teleport button to take your avatar there.

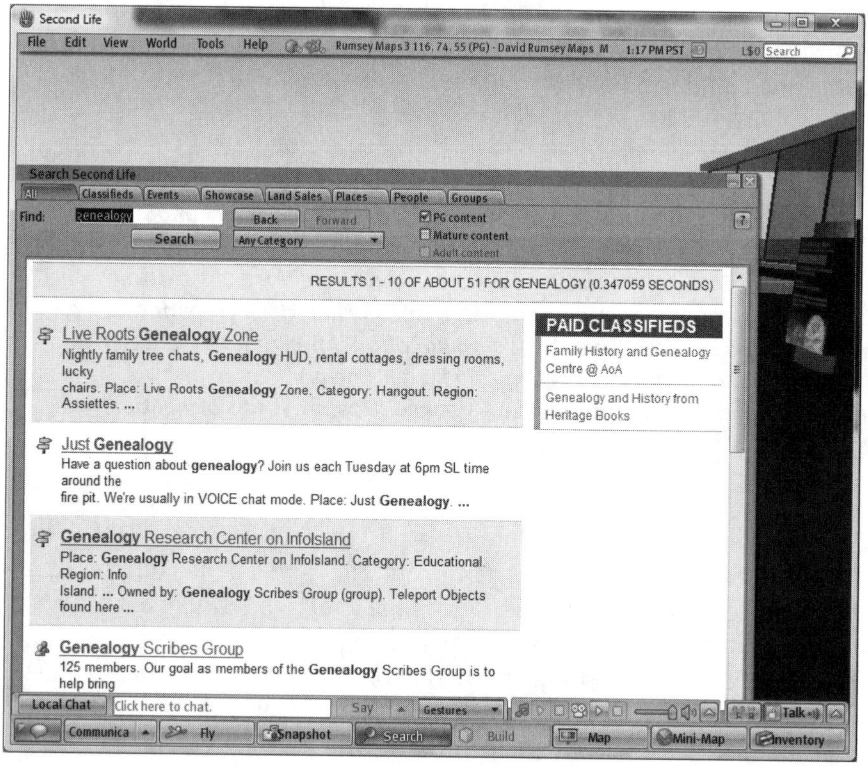

FIGURE 9-6. *Use Search to find genealogy venues, people, and groups in Second Life.*

Coming to Terms with Second Life

The terms used in Second Life include:

- **Avatar** The virtual reality personage you create for yourself after signing up for a free account with Second Life

- **RL** Real life

- **SL** Second Life

- **In-world** Signed on to SL; online with the software

- **SL time** Pacific Time, Daylight Saving or Standard as appropriate for the time of year

- **Voice chat** Turn on your computer speakers to listen to the genealogy discussion in-world. If you have a microphone (best with a headset), you may contribute to the conversation verbally. Those without mics may pose questions by typing in the SL screen, just as in any chat.

- **Teleporting** Using the Second Life command to put your avatar in a different area or room than you are in now

- **Gestures** Commands to have your avatar laugh, wave, pick up an object, and so on

Find the one that interests you and click the Teleport button, and your avatar appears there. I suggest you start with Just Genealogy.

Just Genealogy

This is an area of Second Life (in a region called Wollah) where the scene is a castle including a fire pit with stadium seating for events. Some of the features of this area include Heritage Books marketplace stalls, a gazebo and dance floor, a small three-room cottage, a tent and paraphernalia of a visiting knight, plus a working swing in a blossoming apple tree in the northside garden. All this atmosphere is designed to make Just Genealogy in Second Life a place to learn how to do family history research effectively.

The Just Genealogy owner-avatar has the in-world name Krag Mariner. In real life, he is Craig Scott, CG, who owns Heritage Books. Craig is a well-known genealogical educator and publisher who is most interested in "making people who love genealogy into genealogists." When visiting Just Genealogy, you'll also meet the avatar Clarise Beaumont (who is Pat Richley-Erikson; see Figure 9-7). This avatar develops the schedule of events and coordinates with other genealogy groups in Second Life. Krag and Clarise host a weekly genealogy chat each Tuesday at 7 p.m. "SL time" (which is the same as U.S. Pacific Time, Daylight Savings when applicable).

But the Just Genealogy castle isn't empty the rest of the week. All along the walls of the castle and environs, you will see placards, tartans, and other objects (see Figure 9-8). They are not just decorations; they are clickable links to useful and important genealogy places on the Web—blogs, podcasts, database sites, maps, how-to info, mailing lists, message boards, etc.

FIGURE 9-7. *Krag and Clarise are the avatars that manage Just Genealogy.*

FIGURE 9-8. *In Second Life, objects such as these tartans, posters, and PowerPoint screens can be links to websites.*

Just as an example, one chat about deciphering old handwriting resulted in a discussion of four useful websites; those sites became some of the decorations on the wall that are also links. An image of a modern-day clickable PowerPoint screen describes upcoming topics for Just Genealogy Tuesday night discussions.

The Main Event: Live Chats with Sound and Animation

The chats are the big draw. Though any chat group can be small, usually no more than 20 or so visitors, in general, the participation is active and lively. Sometimes chats can garner up to 80 different visitors. Attendance largely depends on the topic of the week. In a typical recent Tuesday night chat on Just Genealogy, visitors from all over the world, who spoke a variety of languages, decided to speak in

English in the voice chat. One time the topic was using "Eyewitness Reports" to document the life and times of an ancestor. During this chat:

- One person read a letter from his WWI ancestor using the voice function so others could hear.

- A French-Canadian genealogist described an "eyewitness" report he found in a 1587 document, which he was able to post on the chat. He had digitized the document while on his annual research trip to France.

- One person read over the voice chat from *The Civil War Love Letter Quilt*, by Rosemary Young (Krause Publications, 2007) a part of David Coon's letter home to his wife Mary describing camp conditions on March 11, 1864, for the New York 36th Regiment of the Union Army. Burgoyne (Heritage Books, 2006).

That is just a small sampling; much more was accomplished that night! Among all this exciting give-and-take were people who have not met in RL but are friends. Just Genealogy is just one of several established and developing genealogy groups in Second Life.

Another place to visit in Second Life is the headquarters of UGG (Union of Genealogy Groups) in Second Life. Then try the SL Family History Center, where a chat was held on handwriting, using sample images from the Family History Library in Salt Lake City. In Figure 9-9, you can see my avatar attending this discussion led by Clarise.

The United Genealogy Groups, Caladon, LDS Family History Center, West of Ireland, Heritage Books Store, Wonderful Denmark (with interest also in Norway and Sweden), Genealogie Francais, and The Genealogy Resource Center on Info Island are all genealogy areas you can explore on Second Life. As a visitor you can explore a genealogy area's resources and meet with other family historians who've also dropped by between scheduled events. Or just happen upon another genealogist and make a new friend (see Figure 9-10).

FIGURE 9-9.   *Members gather for a chat on handwriting led by Clarise.*

Many other social network services with avatars are popping up on the Internet, and you may eventually want to explore them, too. However, Second Life is one where genealogy has established a firm beachhead, and is creating new communities regularly.

FIGURE 9-10. *Wandering in genealogy areas, you are likely to meet up with others interested in family history.*

Google Wave: Do-It-Yourself Social Networking

If you would like a social network service that combines e-mail, chat, conversations, and documents in one simple format, look at Google Wave (see Figure 9-11). This tool/site/service launched in May 2009, and it didn't take long for genealogists to jump on.

Note

In order to use Google Wave, you must use the Chrome Frame add-in. Also, Wave works best if you are using the Google Chrome, Firefox, or Safari browser. It will work with Microsoft Internet Explorer, but it doesn't like it.

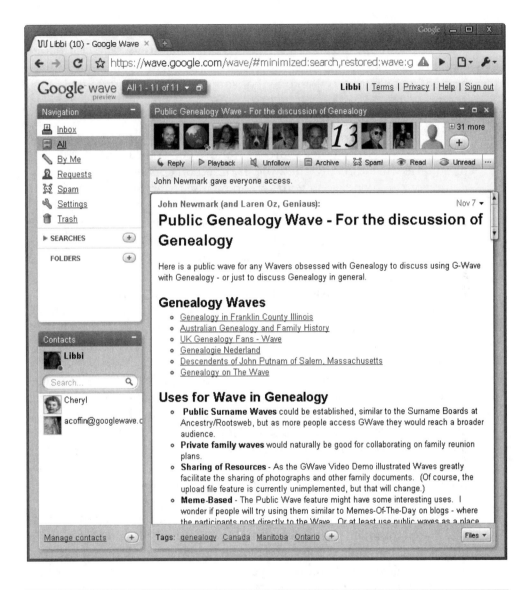

FIGURE 9-11. *Google Wave is a way to social network by creating your own wave and inviting others to it.*

A Google Wave is equal parts conversation and document, where you can communicate and work with other people using richly formatted text, photos, videos, maps, and more. In Google Wave you create a wave and add people to it, or join one that someone else has started; about six genealogy waves already exist. Your member ID on Google Wave is *yourname*@googlewave.com.

Everyone on a wave can use richly formatted text, photos, gadgets, and even feeds from other sources on the Web. You can insert a reply or edit the wave directly. The wave is based on concurrent rich-text editing, where you see on your screen nearly instantly what other collaborators are typing in that particular wave. Google Wave is just as well suited for quick messages as for persistent content—it allows for both collaboration and communication. You can also use "playback" to rewind the wave and see how it evolved.

The Google Wave software is called the Chrome Frame, and you add it to your browser. Google Chrome, Firefox, and Safari browsers work best. Google Wave includes a rich text editor and other functions like desktop drag-and-drop (which, for example, lets you drag a set of photos right into a wave). You can do this with any wave you create or are following.

Here's how following works: When someone adds you directly to a wave, or if you contribute to a wave, you will automatically be following that wave. When you see a public wave that you would like to get updates on, you can choose to follow it by using the Follow button in the wave panel toolbar. You can remove any waves from your inbox with the Archive button, but they will reappear with any update to that wave. You can switch between following and unfollowing a wave as much and as often as you like.

Public waves that are in your inbox simply because you opened them at some point in the past will start to leave your inbox as they are updated. You can also manually remove them with the archive feature, and they will no longer return. If you no longer want a wave you are on for any reason (whether you created it, added to it, or followed it) to show up in your inbox, use the unfollow feature. You can still find waves that you are not following by searching for them or if you have organized them into saved searches or folders.

Following is the first step towards a set of new tools for managing waves in your wave inbox. In the future, Google developers have promised, you will have more control over what kinds of changes will cause a wave to appear in the inbox, as well as better support for groups of wave users. As this develops, you can keep track by looking for the hash tag #wavetips on Twitter.

Wrapping Up

- Social networking services help you collaborate with other genealogists. You can do it by text (the old-fashioned way) or with varying degrees of text, sound, video, animation, and pictures.

- Facebook has several genealogists, and is a convenient way to communicate.

- Second Life is a multimedia social networking experience, with many genealogy lectures and chats happening regularly.

- Google Wave has created several genealogy-related collaborative social networks.

Chapter 10

Social Bookmarking
and Tagging

The Internet has been described as an online world, vast and largely uncharted. One way to find your way back to a place, or leave virtual cookie crumbs so that other genealogy adventurers can follow your trail, is to use tags and social bookmark systems.

When we looked at Twitter, we explored tags a little: Post a message with a hash tag and others can search for it. This is the same sort of idea, using other ways to tag content. Social bookmarking is one of the fun ways to do that. Services such as StumbleUpon and Delicious let you share, organize, search, and manage bookmarks of web resources such as GEDCOM databases. Unlike file sharing, these actual resources aren't shared, but instead bookmarks that reference them, and perhaps a short review to tell others why you liked it.

When you add a tag, description, or review, it can be in the form of metadata (*data about data*) to help other users understand the content of the resource before downloading it for themselves. Your descriptions may be free text comments, votes in favor of or against its quality, or tags that collectively or collaboratively become a folksonomy. *Folksonomy* is a term for user-driven tagging. Just as *taxonomy* is a formal process and science of sorting things into categories, an informal process by which many users classify things with freeform keywords about shared content is folksonomy.

So, now we have several social bookmarking systems, where users save links to webpages to help them remember and share the information, or use a toolbar in a browser to do so. These social bookmarks are usually public. However, sometimes bookmarks can be private, shared only with specific people or groups, shared only inside certain networks, or some other combination of public and private domains. Those granted access to the bookmarks can view these bookmarks chronologically, by category or tags, or with a search engine.

Typically, social bookmark services prefer sorting the bookmarks with tags instead of a browser-based system of folders, as the earliest social bookmarking schemes did (see the box on page 192). However, some services employ category folders or a combination of folders and tags. You can view bookmarks associated with a chosen tag and information about the number of users who have bookmarked and/or reviewed them. Some social bookmarking services also draw inferences from the relationship of tags to create "clouds" of tags or bookmarks (see Figure 10-1).

FIGURE 10-1.   *The San Jose Library system's Delicious bookmarks have a cloud of tags that includes "genealogy."*

Many social bookmarking services have web feeds for their lists of bookmarks, including lists organized by tags. This allows you to become aware of new bookmarks as they are saved, shared, and tagged by others. You will also find features such as ratings and comments on bookmarks, the ability to import and export bookmarks from browsers, e-mailing of bookmarks, web annotation, and groups or other social network features. And, of course, tags that interest you. For example, StumbleUpon has a genealogy category in the drop-down list.

A Short History of Social Bookmarking

Social bookmarking as an idea began around April 1996 with the launch of itList, which included public and private bookmarks. Within the next three years, we had competitive companies such as Backflip, Blink, Clip2, ClickMarks, HotLinks, and others entering the market. They featured folders for organizing bookmarks, and sometimes automatically sorted bookmarks. Blink included browser buttons for saving bookmarks; Backflip let you e-mail bookmarks to others and had "Backflip this page" buttons on partner websites. With no sustainable revenue models, this early generation of social bookmarking companies failed as the dot-com bubble burst.

Fast-forward to 2003, when Delicious (it started as "del.icio.us") explored the frontier of tagging and coined the term *social bookmarking*. Within a year, Delicious got competition with Furl, Simpy, Citeulike, and Connotea (sometimes called *social citation services*) and the now extremely popular StumbleUpon. In 2006, Ma.gnolia, Blue Dot (later renamed Faves), and Diigo popped up. About the same time, Connectbeam included a social bookmarking and tagging service aimed at businesses and enterprises. In 2007, IBM released Lotus Connections for the same market. Sites such as Digg, reddit, and Newsvine offer a similar system for organization of social news. And, of course, all the social networking services (see Chapter 9) have tag and bookmark sharing features.

And genealogists use all of them!

Pros and Cons

When it comes to creating search results that meet your needs, a social bookmarking system has advantages over automated resource location and classification software, such as search engine spiders (see Chapter 6).

These tag-based classifications of Internet resources are created by human beings, who understand both the content and quality of the resource. Search engine spiders, on the other hand, have a set of instructions to help determine the meaning of a resource, and can be fooled with clever tricks such as hidden text. Besides that, sometimes people can find and bookmark webpages before the web spiders do. Finally, a social bookmarking system rates a resource based on how many times it has been bookmarked by users, that is, humans like you. This, in the end, may be more useful to you than a ranking based on how many external links point to it.

Social bookmarking can be useful to access an organized and edited set of bookmarks from various computers, to arrange a large number of bookmarks, and to share bookmarks with contacts. Libraries have found social bookmarking to be useful as an easy way to provide lists of informative links to patrons, as Figure 10-1 showed.

However, they are not a panacea. The folksonomy method of tagging and sorting means that you won't find an "industry standard" set of keywords, structures, or any controls on spelling, grammar, and connotations. Problems such as spelling errors ("geneology"), tags with more than one meaning, synonym/antonym confusion, irregular and quirky tag use, and no way for users to indicate hierarchical relationships between tags can all create confusion. (For example, a site might be labeled as both English and British, with no mechanism to indicate the relationship between the two.)

Another disadvantage is that social bookmarking can also attract corruption and collusion. In a word, spam. Some people use social bookmarking as a tool to make a website more visible. As with webpage keywords, the more often a webpage is bookmarked and tagged, the better chance it has of being found. Spammers will bookmark the same webpage many times or tag each page of a website using popular terms. This means that social networking sites must constantly adjust their security system to keep ahead of abuses.

Surprisingly, and in spite of these clear disadvantages, quite often a simple form of shared vocabulary does emerge in social bookmarking systems. The communal nature of the tagging begins to show a kind of self-organizing dynamic. Even without a centrally controlled vocabulary, the tags that describe different resources eventually converge to an accepted format.

Hansel and Gretel on the World Wide Web

As noted previously, your choices for social bookmarking are varied and wide. And, of course, there are two sides to this coin: bookmarks you make and bookmarks others make for you to find. We'll look at both of these.

Usually in both cases, it is a simple matter of one click, and maybe some typing if you want to add a comment, review, or rating.

Your Breadcrumbs

You will have probably noticed on several sites a little link that says "Share This" (see Figure 10-2). This is one way for you to leave breadcrumbs (bookmarks) for others.

The symbols are for sites such as Delicious, Facebook, and so on. Whichever one or ones you are registered for, you can click the symbol and share that with your friends registered with that same service. For example, to share a news story with friends on Facebook, click the F symbol. You may have to log into your Facebook account, but then you can post the link to your profile, sharing a quick comment at the same time if you like (see Figure 10-3).

Note that you can also use the Facebook applet in your browser, where you simply click an icon in the links toolbar to share a link. Both work the same way, and most of the social networks have this feature.

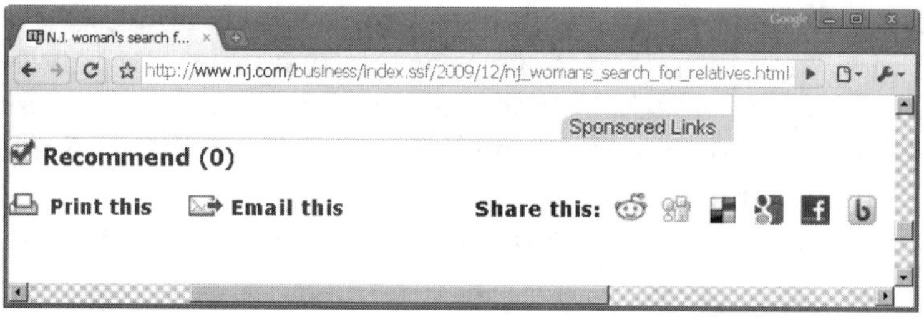

FIGURE 10-2. *Often news, information, and periodicals sites will have several ways for you to leave a social bookmark.*

FIGURE 10-3. *You can share URLs using the link on the page or the Facebook applet.*

Another easy way to share bookmarks is to use a plugin to your browser that connects you to your social bookmarking service. StumbleUpon (SU) is just one example of such a service. StumbleUpon is a free service that helps you discover and share websites with others who have similar interests. The more you use the service, the more likely it is that you'll "Stumble" across pages you like. Go to www.stumbleupon.com and sign up with a valid e-mail, user name, and password.

Download the toolbar and install it in your browser. To do this, go to www.stumbleupon.com/download.php or click on the link in your confirmation e-mail, and the right toolbar for your browser will appear.

Now that your StumbleUpon toolbar is up, you can go to a genealogy site and click the I Like It! icon. Or, if you don't like it, give it a thumbs down. Your browser will pop up a window. The first time of the day you do this, you will have to log in. Also, the program will ask you to type some words it displays to be certain you are not a spammer. Then, it will ask to be sure this is not R-rated. Then your favorite is saved to your StumbleUpon account and posted for others to find. Later if you wish, you can return to your profile and enter a review ("This site is well organized," for example).

Another advantage to this method is that no matter what computer you are using, if you log into your social bookmarking account, you can access your categorized and rated bookmarks. On some social bookmark services, such as Delicious, you can export your current bookmarks from your browser and then upload them onto the social bookmark profile you have set up. If you have more than one computer or use library computers, this can be a real frustration saver!

StumbleUpon does not have a feature to upload your current set of bookmarks from your browser to your SU account. "We deliberately do not provide any facilities for 'batch importing' sites to StumbleUpon," Barry Conway of SU told me. "We want our members to only add quality sites and to review those sites so that other members know why they are recommended. The best way to do this is one at a time, giving a quality review for each site."

Other Genealogists' Breadcrumbs

Let's look at social bookmarks from other genealogists now. I will use StumbleUpon for examples of how to use social bookmarks, but please keep in mind other popular sites such as Delicious and Digg, which also use tags such as "genealogy." They work in much the same way.

Open your browser with the StumbleUpon toolbar. From the toolbar, click All and then select an interest. You will start stumbling only through that interest. (Tip: You can add more interests on your Settings page.) Or, just click the SU button, and random pages based on your favorites, reviews, and interests will start to appear (see Figure 10-4).

The social bookmark sites usually also have a search function. In this example, go to www.StumbleUpon.com and log into your account. Then use the search box with the word "Genealogy." The screen shown in Figure 10-5 is typical of the displayed results. Note that you will see how many people have visited it, how many took time to write a review,

StumbleUpon Toolbar

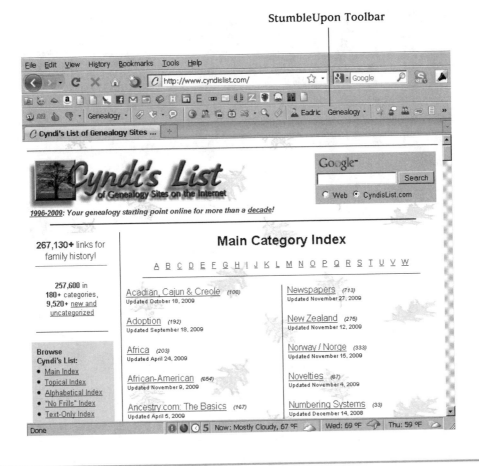

FIGURE 10-4.   *Note in the StumbleUpon toolbar that "Genealogy" appears; this means my stumbling is set to follow links that match that interest.*

sometimes a short excerpt from the page, and so on. But the most useful feature is there on the right: Synonyms for "Genealogy" show you other tags that users might have entered for their favorite sites on this topic, including the misspelling "geneology." Click one of those and you get even more hits, and it might include pages for which the tag is something other than genealogy. Also, try searching for your favorite surnames as well as the tag genealogy to see if, for example, "Spencer Genealogy" has been tagged by someone.

FIGURE 10-5. *Search your social bookmarking site for links tagged "genealogy" to see what other users have liked.*

StumbleUpon also has several social networking tools. You can allow it to search your Gmail, Yahoo! or AOL address books to find people you already know who use SU. You can also join a group to connect with like-minded folks on SU; two you might look into are "Genealogy 101" and "Family Photo Organizing." You can search for other users who use the same tags you do. And when you find other folks who interest you from any of these methods, you can "follow" them, just as you do on Twitter, to keep track of what they are bookmarking, tagging, and reviewing. On SU, this is called following or subscribing, and you can get an RSS feed to help you keep up with your favorites.

> **Note**
>
> *A social bookmarking service can give you almost as many results as a search engine. To narrow it down, combine terms, such as "genealogy" plus a location, a surname, or a type of record.*

Some Social Bookmark Sites to Explore

You want to be certain to explore StumbleUpon, as well as other social bookmark services before you settle on one. Here are some to get you started:

Delicious

As mentioned previously, Delicious (www.delicious.com) is one of the oldest and most popular of the social bookmark sites. Searching for "Genealogy" on this service gets you several tags from "LDS genealogy" to "research genealogy." Another useful feature with Delicious is the ability to filter a search on the tags such as "genealogy" by using other tags such as "reference" or "history." See Figure 10-6 for a sample of such a search.

Faves

Faves (www.faves.com) is blended social networking/bookmarking (see Figure 10-7). Signing up is as simple as StumbleUpon. Then, you save your favorite webpages and find them from any computer. Just like StumbleUpon, you can follow people and topic groups to find webpages that interest you. Then you can build a following of readers who like the

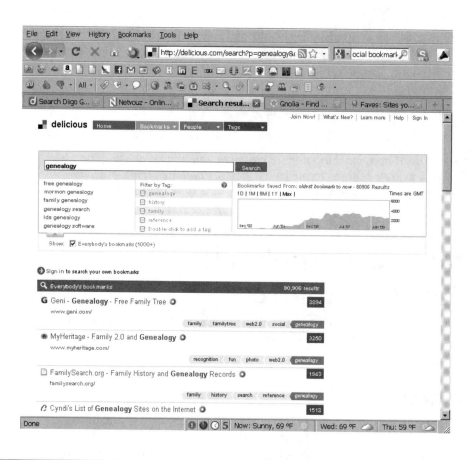

FIGURE 10-6. *Delicious has many bookmarks and tags for genealogy.*

sites you save. Faves also has "topics" that you can follow and add to your Faves home page. Some you might consider are

◆ Genealogy	◆ Divorce	◆ Legal
◆ Backgrounds	◆ Family	◆ Marriage
◆ Census	◆ Government	◆ People
◆ Date	◆ History	

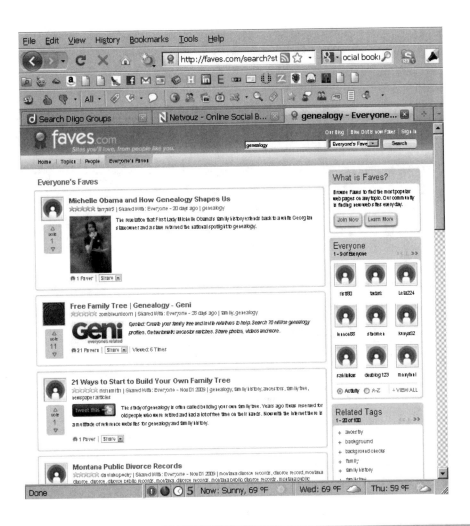

FIGURE 10-7.   *Results of a search for "genealogy" on Faves social bookmarking*

Netvouz

Netvouz (www.netvouz.com) is a social bookmarking service that allows you to save your favorite links online and access them from any computer, wherever you are. In Netvouz, you organize your bookmarks in folders and tag each bookmark with keywords and access them quickly on your personalized bookmarks page. You can share your bookmarks with others or password-protect them for your own privacy.

When you search Netvouz for "genealogy," it gives you a list of tags also used in the bookmarks in your results, giving you a good idea of the folksonomy of the service (see Figure 10-8).

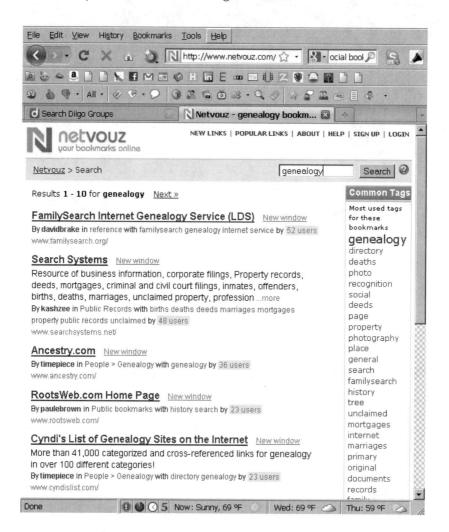

FIGURE 10-8. *Netvouz uses folders and tags to organize your bookmarks.*

Diigo

Diigo (www.diigo.com) has all the features of the previously mentioned services. Where Diigo shines is in the variety of groups (see Figure 10-9). Groups serve as meeting places, bookmark catalogs, and mutual support forums for the members. And, like the others, it is free.

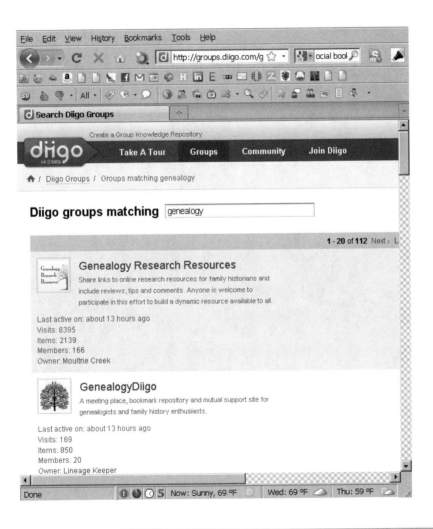

FIGURE 10-9. *Diigo's groups for genealogy range from Florida Genealogy to Genealogy Research support.*

Wrapping Up

- ◆ Social bookmarking services allow sharing of bookmarks.

- ◆ Many of them also serve as social networking sites.

- ◆ Tags and organization are the result of the community of the service.

- ◆ Almost all of the social bookmarking sites have tags for genealogy and related topics, and can allow you to track new or changed bookmarks.

- ◆ Many of these sites also have genealogy-related groups.

- ◆ Some to try are StumbleUpon, Delicious, Faves, Netvouz, and Diigo.

Chapter 11

Blogging Your Genealogy, Sites, Software, and More

In Chapter 3, you read about blogs that can help you learn about genealogy. In this chapter, I will show you how blogging your genealogy can help you communicate your needs, problems, and genealogy happy-dance moments to other genealogists around the world. Blogs can truly be one of the most important tools for your genealogy research!

Amy Coffin, MLS, is the author of the popular blog We Tree. She says of her blog: "I started this blog (1) so I could talk about genealogy without bugging my non-genealogy family and (2) to get my ancestral names out there online, in the chance that someone would be searching for the same names and stumble on my blog. This has happened many times; I just don't always write about it.

"The best success story had to do with my great-grandmother Gertrude Baerecke. I knew all about her, but nothing about her ancestors. The situation remained unchanged for months until one day a woman read my blog and e-mailed me saying she had been researching the Baerecke line. She knew everything about the Baerecke family, except for a woman named Gertrude who was an elusive mystery to her. Would I happen to have any information on Gertrude? Right there the puzzle pieces fit together.

"I really, really, really believe blogs are one of the easiest, cheapest, and most successful ways to advance personal genealogy research. I believe in this tool so much that I came up with 52 ideas (one for each week), which I share freely on my web site: www.amycoffin.com/ Blog_Ideas_Personal_Genealogy.html."

So, are you ready to jump on the blog bandwagon?

Blogging Guidelines

The first thing to know about your genealogy blog is that it has a purpose: to give, share, and relate. The more you do these things, the more you will receive in return. The second thing you need to know is that blogging is ridiculously easy!

A web log, or blog, in plain language, is a journal of thoughts, observations, links, pictures, and comments, published for the entire world to see. It's a dynamic webpage that you can easily change daily, or more than once a day if you wish. In Chapter 6 you learned that web search spiders love "fresh" content, and take note whenever a page changes. So when you blog, you become very findable on the Web!

When you create a blog and often mention the surnames you are searching, you will pop up in the search engines. A visitor may find something on your blog that is of help, or has something that helps you, and there you have online genealogy at its best!

> *Note*
>
> *A dictionary definition for blog is a website that contains an online personal journal with reflections, comments, and often hyperlinks provided by the writer; also "the contents of such a site." The verb "to blog" means to make entries in such a journal. The etymology is short for "web log," and it first started appearing around 1999 (yes, a decade ago!). One who writes a blog is a blogger. The gerund is blogging.*

How to Blog Effectively

Writing a blog is not any harder than any other writing, and no easier! But writing for the Web is a little different than writing a book or a magazine article. This is a point I have made in my presentations about writing in general: When you write for the Web, you must picture your reader leaning forward, ready to take action, even if that action is to click away from here as quickly as interest flags.

Reading a book or a magazine, you tend to be more relaxed, and usually have set aside this time to be reading. Reading something on the Web usually has to do with accomplishing something else, and doing it while in some sort of office chair, or at the least while holding a smart phone. Not relaxed, in other words. Your genealogy blog has to capture the eyeballs and hold them to the end, or until the mouse clicks them away like the heels of Dorothy's ruby slippers. But though that makes it sound like work, it can also be very rewarding.

As Robert Ragan of Treasure Maps Genealogy (www.amberskyline .com/treasuremaps), puts it, a blog can help you use three important keys to getting your genealogy done.

First: Giving back to the world of online genealogy in the form of being generous with your information helps keep you motivated to find even more. And, what goes around comes around!

Second: Working hard at addressing your readers, and using the first person sparingly, keeps your blog from being mere blather. That way, you are focusing outward, not inward, and drawing the reader in. Word your posts, queries, and other requests with "you" and not "I" for better results.

Third: Holding on to *some* of your information encourages readers of your blog to leave comments, ask questions, postulate theories, and exchange their information. It helps it to become an interaction, and that's what the Web 2.0 is all about. In light of this, Ragan also stresses in his web blogs that an offer to exchange and share is the secret to success in blogging. He stresses that "I am willing to share more" should be in all your communications, but especially in your blog.

Beyond those basic genealogy considerations, writing a blog, no matter what the topic, is easier if you follow these guidelines. The first commandment of blogging is to care about the subject. If today's topic is your personal genealogy, let your excitement show. If it's a friend's genealogy success you are writing about, convey that sense of joy. Be passionate.

Part of that is not being formal. Write your blog exactly as you would tell a friend. Because that's what you are doing: telling all your web friends what is new about your search for family history. However, while breezy is good, long-winded is not. Draft a post, and read it over. Look for repeating yourself, wandering off topic, or using needless adjectives. Also give up clichés, unless you are using them as irony. Say it in your own words!

Spell check. Most of the blogging sites and software (see the accompanying box) have a spelling checker. Or write it in your word processor first, spell check, and then paste into your blog software. Learn to love www.dictionary.com.

Line breaks, subheads, boldface, and italics can help you express yourself. Make your blog easy to read so that your reader doesn't click away in frustration or confusion. Part of that is using lists. Bulleted lists catch the eye and make the reader feel efficient. Other times, go with a narrative or a picture so that your blog doesn't look the same every day, making the reader feel, "Oh, I read that already."

Every entry should have a good headline and descriptive tags. Draw those readers in with creative teasers, helping them know what to expect from your posts. This can be as fun as finding a female ancestor!

Software and Services for Blogging

- AOL People Connection (http://peopleconnection.aol .com/blogs) is a social networking and blog service from America Online.

- Blogger (www.blogger.com), from Google, is one of the oldest and most stable of the free online blog services. Google's Blog Search (http://blogsearch.google.com) searches only blogs. Regular Google search will also search blogs, but mix those results with other sites, sorting by relevance.

- LiveJournal (www.livejournal.com) offers you tools for a private journal, a blog, a discussion forum, or a social network all your own.

- TypePad (www.typepad.com) offers professional services in design and so forth, but also a free program, TypePad Micro. Micro is a free streamlined blog, powered by TypePad, and optimized for social media. With it, readers can share content from a TypePad blog with free Micro blogs. Reblogged content links directly back to the original blog.

- WordPress (www.wordpress.org) is a free blogging tool and web log platform. It is also a wonderful site for learning about blogging.

- Writer by MSN is part of the new suite of free communication software in Office Live. Writer connects with all the different blog services mentioned previously. You write your blog in MSN Writer, using its formatting, grammar, and spelling tools, and then post to your blog service.

Success Story: Another Jones Surprise, or Why Genealogists Should Blog

We Tree Adventures in Genealogy. Monday, August 3, 2009, by Amy Coffin, MLIS Texas, United States. Reprinted with permission

In my last entry about Keeping Up with the Joneses, I shared that I was learning about my Jones line. I discovered that they spent some time in Cooke County, Texas, but that I had yet not found the time to learn about the area and its genealogy resources.

In the comments section of that blog post, one of my friends and faithful readers, who also happens to be a very smart librarian, shared with me a link for a Jones Cemetery and asked if these were my Jones folks. They were!

Many of the names in the cemetery are familiar. Duckett and Bostick stand out. Probably anyone from Asheville, North Carolina, has a connection. However, what stood out on that page was a grave marker transcription for:

*JONES, Harriet Elizabeth 8 Oct 1859 – 18 Aug 1861
dau of R. M. and Sarah Neilson Jones (note: no longer found)*

This entry got me excited because R.M. and Sarah are my great-great-great grandparents. Harriet was a child I did not know of! My great-great grandfather, Frank Wiley Jones, had another sister! I went to enter her name in my files and I stopped...

She was born on the same day as my great-great grandfather. He was a twin.

The only evidence I had that Harriet even existed came from the Jones Cemetery transcription webpage. I've yet to find them in the 1860 census. I'm wondering if they were en route from North Carolina to Texas then.

The only reason I now know about it is because I blogged about my Jones line and someone took the time to comment and share what she knew.

This is why all genealogists should blog. We are not islands. So many other folks out there have information to share. You don't have to be an expert writer. Just get your surnames out there. You'll be surprised at what you find ... or who finds you.

Getting Started

Getting set up with a blog is quick and easy on most systems. Generally, you supply a real name and e-mail address; then name your blog and usually choose from some preset design features. WordPress (see Figure 11-1) is just one example; Blogger, AOL, and all the others mentioned in the box earlier in the chapter are just as easy.

Just fill out the forms at WordPress.com. (WordPress.org is for the do-it-yourselfer who wants all the software for designing, writing, posting, uploading, and so forth right on his or her own computer. I am not that person.) The site lets you choose a specific WordPress.com address (e.g., http://PowellGenealogy.wordpress.com); a selection from free, customizable designs; and 3GB (gigabytes) of file storage for pictures, videos, and the like. You can blog as much as you want for free; your blog can be public to the world or private for just your friends. WordPress offers premium features for a fee, such as custom domain mapping if you want to go that far.

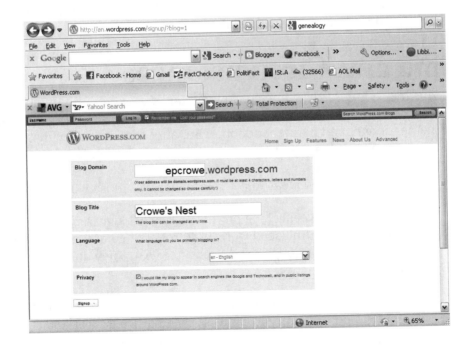

FIGURE 11-1. *WordPress, like most free blogging sites, is easy to sign up with.*

Choosing your theme from the more than 70 available, with different widgets, is time-consuming, but not hard. You can switch themes instantly with just a click of a button. One of the add-ons is the statistics system to give you real-time results on how many people are visiting your blog, where they're coming from, which posts are most popular, and which search engine terms (tags) are sending people to your blog.

When you write a post and add relevant tags, the tags are placed where the search engine spiders can find them. WordPress also uses a program to help you track and avoid spam in your comments, users, and so forth. When you're signed in and leave a comment on WordPress.com, you will see a special page, which notifies you of any follow-ups to your comment so you can easily follow your conversations no matter what blog they're on.

WordPress.com allows you to have a completely public blog, a blog that is public but not included in search engines or the public listings, or a private blog that only members can access. If you want a public blog, but only occasionally post something private, there are per-post password options, too. If you decide to switch to another service, WordPress has an export function that helps you port all your entries to the new site.

All this is in the documentation, and WordPress has user discussion forums and tech help if you need it.

Time and Circumstances

This may all seem very time-consuming, and getting set up can take you the better part of a day as you define for yourself your blog's focus, theme, design, and permanent home. But after that, it really only takes a little bit of each day, or week, or month as you decide, to keep it up-to-date and fresh.

Here are just a few ideas to get your genealogy muse working:

♦ Amy Coffin's weekly blog prompts at www.blogcarnival.com/bc/ submit_6260.html (see Figure 11-2) mentioned at the start of this chapter. Cycle through them year after year: They are perennial topics!

♦ Participate in blog "carnivals." This is when many bloggers all agree to post on a particular topic by a particular date and submit the permanent URL to a database. The carnival is posted on the

FIGURE 11-2. *When you need prompting to write your blog, try some of these ideas.*

declared date, and everyone who wants to can participate in the "moveable feast" of blogs. Here is just one example:

Our first member-submitted idea for the January 2010 edition is The Final Resting Place. This theme comes from Colleen McHugh, author of the Grave Yard Rabbit blog, The R.I.P.PERS. Colleen wants us to investigate how families determine their final resting place. She goes on to say: "In today's mobile society, does one choose a place near where they last lived? Or do they return to the place of their roots? Do they rest in a family plot? If so, and if married, whose family plot? How has the determination of the final resting place changed between the time of our ancestors and now?" Colleen poses some excellent questions, which I'm sure will get a lot of varied responses for this carnival edition. As always, write a blog post that address[es] this edition's theme and submit it to the carnival using the submission form. Submissions for this edition are due by December 25. Be sure to include a short description of your post in the "remarks" section of the submission form (www.thegraveyardrabbit.com/2009/12/call-for-submissions-gyr-carnival.html).

- Manic Monday (things about genealogy that drive you crazy)

- Tombstone Tuesday (pictures or descriptions of interesting/unusual/pertinent tombstones)

- Wordless Wednesday (usually pictures, sometimes a link, sometimes a map)

- Thursday Treasures (heirlooms and their stories)

- Follow Friday (blogs you follow and why)

- Surname Saturday (highlight a surname you are pursuing, where, and when)

- Night Moves (genealogy you found late at night on the Internet)

As you can see, when it comes to blogging, your imagination is your best friend!

Wrapping up

- Blogging is free, fun, and easy to set up.

- Sharing your genealogy on a blog can garner responses from others searching your surnames.

- You need only spend a few minutes a day keeping your blog current.

- Blog entries are best when they are casual in tone, have enough information to intrigue the reader, and are tagged so search engine spiders find them.

- Ideas abound!

Part III

The Nitty Gritty:
Places to Find Names,
Dates, and Places

Chapter 12

Vital Records and Historical Documents

Vital records are the foundation and building blocks of your family history research. These are the records of life: birth, marriage, and death. For everyone you find in your ancestry, you need the time and place of the birth, marriage, and death.

Other important records are naturalization, census records, and land ownership. Other milestones in life can also be included in your genealogy data: baptism, bar mitzvah, graduation, divorce, and so on. More and more, you can find at least clues to these records online; in some cases, you can get digitized versions of the records themselves. Historical documents, such as censuses, diaries, wills, court cases, and government publications, can put flesh on the bones of our ancestors, at least in our imaginations, when they mention individuals.

Such records are usually stored in some form at archives and libraries. In this chapter you'll learn that some things can be found online, while others can be ordered online, and still others you have to visit in person or ask for by mail, but you might be able to print the form you need from an Internet site.

Among the best of the online sites maintained by the United States federal government are the Library of Congress (LOC) and the National Archives and Records Administration (NARA). Both the LOC and NARA sites have been revamped recently, with links to genealogy guides, tips, and resources gathered together for easy access. You'll find these sites useful to help you decide what to ask for by mail or if you should visit in person.

Note

You'll eventually want to visit a NARA branch or the LOC in person because, although many resources are online, not every book or document is available that way.

Other important federal records online are the Bureau of Land Management records of original land grants and patents, immigration records, and naturalization records. Some states and counties also have certain vital records and censuses—sometimes online and sometimes only the contact information for ordering a copy.

This chapter gives you a short overview of what's where and how to access the resources on these sites. Most of the examples I give deal with finding American records; however, vital records are available in many countries, and Chapter 16 will deal with that.

Note

Two excellent sources to consult for addresses are published by Genealogical Publishing Company (www.genealogical.com). One, The Genealogist's Address Book *by Elizabeth Petty Bentley (2009), covers organizations, institutions, special resources, and websites. You will find information about libraries, archives, societies, fraternities, government agencies, vital records offices, professional bodies, publications, research centers, and special interest groups. In the sixth edition, the* Address Book *is arranged by locality and covers mainly U.S. topics, but also includes entries such as the Council of Scottish Clans. Another is Bentley's* County Courthouse Book *(2009), a state-by-state guide to U.S. counties, state court systems, and archives. It is also available from www.genealogical.com.*

Vital Records

In the United States, most birth, adoption, death, divorce, and marriage records will be at the state level, although some counties may also have copies. Usually, you have to write to the organization that has the records and enclose a check to receive a certified copy. You must have a date and a place to go with a name in order to find where an ancestor's vital records are. Only in rare cases can you find the actual document online, unless it is more than a century old and some volunteer group has scanned or transcribed it to be uploaded to the Internet. Furthermore, as discussed in Chapter 1, many professional genealogists insist on a certified copy, if not the original document itself, for proof of genealogy.

To get a certified copy of any these records, write or go to the vital statistics office in the state or area where the event occurred. Addresses and fees are often found online at the state's website. Usually, a fee for each document will cover copying and mailing. Each time you request a record, include a check or money order payable to the correct office and in the correct amount for the number of copies requested; sometimes, a credit card will be accepted. Don't send cash.

When you find information on an office, a phone number is usually included. Before you send your request, be sure to call and verify that the rates haven't changed. Also, in many cases, you can find an online page with the address for obtaining current information, and sometimes you can even order the records online by credit card. Often, you will have to include something like a photocopy of your driver's license as well.

Other steps to take:

- Type or print all names and addresses in the letter.

- When writing for birth or death records, include

    - Full name of person whose record is requested

    - Sex

    - Parents' names, including maiden name of mother

    - Month, day, and year of birth or death

    - Place of birth or death (city or town, county, and state; and name of hospital, if known)

    - Purpose for which copy is needed

    - Relationship to person whose record is requested

    - Daytime telephone number with area code

- When writing for marriage records, include

    - Full names of bride and groom

    - Month, day, and year of marriage

    - Place of marriage (city or town, county, and state)

    - Purpose for which copy is needed

    - Relationship to persons whose record is requested

    - Daytime telephone number with area code

- When writing for divorce records, include
    - Full names of husband and wife
    - Date of divorce or annulment
    - Place of divorce or annulment
    - Type of final decree
    - Purpose for which copy is needed
    - Relationship to persons whose record is requested
    - Daytime telephone number with area code

VitalRec.com is a great place to start. This site has information not only on all U.S. states and territories, but also on Canada, Australia, New Zealand, and several European nations.

The National Center for Health Statistics has a list of where to write for U.S. records at www.cdc.gov/nchs/w2w.htm (see Figure 12-1).

These sources are great for 20th-century records. However, if you need information on earlier centuries, city, regional, and national archives may be your best bet. Use your favorite search engine to look for the terms "vital records" and the geographical area you need. I found the Bedfordshire/Luton, UK, archives site by doing just that. The site's URL is www.bedfordshire.gov.uk/CommunityAndLiving/ArchivesAndRecordOffice.

Note

When requesting information, use the proper form and don't include your whole genealogy; simply include the pertinent data for the record you want. County clerks aren't going to read through a long narrative to find out what they need to do.

In another example, in the state of Tennessee, many vital records, such as births, deaths, and marriages, were not recorded by the state before 1908. Four cities—Chattanooga, Knoxville, Nashville, and Memphis—did keep local records that are now available through the

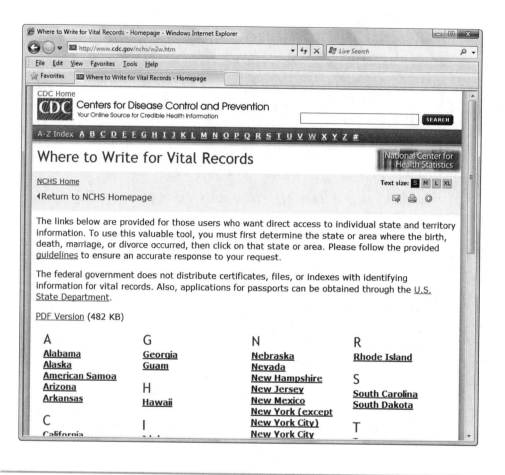

FIGURE 12-1. *In the United States, a good list of sites for records is at the National Center for Health Statistics.*

Tennessee State Library and Archives. Searches of these records can be requested by mail if you know the year of the event (birth, death, etc.). The website for the Memphis Public Library has an online index to Memphis death records that covers the years 1848 to 1945 at http://tempo .memphislibrary.org/dadabik/program_files/sform.php. You can get land grant records, too. The fees for these services range from $5 to $20. Go to the Tennessee State Archives site (www.tennessee.gov/tsla/ index.htm) for the forms and links.

Tennessee is quite typical: Before Social Security, many states did not keep birth and death records, but localities might have. When Social Security was enacted, many people born in the late 19th century had to request that a birth certificate be created for them; marriage records in some states were also lax until Social Security. In these cases, you must ask for a delayed certificate, that is, one that was created at the request of the person involved after the fact.

Library of Congress

The mission of the Library of Congress (www.loc.gov) is to "make its resources available and useful to the Congress and the American people and to sustain and preserve a universal collection of knowledge and creativity for future generations." Today, the LOC has amassed more than 100 million items and become one of the world's leading cultural institutions. The Library of Congress site provides online access to a small portion of the holdings.

The LOC Local History and Genealogy website has four sections that are of particular use to genealogists (see Figure 12-2).The Local History and Genealogy Reading Room page (www.loc.gov/rr/genealogy) has information on how to prepare for a visit to the reading room. It describes what the room holds and allows you to search the card catalog of holdings. You can search these by subject, author, and other criteria.

An important link from this page is to the search hints. As you can imagine, in a catalog of more than 100 million items, finding your particular needle is possible, but tricky. Happily, the LOC catalog uses Boolean terms. Search syntax for keyword searching in the Library of Congress online catalog is similar to that of some Internet search engines—use double quotes for phrase searches and type Boolean operators in UPPERCASE. For example, to get an exact phrase in the subject field, you can enter "Spencer family" or "Madison County Alabama." Do note, however, that the subject field may have county both spelled out and abbreviated as "co." so do search on both. You can search for specific states' military pensions (military pensions Ohio),

FIGURE 12-2. *The Library of Congress has a guide to using the resources there.*

specific countries (Heraldry Ireland), and specific record types (Wills Madison County Alabama). You can search for specific books, too, by putting the title in quotation marks and the author after the connector AND. So, some valid searches are:

```
Wills AND Alabama
Wills AND Mississippi Territory
"military pensions" AND Ohio
Brogan AND presidential
"A to Z" AND Reakes
"civil war" AND women AND 1861
```

Many items do not circulate; however, an interlibrary loan may be possible. Using interlibrary loans, the Library of Congress serves as a source for material not available through local, state, or regional libraries in the United States. A book circulated this way must be used on the premises of the borrowing library; it becomes a temporary addition to that library's reference collection for up to 60 days. Requests are accepted from academic, public, and special libraries that make their own material available through participation in an interlibrary loan system. Participation is usually indicated by membership in one of the major U.S. bibliographic networks (Online Computer Library Center [OCLC]), Research Libraries Information Network [RLIN]) or by a listing in the American Library Directory (Bowker) or the Directory of Special Libraries and Information Centers (Gale). So if you find an item that you feel may help your genealogy search, check with your local public library to see if they can participate. You will need the LOC call number (the LOC does not use the Dewey decimal system), author, title, and date of publication.

The LOC site has many interesting sections you will want to explore. Some of these are listed next.

American Memory

This section contains documents, photographs, movies, and sound recordings that tell some of America's story. The direct link is http://memory.loc.gov.

On the American Memory home page, you can click Browse Collections by Topic to explore other primary source material. The collections are grouped by subject, then time, then place, and then library division. You can also browse by format if you want a sound file or picture. Visiting a collection's home page and reading the descriptive information about the collection can give you more direction in finding what you want.

The drawbacks to the Collection Finder are that it's a catalog you browse—not an index you search—and it doesn't always list every single item in a collection, but instead gives an overview of the topic. For instance, if only a few items in a collection pertain to the broad topic of "agriculture," the collection might not appear under that topic.

Clicking a category is like saying, "I want to see a collection mainly about a certain subject." The complete list of subjects is at http://memory .loc.gov at the link: "More Browse Options." Say you know an ancestor owned a hotel in the early 20th century. In that case, the collection "Hotels 1870-1930" might help you research that ancestor.

Another area of the American Memory section of the LOC for you to explore is the Maps page at www.loc.gov/topics/maps.php. Here you can search collections containing hundreds of digitized maps from 1639 to 1988. You can find city maps, conservation maps, exploration maps, immigration and settlement maps, military maps, and transportation maps, to name a few. And the amazing thing is this wealth of maps is only a tiny part of the LOC's full 4.5-million-item Geography and Map Division holdings.

Research Tools

This section of the site offers many online databases and connections to resources at other sites. The direct link is www.loc.gov/rr.

American Treasures

This section of the site is of interest more for the wonderful historical artifacts found there than for any specific genealogy information. The direct link is www.loc.gov/exhibits/treasures.

> *Note*
>
> *If you're researching African-American roots, you'll want to look at the African-American Odyssey page at http://memory.loc.gov/ammem/aaohtml/aohome.html. This exhibition examines the African-American quest for full citizenship and contains primary source material, as well as links to other African-American materials at the LOC.*

Using the Library of Congress

Click Using The Library of Congress on the home page, and you can click your way through an excellent tutorial on the ins and outs of researching the library in person. If you need to make a trip to the LOC, reading this section first can save you some time and frustration.

The Library Today

This link from the home page tells you about new exhibits, collections, and events at the LOC and its website. Visit it at least once a week, because anything new posted to the website will be announced here. The direct link is www.loc.gov/today.

Research Tools

The Research Tools page at www.lcweb.loc.gov/rr/tools.html takes you to a large set of useful links of interest for researchers, both on the LOC site and on other websites. These include desk references you can use on the Web, the LOC card catalog of all materials (including those not online), and special databases.

The Vietnam Era Prisoner of War/Missing in Action and Task Force Russia Databases at http://lcweb2.loc.gov/pow/powhome.html are examples of databases. This URL takes you to a page that gives you access to a massive database of more than 137,000 records pertaining to United States military personnel listed as unaccounted for as of December 1991. At the bottom of this page is a link to Task Force Russia at http://lcweb2.loc.gov/frd/tfrquery.html, a set of documents dealing with Americans who are believed to have been held in the former Soviet Union.

At the page www.loc.gov/rr/askalib, you can click the Local History/Genealogy link. Here's what you can get here:

♦ Basic research assistance related to genealogy, local history in the United States, and heraldry

♦ Answers to queries requiring resources that are unique to the Library of Congress. You should receive a response within five business days. However, the staff cannot conduct extensive research in genealogy or heraldry for you.

If you cannot find the answers to your questions on the general links, you can e-mail your question to a librarian. Furthermore, certain topics, such as American Memory, have specific times of day when a librarian is available for a live, Web-based chat.

National Archives and Records Administration

The Library of Congress and the National Archives and Records Administration together are a treasure trove for the family historian. However, using these resources can also be like a treasure hunt! Unlike a library, where you walk up to the card catalog computer, type a subject, find the Dewey Decimal system number, walk to the shelf, and get the book, the archive is organized by government agency. Furthermore, what you find in that catalog at the archives may be a book, a manuscript, or a government whitepaper. This complexity means that first-time archive users often need help.

At the NARA, whether online or in person, you can get that help. At many national archives, that is not the case. For example, Britain's Public Record Office has rows of volumes listing the contents of files for the Admiralty, the Foreign Office, and Scotland Yard, but the polite archivist there will simply point you to the right shelf. France's Archives Nationales and Germany's Bundesarchiv operate the same way. Though the NARA has a long tradition of helping researchers one on one, that may not be the case for long if funding woes continue.

Freedmen's Bureau

Archivist of the United States Allen Weinstein announced in early 2007 that the National Archives completed the five-year project to preserve and microfilm the field office records of the Bureau of Refugees, Freedmen, and Abandoned Lands (the Freedmen's Bureau). Now the LOC has 1,000 rolls of microfilm reproducing over one million Bureau field office records from the former Confederate states, the border states, and the District of Columbia. All of the microfilm series of the field office records are available free of charge for research at the National Archives Building in Washington, D.C., and at the National Archives 13 regional archives nationwide.

Following the Civil War, the Freedmen's Bureau helped former slaves make the transition from slavery to freedom by issuing food and clothing, operating hospitals and refugee camps, establishing schools, helping legalize marriages, supervising labor agreements, and working with African-American soldiers and sailors and their heirs to secure back pay, bounty payments, and pensions. The records created during the course of these activities are a rich source of documentation of the black experience in late-19th-century America, and are essential for the study of African-American genealogy and Southern social history.

These are available for $65 per roll for domestic orders and $68 per roll for foreign orders—details on how to order are on the website. Also, don't miss the section of American Memory that is devoted to African-American research. It has several pages describing how to research African-American and Native American genealogy in the NARA site that may help you.

> ### Note
> *Included in these extraordinary records are registers that give the names, ages, and former occupations of freedmen, as well as names and residences of former owners. For some states, marriage registers provide the names, addresses, and ages of husbands and wives and their children. There are also census lists, detailed labor and apprenticeship agreements, complaint registers, rosters with personal data about black veterans (including company and regiment), and a host of documentation concerning the social and economic conditions of the black family.*

Other NARA Areas to Explore

You can click the Research Room link in the navigation bar to the left of the home page and go to Genealogy from there, or you can go straight to www.archives.gov/genealogy. Here you'll find information for beginners, such as the About Genealogy Research page and a list of research topics in genealogy with links to NARA resources that deal with them.

More advanced genealogists will want to read about the census catalogs, the online catalogs, Soundex indexing, and the latest additions to the collection. All genealogists should read the frequently asked questions (FAQ) file and the latest list of genealogy workshops. After touring this general help area, you're ready to tackle the specific resources on the NARA site.

Access to Archival Databases

You can search various subsets of the NARA holdings from their Web databases, starting at http://aad.archives.gov/aad. The Access to Archival Databases (AAD) is a searchable set of records preserved permanently in NARA. These records identify specific persons, geographic areas, organizations, and dates over a wide variety of civilian and military data, and have many genealogical, social, political, and economic research uses. Among the most popular of these databases are

♦ World War II Army Enlistment Records

♦ Records of Prime Contracts Awarded by the Military Services and Agencies

♦ Records on Trading of Securities by Corporate Insiders

♦ World War II Army Enlistment Records

- Records About the Proposed Sale of Unregistered Securities by Individuals

- Data Files Relating to the Immigration of Germans to the United States

- Central Foreign Policy Files

At www.archives.gov/research/african-americans, you can find a guide to researching African-American and Native American genealogy. For further information about all of NARA's electronic records holdings, including those not in AAD, see the Electronic and Special Media Records page (www.archives.gov/research/electronic-records/index.html) or NARA's online catalog, ARC.

ARC

The Archival Research Catalog (ARC) at www.archives.gov/research/arc is the online catalog of about 50 percent of NARA's nationwide holdings in the Washington, D.C. area, Regional Archives, and Presidential Libraries.

You can do keyword, digitized image, and location searches on this catalog, and in the advanced search, look for organizations, persons, and topics. The NARA staff is working to expand the catalog, and eventually it will reflect all the holdings. Check this site about once every two weeks to see the updates on what has been added.

Part of what is so wonderful about this updated catalog is the quick access to specific collections, such as the Guion-Miller Roll Index and the Index to the Final Rolls (Dawes)—two censuses of Native American populations from the 1800s and early 1900s—the World War II Army and Army Air Force Casualty List, and the World War II Navy, Marine, and Coast Guard Casualty List.

ALIC

The Archives Library Information Center (ALIC) is for professionals such as NARA staff and librarians nationwide. Its website is www.archives .gov/research/alic.

ALIC provides access to information on American history and government, archival administration, information management, and government documents to NARA staff, archives- and records-management professionals, and the general public.

On the ALIC page, you'll see links to quick searches of the book catalog, NARA publications on research, and special collections. On the right side of the page is a set of links under What's New In ALIC For Genealogists? (see Figure 12-3). Here you'll find the latest additions, such as a listing of genealogical CD-ROMS.

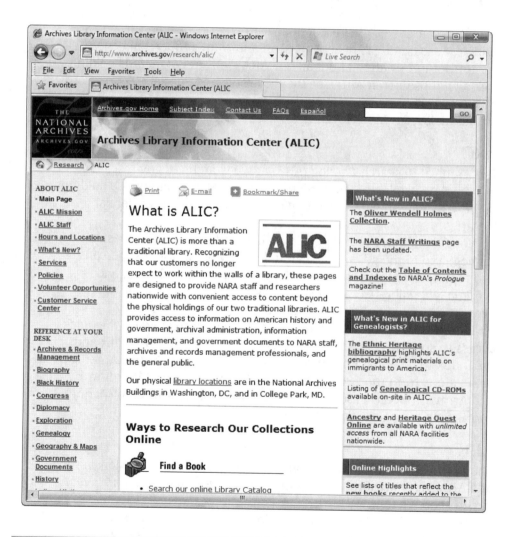

FIGURE 12-3. *Check the ALIC page for what's new for genealogists on the right side of the page.*

On the left of the page, under Reference At Your Desk, you'll see a list of topics, including Genealogy and History. The former has general links to NARA pages already covered in this chapter, as well as links to other websites that can help with genealogy. The latter does the same for general history sites.

ERA

The Electronic Records Archives (ERA) will theoretically be helpful to genealogists a hundred years from now. The goal is to preserve the electronic records of the government, such as memos, e-mails, presidential speeches, and so on. As such, it has only recent records.

It's been four years since the National Archives and Records Administration first began building ERA. The program is designed to digitize existing government paper records and to make electronic archive items available digitally. ERA is a complex and multiple-year project to move the government beyond simply warehousing paper. It reached an important milestone recently, according to Assistant Archivist and NARA Chief Information Officer Martha Morphy. "We have transferred the electronic records," she told Federal News Radio, "from the (George W.) Bush '43' Administration into the system, and we're able to provide access to those records to those who have legal rights to the records."

The project is ongoing, and will include records from:

♦   The U.S. Patent and Trademark Office

♦   The National Nuclear Security Administration

♦   The Bureau of Labor Statistics

♦   The Naval Oceanographic Office

Microfilm Publications Search

From the NARA Genealogy page, you can click Search Microfilm Catalogs. The catalogs list the various microfilms you can purchase, rent, or view onsite from NARA, These 3,400 microfilms can be searched by keyword, microfilm ID, record group number, and/or NARA location. Most of NARA's microfilm lists and descriptive pamphlets are not online. By searching for microfilm publications in the Microfilm Publications Catalog, however, you will be able to find out if a roll list or descriptive pamphlet is available. You will need to contact one of the NARA locations listed in the Viewing Location field(s) of the microfilm publication description to find out how to get a copy of the descriptive pamphlet or roll list.

Of particular interest is the Genealogical and Biographical Research catalog. This edited list of NARA microfilm publications is available online only as of this writing at www.archives.gov/publications/microfilm-catalogs/biographical/index.html. It lists the land records, tax records, court records (including naturalization!), and war records available on microfilm.

Federal Register Publications

The *Federal Register* (www.archives.gov/federal-register) is a legal newspaper published every business day by NARA. It contains federal agency regulations; proposed rules and notices; and executive orders, proclamations, and other presidential documents. NARA's Office of the Federal Register prepares *The Federal Register* for publication in partnership with the Government Printing Office (GPO), which distributes it in paper form, on microfiche, and on the World Wide Web.

Prologue

The quarterly NARA magazine *Prologue* has a webpage you can link to from the NARA home page, or you can go directly to www.archives.gov/publications/prologue. Special issues, such as the 1997 "Federal Records in African-American Research," may be posted almost in their entirety, but usually a regular issue has one or two features on the website, plus the regular column, "Genealogy Notes." A list of previous columns can be found in the navigation bar from the *Prologue* page. This site is worth bookmarking.

Some Advice

Much of what is available on the LOC and NARA sites would be most helpful for intermediate to advanced genealogists. The best way to use these sites is to have a specific research goal in mind, such as a person's military record or a name in a Work Projects Administration (WPA) oral history from the 1930s. The beginner will find the schedules of workshops on the NARA site and the how-to articles on the LOC site helpful, as well as the schedule of NARA workshops and seminars around the country.

Government Land Office

I just "glowed" when I found this resource, the Government Land Office (GLO) site. You can search for and view online original land grants and patents between 1820 and 1928, and order copies from the site.

> ## Note
> *Land patents document the transfer of land ownership from the federal government to individuals. These land patent records include the information recorded when ownership was transferred.*

Land Patent Searches

Go to www.glorecords.blm.gov, and click Search Land Patents in the navigation bar. Type the state and name you are looking for, and you'll get a list of matching records. For individual records, you can see a summary, the legal land description, and the document image.

You can also order a certified copy of a record you find. In addition, you will find a link to a glossary page with details on what the search fields mean. This site does not cover the 13 colonies, their territories, and a few other states, although the site does have resource links for most states. This is because in the early years of the United States, the Congress of the Confederation declared it would sell or grant the unclaimed lands in "the West" (that is, what is now Alabama, Michigan, parts of Minnesota, Mississippi, Illinois, Indiana, Ohio, and Wisconsin). The United States could then sell this unclaimed land to raise money for the Treasury. In turn, the United States gave up its claims to any land within the boundaries of the original colonies.

When you are researching these records, please remember that things were hardly organized in the first 50 years of our nation. Click the FAQ link for some good tips on what to look for. Here's a good example of the kind of help you'll find in the GLO FAQ:

Q. What is the Mississippi/Alabama and Florida/Alabama "Crossover?"

A. The St. Stephens Meridian and Huntsville Meridian surveys cross into both Mississippi and Alabama, creating situations where the land offices in St. Stephens and Huntsville, Alabama, and in Columbus, Mississippi, sold lands in both states. We suggest that anyone researching that area take a look at the databases for both states. The original state line between Alabama and Florida did not close against the Tallahassee Meridian survey (which covered all of Florida), but rather against the earlier St. Stephens Meridian survey in south Alabama. The state line was later resurveyed, creating a situation where some Tallahassee Meridian lands fell across the border into Alabama. We suggest that anyone researching that area take a look at the databases for both states.

Survey Plats

One of the best resources on this site is the database of survey plats, searchable maps of the original townships. This means that if you have a land grant image, which gives the boundaries, you will be able to see a small map showing the land. The drawings were created to represent survey lines, boundaries, descriptions, parcels, and subdivisions mentioned in every federal land patent.

Getting Certified Copies

With the online shopping cart, you may request certified copies of land patents, either electronically or through the mail. Hard copy will be on a letter-sized sheet of paper (8.5 × 11 inches) of your preference (plain bond or parchment paper).

Census Records

Census records are available in a variety of forms, both online and offline. For countries beyond the United States, check out Census Links, www.censuslinks.com, which has transcriptions of censuses, such as "Roll of Emigrants That Have Been Sent to the Colony of Liberia, Western Africa, by the American Colonization Society and Its Auxiliaries, to September, 1843" and "Ecclesiastical Census of Revilla (Mexico) 1780."

Another good source is the Archives of Canada. The first census in Canada was in 1666 by Intendant Jean Talon, who listed 3,215 inhabitants. Talon is considered the "father" of modern census-taking in Canada. Regular censuses did not begin in Canada until 1841, however. Several Canadian censuses are searchable online at www.archives.ca.

Use your favorite search engine to search for "census" and the country you are looking in to find other census resources. For example, Brazil's census information has an English page at www1.ibge.gov.br/english/default.php.

Note

A fire in 1921 destroyed many of the original records of the 1890 Census in Washington, D.C. An account of this incident is on the NARA site at www.archives.gov/genealogy/census/1890/1890.html.

Success Story: Stepping Back Through the Censuses

The Internet is one of the few spaces in genealogy that is friendly to people not running Windows, so instead of using CD-ROMs, I subscribe to Images Online at Ancestry.com for easy access to the handwritten census pages. Reading originals instead of relying on transcribers and indexers was part of my success in finding my great-great-grandparents.

Tracking my family back through ten-year steps is what worked for me. I had inherited a genealogical chart of my male Downs/Downes line in Connecticut, showing the names of the wives but nothing else about them. So I knew only that my great-grandmother was supposed to be a Charlotte Smith. First, the 1900 Census showed my grandfather living with a Charlotte Thompson, described as "Mother" and shown as being born in 1849. The step back to 1890 had to be skipped, of course, because of the destruction of those records. Then the 1880 Census showed my grandfather at the age of five living in Oxford, Connecticut, with a Jane M. Burnett, who called him her grandson. This allowed me to leapfrog over the puzzle of my great-grandmother Charlotte and jump directly into the puzzle of my great-great-grandmother Jane. I reasoned that for Charlotte to have been a Smith, it was necessary for this Jane M. Burnett also to have been a Smith when Charlotte was born, so I went to the 1850 Census in search of Jane M. Smith.

The 1850 schedules list everybody by name, but the index lists mostly heads of household—meaning that almost all wives and children are invisible until you read the original pages. After spending two months following the wrong Jane M. Smith with no baby Charlotte, I abandoned the index and started wading through every name in Oxford and then in the surrounding towns. In 1860 Naugatuck, I found a Jane M. Smith whose age fit that of Jane M. Burnett, but still no Charlotte. Tracking that family back into the 1850 Census, I couldn't find them in Naugatuck or in Oxford, but I did find them next door in Middlebury. And there, finally, was one-year-old Charlotte along with Jane and—for the first time with certainty—my great-great-grandfather David S. Smith. Since then, the census has helped me to solve many parts of the puzzle. The next steps—back to 1840 and beyond—will be much more difficult, because those earlier schedules do not list names of family members except for the head of household, but I am very happy with my success so far.

—Alan Downes

The U.S. Census Bureau

The U.S. Census Bureau generally provides only summary and statistical information for the first 72 years available on microfilm, for research at the U.S. National Archives and Records Administration in Washington, D.C.; at Archives Regional Centers; and at select federal depository libraries throughout the United States. In addition, these records are available at various other libraries and research facilities throughout the United States. Additional important information at the Census Bureau site is in their FAQ at www.census.gov/genealogy/www/ faqgene.txt.

CDs and Microfilms

Several vendors provide CD-ROMs and microfilm of census records—sometimes images of the actual census form and sometimes transcriptions. Here's a list of some of these vendors:

- ♦ AllCensus.com

- ♦ Ancestry.com

- For the United Kingdom, you can order certificates online from the General Register Office, including birth, marriage, civil partnership, death, adoption, and commemorative certificates, at www.gro.gov.uk/gro/content/certificates. You can look at the page www.direct.gov.uk for information on birth, marriage, civil partnership, death, adoption, and stillbirth records and registrations, as well as guidance on researching your family history and the General Register Office Indexes.

- CensusDiggins.com

- CensusFinder.com: U.S., UK, Canada, and Native American

Online images of census records can be found at:

- Everton.com

- FamilySearch (LDS—the abbreviation for The Church of Jesus Christ of Latter-day Saints)

- Genealogy Today

- HeritageQuest (available at many public libraries)

Your local library, LDS Family History Center, or genealogy club may also have copies of these microfilms and/or CD-ROMs with census images.

Online Searches

Ancestry.com and Genealogy.com have subscription-based services that let you search indexes of U.S. federal censuses and view the original pages. These are usually worth the money for at least a year's subscription, once you know what you are looking for.

The UK 1901 census is available for searching online at www.1901censusonline.com. This site had a disastrous beginning: When it first went online, it had over a million hits in the first hours, the server crashed, and it was months before it was back up. They finally got it all on servers able to handle the traffic, and now several UK censuses are available besides 1901: 1891, 1871, 1861, 1851, and 1841 census records and Birth, Marriage and Death (BMD) indexes. The censuses, like U.S. censuses, ask different questions for different counts, such as occupation and place of birth. Other records are available, too, as this list shows:

- Address search: Find out who lived in your house in 1901.

- Place search: Look at who was in which enumeration district in 1901.

- Institution search: See who lived in hospitals, barracks, orphanages, etc., in 1901.

- Vessel search: Locate a naval or merchant vessel in the 1901 census.

- Reference number: Use this search if you know the National Archives census.

Like Ancestry.com and Genealogy.com, you can search the indexes for free, but looking at the actual record costs a fee. Unlike Ancestry.com and Genealogy.com, you can pay per record, put your subscription on hold, and buy a set of voucher lookups. Viewing transcribed data costs 50 credits for an individual and then 50 credits for a list of all other people in that person's household. Viewing a digital image of the census page costs 75 credits.

Transcriptions

As mentioned earlier, www.censuslinks.com is one way to find census transcriptions from around the world. Also check Cyndi's List at www.cyndislist.com/census.htm.

Some Census Sites

Other census sites that are more local in nature are

- The Ayrshire Free Census Project aims to transcribe all 19th-century Ayrshire census records and upload them to a free-to-view online database. This is part of FreeCEN: UK Census Online Project at www.freecen.org.uk.

- Massac County, Illinois History and Genealogy (www.genealogytrails .com/ill/massac/censusindex.html) is an ongoing project to transcribe records of births, cemetery records and tombstones, census pages, death records, land grants, marriages, obituaries, biographies, and wills for this specific area.

- 1920 Yavapai County, Arizona Census Index online (www.sharlot.org/archives/gene/census/index.html) is a local project. The Sharlot Hall Museum in Prescott, Arizona, has posted transcriptions of the 1870, 1880, 1900, and 1920 Yavapai County census indexes. Genealogists can search the 1870, 1880, and 1900 census indexes for names and partial names and also get page numbers.

- African-American Census Schedule (www.afrigeneas.com/aacensus) is a volunteer project to transcribe pre-1870 census schedules.

- Transcriptions of censuses around the world are at the USGenWeb project at www.us-census.org (see Figure 12-4). Click Census Surname Search from the USGenWeb home page, and then use the form to search all the census records or to narrow your search by state or year. And consider volunteering, as the work is far from complete!

As mentioned previously, an important aspect of online genealogy is giving back to the resources on the Web. A great way to do this is to participate in the Census Project shown in Figure 12-4. The USGenWeb Census Project was created to coordinate a U.S. federal census transcription effort. The mission is to recruit and guide volunteer transcribers in achieving the goal of providing free access to online research data for everyone. Each transcription will bear the transcriber's copyright and will be housed in the Census FTP Archives, maintained free of charge for all researchers to use. It's an ambitious project, and the 1930 Census reel numbers and enumeration district descriptions have been added to the project. It will take a lot of folks to complete this project; try to be one of them!

State and Local Sources

Besides the U.S. federal census, some state and local governments took censuses for tax purposes. Such states include Illinois, Iowa, Kansas, Massachusetts, Michigan, Minnesota, New Jersey, New York, and Wisconsin, to name a few.

You can often trace the migration of families in America when state census records are used with other records, such as the federal census after 1850; family Bibles; death certificates; church, marriage, military, probate, and land records; and other American genealogical sources. A major reference source is *State Census Records* by Ann S. Lainhart (Genealogical Publishing Company, 1992); also check FamilySearch or

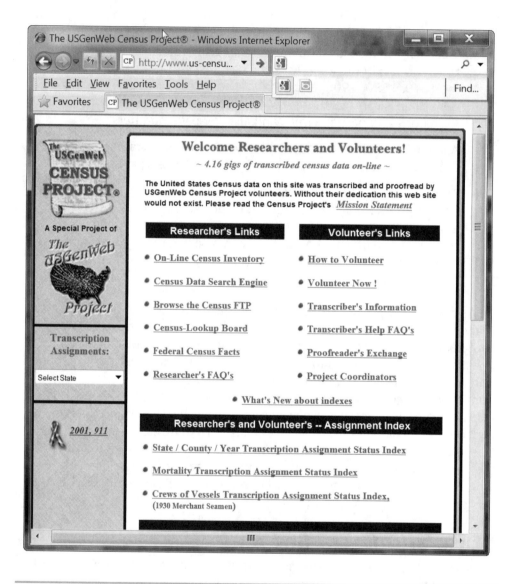

FIGURE 12-4. *Use and contribute to the USGenWeb census transcription project at www.us-census.org.*

the catalog of a library under your state of interest and then under the headings "Census Indexes" and "Census."

Search the Internet to see if state and local censuses have been indexed. See especially the AIS Census Indexes at Ancestry.com (searching Ancestry's indexes is free; seeing the original record is for paying subscribers only).

State Archives and Libraries

Many state archives and libraries have vital records and census information. For example, www.nysl.nysed.gov/genealogy/vitrec.htm is a guide to getting genealogical records from the state of New York. The Alabama Archives has a list of available census information from the state's early years at www.archives.state.al.us/referenc/census.html. Search for the state you need, along with "census" or "archives," to find such sources.

Other Sources

Sometimes you can't find a birth, marriage, or death record in the "official" sources. In these cases, you can look in county and city court records, newspapers, cemetery and funeral home records, and local libraries. These sources can give you clues to parentage, marriages, and burials, which can help you discover where the records may be located—or that the records were destroyed in some way. Some other sources—both official and private—are working to make documents available online.

Footnote

Footnote.com digitizes historical documents, and works in partnership with NARA. At Footnote.com, you will find millions of images of original source documents, many of which have never been available online before. Hundreds of the documents are free, and if you find something you know the background on, you can comment on and annotate it. You can also create your own story page, pulling images from the collection to it.

Launched in January 2007, it has added about 2,000,000 items a month, most of them handwritten. You can browse or use a search box (you can do a Boolean search) to find military records, naturalization records, and more. As of this writing, only U.S. documents are being scanned and indexed, but Justin Schroepfer of Footnote said that soon more countries will be included. American Milestone Documents,

Project Blue Book, Pennsylvania Archives documents from 1664 to 1880, and all indexed information and previews of all of the images are free. You are also invited to scan and upload your own historical documents, whether they are photographs, diaries, bible records, and so on. Access to other documents is by subscription: $8 a month, $60 a year, or $2 an image. Some of the free collections available include

- The Ratified Amendments XI-XXVII of the U.S. Constitution

- Copybooks of George Washington's Correspondence with Secretaries of State, 1789-1796

- Naturalization Petitions of the U.S. District Court for the District of Maryland, 1906-1930

- Naturalization Petitions for the Middle District of Pennsylvania, 1906-1930

- Naturalization Petitions for the Eastern District of Louisiana, New Orleans Division, 1838-1861

- Presidential Photos of Coolidge, Eisenhower, Truman, and Roosevelt

- World War II Japanese Photos

- The Case File of the *United States v. The Amistad*, 1841

Bible Records Online

Bible Records Online (www.biblerecords.com) is a site dedicated to transcribing and digitizing the contents of records inside family Bibles and in other important documents from as early as the 1500s through today. Often, these were the only written records of births, marriages, and deaths of a family, but they are usually inaccessible, except to the person who owns them.

At www.biblerecords.com, you can browse or search by surname. To submit your own family Bible records, go to www.biblerecords.com/submit.html. Tracy St. Claire, the site's administrator, has a standard format for the transcriptions to make them easy to read and compare. If you can submit a scan of the original, that is wonderful, but she will take a transcription alone. The site also has a forum and a place for scans of photographs or other items people typically slip into the family Bible as keepsakes.

Internmen

This is another volu   , uploaded burial records, at
www.interment.net   be and upload records of every
bit of data they can   etery. The records include the
official name of the   n of the cemetery (town, county,
state, country, etc.),   ddress of the cemetery or
driving directions; th   on was compiled and how
(tombstone inscriptio   revious transcriptions); how
complete the list is; a   compilers. As of this writing,
almost four million re   for searching or browsing.

You can also subs   f all new cemetery
transcriptions publish   y) and of the Cemetery Blog
news and articles from   of the site.

Obituaries a

Sometimes you can find   istics in obituaries, although
one must be cautious. M   ed obituaries had minor
errors because the family   rly at the funeral home. I
suspect that is the case w   . Still, the parents and
progeny were correct, eve   ulars were not.

Go to Cyndi's List and   age (www.cyndislist.com/
deaths.htm) for a good r   pecialize in obituaries.

Once you have a place   m an obituary, if your
ancestor died in the 20th   ok at the Social Security
Death Index (SSDI) as a m   ata. This is public record,
and you can search it for f   web.ancestry.com. The
results will give you the off   date, where the Social
Security number was issue   residence at the time),
and where the last paymer   the place of death at
the time). With this informa   state's vital statistics
department to get a copy of   icates, which are
primary sources.

Other sites with SSDI loo

- FamilySearch.org has   he SSDI at
  www.familysearch.org   _ssdi.asp.

- Genealogy.com (home   offers the SSDI for
  free, but only as part c   y Finder search.

The advantage is that you can search many resources at once, but the disadvantage is the overabundance of results to weed through. You also can't search without knowing the last name.

- GenealogyBank.com (access is free at many libraries) has over 84 million records, updated weekly, and is a quite good source for recent deaths.

- NEHGS - Social Security Death Index Free Access at www.newenglandancestors.org/research/Database/ss/default.asp. For finding someone who died recently, this free Social Security Death Index search offered at NewEnglandAncestors.org is also very good.

- Railroad Retirement Board (www.rrb.gov/mep/genealogy.asp) is the place to look if your ancestor worked for a railroad company and was covered by the Railroad Retirement Act (after 1936).

- Search the Social Security Death Index (SSDI) in one step at http://stevemorse.org/ssdi/ssdi.html. Steve Morse has created a practical search form that augments the search logic of many of the free SSDI search engines on the Web. You can choose which of several SSDI databases to search. This easy SSDI search interface is a favorite of mine.

Wrapping Up

- Vital statistics are the milestones of life: birth, marriage, sometimes divorce, and death.

- Most states have good vital statistics starting from 1938 (the beginning of Social Security). Prior to that, you may have to get creative, looking at obituaries, census records, family Bible sites, and other sites.

- The Library of Congress and National Archives and Records Administration have several resources, guides, and databases to help genealogists.

- Many sites have transcribed and scanned original documents, indexed for searching by surname: Bibles, cemetery records, and so on. Some are free and some are subscription-based.

Chapter 13

The Church of Jesus Christ of Latter-day Saints

The genealogy research work of the members of the Church of Jesus Christ of Latter-day Saints (LDS) is unsurpassed in scope and size. Every genealogist needs to know how to use this wonderful resource. Some of the data are offline and some are online, but it is all helpful.

All these databases are submitted by LDS church members as well as others around the world. About ten years ago, all data was accepted, but this led to duplicates and misinformation being included. Now, submitters must include documentation for their data (original records, interview date and time, and so forth), so the newer uploads are more reliable than the earlier ones.

FamilySearch Internet

The FamilySearch Internet Genealogy Service (www.FamilySearch.org) is a site sponsored by LDS to help people find and share family history information. Launched in May 1999, it is a genealogy database, a catalog to the Family History Library in Salt Lake City, a place to get a free website for your own genealogy, and an education center, with publications and lessons online to help you learn what you need to do next in your family history research. And it is free!

The whole site is designed to encourage you to find your ancestors and preserve your family histories. The LDS has been actively gathering and preserving genealogical records worldwide for more than 100 years. The databases contain more than 400 million names of people who have died. These names are mostly from the United States, Canada, and the British Isles, and have taken decades to compile. In addition, years have been spent developing, engineering, and improving core internal systems to provide this resource. Using the site (the opening page is shown in Figure 13-1) is free, although you can order some products, such as databases on CD-ROM and research guides.

Here's a short list of the main resources on the site:

♦ Censuses: The 1880 United States, 1881 British Isles, and the 1881 Canadian censuses, just to name a few. This is an ongoing project, and more are available each month.

♦ The International Genealogical Index, or IGI (explained later in the chapter)

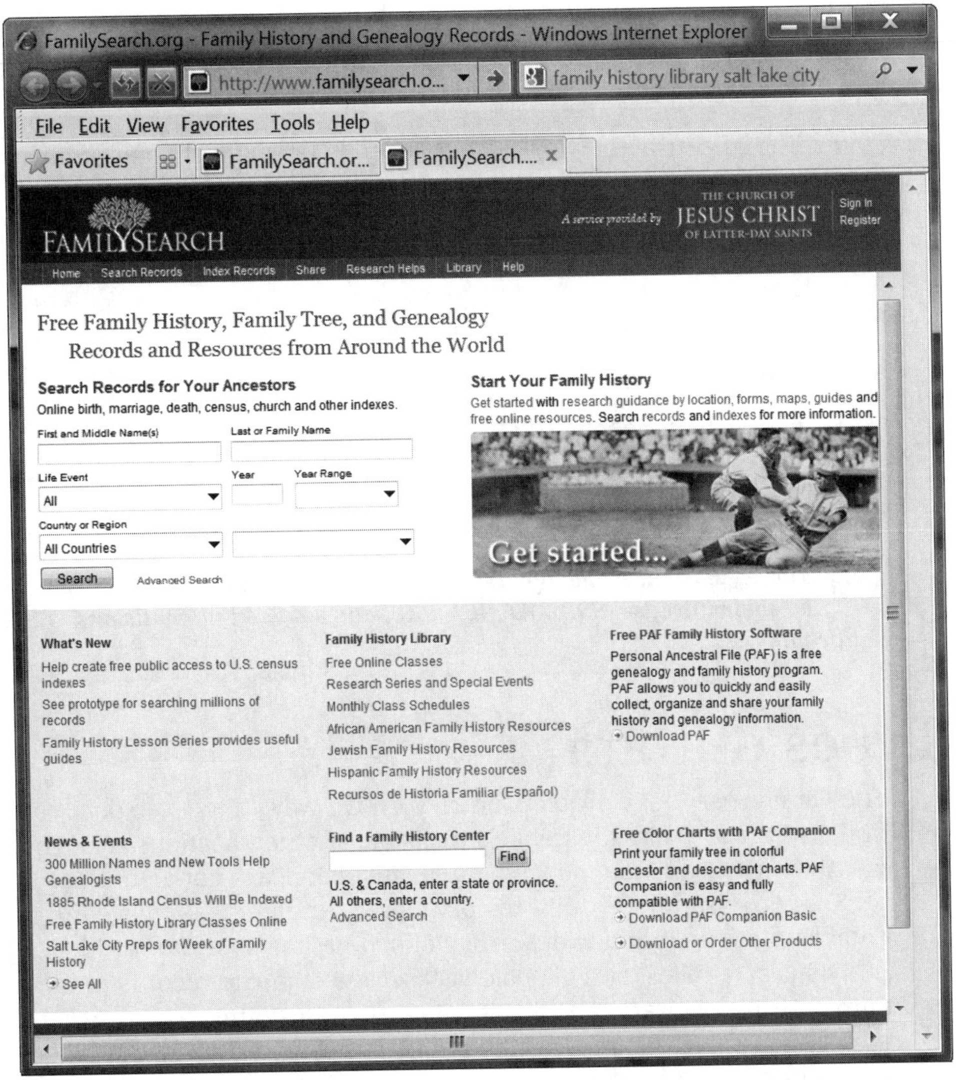

FIGURE 13-1. *The FamilySearch website is one of the most important online genealogy resources.*

- The Pedigree Resource File, or PRF, which is the collection of genealogical information uploaded to FamilySearch since its launch in 1999 (explained later in the chapter)

- The Ancestral File, or AF, (explained later in the chapter), which is a collection of genealogies submitted by members and nonmembers of the LDS

- The U.S. Social Security Death Index, or SSDI

- The Vital Records Index for Mexico and Scandinavia

- Family history websites uploaded by users of the site

- Pilot Family Search, the future of the site

Note

You'll find that genealogists online often refer to these databases by their initials—SSDI, AF, IGI, PRF, and so on—in e-mails and forum posts.

Types of Data

The FamilySearch site protects privacy in two ways: First, the data you find on the site is already publicly available at other locations, though not always available online. Second, living people are not identified.

The records in the Family History Library and in the FamilySearch databases come from a wide variety of sources, all over the world. Individuals, families, and genealogical societies donate records to the Family History Library. The library also purchases other records, such as the U.S. Social Security Death Index, census records, and published family or county histories. Most of the microfilm collection has been produced by the Family History Department's own international effort to microfilm original sources. You can also search a Vital Records Index for Mexico and Scandinavia, built by the same volunteers.

An index to many of these records is available online through the Family History Library Catalog, on the site, and at local Family History Centers (FHCs). Furthermore, Family History Department employees are currently supervising microfilming projects in 47 countries.

Often, what you get in a search is a reference to a document on microfilm that you can rent or buy or view at a local FHC.

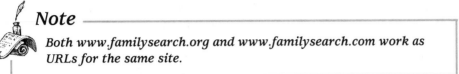

Note

Both www.familysearch.org and www.familysearch.com work as URLs for the same site.

FamilySearch Internet Genealogy Service is designed to be a *first* step in searching for family history information. That means you will more often find pointers to information on this site than the actual information, though, of course, a lucky strike is not out of the question!

When you're searching LDS proprietary sources, the first screen doesn't give you the information itself. The search results simply tell you if the information you need is available, with links to the website, Family History Library Catalog citation, IGI, AF reference, or citation in one of the CD-ROMs the LDS has for sale.

This is more helpful than it sounds, however. Just finding a match in the Family History Library Catalog can save you hours of research. Some FHCs are so busy, patrons are only allowed one hour a week at the computer! Searching the catalog before you go can make your trip much more productive. Finding a reference in the CD-ROMs might tell you whether it's worth the price for you to order it. Finding a reference in the IGI or AF can tell you if someone else has already found the primary record or source you're looking for, and sometimes how to contact the person who found it. In short, this can save you a lot of time and travel.

With the exception of the census records being indexed, you will often find these records are not primary (original record) sources. Most of the records in the FamilySearch Internet Genealogy Service are abstracts. If you find a reference to a record you want in the LDS sources, you usually can get a complete copy of it from an FHC. FHCs are located throughout the world and have many of the records found in the FamilySearch Internet Genealogy Service. You learn more about FHCs later in the chapter in the section called "A Visit to a Family History Center."

Note

The records being indexed by volunteers are available online as images, and are an exception to the usual results in that they point to actual records on the site. However, this is a work in progress and the collection is spotty in coverage; volunteer to help with the indexing to speed up the rate at which these records become available!

Another big advantage to this site is that it has more international data than most online sources. Although the greatest part of the data is from English-speaking countries, you can find some information from every continent. Asian sources are the most limited, whereas North American and European sources are the most abundant.

Some Background

Mormons consider it a religious duty to research their family history. The Church teaches that families are eternal, and for more than a century and a half, members have been encouraged to identify their deceased ancestors. A detailed explanation can be found at the LDS website, www.lds.org.

One of the LDS Church's objectives is to build its copyrighted databases and to continually improve their accuracy and the software used to search them. The result is a huge database of names with births, christenings, and marriages with their dates. The data is archived at the Church's headquarters in Salt Lake City, Utah, and distributed in microfilm, microfiche, and CD-ROM to their many Family History Centers throughout the world. The Family History Department maintains a climate-controlled underground storage facility to safeguard master copies of all its microfilm records. The storage facility, built literally into a mountainside, is about 25 miles from downtown Salt Lake City.

Note

The AF offers pedigrees, but the IGI doesn't. The PRF is all secondary material submitted by volunteers.

International Genealogical Index

The International Genealogical Index (IGI) lists the dates and places of births, christenings, and marriages for more than 285 million deceased people and makes otherwise difficult-to-access information searchable online. Its best use is to find an individual in your family tree and a living person's contact information to exchange data with. The index includes people who lived at any time after the early 1500s up through the early 1900s. These names have been researched and extracted from thousands of original records, mostly compiled from public-domain sources.

The IGI contains two basic kinds of entries: submissions by individual LDS members of data on their ancestors (older submissions may not be as accurate as newer ones) and submissions from the extraction program, which is a systematic, well-controlled volunteer program of the Church. Members all over the world extract birth or christening dates, as well as marriage dates and locations from microfilms of original parish and civil records. The source of the data from information provided for each entry is on the CD-ROM version of the IGI, although not necessarily the web version. But always remember, the IGI is only an index. You should go to the source document to verify the information.

A typical search will turn up lots of hits, so it is best to limit your search for a name with a date and an event (birth, marriage, or death, for example) and, if possible, the most narrow geography. You must specify a country at least; narrowing by state helps even more. FamilySearch will not search for middle names unless you select the Use Exact Spelling check box, but if you use that search option, you cannot also search using any other option. You may not get the results you want if you list parents' names and a spouse's name in the same search. Most records from the IGI contain either parents' names or a spouse's name, but not both. Often, the immediate family group (husband, wife, children) is what you find.

You will find some duplicate records in the IGI; in most cases, the duplication is caused by multiple people submitting the same name with slight variations in the data. If you decide to contribute data to IGI, contact other family members who are working on the same family lines to help keep these duplications to a minimum.

The IGI on CD-ROMs that you view at the local Family History Center and the Internet version have the same data, but the Internet and Family History Center versions display that data differently: The Internet version displays all events and relationships. The CD-ROM version displays only one event per entry. The Internet version also is updated more frequently and contains more information. With both, if you want to look at the documents in microfilm, you order by film number or find it at your local FHC.

> **Note**
>
> *Need to know where your local Family History Center is? Check the phone book under "Churches—LDS," or go to www.familysearch .org/eng/library/FHC/frameset_fhc.asp and search using the drop-down boxes.*

Ancestral File

The Ancestral File contains a compilation of genealogies of families from around the world and records that have been contributed by thousands of people, including users of the Church's Family History Library and Family History Centers. The information—mostly data about people who have died—is linked into pedigrees to show both ancestors and descendants of individuals. The file contains more than 35 million names.

You must at least enter an individual's last name (unless you search for children of the same parents or search by Ancestral File number). Like the IGI search, middle names don't count, unless you specify exact spelling, and then you cannot use other parameters. You may search for any combination of first and last names for the individual, parents, and spouse. You may also search for just a last name. For common surnames, fill in additional fields to improve your search results. You will get better results if you enter an individual's first name and last name. Last names are standardized so that spelling variations are retrieved in the results.

The results will have family and spouse information, as well as the submitter's information. This is usually a mailing address, sometimes with phone and fax numbers as well. You would use this to write a query letter, offering what information you have in exchange for the details on the source of the material submitted.

Pedigree Resource File

The Pedigree Resource File (PRF) is a searchable database of submissions from FamilySearch Internet users. The PRF grows at the rate of 1.2 million names per month. Forty percent of the database is from outside North America and the British Isles. You can search it online or at a local FHC on CD-ROMs that are updated every six months. The PRF contains compiled pedigrees submitted by users of FamilySearch or gathered from printed family histories and other sources, including government archives. The PRF is becoming a reservoir of names to help individuals identify and link their ancestors. It is similar to the Ancestral File, but they do not overlap completely. Unlike the Ancestral File (which simply has the name of the person who submitted data), it contains notes and source documentation, which varies in thoroughness.

Social Security Death Index

The Social Security Death Index (SSDI) can help you find people who died after 1938. You will find that some sites charge you for this search, but on FamilySearch, it is free.

You can search for just a last name, but for common surnames, it is best to fill in additional fields to improve your search results. You will also get better results if you enter an individual's first name and last name. Last names are standardized so that spelling variations are included in the results.

To search for a woman, use the surname she registered with the Social Security Administration. If the woman was married, search using her married name. Areas under U.S. administration for Social Security number issuance include Canal Zone, Canton Islands, Caroline Islands, Mariana Islands (other than Guam), Marshall Islands, Midway Islands, and Wake Islands.

Where it gets tricky is which event you choose to search by. If a birth is the selected event, you will want to search for where you think the Social Security number was issued (which may not necessarily be the birthplace). If a death is the selected event, FamilySearch Internet Genealogy Service will search for the state or territory of the ZIP code at time of death. If you select all events (birth, marriage, and death), FamilySearch Internet Genealogy Service will search for both location of Social Security number issuance and location at the time of death.

Using These Resources

The IGI, the AF, and the PRF are unrelated because data entered in one file doesn't necessarily show up in the other file. Each has a value of its own, and all files are worth searching. The advantage of the AF is that you can get pedigrees from it. The advantage of the IGI is that it provides more detailed information. The PRF has the work of other genealogists, which makes it one or two times removed from the original sources, but it's useful nonetheless. They all will help you find other people searching your surnames.

It used to be common wisdom that the IGI was a little more reliable than the AF, because although errors turn up in both, the IGI is closer to the original records (data is normally entered into the IGI first), and it had better bits and pieces of information, especially its references to where the information originated. Since about 2003, however, controls on all the databases have improved and documentation has been added. Although errors do exist, the percentage seems low. Plenty of genealogy books printed in the past 100 years have more errors than these databases.

Treat the PRF, AF, and IGI the same way you treat a printed book about a surname—with informed caution. Used as an excellent source of clues, they can always be crosschecked with primary records. Just remember: Although the computer increases the amount of data you can scan, making your work much easier, it doesn't necessarily improve accuracy. Human beings are still the source of the data.

Success Story: FamilySearch Proves a Family Legend

I had the names of my great-grandfather, his two brothers, and both parents—along with the name of the little town they were born in and raised in Wales. For three years, I searched for evidence of the parents who were presumably named Hugh Jones and Mary Ellen Williams. The information was furnished by their grandson.

In the quest to acquire as much evidence as possible on every person in my line, I ran a query on the LDS site. Some of this information was transcription, and some was by submission of family group sheets (without source citations). I was fortunate to find what could potentially be my great-grandfather's christening record as a transcribed set of bishop's records for the parish. Correct place, correct year, wrong parent names—or so I thought. I was able to run a query using the parents' names only so that I could find all birth records in that county where these two names appeared as mother and father. Sure enough, each of the other two boys and a bonus daughter appeared. The parents were Moses Jones and Elizabeth Jones.

Subsequent research further supports the information. In fact, both died before the grandson informant was even born! Perhaps he mistook an "adopted" set of grandparents as his own ... who knows? Three years of trying blown away by a total of five minutes' worth of Internet research. I use the Internet for a large portion of my research.

—Heather Jones DeGeorge

FamilySearch Labs

The FamilySearch team has been working on expanding access to the LDS records for quite a while. Over 20 years ago, the church set up local FHCs around the world. In 1988, they started selling the databases on microfiche. In 1991, the Church released them on CD-ROM to their local centers, and later to societies and libraries. The New England Historic Genealogical Society has a complete set at their library in Boston, as does the California State Sutro Library in San Francisco.

Right now, as you are reading this, programmers at FamilySearch Labs in Salt Lake City are devising several ways to enhance the FamilySearch experience. At http://www.familysearchlabs.org, you can give this beta software a test run, and it's really fun. You can also keep track of all the latest bells and whistles at http://labs.familysearch.org/blog, where the developers are busy making the future of online genealogy even more exciting.

FamilySearch Beta

In late 2009, the LDS software engineers rolled out an entirely new, rebuilt, souped-up, hot-off-the-presses search feature in the FamilySearch beta. "It isn't perfect yet," the programmers wrote in the blog, "but we hope it is a step forward and would love to get your feedback. Give the updated FamilySearch beta a whirl and let us know what you like and don't like."

The address of the beta version of what will be the future of FamilySearch is http://fsbeta.familysearch.org. This new version will have auto-complete features, so that instead of choosing from a long list of locations, for example, you can input "New York" and it fills in "New York, United States" for you. The results will have a short list of the resources where there is a match. Choose the census result and you have an option to save an image of the census record of 1850. The beta also sorts the results better based on relevance than the current site.

Record Search

Record Search at FamilySearch labs is where you can search the latest results in the ongoing volunteer effort to index census, church, and civil records from around the world.

Note that in the figure, the site says that records from Argentina, Guatemala, and Germany as well as the United States were recently added. Each month, more and more records are added from around the world, so check back often.

England Jurisdictions 1851

The England Jurisdictions 1851 project shortens your research chores by bringing data from several aids into one searchable form. You access the data by clicking in a parish boundary. Features include contiguous parish and radius search lists and relevant jurisdictions as they existed in England in 1851. Data includes changes to parishes prior to 1851 and lists of nonconformist denominations in a parish. This feature requires Internet Explorer 7, Firefox 3, or Safari 3 or newer.

Research Wiki

Research Wiki is the experimental social information exchange for FamilySearch. FamilySearch Wiki is a large, online library with thousands of articles and how-to instructions about researching family history. To learn more about the wiki, click the Getting Started link, but it is really very simple and much like the famous Wikipedia. The difference is that this wiki is strictly for family history topics. From this beta site you can connect with others in the new Community Center, or look at the wiki's new pages, recent edits, new features, and new images. You can also participate by editing an existing page or creating a new one.

Standard Finder

With Standard Finder you search for a standardized name, date, or place based on your input. The Standard Finder presents the standards that will be used in future releases of new FamilySearch. With filtered results, you see what the programmers think the best match would be; without the filters, you see all the possible standards. Then send them feedback on how the system can do better.

Forums

The Forums page is where you can read up on the latest information on all FamilySearch products for family history. As described in Chapter 8, these forums are messages on topics about using FamilySearch or just genealogy in general. Through the forums, anyone can ask questions about FamilySearch features, research techniques, hints and tips, or even about specific families in specific locations. And anyone who knows the answer can reply. Instead of a limited number of support agents available to answer the questions, there will be tens of thousands of users collaborating together. You can also find forums for Family History Consultants or leaders assigned to foster local family history participation.

Community Trees

Ever wish you could reconstruct the families that lived in your ancestral village in the 1750s? FamilySearch Community Trees can help you. FamilySearch worked with people with the expertise to piece together the families that lived together historically in a community, then on how to present that graphically. The programmers are experimenting with ways to make these lineage-linked trees more available and expand the number of people helping with this effort.

FamilySearch Indexing

This is where you can give back to the world of online genealogy. Using this software, you can extract family history information from digital images of historical documents to create indexes that assist everyone in finding their ancestors. This could be census pages, church records, vital statistics records, and so on.

Note _____

The New Family Search and its Family Tree Browser are for members of the LDS church only as of this writing.

As the years go by, the FamilySearch site is offering more and more access through new and exciting interfaces. The Mormons are cautious, though, and they take small steps, one at a time, with lots of feedback from people like you. The LDS Church is still working on more reliability, more accuracy, and more controls on privacy for living people, and it works hard to present a useful, viable program and database for its members and the rest of the world. The main concern of the LDS Church is to avoid turning out a bad product.

So that's what's brewing for the future. But the FamilySearch site is full of things you can use right now. We already looked at the databases, so let's examine what else you can find there.

A Tour of the Site

At the top of the home page you will see the tabs: Home, Search Records, Index Records, Share, Research Helps, Library, and Help. Each one has treasures!

Search Records

If you put in the name and a place for one of your ancestors from the home page, you can search all FamilySearch records, databases, and library holdings. But if you go to the Search page, you can fine-tune your search to just one database or to just Family History websites registered with FamilySearch.

You will also find a link to a helpful document called "Tips on How to Search for Your Ancestor," which gives you the syntax for successful searches on the site. It is important to note that you cannot search for only a first name. Also, unless you check the Use Exact Spelling option, it will not search on middle names. Using the exact spelling option, the search will look for the individual's first, middle, and last name exactly as you listed it. If you check Use Exact Spelling, you may not list parents, spouse, event, year, or country.

Index Records

This is where you can download the software to help preserve the key life events of billions of people. Using the online indexing system, volunteers from around the world transcribe records from the convenience of their homes, quickly and easily. The indexes are then posted for free at familysearch.org. This includes millions of rolls of microfilm with census, vital, probate, and church records from more than 100 countries for indexing projects. Governments, churches, societies, and commercial companies are also working to make more records available. You can help, too! There are current U.S. census projects and upcoming England and Wales census projects. At https://fch.ldschurch.org/WWSupport/Courses/FamilySearchIndexing/Version20/en/Index/Index.htm is a great video showing you how to do it.

Indexing is as fun as it is simple. You download the program, which must have the latest Java applet to run, after you register your e-mail and password. The program has you log in; then you can choose to download the image to your disk or work online. Download a batch, which is a small portion of a project, and the program will guide you through typing in from the image (see Figure 13-2).

Share

Under Share, you can register as a FamilySearch user and upload GEDCOMs for others to search.

Research Helps

This is one of the greatest things ever put on the Web. The LDS Church has guidebooks on every kind of research you can imagine: specifics for geographical locations, how to write letters asking for information, worksheets for specific censuses for different countries, and step-by-step guides. All these are free online, and all can be downloaded in PDF format or read online. Or, for a small fee, you can order a printed copy instead of printing it out yourself.

Library

The Library tab has four sections that give you practical information.

♦   The Family History Library section has background information about the library's hours, patron services, and record collections. You can also get tourist information to help you prepare for a trip to the library in Salt Lake City, Utah.

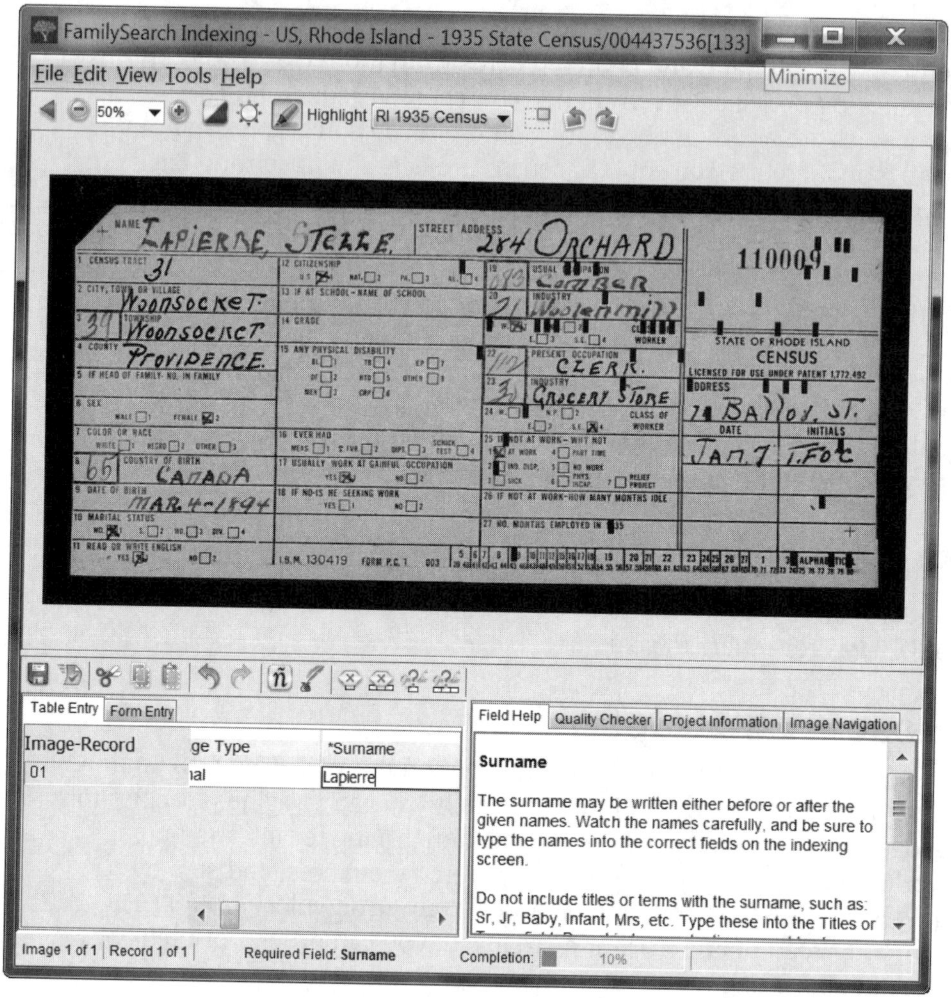

FIGURE 13-2. *The indexing program highlights the image portion that has the text for you to type in the table. It's easy and interesting!*

- ♦ The Family History Centers section helps you locate a Family History Center in your area. You can also learn about the services and resources that are available to the public at Family History Centers.

- The Family History Library Catalog section is used to find the call numbers for books, microfilms, and microfiche records in the Family History Library. You can also find information about library collections and new acquisitions.

- The final section provides information on library classes, genealogical institutes, conferences, and publications.

If you find something in the main library catalog, you can ask your local FHC to borrow it for a time for you to read and study. The Family History Library has the largest collection of genealogical materials in the world, which includes microfilms, microfiche, books, maps, charts, CD-ROMs, and more. The items range in date from 1550 to 1920 and include

- More than 2.4 million rolls of microfilm

- More than 742,000 microfiche

- More than 300,000 books, serials, and other formats

Another important part of this section is a guide to using the FHL in Salt Lake City. Read this, and follow it. You should study and prepare before you travel to the main library. The materials available are so vast and varied, you can be overwhelmed. I have literally witnessed hopeful researchers leave in tears because they had not mapped out a research plan before arriving.

But also remember that the local FHC is a branch of the main library. Use this section to prepare for a trip there, too.

Help

For almost everything you find on FamilySearch, there is a help topic explaining how to use it and when. Anytime you find yourself confused about a resource on the site, come to the Help tab and look down the alphabetized list on the left.

> **Note**
>
> *The contact information for the main Family History Library is 35 North West Temple Street, Salt Lake City, UT 84150-3400; Phone: (801) 240-2331 or 866-406-1830, Fax: (801) 240-5551, E-mail: fhlldschurch.org*

Freedman's Bank Records

You can buy some records collected by the LDS Church on CD-ROM; one such resource is the Freedman's Bank Records CD-ROM. First released in this form in February 2001 by the LDS Church, this database contains biographical information on the roughly 500,000 African Americans who deposited money into Freedman's Bank following the Civil War. It is estimated that eight to ten million African Americans living today have ancestors whose records are contained in the Freedman's database. This CD-ROM has records that cover 1864 to 1871 and document the names and family relationships of those who used the bank. The information contained in these records is rather fragmentary by normal genealogical standards, but they are some of the very few records that document these individuals, and they are a vital source of information for those with African-American ancestry. There are approximately 480,000 names in the file, which have been entered in a pedigree-linked GEDCOM format. This means that they are indexed for searching; before this CD-ROM, the records were available but unindexed, making them hard to use. It took 11 years to complete the indexing and formatting for the CD-ROM. The Freedman's Bank Records CD-ROM costs $6.50 as of this writing. It can be ordered at www.familysearch.org or by calling Church Distribution Centers at (800) 537-5971.

A Visit to a Family History Center

Family History Centers are to genealogists what candy stores are to kids. There are big ones and little ones, elaborate set-ups, and simple ones. But they all have something to help your search, and going to one is usually a treat.

The best way to find a Family History Center near you is to look in the White Pages of the phone book for the nearest Church of Jesus Christ of Latter-day Saints. Call them and find out where the nearest FHC is and the hours. Honestly, because the hours vary so much from place to place, the best time to call is Sunday morning around 10:00 A.M. Everyone's at church then!

If you call any other time, give the staffers lots of rings to answer the phones, which might be on the other side of the church from the FHC. Another easy way: Use the search box on the FamilySearch.org main page. Scroll down about halfway on the page, and you'll see a box to input your ZIP code. For a more detailed search, go to www.familysearch .org/Eng/default.asp.

Note

Some FHC directors insist that if you use a disk to take home information, you buy one from the FHC. This is to prevent accidentally introducing a virus to the system. Similarly, while Wi-Fi may be available in a certain FHC, if your laptop has a virus, you will be asked to take out your connection card.

All FHCs are branches of the main LDS Family History Library in Salt Lake City. The typical FHC has a few rooms at the local Mormon Church, with anywhere from one to ten computers; a similar number of microfilm and microfiche readers; and a collection of atlases, manuals, and how-to genealogy books. Figure 13-3 shows the FHC in my neighborhood in Navarre, Florida. Others in bigger towns are larger and more elaborate. It's a cozy place, open two nights a week, but it's a branch of the library in Salt Lake City just like the big ones in cities such as New York and Los Angeles. Exciting things are happening there.

WorldVitalRecords and Ancestry.com

More than 4,500 FamilySearch Family History Centers throughout the world have free access to WorldVitalRecords.com's genealogical records and resources as a result of an agreement signed between FamilySearch and WorldVitalRecords.com in May 2007.

FIGURE 13-3.   *My local FHC has four computers, two film readers, one fiche reader, and a small collection of books, CD-ROMs, fiches, and films as well as some printed versions of the Research Guides for you to use.*

WorldVitalRecords.com has collections of genealogical materials, including vital, land, immigration, and military records; newspapers; international databases; and a collection of reference material. WorldVitalRecords.com also partnered with Everton Publishers last year to provide the Everton Genealogical Library, containing numerous databases, as well as 60 years of the Everton Genealogical Helper and 150,000 Everton pedigree files and family group sheets. In addition to making all WorldVitalRecords.com content free, each FHC has FamilyLink.com, a new social genealogical website that enables individuals to connect with genealogists from more than 1,600 cities.

WorldVitalRecords.com was founded by Paul Allen, who also founded Ancestry.com. Ancestry.com is available through all FHCs as well. The full services, as the FHC is the "subscriber," can be searched at any FHC. The results you get will have to be e-mailed, printed, or saved to a disk for you to take home.

Kindred Konnections

This database has Canadian, U.S., New Zealand, and UK genealogy records; extracted vital records from those countries; and a database of GEDCOM files uploaded by users, as well as information from files indexed from the Internet. It also has a program that will search your GEDCOM and all the ones on the site, looking for matches. From a Family History Center, you have the same access as if you had a subscription.

Godfrey Memorial Library

The Godfrey Memorial Library was founded in Middletown, Connecticut, in 1947 as a genealogy library. It has approximately 200,000 books and periodicals in its collection, including state and local histories, international resources, family histories, biographies, records by religious organizations, church records, funeral records, cemetery records, military records, maps, etc. And you can search it all from an FHC!

Heritage Quest Online

This has been available through most public libraries for a while and now from FHCs as well. You can search census records, the Periodical Source Index, Revolutionary War records, Freedman's Bank, and the full text of several thousand books.

Footnote

This is a wonderful place, which is also available from some public libraries. It is a site for scanned and indexed documents, maps, and images. It is a way to search original source material not found in other places. And, at a FHC, you can search it for free.

Other Services

Research help from volunteer staff. Staff members will not do research for you, but they can give you an orientation about the center, answer some research questions (research expertise in each center varies), help you use center resources, and order microfilms and microfiche from the Family History Library. Most centers have a small collection of published reference sources that includes research helps, genealogies, histories, gazetteers, atlases, and maps. A few centers have large collections of these resources that many a public library would envy!

A typical FHC will have a running copy of Personal Ancestral File so that you can give that genealogy program a test drive. Many offer training classes in genealogy and in the use of LDS resources. Some centers offer training on the programs, some insist they train you before you start using the computers, and some only help if you ask. The FHC computers usually run Windows. In the typical FHC setup, you must reserve a computer, and you're given a certain block of time to use it. Printouts of what you find usually cost a nickel a page. Because the larger, busier FHCs may require you to make a reservation, before you make a trip to the one near you, check out FamilySearch Internet Genealogy Service and determine which resources you need. Make a list of your research chores before you go. This can save lots of time!

Wrapping Up

- ◆ The LDS Church is the largest online resource for genealogy.

- ◆ The FamilySearch Labs site has the latest in features and experimental programs such as the Genealogy Research Wiki.

- ◆ The Indexing program has projects you can search and help index.

- ◆ Family History Centers are where you can view microfiches and microfilms of actual records, as well as order copies of records. Most FHCs also have Internet access, including access to subscription online databases.

Chapter 14

Ellis Island Online: The American Family Immigration History Center

Are you one of the 40 percent of Americans who can trace an ancestor to the immigration center at Ellis Island? If so, you definitely want to check out Ellis Island Online at www.ellisislandrecords .org (see Figure 14-1). This site is the best thing to happen to online genealogy since the launch of FamilySearch. The interface has improved

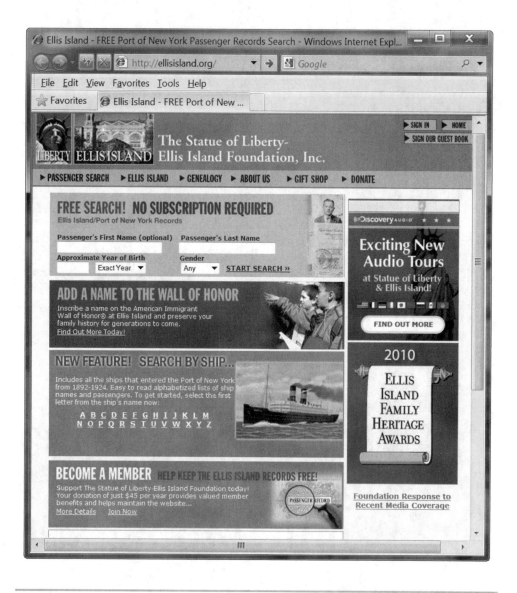

FIGURE 14-1. *Immigration records from 1892 to 1924 are available at EllisIsland.org.*

in the last few years and is easier to navigate. The response to search input is fast, and the results are easier to understand than when the site first launched.

The grand opening was on April 17, 2001, and included appearances by Tom Brokaw, Charles Grodin, and Joel Grey; a search for Irving Berlin's immigration records involving his daughters and great-grandson; an overview of the Family History Center's Family Scrapbook activity; and a presentation by Foundation Founding Chairman Lee A. Iacocca. It was also the first annual Ellis Island Family History Day, an event that's co-sponsored by the Foundation, the National Genealogical Society, and America's governors. That date was chosen because April 17, 1907, saw the largest number of immigrants ever processed on one day at Ellis Island—11,747 people, more than twice the usual number. This record-breaker will be honored every year.

Just for Genealogists

The newly redesigned site has several sections to help you with your genealogy, called the Genealogy Learning Center. The following sections describe the various features.

Genealogy Getting Started Tips

This section for beginners to family history research serves as an online "Genealogy 101" to guide you through the basic steps. This step-by-step approach will help you to grasp quickly the key concepts of all levels of genealogy research.

Genealogy Charts and Forms

The section has several different downloadable documents for you to print, copy, and share freely with others as you organize your family data. These include multigeneration Pedigree Charts, Family Group Sheets, and other documents in PDF format, and should be accessible by most computers. You have to print them out to fill them out.

Locating a Genealogy Society

Any aspect of genealogy research has a corresponding genealogy society: surname, geographic area, historical, ethnic heritage, and family societies have been the foundation of American genealogy for more than a century. To connect you with an area of particular interest, the site has a page called the Ellis Island Society Links Network.

Hiring a Professional Genealogist

This section contains information about professional genealogists and why you may want one. Through an alliance with the Association of Professional Genealogists, this page will connect you with individuals skilled in different geographic, ethnic, and other areas of research specialty.

Helpful Websites for Genealogy Research

Whether you search the Web for the terms genealogy, family history, family tree, or even the popular misspelling (geneology), you'll notice there are more Internet sites dealing with genealogy than you could possibly visit, with more being published every day. This section introduces you to just a few of the places online that you are likely to find of general interest relating to your family history research.

Family History Center

The Family History Center is available on this website, as well as on a first-come, first-served basis or by appointment at the Ellis Island Immigration Museum itself. The Family History Center has an electronic database of immigrants, passengers, and crew members who entered the United States through the Port of New York between 1892 and 1924, the peak years of Ellis Island processing. The data, taken directly from microfilms of the ships' passenger manifests provided by the National Archives and Records Administration (NARA), was first made available electronically on this site. It was extracted and transcribed through the efforts of 12,000 volunteers from The Church of Jesus Christ of Latter-day Saints (LDS), who spent 5.6 million hours on the project. With more than 22 million records, the countries with the highest representation in the database are Italy, Austria, Hungary, Russia, Finland, England, Ireland, Scotland, Germany, and Poland.

Using the Site

The site has two parts: free services and services available only to Foundation members. Even without the free registration, however, you have access to several areas. "The Immigrant Experience" has two sets of articles on the population of the United States. "Family Histories," the first set, gives real-life examples of people whose ancestors passed through Ellis Island. "The Peopling of America" is a companion series of articles showing the timeline of people coming to the United States from all over the world, beginning with those who crossed the Bering Straits 20,000 years ago. You can also look at a history of Ellis Island and a timeline that begins in 1630. All of these would be a great help to a student writing a paper on Ellis Island!

However, to gain access to the free searches, you must register. This involves choosing a logon name and password and giving your name and address; when you return, cookies on your computer will allow the site to show you saved searches.

Free vs. Paid Membership

If you register as a regular user, which is free, you can keep copies of the passenger records, manifests, and ship images in "Your Ellis Island File." This can be opened on the computers at Ellis Island or on the website. You can purchase copies of these documents at the online gift shop or at the interpretive shop on Ellis Island.

If you join as a Foundation member at $45 per year, you can:

- Annotate passenger records in the Ellis Island Archives

- Create and maintain your Family History Scrapbook

- Order one free copy of your initial Scrapbook (printout or CD-ROM)

- Receive a 10 percent discount at the online gift shop or at the Center

- Possibly get a tax deduction (check with your accountant)

- Your membership also helps to support the work of The Statue of Liberty-Ellis Island Foundation to preserve and protect the sites and their records.

Searches

As a registered user (remember, registration is free), you can use the Passenger Search. Simply put in a first and last name at the opening screen, and then click Search Archives. If you want to perform a more targeted search, click Passenger Search at the top of the page, and then click New Search. On that search page, you can input a first and last name, and then choose Male or Female (or don't use gender at all).

As the site says, if at first you don't succeed, don't give up! Remember that many passengers' names were misspelled, so try clicking the "close matches" or "alternate spellings" boxes at the top of the page to ask the system to search for spellings that have similar sound values (e.g., Dickson and Dixon would sound the same). If the results list is too long, refine the search using the bar on the left of the screen, filtering for year of arrival, ethnicity, and so on. Choosing one of the names gives you a screen where you can choose to see the original ship's manifest.

The information on passenger records comes from passenger lists, called ship manifests. Passengers were asked a series of questions; their answers were entered into the manifests. Ellis Island inspectors then used the manifests to examine immigrants. Click the links on the left to view the passenger's ship and the manifest with the passenger's name. On some passenger records, click to read information added to the Community Archive by members of the Foundation. (If you're a Foundation member, you'll be able to add annotations of your own.) To save the passenger record, click Add To Your Ellis Island File. As a registered member, you can access this file at a later logon.

You can look at the transcription of the ship's manifest to see who is recorded near the person. You must look at two images for the complete records, which often run across both pages of the original books.

Click the Ship link to view details about the vessel, as described previously. Registered members can save their searches and results in an online file for later reference and use. All of these images, as well as an official Ellis Island Passenger Record, can be ordered in hard copy.

The Ellis Island search form lets you enter just the leading characters of the last name. It also allows you to search on ethnicity, ports, and ships. However, the search on the Ellis Island site requires you to first have an exact spelling match, whereas the Morse form (see the following section) does not. For example, suppose you are searching for a Polish immigrant named "Hoffman." To make sure you also get hits for "Hofman" (with a single f), you can do the search by entering only the first three letters—Hof. Then from the Ellis Island search page, you would click Edit-Ethnicity.

Community Archives

On the Ellis Island site, only members of the Foundation can create annotations to the records, but all registered users of the website can view them. Annotations supplement information in the record, telling more about the passenger's background and life in the United States. This information has not been verified as accurate and complete—it's simply what the annotating member believes to be the facts. Click View Annotations on the passenger record (if no View Annotations button exists, the record hasn't yet been annotated). If you're registered with the site, you'll see a list of annotations. If you haven't yet registered, a screen will appear so that you can.

Ellis Island Family History

If you have paid for a membership to The Statue of Liberty-Ellis Island Foundation, you can contribute Family History Scrapbooks on the website or at the American Family Immigration History Center itself on Ellis Island.

Scrapbooks

Family Scrapbooks combine member-submitted pictures, images from the Ellis Island archives, written stories and memories, and sound recordings. Members can choose to keep the Scrapbook private or add it to the publicly available Ellis Island Family History Archive. When you visit the Center, you can use a scanner, a camera, and recording equipment there.

When you begin your Scrapbook, you have 16 pages to work on, including a title page and an author page. Ten of those pages have space for your images, and four have space for an image from the Ellis Island Foundation archives. The site's documentation suggests that you decide on a particular story or theme for your Scrapbook. Begin with a passenger search in the archives to find passenger records, ship images, and ship manifests to save in Your Ellis Island File and add to your Scrapbook, for example.

If you're a paying member, you can click Family Scrapbooks on the main menu and then click Start New Scrapbook (if this is the first time) or Create New Scrapbook (if previous Scrapbooks exist). You choose a style and create a title page and an author page. Once you complete those steps, you'll see the Scrapbook's table of contents. From there, you compose the pages.

The Scrapbook pages can accept both pictures and audio recordings. The easiest way to do this is to gather everything you want to upload into one directory, or perhaps to your desktop, to make them easier to find. On a Scrapbook page, under Add An Image, click Your Computer. In the Upload Image window, you can browse the local computer for the file or simply enter the filename. The files are uploaded one at a time, and they can be 180KB or smaller. If a file is larger than 210 × 210 pixels, it will be resized proportionally. If a file is smaller, it won't be resized.

When you click Use Selected Image, the picture will appear on the page and the window will close. Members can also add files from the Ellis Island Library by clicking Our Library on a Scrapbook page under Add An Image.

Your Ellis Island File may also contain passenger records, ship images, and ship manifests you saved during a passenger search. Click the left and right arrows to review the images in Our Library or Your Ellis Island File, and then click Use This Image to add an image to the page. On a Scrapbook page, under Add Audio, click Your Computer, and choose an audio file. You can upload files up to 1.8MB in size. Then enter a title for the audio file. When you click Use Selected File, the title assigned to the file appears on the page and the window will close. To remove an audio file, under Remove Audio?, click Delete This Audio File.

At the online gift shop, paid Foundation members can order one free copy of their Scrapbooks, choosing either a high-quality printout or a CD-ROM copy. Additional copies are available for purchase. At the table of contents, click Purchase Scrapbook.

Visiting in Person

You can also take care of these tasks on site at the museum, but you have to make an appointment within 90 days of your arrival. Click Schedule A Visit in the navigation bar at the top of any page on the site. You can simply choose to perform a passenger search ($5 entry fee to the museum) or to work on a Scrapbook (as with the online version, you must be an annual member of the Foundation to work on a Scrapbook). You select the things you want to accomplish on your visit, list the number of people in your party and whether any will need wheelchair assistance (up to seven people), and then select the date and check-in time. Your appointment time will be assigned at check-in. You'll get a confirmation number at the end of the process to present at check-in. Print a copy to present at the desk. The screen also gives you links to articles on how to research and gather information for either a search session or a Scrapbook session.

Morse's Forms

This search on the Ellis Island site is better now than it was the first summer the site went online, but it still has many steps. Dr. Stephen Morse, with collaborators Michael Tobias, Erik Steinmetz, and Dr. Yves Goulnik, created One-Step Search Tools for the Ellis Island site at www.stevemorse.org. This project has several different search forms that overlap to a degree. Though this may get you a bit confused about which one to use, I suggest using several of them in this order:

- Ellis Island white form (1892–1924) is the main form for searching for Ellis Island passengers.

- Ellis Island gold form (1892–1924) is an enhanced form for searching for Ellis Island passengers.

- Ellis Island manifests (once known as "Missing Manifests") (1892–1924) searches by direct access the Ellis Island manifests.

- Ellis Island ship lists (1892–1924) allows you to search for the names of specific ships in the Ellis Island microfilms.

- Ellis Island additional details (1892–1924) searches the additional passenger information.

Note

As an aside, Dr. Morse's pages are so much better at finding things than the Ellis Island site that I think they should pay him to substitute his code for theirs. However and alas, they haven't asked my opinion.

The forms on this site can search by town of origin, use "sounds-like" codes, and can search microfilms that are in the index but that are not accessible through the Ellis Island site's algorithms. An article on using these forms is at www.stevemorse.org/onestep/onestep.htm with tips and explanations. It is definitely worth your time to read this article before you start, but I'll provide a quick overview here.

White Form

The first form on the site, called the white form, searches all passengers, has a restricted town search, and has a somewhat-restricted "sounds-like" (similar to but not Soundex) search.

Note

This form will also search other ports and immigration records! Just use the drop-down box to choose.

On this form, you must input exact spelling matches for the ports. You can find those spellings in the links at the bottom of the form, which sorts the more than 700 port names by country. You can also enter a town name at the bottom under Advanced Search Features. In this case, you can enter just the starting letters of the town name, but the advanced search has a serious flaw: It doesn't do a real town search, but instead downloads all matches, regardless of town, and filters for your match on your computer.

The white form allows you to perform "sounds-like" searches on the last name only, but it does not use Soundex. Instead, it generates a list of all names that are known to be in the database that sound like the name you are interested in. Then it searches for all passengers with those names. While this looks only for names known to be in the database, it also misses some similar-sounding names, for example, Spenser and Spencer. The town search and name search are mutually exclusive on the white form. You can do one or the other, but not both at the same time.

Gold Form

The search engine for the gold form has no requirement on the last name field. You can specify only the first character, or you can even leave the last name out completely. In any case, there will be only a single search performed on your behalf and the results will appear relatively quickly. In the gold form, you can also search for traveling companions, exact dates, and marital status, and better control the display of results.

Ellis Island Manifests

One of the most useful features of the Morse site is the Ellis Island Manifests feature, formerly known as the "missing" manifests. Now these manifests were not really "missing" because they have been microfilmed and even indexed. But the search on the Ellis Island database will not find them because, for some strange reason, the HyperText Markup Language (HTML) links to them are wrong. To make best use of this page, take your results to the Ship-Lists page (www.stevemorse.org/ellis/boat.html). That page will allow you to go directly to the exact image of the records for any ship arrival.

Usually, you will use this form if you have found your ancestor and a date, but the image did not appear when you looked at the individual result, or you got a picture of the wrong page of the manifest instead of what you wanted. But since you have the ship and date, you can use the Direct Access To Manifests form for the particular arrival port and view the manifest.

It's something only a Web wonk would understand, but Alex Calzareth discovered that the images are in the Ellis Island database even though the links to them aren't, and Michael Tobias figured out a way to catalog these images with bad HTML links, and Yves Goulnik figured out how to find the start and end of each roll of film as represented in the image database. Then Dr. Morse put it all together into this search page.

Now that was a lot of technical stuff, but this should deglaze your eyes: What it means is that this page can find images of ships' manifests that the Ellis Island search will not find. You can search for all arrivals of a certain ship, or all ships arriving in a certain date range, or all ships leaving a certain port in a date range. Use of this Missing Manifests page is greatly simplified if you know the roll and frame number for your ship, which may be listed in the Ellis Island results, or you can get them from other forms on Morse's site.

Ship Lists

Once you have your ancestor's information from the Manifest search, take that data to the Ship Lists form. Here, you can search for all arrivals of a particular ship, for all arrivals between specific dates, for all ships coming from a particular port, and more.

Steve Morse's step-by-step directions are at http://stevemorse.org/ellis/faqb2.htm.

A roll might contain several days' worth of ship landings. You will see a date on the "Direct Access to Manifests" form: that is the date of the first ship arrival on that roll. It is not the date of the arrival of the particular ship corresponding to the frame you are looking at.

Now, certain lists come back as "inaccessible." Sometimes the staff at the Ellis Island Foundation accidentally failed to upload the manifest images for a certain ship (or for an entire roll). The manifest does exist on the original microfilm roll, and you can view it at many libraries or at NARA. Just be sure to write down the identifying numbers from the result. You can also view it using the All-New-York-Ship-Lists form or All-New-York-Manifests form, both of which access the images from Ancestry.com instead of EllisIsland.org.

Ellis Island Additional Details

When you use the gold and white forms, there is a check box for passenger ID. If you use that, you will find that every passenger in the Ellis Island database is assigned a 12-digit passenger ID. You can also see the passenger ID by moving the mouse cursor over any of the links for the particular passenger on the Ellis Island site as well, or when you click the link for one. If you have followed a link to a particular passenger on ellisisland.org, look at the address bar of your browser.

Other Morse Ellis Island search forms search for passengers in the Ellis Island database and display a limited amount of information on each passenger found. Specifically, they give the passenger's name, age, year of arrival, and place of residence. This form allows you to view additional details on each passenger found, such as sex, marital status, ethnicity, port of departure, and full date of arrival.

The gold Morse Ellis Island search form can show you all or a subset of these details directly if you use the check boxes to specify which ones you want. But with this form, you don't have to navigate through several pages to obtain the information. Also, it makes it convenient to copy the information into a spreadsheet. Another advantage of this form is that it can be set to display the details for companions traveling with the passenger found.

For this Additional Details form, you enter that passenger's ID in the field, as well as your user ID and password for Ellis Island (remember, you can sign up there for free); then click the Show Details button next to that field. It takes a while for the form to do this search, so be prepared for a wait.

You might want to get the additional details on all the passengers in the list rather than just on a single passenger in order to get details on traveling companions. You can do that by copying and pasting the entire results page into the large box on this form. But if you are using the white or gold form, you must indicate on that form that you want the passenger ID to be displayed.

Another way to do this is to view the source code of the results page and then copy and paste that source code into the large box on this form. Then you would click the Show Details button next to that large box rather than the one that is next to the individual passenger ID field. This method will work even if the passenger ID is not one of the items displayed on the results page.

To view the source code, go to the View menu and select Source (Internet Explorer) or Page Source (Firefox). Furthermore, for the white form, there is a button that says View Source. The source code obtained from that button is different from the code obtained from the View/Source menu item, but either source code can be pasted into the large rectangle and the detailed results obtained will be the same.

Other Forms

Morse has several other forms for searching the Ellis Island database; Ancestry.com (you have to input your ID and password for your paid subscription for those); and several other ports of immigration, including Baltimore, Galveston, Philadelphia, and more. He also has helps for census forms, calendars, and translations. His site, www.stevemorse.org/index.html, is a bookmark you must have!

Wrapping Up

♦ Ellis Island Online is a wonderful resource on the Web.

♦ You can search for immigrants from 1892 through 1924—the peak years of Ellis Island's processing—by name, date, and ship.

♦ You can upload pictures, sounds, and text to an online scrapbook if you're a member of the Statue of Liberty Foundation (it costs $45 to register) or if you visit the museum itself in New York.

♦ Stephen Morse and several others have created alternative search forms for the Ellis Island data, as well as other ships' lists and sites.

Chapter 15

Online Library Card Catalogs and Services

Despite all the wonderful things appearing online, many of your genealogical expeditions will still be in libraries. However, the online world can help you here, too. One of the wonderful things about the online world is the plethora of libraries now using online card catalogs (OCCs). This greatly speeds up your search while you're at the library. Not only can you perform an instant search of all of a library's holdings (and, sometimes, even place a hold on the material), but also, with many terminals scattered throughout the building, you needn't look up your subject, author, or title on one floor and then repeatedly run to another floor to find the referenced material. If your local library hasn't computerized its card catalog yet, it probably will soon.

And, oh, the joys of looking in the card catalog before you actually visit the library (and in your pajamas at that!). You know immediately whether that library owns the title. With a few more keystrokes, you can find out whether the title is on the shelf, on reserve, on loan to someone, or lost without a trace. You can find out whether the book is available by interlibrary loan or found in a nearby branch library. Then, you can, if you want to, get dressed and go to the library to pick up your resource!

You can connect to most online card catalogs through the World Wide Web with a browser interface. In many cases, it will look exactly as it does in the library itself.

Connecting to OCCs by Web Browser

Modern libraries use computerized card catalogs all around the world. In fact, the site LibWeb (http://lists.webjunction.org/libweb) has links to more than 8,000 different library pages in Europe, the Caribbean, and Asia, and is updated daily by Thomas Dowling.

Similar sites are at:

♦ A2A (www.nationalarchives.gov.uk/a2a) is a searchable collection of archive catalogs in England and Wales from the eighth century to the present. Type a word or phrase into the box; you can limit the search to specific archives or to English or Welsh counties, as well as specific dates.

- Catalogue Collectif de France (www.bnf.fr/pages/zNavigat/frame/
version_anglaise.htm?ancre = english.htmr) will let you use one
interface to query the three largest online library catalogs in
France, including the printed and digitized holdings of the
national Library of France, the University SUDOC (System of
Documentation) of French universities, and local libraries across
France. It includes books printed from 1811 to the present in
more than 60 public or specialized libraries.

- Don't forget the Google Book Search at http://books.google.com/
books! It can show you if a library has a book that matches your
search terms.

- LibDex (www.libdex.com) is a worldwide directory of library
home pages, Web-based online public access catalogs (OPACs),
Friends of the Library pages, and library e-commerce affiliate
links, with a page for you to browse by country.

- Lib-Web-Cats (www.librarytechnology.org/libwebcats) is a directory
of libraries worldwide. While the majority of the current listings
are in North America, the numbers of libraries represented in
other parts of the globe are growing.

- National Libraries Catalogue Worldwide (www.library.uq.edu
.au/ssah/jeast) from the University of Queensland, Australia,
allows you to access the websites and online catalogs of national
libraries across the world.

- The European Library (http://search.theeuropeanlibrary.org/
portal/en/index.html) searches the content of European national
libraries.

- UK Higher Education and Research Libraries is maintained by Ian
Tilsed of the University of Exeter at http://as.exeter.ac.uk/library/
about/other. Here you will find links to lists of online academic
libraries, public and national libraries in the United Kingdom, and
more.

- WorldCat (www.worldcat.org) is the world's largest network of
library content and services, currently indexing the resources of
around 10,000 libraries. It has an application for searching the
catalog from your smart phone, too!

Of course, some of those libraries are more concerned with engineering or agriculture or biology than they are with genealogy. The following is a tour of U.S. libraries that have extensive genealogy collections and are worth searching.

The Library of Congress Card Catalog

The Library of Congress Online Catalog has about 14,000,000 records of books, serials, computer files, manuscripts, cartographic materials, music, sound recordings, and visual materials in one database with cross-references and scope notes. As an integrated database, the online catalog includes 3,200,000 records from an earlier database. These catalog records, primarily for books and serials cataloged between 1898 and 1980, are being edited to comply with current cataloging standards and to reflect contemporary language and usage.

Many items from the library's special collections are accessible to users but are not represented in this catalog. In addition, some individual items within collections (microforms, manuscripts, photographs, etc.) are not listed separately in the catalog, but are represented by collection-level catalog records. You can use the simple search on the far left, or use Boolean terms and limiters in the middle and the right.

Library Holdings, Location, and Status Information

Each catalog record indicates where onsite users should request library materials. Other users should consult the interlibrary loan policy for the Library of Congress. Records in the online catalog will generally indicate that the library holds one copy of a work, even though additional copies may actually be available in the library's collections. Library staff will begin entering information about additional copies in the near future. The library will also be incorporating more detailed information about serials holdings, indicating which issues are available and where they should be requested.

In addition to holdings and location information, the catalog record supplies information on the circulation status of library materials. Some circulation information may not be complete, since many materials in the library (including many special collections materials) are not handled by the circulation system at this time.

Other Databases and Electronic Research Tools

In addition to the Library of Congress Online Catalog, users have access to recent issues of the Handbook of Latin American Studies (HLAS). HLAS is accessible by visiting HLAS Web at http://hlasopac.loc.gov. Other electronic research tools, some of which provide supplementary access to the library's collections, can be found on the Library of Congress website.

Don't Miss These Library Sites

Genealogy sections in libraries can be a small section or an entire floor, or even the library's reason for existence. Here are some card catalogs to examine from home.

Anne Arundel County Public Library (Maryland) has the Gold Star Collection, which contains about 700 titles dealing with Maryland, including some Anne Arundel County genealogy. In their special collections are several Maryland family histories and local histories. The library catalog is located online at www.aacpl.net.

California University and State Libraries MELVYL (California) is a searchable catalog of library materials from the ten UC campuses, the California State Library, the California Academy of Sciences, the California Historical Society, the Center for Research Libraries, the Giannini Foundation of Agricultural Economics Library, the Graduate Theological Union, the Hastings College of the Law Library, and the Lawrence Berkeley National Laboratory Library. And every single one of those institutions has a history/genealogy section. The California State Library, for example, has books, maps, manuscripts, diaries, newspapers, and photographs pertaining to California history and genealogy. See the collection guide at www.library.ca.gov/research/index.html#cal. In the California Information File, you will find an index to almost 1.5 million items, including newspapers, periodicals, and books about California persons, places, and events. The collection also has federal census records (1850 to 1930) and Soundex listings through 1920 for California, a transcription of the 1852 state census of California (separate from the national one), California cemetery transcriptions made by the Daughters of the American Revolution (DAR) and DAR indexes to early California vital records and wills, and more.

Connecticut State Library (Connecticut) has not only genealogy and local history of Connecticut, but also of the rest of New England. Their special collections include Connecticut town vital records to about 1900. The state library's catalog can be accessed through the state library home page at www.cslib.org or through CONSULS, the Catalog of Connecticut State University and the State Library at http://csulib.ctstateu .edu. To limit your searching to state library holdings, choose the last option, Change Library Catalog, on the first menu screen. Then choose Search The State Library Only. Be sure to check out the links and resources on the History and Genealogy page at www.cslib.org/handg.htm.

Samford University Library (Alabama) does not have quite the scope of the Birmingham Public Library with regard to Alabama history, but because of the annual Institute of Genealogy and Historical Research held here has quite a collection of all things Alabama. The website is http://library.samford.edu.

The Allen County Public Library (Indiana) at www.acpl.lib.in.us/ genealogy/index.html has one of the best genealogical collections in the country. The link to the genealogy page gives you an overview of this wonderful genealogists' treasure house. More than 50,000 volumes of compiled genealogies, microfilms of primary sources, and specialized collections, such as African-American and Native American, make this library one you must see. But like the Family History Library in Salt Lake City, you must first plan your visit, or you will be overwhelmed. Search the catalog online for the names you need to see if they have something for you!

The College of William and Mary Library (Virginia) is one of the oldest universities in one of the oldest states, and the collection is astounding. The special collections include Virginia tax lists for the 1780s; census microfilms for Virginia (1815–1920), North Carolina (1790–1850), and other states (1790–1820); and compilations of Virginia county, marriage, land, probate, church, military, emigration, and immigration records. The library's catalog is located at http://lion.wm.edu/uhtbin/cgisirsi /pFhG477g0e/SWEM/183510069/60/502/X. Manuscript collections are listed in the online library catalog. In addition, the Reference Department will do limited research in response to phone, fax, or e-mail questions. They will check to see if the library has materials on a certain subject, and they will consult an indexed book or collection for a specific name (see www.swem.wm .edu/resources/genealogy/research.cfm). Finally, this site has excellent guides to researching genealogy in Virginia and

to this collection. Look at www.swem.wm.edu/resources/genealogy/
key-guides.cfm and www.swem.wm.edu/resources/genealogy/index.cfm.

The Daughters of the American Revolution Library (General) at
www.dar.org/library has more than 160,000 books on American
genealogy, and it's open to the public.

The Library of Virginia (Virginia) is home to a set of powerful online
card catalogs, located at www.lva.lib.va.us/whatwehave/index.htm.
This site has scanned images of Civil War records, family Bible records,
letters, and other material, all indexed and searchable by name. I ran a
test with "genealogy and Powell" as the search terms. If I want to refine
my search further, I could also use Boolean terms, such as AND, NOT,
and so on. Overall, the Library of Virginia's card catalog is easy to
understand and read—and, I might add, a pleasure to work with.

**The New England Historical and Genealogical Society Lending
Library** (General) at http://www.newenglandancestors.org/25.asp is
available to members only. Consider joining if you have any New
England ancestors!

The New York Public Library (New York) contains a genealogy
section called The Milstein Division. This department collects materials
documenting American history on the national, state, and local levels,
as well as genealogy, heraldry, personal and family names, and flags.
The card catalog of the research library (nicknamed CATNYP) is
searchable at the top of every page in the site.

The Newberry Library (Illinois) in Chicago at www.newberry.org/
genealogy/collections.html has more than 17,000 genealogies. Search
the catalog to see if you need to make a visit!

The Sons of the American Revolution Library Catalog (General) at
http://sar.library.net can tell you if this collection has genealogies of
interest to you. The SAR Library maintains a noncirculating collection of
genealogy and American Revolutionary War history and military
records. It is located at 1500 South Fourth Street, Louisville, Kentucky,
40203. The library collection includes family genealogies, state and
county history, and vital statistics, with many New England records;
federal census records (complete through the year 1860 for every state;
some records through 1920); Revolutionary War pension applications;
and a special George Washington collection containing books, journal
articles, and manuscripts.

The University of Illinois at Urbana-Champaign Library Catalog
(Illinois) at http://uiuc.libguides.com/genealogy offers an outline of the
UIUC online catalog, describing its major collections, and a helpful guide

to American genealogy research. Note that the university also has extensive collections of material originating outside the United States that may be helpful for genealogical research once you get "back to the boat."

The Filson Historical Society library (www.filsonhistorical.org) has material on the history of the entire Ohio Valley, especially the significant stories of Kentucky and the Ohio Valley history and culture. If you have any genealogy in that area, a personal visit to the Filson is something you will never forget. The library has 50,000 titles, a 1.5-million-item manuscript collection, a collection of 50,000 photographs and prints, and a museum with 15,000 items. The library has such items as original manuscripts, portraits, landscapes, photographs and prints, genealogical materials, printed family histories, local business records, and other primary historical materials about Kentucky, the Ohio Valley, and the Upper South. Search the catalog of the Filson at http://filson.ipac .dynixasp.com.

The Ohio Historical Society (Ohio), located at www.ohiohistory.org, has newspapers, federal census records, county histories, and family histories. Government records holdings include the archives for the state of Ohio and local government records from counties of central Ohio, as well as statewide death certificates (1909–1953). The library catalog is located at www.ohiohistory.org/occ/menu.htm.

Where to Find More Online

There are more online library resources than you can shake a stick at. Be sure to Google the geographic area you need, plus "library" and "catalog." You are certain to get some hits! Also search for the name of a state and "public library" because many states have a network of their libraries.

Card Catalogs

Librarians love to make lists and catalogs for each other! Try some of these:

♦ **Gateway to Library Catalogs** (www.loc.gov/z3950) is a page by the Library of Congress. In addition to links to the LOC catalog, you will find an alphabetical list of catalogs around the world. Also, check out the Research and Reference Services page for librarians at www.loc.gov/rr.

- **National Union Catalog of Manuscript Collections** (NUCMC) can point you not only to library card catalogs, but also to archives and repositories with websites. You can find it at www.loc.gov/coll/nucmc.

- **The Library of Michigan** website has a database with the locations of more than 3,700 Michigan cemeteries and lists sources at the library where a researcher can find the names of those buried in each cemetery. The database can be found at http://michigancemeteries.libraryofmichigan.org.

- When you visit **USGenWeb** (www.usgenweb.com), look under the state and then the county you're researching to see if the library catalog is linked.

- **The WWW Library Directory** (www.travelinlibrarian.info/libdir) is a list of library websites sorted by geography, not topic. However, it's useful and international in scope.

Using Your Local Library Online

You can do more than just peruse the card catalog of your local and distant libraries! Find out if your local library offers online services for home use as well. Usually, the login to use these will be some combination of your local library card number and your identifier with their system (name, phone number, etc.)

PERiodical Source Index on Microfiche (PERSI)

The PERiodical Source Index (PERSI) is a subject index to articles in genealogical periodicals and journals. Remember using the Reader's Guide to Periodical Literature (RGPL) in high school for writing research papers? PERSI is the same idea, targeted to genealogy sources. Using PERSI can help you find genealogy articles fast, saving you many hours of searching in usually unindexed periodicals. The PERiodical Source Index is published by the Allen County (Indiana) Public Library Foundation in a joint effort with the Genealogy Department of the Allen County Public Library (see the earlier section).

Note

The Family History Library produces a microfiche version of PERSI with the permission of the Allen County Public Library for use in the Family History Library and its family history centers (see Chapter 13). This means you can access it online from the FamilySearch.org site or from your local FHC. Some local libraries also offer it: to find out if yours does, go to the WorldCat (see the earlier section) page at www.worldcat.org/oclc/15689202&referer = brief_results, enter your location, and the bottom of the page will list, in order of proximity, the libraries nearest you that offer PERSI. PERSI search is also available on Heritage Quest Online, offered by many local libraries.

With PERSI, you can look at indexes to articles in more than 2,000 periodicals, about 50,000 articles in all. This includes the majority of English-language and French-Canadian genealogical periodicals. The index pointers are locality, family (surname), and research methodology. It is important to note that PERSI is not an every-name index, nor does it include the actual articles. Like the RGPL, it points to the publication, date, and author, but only of major articles. It does not index queries, Ancestor Charts, Family Group Sheets, book reviews, or time-sensitive material such as society officers, membership lists, and meeting notices. And, it does not include page numbers, unlike the RGPL.

There are two PERSI indexes:

- The retrospective index, also known as the 1847–1985 Index. The Family History Library reference is FHL fiche 6016863 for this section. It indexes articles in journals from 1847 through 1985. The 1989 edition indexes every issue of about 200 popular genealogical periodicals. Other periodicals will be added yearly until 1993. Eventually, about 2,000 journals will be indexed.

- The Annuals Index (FHL reference: fiche 6016864) is a cumulative index to virtually all genealogical journals dated 1986–1990.

You can search PERSI by:

- **People** Articles are indexed by surname in this section. These articles contain information on individual families, cemeteries where all burials are of the same surname, and family Bible records. However, family group records, Pedigree Charts, and surname journals are not indexed in PERSI.

- **Places** Articles about records of specific localities are indexed in one of three locality sections: U.S. Places, Canada, and Foreign Countries. Each section has a similar arrangement in which the articles are listed first by the locality and then by the record type.

- **How To's** Articles in this section offer research methodology advice, such as what information you find in church records or how to trace women in a pedigree.

- **Periodical Name** If you know an article appeared in, say, *Genealogical Helper*, you can search for keywords only in that publication.

PERSI also identifies different kinds of article subjects: biography, cemeteries, census, church, court, deeds (land and property), directories, history, institutions, land (not including deeds), maps, military, naturalization, obituaries, other, passenger lists, probate (not including wills—that is, adoptions, and so on), school, tax, vital records, voter, and wills (probate).

Note

- *Search both the annuals and the 1847–1985 indexes.*

- *Your family's surname may not have been the main topic of an article. Try searching for related families.*

- *In the U.S. Places section, look for statewide articles, listed before the county articles.*

- *PERSI does not index most articles by secondary topics. Also, the title of an article may not indicate its entire contents.*

Sample Search

In Figure 15-1, I have searched PERSI on Heritage Quest for "Powell" and "South Carolina," getting three results. The article title, the journal, and date are listed with each result. Remember, this is not going to be a link to the actual article, but to the details on the publication that has the article.

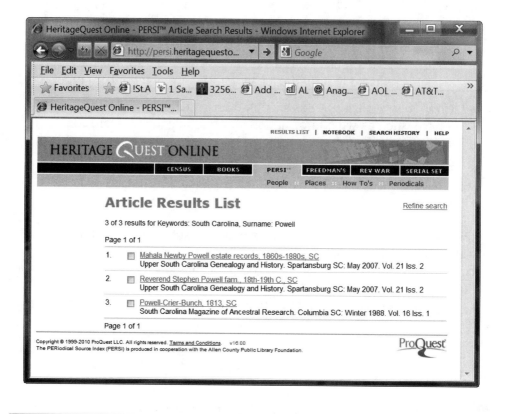

FIGURE 15-1. *Search PERSI for name and location, and results are presented most recent first.*

So, I click the link for the title, getting details on the date, volume, and number. To read the actual article, I can click the title again and see whether the journal in question is held at a library near me (Figure 15-2). I can also search for the title of the journal in my local library catalog. If it is there, I can copy the call number from my local library's catalog and go see about reading and copying the article (the journal in question may not circulate, so I may have to read it there.)

I can order a copy from Allen County Public Library, too. To do this, I have to write a letter addressed to:

Allen County Public Library
P.O. Box 2270
Ft. Wayne, IN 46801

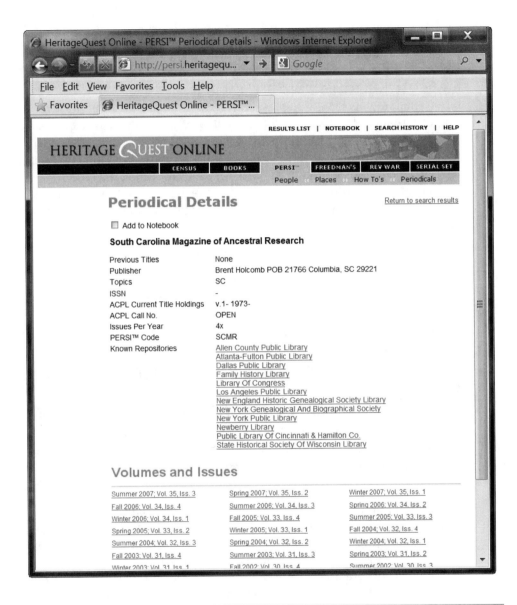

FIGURE 15-2. *This screen shows me other libraries that have the journal in my results.*

My letter would have the full entry from PERSI and the name of the journal. Heritage Quest has a handy form to fill out and print for this. Up to six articles can be requested by each letter. The charge is $7.50 for each letter, prepaid, plus $0.20 per page copied to be billed later when the copying is sent back. I cannot send this request by phone, fax, or e-mail and it will take six to eight weeks to receive a response.

An alternative is the Family History Library. Most of the periodicals in PERSI are available at the Family History Library. Look in the Author/Title section of the Family History Library Catalog. If the periodical has been microfilmed, you can order a copy to use at a local Family History Center. However, most genealogical periodicals are under copyright and are not microfilmed.

I can also write to the publisher to get a copy of an article. Names of publishers are listed with the periodical in most library catalogs, including the Family History Library Catalog. Often, the publishers are genealogical or historical societies, and their addresses are listed in *Directory of Historical Organizations in the United States and Canada,* published by the American Association for State and Local History.

Other Library Online Services

Success Story: Local History Online

Marian Pierre-Louis is a house historian and a realtor. Those two jobs combined mean that she gets to see a lot of old houses. Nothing makes her happier. Marian also regularly lectures on African American and New England genealogy.

"My local library posted vital records from 1850–1900," Marian said. "While it doesn't show images, it's a very easy-to-scan chart (transcription). I use it all the time. Actually, they have a whole portal of local history for our town! (Search Facebook for "medwaylib.org" to see the pages).

I've also had great luck with Heritage Quest and Sanborn Maps through the library. My library is now offering Ancestry, too, but I have my own subscription."

Many local libraries have an abundance of online services for genealogists, some of them available from home, some from the library computers. Among my favorites from my local library are:

♦ **America's GenealogyBank (NewsBank)**   More than four centuries of rare documents and records, including historical newspapers, books, pamphlets, and genealogies, plus selected material from the American State Papers and U.S. Serial Set, the complete Social Security Death Index, and more than 29 million obituaries.

♦ **America's Obituaries & Death Notices** (NewsBank)   An easy-to-use interface allows searching by name, date range, or text such as institutional name, social affiliation(s), geographic location(s), philanthropic activities, etc.

♦ **Ancestry Library Edition** (available only inside the library) Ancestry Library Edition (ALE) gives individuals something truly priceless: the chapters of their own authentic, unique family stories. The world's largest online collection of family history records and resources, ALE is a popular research tool. It offers a wide variety of unique content to help users trace their family lineage.

♦ **Heritage Quest Online** (available both inside the library and from home for library card holders)   This has digital, searchable images of U.S. federal census records with the digitized version of the popular UMI Genealogy & Local History book collection, U.S. federal census records from 1790–1930, more than 22,000 family and local history books, Revolutionary War Pension and Bounty Land Warrant application files with records for more than 80,000 individuals, and Freedman's Bank Records containing key African-American data.

♦ **ProQuest Obituaries** (available both inside the library and from home for library card holders)   This service offers more than 10.5 million obituaries and death notices in full-image format from uninterrupted historical archives of top U.S. newspapers. With content dating as far back as 1851, this wholly unique database provides researchers with valuable clues about their ancestors in the United States, including proper full name, maiden name, spousal information, relatives' names, occupation, religion, cause of death, and more.

♦ **GenDisasters: Events That Touched Our Ancestors' Lives**   This service contains information on the historic disasters, events, and tragic accidents our ancestors endured, as well as information about their life and death. Database and records are searchable by surname and location.

- **Roots Television**   You'll find videos covering everything from DNA stories, to Flat Stanley's Family Tree, to the lectures from the latest Genealogy and Technology Conference. We're defining "roots" broadly—really broadly—so you don't have to be a genealogist to find something of interest here.

- **RootsWeb**   Finding our roots together.

- **Sanborn Fire Insurance Company Maps of Florida**   These maps were created for insurance purposes from 1860 through 1923. They show the size, shape, and construction of buildings, dwellings (including hotels and churches), and other structures such as bridges, docks, and barns. The maps include street names, property boundaries and lot lines, and house and block numbers.

Wrapping Up

- Going to the library in your pajamas is fun!

- You can search the card catalogs of many libraries across the world from the Internet.

- Some libraries have begun scanning images and actual text of their genealogical holdings.

- Some libraries participate in interlibrary loans of books and microfilms.

- You can search for such libraries at several sites across the Internet.

- State libraries and provincial libraries are excellent online resources.

- Librarians like to maintain lists of online libraries for each other. You can use them, too!

- Beyond the card catalog, many local libraries allow you to use databases and indexes such as PERSI and Heritage Quest from your home as well as from the library. Check with your local librarian for details!

Chapter 16

International Genealogy Resources

Sooner or later, you'll get "back to the boat"—that is, you'll find your original immigrant in a certain family line. The first immigrant in your family might have arrived just a generation ago or centuries ago. Either way, that doesn't have to mean your genealogy is "done." Although finding where he or she boarded won't tell you a birthplace, it is a beginning.

Of course, if your time frame for immigration is right, you can use the Ellis Island site, as covered in Chapter 14. Immigration before and after the 1892 to 1924 time frame is not so easy as Ellis Island, but quite possible nonetheless. Here are some places for you to start:

- Check out Cyndi's List for links to ships' passenger lists projects at www.cyndislist.com/ships.htm.

- Search the Ellis Island site.

- Investigate the Immigrant Ships Transcribers' Guild at www.immigrantships.net.

- Check out the Ships List (www.theshipslist.com), which not only has passenger lists, but also newspaper reports, shipwreck information, and information on shipping lines.

- Search the National Archives and Records Administration (NARA) microfilm catalog for immigration records for arrivals to the United States from foreign ports between approximately 1820 and 1982. See www.archives.gov/genealogy/immigration for details on how to order microfilms that match.

- Look at naturalization records at the NARA page (www.archives.gov/genealogy/naturalization), state archives, and county and state courts.

- Check out the Genealogy page at the U.S. Citizenship and Immigration services: go to www.uscis.gov and click the Genealogy link on the bottom of the panel on the left.

Note

Remember to give back to the Internet by getting involved in a project such as the Immigrant Ships Transcribers' Guild project.

USCIS Genealogy Program Frequently Asked Questions (FAQs)

The United States Citizenship and Immigration Genealogy Program is a way to pay the government to do research on immigrant ancestors. After the program launched in August 2008 there was a tremendous response, and the turn-around goal became to respond to all requests within 90 days.

The program accesses records from five different types of agency records:

- Naturalization Certificate Files (C-files) from September 27, 1906, to April 1, 1956

- Alien Registration Forms from August 1, 1940, to March 31, 1944

- Visa files from July 1, 1924, to March 31, 1944

- Registry Files from March 2, 1929, to March 31, 1944

- Alien Files (A-files) numbered below 8 million (A8000000) and documents therein dated prior to May 1, 1951

An Index search costs $20 and uses data you provide to come up with record citations. You also get instructions for how to ask for those records from the USCIS or National Archives, which costs between $20 and $35. If you do not have the right file number, you have to first do an index search.

If you have questions about index search results or record copies that you have already received, e-mail Genealogy.USICS@dhs.gov and include your case identification number in your message.

Following the Past

Of course, the next step is to start researching in "the old country," outside the United States, Canada, or whatever country where you live. Can you do this online? Well, that depends on the country. Some countries do, indeed, have online records for you to search, especially those countries where English is spoken. But some countries only have sites with the most general information, and you'll be lucky to find the address of the civil records offices. You'll probably wind up doing a combination of online and postal mail research and possibly some in-person research, too.

One thing that can help is the book *International Vital Records Handbook: Birth Marriages and Deaths* by Thomas Jay Kemp (Genealogical Publishing Company, 2009). At this writing, the fifth edition is the latest. From Afghanistan to Zimbabwe, from Alabama to the U.S. Virgin Islands, Kemp has gathered not only the right offices and phone numbers and address, but if a website or fax applies, he has included that, too. Each entry has information on whether that government entity will release records for genealogy research and the costs for each. Most important, Kemp has done the research for what records are released for genealogy research for each entry and included the proper form in "camera-ready" format (that is, ready to be photocopied and mailed in.)

If your local library does not have this important resource, you can order it from Genealogical Publishing Company at www.genealogical.com.

Beyond the Boat

In many of the places covered in previous chapters, you can find links to sites for genealogy beyond the United States. For online links, I recommend starting at Cyndi's List at www.cyndislist.com and RootsWeb at www.rootsweb.org. Other good places to look are:

National Archives

A country's national archives might have a webpage describing genealogy how-to's for that country. For example, I recently searched for "Poland National Archives" in Google. Quickly, I found the English version of the archives' website (www.archiwa.gov.pl/lang-pl.html) and clicked on the flag beside the word "English". This site has pages that explain how to start a genealogy search (see Figure 16-1), what to ask for, and where to look for records.

FIGURE 16-1. *The National Archives of Poland site has pages on how to do genealogy in that nation.*

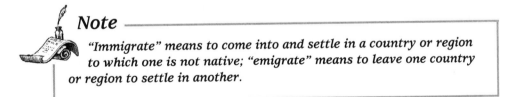

Note

"Immigrate" means to come into and settle in a country or region to which one is not native; "emigrate" means to leave one country or region to settle in another.

Note

Be sure to look at FamilySearch for research guides to the country you need.

Genealogical Societies

Search in any major search site (Yahoo!, Google, Bing, and so on) for the country of origin for your immigrant and "genealogy." Often, at the top of the list will be a genealogical society devoted to that particular nationality. These organizations can help you learn how to conduct research in those countries. Each place has its own method of recording vital statistics, history, and other information.

LDS Research Guides

Before you start looking for records, you need to know what those records are called and who keeps them. The Church of Jesus Christ of Latter-day Saints (LDS) has developed pamphlets on researching immigrants and ancestors around the world. These Research Guides are indispensable for these tasks. They are free to download online, or you can order hard copies for a nominal fee from any Family History Center. Look in the Yellow Pages or in the White Pages for The Church of Jesus Christ of Latter-day Saints for a Family History Center near you.

The first one to read is the guide "Tracing Immigrant Origins," a 49-page outline of tips, procedures, and strategies found online at www.familysearch.org/Eng/Search/RG/guide/tracing_immigrant_origins .asp or available in hard copy from a Family History Center for a small fee.

Other Research Guides give you step-by-step pointers on the best way to pursue historical records in a particular state, province, or country. The letter-writing guides tell you what you need to know before you write the letter, where to write, how to address the envelope, how to enclose return postage, and include a sample letter in the appropriate language. Arm yourself with the research outlines and, if available, a letter-writing guide for the appropriate country before you begin. Also, look at the LDS "word lists" for various languages; this can help you recognize the words for "birth," "marriage," "death," and so on in the records, even if you can't read the language.

WorldGenWeb

The WorldGenWeb Project was created in 1996 by Dale Schneider to help folks researching in countries around the world. The goal is to have every country in the world represented by a website and hosted by researchers who either live in that country or are familiar with that country's resources. The site is www.worldgenweb.org.

When the WorldGenWeb Project launched on the Internet 15 years ago, volunteers were recruited to host country websites. By coordinating with the USGenWeb Project, soon the major countries in the world had websites. Throughout the next year, WorldGenWeb continued to grow. In 1997, the WorldGenWeb Project moved to RootsWeb. The support of the RootsWeb staff helped WorldGenWeb expand to its present size. Divided into 11 regions (Africa, Asia, British Isles, Central Europe, Caribbean, Eastern Europe, Mediterranean, Middle East, North America, Pacific, and South America), WorldGenWeb provides links to local sites with local resource addresses of county/country public records offices, cemetery locations, maps, library addresses, archive addresses, association addresses (including Family History Centers or other genealogical or historical societies), and some history and culture of the region. Other resources may include query pages or message boards, mailing lists, historical data (including census records), cemetery records, biographies, bibliographies, and family/surname registration websites.

Between RootsWeb and WorldGenWeb, you should be able to find something about the country you need to search.

Translate a Site

Don't be frustrated if you find a country's archive but can't find an English button, as I did on the Polish site. You can translate a page at most of the major search sites.

♦ Use the option "Translate A Page To English" using Bing Translator at www.microsofttranslator.com. Paste the original text in the left box, and choose the language to translate to in the box on the right.

♦ Google Translate at http://translate.google.com, Google's free online language translation service, instantly translates text and webpages. This translator supports English, Afrikaans, Albanian, Arabic, Belarusian, Bulgarian, and more.

♦ Yahoo! Babel Fish Text Translation and Web Page Translation at http://babelfish.yahoo.com lets you can translate a webpage or compare a translated webpage with the original by clicking View Page In Its Original Language.

♦ Several browsers, for example, Firefox, have add-ons that translate pages on the fly for you. Check your browser's help file.

Country-Specific Sites

In addition to the places mentioned so far, there are many good starting places for an international search. Some are general and provide all sorts of international research, and some are for specific locations. The following sections describe some to get you started.

Asian Genealogical Sites

♦ **The Singapore Genealogy Forum** (http://genforum.genealogy .com/singapore) allows Singaporeans of all races to look for their relatives and ancestors.

♦ **The AsiaGenWeb** (www.worldgenweb.org/index.php/ asiagenweb) is part of WorldGenWeb and has some sites, but needs hosts for many more.

♦ **Origin of Chinese Surnames** (www.yutopian.com/names) is a fascinating page with the most common Chinese surnames and their history.

European Genealogical Sites

There are many sites where you can research your European roots. I recommend you start with the following:

♦ **Europe Genealogy Links** is a list of sites sorted by country and resource at www.genealogylinks.net/europe/index.html. You will find links to cemeteries, censuses, GenWeb pages, and personal sites.

♦ **Benelux (Belgium, Netherlands, Luxembourg)** Digital Resources Netherlands and Belgium (http://geneaknowhow.net/digi/ resources.html) is one place you can find resources from the Netherlands and Belgium, including more than 350 Internet links to online resources (with more than 150 passenger lists), nearly 900 online resources on Dutch and Belgian bulletin board systems, and hundreds of digital resources.

♦ **Family Explorer Benelux** (http://freepages.genealogy.rootsweb .ancestry.com/~jberteloot) is a list of links to databases, mailing lists, and other Benelux resources.

♦ **The Federation of East European Family History Societies** (FEEFHS) (www.feefhs.org) was organized in 1992 to foster family research in Eastern and Central Europe without any ethnic, religious, or social distinctions. You'll find a forum for individuals and organizations focused on a single country or group of people to exchange information and be updated on developments in the field. While it primarily serves the interests of North Americans in tracing their lineages back to a European homeland, it welcomes members from all countries. The site has historical maps, information on conferences and workshops offline, information on organizing tours to Europe for hands-on research, and a quarterly e-mail newsletter.

♦ **The Ukrainian Roots Genealogy Webring** begins at http://ukrcommunities.8k.com/ukrroots.html. The webring is a community of webpages on Ukrainian genealogy research. The pages are personal home pages of people who want to share information that they have accumulated on their family history and Ukrainian heritage. You'll also find pointers to sources of information that would be of help to others doing research into their Ukrainian family history.

♦ **Eastern Slovakia, Slovak, and Carpatho-Rusyn Genealogy Research** (www.iarelative.com/slovakia.htm) has articles, links, message boards, and transcribed records.

France

Interest in French genealogy online is growing rapidly. This short list will get you started.

♦ Besides the usual sites, such as Cyndi's List and WorldGenWeb, check out FrancoGene at www.francogene.com. At Francogene, you'll find Quebec's pioneers and resources in Europe, genealogy sites in former French colonies around the world, such as Quebec and Haiti, as well as links to genealogy societies and institutions.

♦ Much like Ancestry.com in the United States, Genealogy.tm.fr (www.genealogy.tm.fr) is a for-fee site that allows you to search documents and records in French. This was started in 1994, when Laurent Fondant began his own genealogy and found a need to transcribe, index, and scan documents. You pay a subscription for a period to access the documents you find in searching indexes. You can search for the geographic distribution of your surname in France (based on censuses from 1891 to 1990) at www.geopatronyme.com.

♦ Nomina (www.culture.fr/genealogie) is a meta-search of 13 million names in genealogy databases (GEDCOMs), marriages records, and military records. You can search them all at once or narrow it down to one of four categories.

♦ Genealogie.com is much like Genealogy.com in the United States (www.genealogie.com). People upload their data for searching and exchanging information.

Germany

The Germans keep wonderful records, but wars and other disasters sometimes left holes in the lexicon. Still, using these sites may be helpful.

♦ **Genealogy.net** (www.genealogienetz.de/genealogy.html) is a treasure trove of information. From the home page, you can find the monthly newsletter in German, information on genealogical research in local regions, links to 35 different German genealogical societies, 60 mailing lists, a FAQ on German genealogy, a GEDCOM database, a gazetteer, a list of heritage books, and much more. Most of it is in German, so remember the translations sites mentioned earlier! You can search many of these databases with just one query in the meta-search engine.

♦ **GermanRoots** (www.germanroots.com) offers tips, links, and research hints. It has lists such as "The Best German Resources," "The Best General Resources," "History, Language, and Culture," and a basic guide for research in German genealogy by Joe Beine.

♦ The **telephone** book for Germany can be found at www.dastelefonbuch.de.

♦ **Kartenmeister** is a free online gazetteer of German place names at www.kartenmeister.com/preview/databaseuwe.asp.

Italy

Italians love genealogy! Again, this is a short list to get you started.

- The **Italian Genealogy Homepage** (www.italgen.com) is the place to start when researching your genealogy in Italy. This page includes links to how-to articles, discussion groups, and history.

- Visit **D'addezio**, or The Italian Heritage and Genealogy page, at www.daddezio.com. It has links to atlases, cemeteries, genealogy articles, genealogy newsletters, genealogy software reviews, genealogy supplies, helpful organizations, history and culture resources, information on coats of arms, local (Italian) societies, maps, military records, passenger lists, research services, surname studies, vital records, and more.

- The **Italy World Club** has a page with links to archives in Italy by region at www.italyworldclub.com/genealogy.

Spain

The Spanish Empire in the New World as well as in Europe left many records that family historians can use. Here are some examples.

- The place to start is the **Society of Hispanic Historical and Ancestral Research** at http://shhar.net. This organization is nonprofit and all-volunteer, and is dedicated to family history. Besides good pointers for beginners and a message board, this is the only site I've seen with information on African-Hispanic families. The books and journals are worthwhile, too. Don't miss the monthly online magazine at http://shhar.net/somos_primos.htm.

- **Spain Genealogy Links** (www.genealogylinks.net/europe/spain/index.html) has tips, data, and links about Spain and more.

- A site called **EuroDocs** from Brigham Young University has a page on Spanish history at http://eudocs.lib.byu.edu/index.php/History_of_Spain:_Primary_Documents. This has transcribed Spanish documents ranging from the Visigothic Code to wills of individuals.

- A list of mailing address for archives and libraries in Spain is on the Genealogy Forum at www.genealogyforum.rootsweb.com/gfaol/resource/Hispanic/SpainNA.htm.

Portugal

Portuguese ancestry is almost as widespread as Spanish. Online resources are not as prevalent, however.

- Doug da Rocha Holmes' page at http://www.dholmes.com/ rocha1 .html, called Portuguese Genealogy Home Page, is dedicated to Portuguese genealogy. The site proclaims, "This website was created with the Portuguese genealogist in mind. It is for anyone and everyone whose passion has become the search for their Portuguese ancestry no matter where they came from in the former Portuguese territories. Many projects are underway which will be of great interest to anyone concerned with this field of study. Check back from time to time to see the new developments."

- **LusaWeb** is a site dedicated to Portuguese culture, ancestry, and more at http://www.lusaweb.com/. This is an organization with dues, like many genealogy societies. It is a place to celebrate common heritage, to learn about Portuguese history and traditions, and to share the memory of our Portuguese ancestors.

- **The Portuguese-American Historical & Research Foundation** has a page for genealogy questions and answers at www.portuguesefoundation.org/genealogy.html.

- **The National Library of Portugal** is online at www.bnportugal.pt, in Portuguese, of course. Remember to use the translation tools mentioned previously!

 ### Note

Most European national libraries are searchable from The European Library webpage at www.theeuropeanlibrary.org/portal/index.html.

Scandinavia

Census records of Norway are being transcribed and posted by volunteers at these pages, which also have good information on research in Norway:

- **The Digital Archives** is a public service from the National Archives of Norway. Here you can search transcribed source material for free at http://digitalarkivet.uib.no. Click the English button at the bottom to read it in English.

- **Norwegian Research Sources** (www.rootsweb.ancestry.com/ ~ wgnorway/NorLinks3.htm) is an excellent starting place. It has links to articles on the Ancestors from Norway site and "Basics of Norwegian Research," among other things.

- **Ancestors from Norway** (http://homepages.rootsweb.ancestry .com/ ~ norway) was created in 1996 to document and inform Norwegian ancestry. It now has excellent articles on research, links to more than 100 sites with information and records, and even recipes!

- **The Norwegian Emigration and Genealogy Center** offers information in Norwegian for descendants at www.emigrationcenter.com.

Note ———————————————————————————

Are you finding lots of good information? Have you backed up this week? This month? This year?

- **Martin's Norwegian Genealogy Dictionary** (www.martinroe.com/ eidhalist.htm) can help you decipher words for relationships, occupations, and so on.

- **ProGenealogists** has a page for most European countries, including one for Denmark at www.progenealogists.com/denmark.

- **Swedish Genealogical Society of Minnesota** (www.rootsweb .ancestry.com/~ mnsgsm) has queries, data, a few transcriptions of records translated into English, and meeting dates of the society.

United Kingdom

Genealogy is as popular in the United Kingdom as it is in the United States. Here are some good starting places for online information.

- **The United Kingdom (UK) and Ireland Genealogy site** (www.genuki.org.uk) is the best starting point. This site has transcribed data, such as parish records, plus links to individuals' pages where genealogy research (secondary material) is posted. Look at the index page (www.genuki.co.uk/contents) for specific counties, surnames, and so forth.

- **The Free BMD (Free Birth, Marriage, and Death Records) Project** (http://freebmd.rootsweb.com) provides free Internet access to the Civil Registration Index information for England and Wales from 1837. The transcriptions are ongoing, and the updates are posted once or twice a month. *You can volunteer to help!*

- **The National Archives of Ireland** has a genealogy how-to page at www.nationalarchives.ie/genealogy/beginning.html. From the site, you can search the indexes of 1901 or 1911 census returns; 1840s, 1850s, and 1860s Primary Valuation (also known as Griffith's Valuation); and 1820s or 1830s Tithe Applotment Books. There are also some marriage records, although a certain number of records were destroyed in "The Troubles."

- **The UK National Digital Archive of Datasets** (www.ndad .nationalarchives.gov.uk) has archived digital data from UK government departments and agencies. The system has been available since March 1998 and provides open access to the catalogs of all of its holdings, as well as free access to certain datasets when you register online.

- **The National Archives of Scotland** (www.nas.gov.uk) has records from the 16th century. The family history page at www.nas.gov.uk/ familyHistory has good how-to information. You can download PDF files of fact sheets on adoption, deeds, wills, and other topics.

Australia and New Zealand

Australia is rich with genealogy websites. Start with Cyndi's List at www.cyndislist.com/austnz.htm. Other sites include

- **The Society of Australian Genealogists** (www.sag.org.au) offers materials, meetings, and special interest groups. The library catalog is online as well. This group has been helping people with Australian genealogy since 1932.

- **The Dead Persons Society**, a site for genealogy in Melbourne, Australia, has a graphic of dancing skeletons at http://home.vicnet .net.au/ ~ dpsoc. It has guides to searching Australian provinces; databases of cemeteries, census and other records; and general articles on Australian genealogy.

- **Convicts to Australia,** a guide to researching ancestry during the time when Australia was used as a large prison, can be found at www.convictcentral.com/index.html. The site has some how-to guides, many census and ships' passenger lists, and more. However, the site cannot handle individual questions or requests for research help.

- **The KiwiGen Genealogy webring** has links to New Zealand genealogy at http://g.webring.com/hub?ring = kiwigen. With 42 sites ranging from single-family genealogies to geographically based ones, it is a useful site for amateur and professional genealogists alike.

- **The National Archives of Australia** (www.naa.gov.au) has an entire section on family history and what records to look for.

Africa

- **South African Genealogy** (www.sagenealogy.co.za) is dedicated to helping folks find South African ancestors. "Here you will find lists of passengers arriving or departing the port of Cape Town mostly during the 1800s, books and CDs of colonial records and local history, links to specialist South African and International genealogical websites and more … all aimed at making your South African Family History research a little easier," the site says.

- **Conrod Mercer's** page (http://home.global.co.za/ ~ mercon) is a personal collection of tips on doing South African (white) genealogy.

- **The African Atlantic Genealogical Society** (http://freepages .genealogy.rootsweb.ancestry.com/ ~ gfli/africanatllantic.html) has newsletters, queries, and census data to help you get started.

You may want to check out Cyndi's List (search for the African nation of interest) and WorldGenWeb first.

North America

The following sites are good places to start to search for information on ancestors from Canada and Mexico.

Canada

Canadian history is as long and varied as U.S. history. Here are some good starting places.

- **Canadian Genealogy and History Links** (CGHL) (www.islandnet.com/ ~ cghl) lists online sites for vital records, genealogies, and general history, sorted by province. The CGHL search engine will look for your search term in the descriptions or titles of pages listed on the site. For example, if you are looking for "Powell," you'll find one match to a personal genealogy page with Powells on it.

- **Immigrants to Canada** (http://jubilation.uwaterloo.ca/ ~ marj/ genealogy/thevoyage.html) offers information extracted from various government records, as well as from shipping records. You can read and search such documents as ships' lists, immigration reports, and first-person accounts. It also has links to other genealogy sites. It is from the University of Waterloo.

- **The Canadian Genealogy Centre** (www.collectionscanada.gc.ca/ genealogy/index-e.html) is a page from the National Archives and Library of Canada. You can read a PDF file of the free booklet, "Tracing Your Ancestors in Canada," which describes the major genealogical sources available at the National Archives and other Canadian repositories. You also want to see the main page, www.collectionscanada.gc.ca/index-e.html, which combines the Archives and Library of Canada sites.

Mexico

Mexican records are fairly detailed when it comes to church matters (births, baptisms, marriages, burials, and so on). Some states in Mexico have less information on civil matters, however.

- **Archivo General de la Nation** (www.agn.gob.mx) is the National Archives of Mexico site. It's as rich and deep as the NARA site in the United States. Note that the site is in Spanish.

- **Archivo Historico de Arzobispo** (www.arquidiocesismexico .org.mx) has the archives of the Archbishop of Mexico, a treasure trove of Church records. This site is also in Spanish and has a corresponding Facebook page at www.facebook.com/pages/ Distrito-Federal-Mexico/Archivo-Historico-del-Arzobispado-de-Mexico/204431596423.

- **The Texas General Land Office** has a page at www.glo.state.tx.us/ archives/archives.html for their archives. This state office has records dating back to Spanish times. The page tells you how to write for these records, including the proper addresses and what is available. It also has a searchable catalog of historic maps of the region.

- **The Genealogy of Mexico** (http://garyfelix.tripod.com/index1 .htm) is one genealogist's compilation of starting places. He covers the conquistadores, coats of arms, a DNA surname project, and more.

- **The Hispanic Genealogical Society of New York** (www.hispanicgenealogy.com) includes Mexico, Puerto Rico, and other North American Hispanic genealogy. You can learn about their regular meetings and publications, as well as find links to resources.

A Success Story: German Ancestry Discovered

Denzil J. Klippel had quite a bit of success in his international genealogy search, but it didn't happen overnight. Denzil started with what he knew, researched back to the boat, and finally found his family's village of origin. How he did this is fascinating.

Denzil only knew his parents, his grandmother on his mother's side, and her brother and sister. "In the beginning, I didn't take advantage of the resources on the Net like DearMYRTLE and so forth, and ask questions. But I soon learned everyone in the online genealogy community is willing to help answer questions. We don't need to reinvent the wheel—just ask if anyone has done this or that," Denzil says. So he did eventually ask DearMYRTLE, who pointed him to research at a local Family History Center (FHC). Denzil visited a local FHC in New York City.

There he found his grandmother's family, but not his grandmother, on one of the microfilms. Requesting the name and address of the submitter, he contacted him with a query, including his e-mail address. Soon, another researcher contacted him by e-mail, and everything began to fall together. Denzil sent for his father's death certificate (New York) and found his place and date of birth (California). Then he found his father's father's place of birth (upstate New York), as well as his father's mother's maiden name (Settle) and place of birth (California). He was able to order some of these records online through various vital records sites maintained by these states.

Note

Denzil could have searched the Family History Library Catalog at FamilySearch.com before going to the FHC.

"After going back to my great-grandfather and finding he came from Germany, I hit a brick wall. Not knowing what to do, I went to one of the search engines—Yahoo!—and put in the name Klippel. It gave me 6,000 places where the name appeared on the Net, most of them regarding an illness discovered by a Klippel. I captured all of the Klippel e-mail addresses and sent them a message saying I was researching the Klippel family name and, if they were interested in working with me, perhaps we could find some common ancestors or at least discover where the Klippels originated."

Denzil says he does not recommend this approach, however. "This shotgun approach never works," he said. What did work, though, was searching for the surname on Google and looking for the genealogy sites. After e-mailing people with Klippel genealogy sites, as opposed to every Klippel he could find online, Denzil heard from people who had been searching the line. Several were cousins he didn't know he had, and since that time, he now calls all Klippels he comes in contact with "cousin." "One of these cousins had the name of the town in Germany where my Klippel line came from (Ober-Hilbersheim). I found this village had a website and sent a letter to the mayor. He responded via e-mail and said he knew of my line and told me there were still Klippels living in the village," Denzil said. "In the meantime, other Klippels in Europe contacted me, and before I knew it, I was planning a trip to visit some of them and Ober-Hilbersheim. When they heard I was going to visit, they all said I had to stay with them. I bought my airline tickets online via Priceline.com and my train pass online."

Now Denzil was really into the in-person, offline mode! Through electronic and regular mail, he made appointments at all the archives he planned to visit in Germany. When he arrived, they were ready for him and, in most cases, they'd already done all the lookups. As Denzil gathered the research material, he mailed it home to himself. This was important insurance against losing or misplacing any of the papers during his sojourn. "My trip started in Ober-Hilbersheim, and I stayed with the mayor. He took me to all the archives and helped me get all the Klippel family history back to 1650! My distant cousins in the village welcomed me with open arms. I then went to the Netherlands and stayed with the Klippels there, and they took me to the Island of Tholen, where the first Klippel came from in the 1400s. Then on to Hamburg to visit Helmut Klippel and the archive there," Denzil said.

"And last, but not least, on to Sweden to stay with Alf Klippel, who had given me a wealth of information about the origins of the Klippel name via e-mail and did most of the translating of the old German documents I had been receiving over the Net." It took some footwork and perseverance, but after seven years, Denzil feels he accomplished a lot in his international search, and the online resources made it possible.

Note

You can find where to write for many vital records at The National Center for Health Statistics page (http://www.cdc.gov/nchs/nvss.htm).

Wrapping Up

- ◆ Once you find your immigrant ancestor, you can use archives and ships' passenger lists to identify the home town.

- ◆ Many national archives have webpages describing research techniques for that country.

- ◆ At FamilySearch, you can download and print research guides for immigrant origins and for specific countries, as well as word lists of genealogical terms in non-English languages.

- ◆ You can find specific sites for genealogy of many nationalities.

- ◆ Translating pages are found at most web search sites.

Chapter 17

Ethnic Genealogy Resources

The international sources cited in Chapter 16 can also help you with ethnic research within the United States and Canada for a well-documented ancestry. For some groups, however, the search is a little more complex.

Special Challenges

Sometimes you need to search unexpected resources based on other genealogies, history, and, yes, the infamous "family legend." None of these things alone will solve your special challenges of ethnic research, but taken together, they might lead to that one document, vital record, or online resource that solves the puzzle.

African-American genealogy often presents special challenges. When researching the genealogy of a former slave, it's necessary to know as much about the slave owner's family as you do about the slave. Wills, deeds, and tax rolls hold clues to ancestry, as do legal agreements to rent slaves. Tracking down all these items can be difficult. You need to know the history of the region and the repositories of the records, and you need to consider family legends to be clues, not answers.

As another example, Native American genealogies are also difficult, because in many cases, very little was written down in the 18th and 19th centuries. A genealogist must contact the tribe involved and look at many different kinds of records. Mixed ethnic heritages, such as Melungeon, are problematic to research because these mixed groups suffered from stigma for many years. If you are researching a Melungeon family line, the true genealogy may have been suppressed or even forgotten by your ancestors. These special cases have led to many online resources.

The sites mentioned in this chapter provide good information on how to begin to search for specific genealogy information, as well as the history and culture of different groups. The challenges you will face can be discussed in the forums and mailing lists; you will often find tips on which records to seek and how to get them. Don't forget, however, that new pages are being added to the Web all the time. Search for "genealogy" plus the name of whatever ethnic group you're seeking on your favorite search engine about once a month to see if new information has become available.

And stay on the mailing lists and newsgroups for the ethnic groups; when you hit a brick wall, perhaps someone on the list can help!

African-American Genealogy

African-American genealogy presents some special challenges, but online genealogists are working hard to conquer them. Search for "African-American genealogy" in any search engine and you'll find many good resources. Also try these sites as starting places. To begin, the African-American Research Area (www.archives.gov/research/african-americans) on the National Archives and Records Administration (NARA) site provides a list of articles and other resources not to be missed.

Note

You will find many African-American resources in the "Caribbean" section later in the chapter, and you'll find plenty of Caribbean information among the African-American genealogy pages listed in this section.

AfriGeneas

AfriGeneas, at www.afrigeneas.com, is the major portal for African-American research. Transcribed records, discussion groups, monthly articles, and more will help you get started. The site has a searchable database of surnames in addition to slave data from descendants of slaveholding families, as well as from other sources, both public and private. Tips and topics to help people in their search for family history are distributed through mailing lists, chats, newsletters, and the Internet. Volunteers do all of this; they extract, compile, and publish all related public records with any genealogical value. The site also maintains an impressive set of links to other Internet resources to help African Americans in their research.

The sections of this site are an important body of work. They include:

◆ **E-mail** AfriGeneas has a page for you to create an e-mail account through Google Mail so that your address is < *yourname* > afrigeneas.com. The advantage: You can use this address only for genealogy and not for other correspondence. That way, you don't have so much worry about spam coming in with the stuff you really want to read.

♦ **Search** The search page lets you search the mailing list, surnames, death records, and the entire site for your surnames or places of interest.

♦ **Records** This drop-down menu helps you search the census records, death records database, library archives, marriage records database, photos, slave data collection, surnames database, state websites, and world websites of the AfriGeneas collection. Be sure to read the page "African American Genealogy: An Online Interactive Guide for Beginners" by Dee Parmer Woodtor, author of *Finding a Place Called Home: An African-American Guide to Genealogy and Historical Identity* (Random House Reference, 1999). This step-by-step guide to genealogy in general and African-ancestored genealogy in particular is full of good advice.

♦ **Resources** Under this heading on the navigation bar, you can find a site map with every page on the site and a What's New link. It also can take you to the Beginner's Guide, a slideshow-like presentation that steps you through online genealogy. It's a no-nonsense approach, showing what can and can't be done online. It also includes some success stories. The Resources tab also has links to state resources, a clickable map with links to each state in the United States with history, links to state resources, and queries. The World Resources link does the same for other countries, such as the Bahamas. Volunteers are actively being sought for other countries. From the Resources tab, you also have access to some important databases:

   ♦ **Forums** This drop-down menu lists the major topic divisions, from African-native connections to surnames and family research, and the mail lists. You can also choose to look at the most recent posts in all topics for a quick catch-up on what's going on in the different forums.

   ♦ **Chat** The AfriGeneas Chat Center is open 24 hours a day, seven days a week, for any AfriGeneas member who cares to use it, except during times set aside for regularly scheduled or special chats, and the menu will take you to a chart of when those are. Use is specifically restricted to discussion of African-American or African ancestored genealogical or historical topics. If anyone abuses the privilege, off-hours access to the chat spaces will be curtailed by AfriGeneas.com. To reserve a room, host a chat, or make comments about or suggestions for future chats, you contact the chat manager at forumafrigeneas.com

♦ **Resources** This menu has links to books, guides, directories of sites, links to genealogical and historical societies, humor, history, and the help desk, to name just a few. You could spend a week just exploring the items under this drop-down menu!

♦ **Stores** This menu links you to both the onsite bookstore and Amazon.com.

Among the most valuable resources on this site are

♦ **Slave Data** This area will help you find the last owned slave in your family. Records kept by the slave owner are frequently the only clue to African-American ancestors, particularly during the period 1619 to 1869. The site is also designed to help descendants of slaveholders and other researchers. Users share information they find containing any references to slaves, including wills, deeds, and other documents. This site also houses a search engine and a form for submitting any data you might have. To use the database, click the first letter of the surname you're interested in. This takes you to a list of text files with surnames beginning with that letter. Now click a particular file name. The text file may be transcribed from a deed book, a will, or some other document. The name and e-mail address of the submitter will be included, so you can write to that person for more information, if necessary.

♦ **Census Records** These are transcribed census records. As a file is submitted, it's listed at the top of the What's New list on this page. Not all states have volunteers transcribing right now, so you can only click those states that show up as a live link.

♦ **News Briefs & What's New** These are located on the home page and keep you updated on the latest news and additions.

Note ————————————————————————

AfriGeneas also has a Facebook page, www.facebook.com/afrigeneas, where queries, news, and reviews are posted regularly. Be sure to become a fan!

Africana Heritage

A project at the University of South Florida (USF), this site is at www.africanaheritage.com. The USF Africana Heritage Project is an all-volunteer research project and website sponsored by the Africana Studies department at the University of South Florida. The volunteers concentrate on recovering records that document the names and lives of slaves, freed persons, and their descendants and then share those records on the free site. Volunteers search the University of South Florida's library holdings, other library holdings, academic archives, plantation journals, public records, Freedman's Bureau records, early church records, oral histories, family Bible records, Internet research, and information contributed by genealogy researchers, historians, and community members. In 2007, USF announced a collaboration with WeRelate.org on historical research sponsored by the Magnolia Plantation Foundation of Charleston, South Carolina. Magnolia Plantation is funding genealogical research in the plantation journals of the Drayton family of Charleston. The USF Africana Heritage Project will reconstruct the lineages of enslaved communities on Drayton family plantations and build family files that anyone can access for free on the Internet.

Readers are invited to share documents with the site, and material is there from readers, scholars, archives, universities, and historical societies. For more information, contact Toni Carrier, Founding Director, USF Africana Heritage Project, 4202 E. Fowler Avenue, FAO 270, Tampa, FL 33620, e-mail: infoafricanaheritage.com.

More Good Resources

Other good African-American sites include the following:

♦ **African American Genealogy on the Web,** from Princeton University at www.princeton.lib.nj.us/history/index.html, has links to several good sites, as well as information on singer/actor Paul Robeson. Please note, however, that materials on the

Princeton pages are exact transcriptions from the historical sources, which may have offensive language, negative stereotypes, and/or graphic descriptions reflecting the culture of an earlier time. Nevertheless, they are part of the historical record accessible to genealogists, local historians, and other interested readers. The data are compiled and transcribed by Terri Nelson. Please send suggestions, comments, or corrections to tnelson@princetonlibrary.org.

- **The Afro-American Historical and Genealogical Society (AAHGS)** is a group for the preservation of the history, genealogy, and culture of those with African heritage. The society's main emphasis is in recording research (as in transcribing sources and so on) and sharing completed genealogies. You'll find AAHGS at www.aahgs.org. They have an annual conference, local chapters, a journal, and newsletter.

- **Slaves and the Courts** (http://lcweb2.loc.gov/ammem/sthtml) is an online collection of pamphlets and books at the Library of Congress about the experiences of African and African-American slaves in the United States and American colonies. It includes trial arguments, examinations of cases and decisions, and other materials concerning slavery and the slave trade. You can locate information by using the collection's subject index, author index, or title index, or you can conduct your own search by keyword. You can look at the items as transcriptions or as images of the original pages. Knowing this sort of history can often give you a clue as to where to look for other records.

- **U.S. African-American Griots**, at http://www.rootsweb.ancestry.com/~aagriots/, discusses the storytellers, or griots. Their roles are hereditary, and their surnames identify them as griots, and they sing and tell the histories of their tribes. The site helps other to pursue African American ancestry by being a central depository for African American records of historical importance. Resources held here are organized by States and Projects (databases for individuals and records pertaining to groups of people).

- **The Freedman's Bureau Online**, at www.freedmensbureau.com, allows you to search many records. The Freedman's Bureau took care of education, food, shelter, clothing, and medicine for refugees and freedmen. When Confederate land or property was confiscated, the Freedman's Bureau took custody. Records include personnel records and reports from various states on programs and conditions.

- ◆ **The African-American Genealogical Society of Northern California** is a local group, but its website has monthly articles, online genealogy charts, discussion groups, and more. It is worth a visit. Find it at www.aagsnc.org.

- ◆ **AAGENE-L** is a moderated mailing list for African-American genealogy and history researchers. Subscribe to the list by sending a message to aagene-l@upeople.com with SUBSCRIBE in the subject line. Details can be found at http://ftp.cac.psu.edu/~saw/aagene-faq.html.

Arab Genealogy

- ◆ **Linkpedium** (a social bookmarking site) has a page of Arab Genealogy links at www.linkpendium.com/genealogy/USA/sur/surc-A/surc-Ara/sur-Arab.

- ◆ **Genforum** has a discussion group on United Arab Emirates genealogy at http://genforum.genealogy.com/uae.

- ◆ Check **Cyndi's List** page, The Middle East, at www.cyndislist.com/mideast.htm, for a list of sites dedicated to related history, culture, and genealogy research.

Australia and New Zealand

- ◆ **The Aboriginal Studies WWW Virtual Library** (www.ciolek.com/WWWVL-Aboriginal.html) has links to resources and articles concerning Australian aborigines.

- ◆ **The WorldGenWebPage** (www.rootsweb.ancestry.com/~nzlwgw/resources.html) has links to many resources about New Zealand genealogy.

- ◆ **The National Library of Australia** has a page on genealogy, located at www.nla.gov.au/oz/genelist.html, that includes links to many specific ethnic and family sites.

♦ **The Australian Institute of Aboriginal and Torres Strait Islander Studies** (AIATSIS) has a page just for family historians, located at www.aiatsis.gov.au/fhu/start.html.

Caribbean Genealogy

♦ **Caribbean Genealogy Resources**, located at www.candoo.com/genresources, provides links to archives, museums, universities, and libraries with historical and genealogical information for countries in the Caribbean. Another page from this site is www.candoo.com/surnames, which is a list of Caribbean surnames. The text files list surnames, places, and dates, as well as e-mail contact information for researchers looking for them.

♦ **WorldGenWeb** has a Caribbean page at www.rootsweb.com/~caribgw. Search RootsWeb for mailing lists for related queries and discussions.

♦ **British Virgin Islands Caribbean GenWeb** (www.rootsweb.ancestry.com/~bviwgw) has general resources, online records, query boards, and a mailing list. The following offices hold BVI records that are relevant to family research. Although they do not all have adequate space and staff to accommodate public searches, if you make an appointment, the appropriate officer would likely find a way to assist you with your search:

   ♦ The General Civil Registry Office holds records of births, marriages, deaths, and wills from 1859 to the present. The Anglican and Methodist churches hold records of baptisms, marriages, and deaths as follows: Anglican Church: baptisms (1825 to 1861), marriages (1833 to 1946), and burials (1819 to 1867); Methodist Church: baptisms (1815 to 1895 and 1889), marriages (1877 to 1934), and burials (1845 to 1896).

   ♦ The Inland Revenue Office records ownership of houses, land, and other property.

   ♦ Tax lists containing pertinent information are published annually.

- The Land Registry holds property identifiers, including indexes and maps from 1972, public library information (newspapers from 1959 and various name indexes), BVI history books, and, from the Survey Department, ordinance maps from 1953 and boundary maps from 1975. You can write to them at The Archives Unit, Deputy Governor's Office, Burhym Building, 49 deCasro Street, Road Town, Tortola. (284) 468-2365 (phone) and (284) 468-2582 (fax).

- **Caribbean Genealogy-Resources-Microfilm Indexes** (www.candoo.com/genresources/microfilms.htm) is a list of surnames in the Caribbean listed by surname and researcher.

- **Genforum.Genealogy.Com** (http://genforum.genealogy.com) features a forum finder, and you can search by surnames. It also offers information on general genealogy topics, such as immigration, emigration, migration, religions, and wars.

Creole/Cajun Genealogy

The Acadians/Cajuns were the French settlers ejected from Nova Scotia by the British in the mid-18th century. Some went to Quebec, and some to Louisiana.

"Creole" means different things in different places. In Latin America, a Creole is someone of pure Spanish blood. In the Caribbean, it means a descendant of Europeans; in the Guineas, it means someone descended from slaves, whether African or native to the islands. In the southern United States, the term refers to aristocratic landowners and slaveholders before the Civil War, part of the overall French/Cajun culture of the Gulf Coast. For almost all Creole research, parish records are your best bet—those and mailing list discussions!

- **Acadian-Cajun Genealogy and History** (www.acadian-cajun.com) publishes records, how-to articles, history, mailing lists, maps, genealogies, and more.

- **The Encyclopedia of Cajun Culture** (www.cajunculture.com) will give you good background information.

- **Acadian Genealogy Homepage** (www.acadian.org) has census records, books, maps, and more.

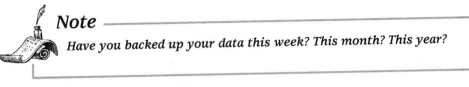

- **The Cajun and Zydeco Radio Guide** also has a list of family histories that have been posted to the Web at www.cajunradio.org/genealogy.html.

- **Acadian/Canadian GenWeb** is at http://acadian-genweb .acadian-home.org/Links.html.

- **The Louisiana Creole Heritage Center** is located on the campus of Northwestern State University in Natchitoches, Louisiana, and on the Web at http://creole.nsula.edu.

- **The Confederation of Associations of Families Acadian** (www.cafa.org) promotes the culture and genealogy of Acadian families in America.

- **Search RootsWeb's** list of mailing lists; there are several for Acadian/Cajun research and data in Louisiana and Canada.

Cuban Genealogy

- Good pointers, tips, and exchanges on Cuban genealogy can be found at the **Cuban GenWeb** (www.cubagenweb.org).

- The Cuban Genealogy Club of Miami at www.cubangenclub.org/ has a page of links and some digitized books on Cuban history.

- The Cuban Genealogical Society has a page on RootsWeb at www.rootsweb.ancestry.com/ ~ utcubangs/.

- The University of Miami has a Cuban Family History and Genealogy Project with a genealogy research kit at cubanfamily.iccas.miami .edu/genealogy_kit.htm.

Doukhobors Genealogy

The history of this small sect of Russian pacifist dissenters is outlined in an article at www.rootsweb.ancestry.com/ ~ cansk/Saskatchewan/ ethnic/doukhobor-saskatchewan.html. The RootsWeb message boards at Ancestry.com have several topics on this group as well.

Gypsy, Romani, Romany, and Travellers Genealogy

- ♦ **The Gypsy Lore Society** maintains a list of links on Gypsy lore, genealogy, and images at www.gypsyloresociety.org.

- ♦ **Romani** culture and history are covered at www.romani.org. This is one of a webring of Romani sites.

- ♦ Learn about the Irish Travellers at these sites:

  - ♦ **Travellers' Heritage** (www.travellerheritage.ie/asp)

  - ♦ **Traveller Heritage** (http://www.travellerheritage.ie/asp/)

Hmong Genealogy

The Hmong people came to the United States from Laos at the end of the Vietnam War. The Hmong home page at www.hmongnet.org has culture, news, events, and general information. The Hmong Genealogy page (www.hmonggenealogy.com) has information as well.

Quaker and Huguenot Genealogy

- ♦ **Huguenot Genealogy - Who were the Huguenots?** (www.huguenottrails.com/who-were-the-huguenots.html) is a good reference source for the history of this group.

- ♦ **My Quaker Roots** (http://robt.shepherd.tripod.com/quaker1.html) is a personal site covering New England families of Maris, Palmerton, Jenkins, Smith, Nichols, Newlin, Rogers, Kinsey, Sherman, Palmer, Pugh, Fawkes, Mendenhall, and other Quakers.

- **The Huguenot Society of America**
  (http://huguenotsocietyofamerica.org) has a website; an e-mail
  newsletter is located at www.huguenotstreet.org.

- **The Quaker Collection** (http://freepages.genealogy.rootsweb
  .ancestry.com/ ~ jrichmon/qkrcoll/qkrcoll.htm) features a collection
  of Family Group Sheets on the founders of certain larger Quaker
  families.

- **The Quaker Corner** (www.rootsweb.ancestry.com/ ~ quakers/
  index.htm) has many resources for Quaker genealogical research.

Jewish Genealogy

The first site to visit for Jewish genealogy is **JewishGen.org**
(www.jewishgen.org). Mailing lists, transcribed records, GEDCOMs, and
more are at the site. You can also find links to special interest groups,
such as geographic emphasis or genetics. Your next stop should be **The
Israel GenWeb Project** website (www.israelgenealogy.com), which
serves as a resource to those researching their family history in Israel.

Sephardim Genealogy

Sephardim is a Hebrew word assigned to the Jews of Spain and Portugal.
They were at one time the largest minority on the Iberian Peninsula.
Late in the 15th century they were given the options of conversion,
death, or exile. **Sephardic Genealogy** (www.SephardicGen.com) has
links to articles and historical documents, as does **Sephardim.org**
(www.sephardim.org), which has an article on Jamaican-Jewish history.
Canadian-Jewish genealogists should begin at the **Jewish Genealogical
Society of Montreal** (www.jgs-montreal.org), which contains a history
of the first Jewish settlers there. Another site is **Etsi** (http://www.oocities
.com/etsi-sefarad/), a Sephardi Genealogical and Historical Society founded
in 1998 in Paris.

   **The Foundation for the Advancement of Sephardic Studies and
Culture** is at www.sephardicstudies.org. For nearly 40 years, the
foundation has been dedicated to preserving and promoting the
complex and centuries-old culture of the Sephardic communities of
Turkey, Greece, the Balkans, Europe, and the U.S. emigration, and the
devastation of the Holocaust.

Native American Genealogy

- **Indians/Native Americans** on NARA is a reference page with links to various government records resources. It can be found at www.archives.gov/research/alic/reference/native-americans.html. A good source on culture and heritage is a search engine called Native Languages of America, located at www.nativelanguages.org. The Congress of Aboriginal Peoples is a site that presents categorized links to Canadian aboriginal, Native American, and international indigenous sites on the Web. The genealogy page is at www.abo-peoples.org.

- **The African-Native American History & Genealogy** webpage (www.african-nativeamerican.com) is mostly concerned with the history of Oklahoma and surrounding areas.

- **Access Genealogy's Native American Genealogy** page, located at www.accessgenealogy.com/native, has transcribed records and a state-by-state list of online sites.

- **All Things Cherokee** is a site about many aspects of Cherokee culture, genealogy included. The genealogy page is at www.allthingscherokee.com/genealogy.html. All Things Cherokee started out as The Cherokee Genealogy Page and expanded, but genealogy is still a major emphasis.

- **The Potawatomi** has a site at www.potawatomi.org with a history of the tribe.

- **The Cheyenne Ancestors** (www.cheyenneancestors.com) is a site containing a database of some ancestors, a bibliography for further study, and Montana links.

Many other tribes also have sites. Simply use any search engine for the tribe name, plus the word "genealogy," and you'll likely get a hit.

Melungeon Genealogy

The origins of the people and even the name are controversial, but the Appalachian ethnic group called Melungeon seems to be of European, African, Mediterranean, and Native American descent. One legend is that Sir Francis Drake marooned Portuguese, Turkish, and Moorish prisoners on the North Carolina shore in the 1560s. Melungeons are documented as far back as 18th century in the Appalachian wilderness. They are found in the Cumberland Plateau area of Virginia, Kentucky, North Carolina, West Virginia, Tennessee, and, some argue, North Alabama.

A Success Story: Understanding Family Stories

"As the family story goes, there was a young girl, early teens, that came to live with the family," Russ Worthington, a genealogist who lives in New Jersey, said. "It was thought, by her features, that she was Native American. The woman of the house died several years after this young girl came into the house and the husband married the young girl. Her full name has yet to be found. Was she a Native American or not? A little research by the family indicated that this young lady may have been Melungeon. The family was living in the coal mining area in Tennessee. I had done some research about Melungeon and had read some articles from a couple of websites.

"Having participated in a Church Mission trip to the Appalachian area of Southwestern Virginia for a couple of summers, I came across a book called Do, Die, or Get Along – A Tale of Two Appalachian Towns *by Peter Crow (University of Georgia Press, 2007). It was specifically about the area where the Mission Trip was working on houses. Being interested in genealogy I was interested in the history of the area, trying to understand something about the culture of the families in whose houses we were working in. I started to read the book, and on page 2 I read:*

> It was just sort of an unspoken truth around here for years that these days, curly-haired, dark-skinned, olive-skinned children that came to school—every one of them has the same story: 'My grandmother was full-blooded Cherokee' … Where are these Cherokees? I've never seen one.

Russ said that finding this bit of information helped him understand the old family stories much better. So did these two sites:

- ◆ Melungeon Heritage website (www.melungeon.org)
- ◆ "Mixing in the Mountains" by John Shelton Reed (www.melungeon .org/node/262)

"Knowing that the area appears to be correct and my ancestors were in the coal mining area, the description was consistent, other family researchers and I agree that she was Melungeon. We are also aware that we may never find her complete name [or] date of birth. But reading about what Melungeon is and experiencing the culture [today] puts her family life into perspective.

"There are a number of authorities mentioned in *Do, Die, or Get Along*, most of whom have Melungeon blood lines. For the moment, I will leave this 'brick wall' standing, as I don't expect to find any more documentation. I can and have experienced a small piece of the environment [in which] this young lady lived," Russ concluded.

Melungeon genealogy took on new and exciting relevance with the publication of *The Melungeons: The Resurrection of a Proud People* by Dr. N. Brent Kennedy (Mercer University Press, 1997). One interesting theory in the book is that Abraham Lincoln bears the Melungeon characteristics of his mother, Nancy Hanks (see also "The Legend of a Mountain Girl and Her Baby" at www.melungeons.com/articles/mar2005.htm).

One of the best places to start is the Melungeon Heritage Association mentioned by Russ Worthington previously at www.melungeon.org.

The Melungeon Resource page includes a FAQ file, located at http://homepages.rootsweb.ancestry.com/ ~ mtnties/melungeon.html.

The Appalachian Mountain Families page includes information on Melungeons and is located at http://freepages.genealogy.rootsweb .ancestry.com/ ~ appalachian.

Some rare diseases are characteristic of Melungeons. **The Melungeon Health Education and Support Network** (www.melungeonhealth.org) describes some of these diseases and has links to resources about them.

Wrapping Up

- Many ethnic groups have started mailing lists, newsgroups, and history sites.

- Once a month, use your favorite search engine to find new sites.

- Stay on mailing lists to discuss your ethnic "brick walls."

Chapter 18

The National
Genealogical Society

The National Genealogical Society (NGS) is one of the most important genealogical societies in the United States. A service organization that leads and educates the national genealogical community and assists members in tracing family histories, it is more than 100 years old.

On its website (www.ngsgenealogy.org), you'll find announcements of NGS seminars, workshops, and programs; information on its home-study course; youth resources; and other NGS activities. This is an excellent site for learning genealogy standards and methods.

NGS was organized in Washington, D.C., in 1903. The preliminary first meeting was held on April 24, and the formal organization was effected on November 11. Now, the NGS has more than 17,000 members, including individuals, families, genealogical societies, family associations, libraries, and other related institutions.

National Genealogical Society

The NGS is one of the best broad-based organizations for family history. Its workshops, meetings, and publications are invaluable. You can see its home page in Figure 18-1.

On the home page, you'll find links to the newest and most relevant items on the site, including upcoming meetings, trips, courses, and competitions. You need to create a profile on your first visit. This is not the same as joining for $60 a year as an individual. It simply adds some cookies to your browser so that the site can show you where you've visited and where you haven't. The profile also lets you shop the NGS store for books, maps, courses, and membership. On every page of the site, you'll find a navigation bar at the top that leads to the following sections.

Note

It seems intuitive to use www.ngs.org as the Uniform Resource Locator (URL) for this organization, but the National Geographic Society got there first.

References for Researching

Some of the features in References for Researching are available to nonmembers. For example, you can learn how to interpret the information in certain records and put it together to draw a logical conclusion, record it so you know where it came from, and follow the

FIGURE 18-1. *The National Genealogical Society website has searchable data as well as information about the organization.*

next logical step to find more relevant information from their tutorials for beginners.

Nonmembers may also read selected NGS articles from the *NGS Quarterly*, *NGS Magazine*, or "UpFront with NGS."

NGS Standards and Guidelines is another section of this area. This has PDF files of the recommended set of Genealogical Standards and Guidelines for the benefit of those who wish to improve their skills and performance in genealogical pursuits. They are reproduced in this book in Appendix A by permission. Just reading these guidelines is a good primer in how to do family history the right way!

NGS Book Loan Collection, located at the St. Louis County Library (SLCL) in St. Louis, Missouri, has more than 20,000 books, and new

---

Some Membership Benefits

- **Family History Skills** Start your family history quest or brush up on genealogy basics by reviewing the free online course for members of the National Genealogical Society.

- **Member Periodicals** These include the *National Genealogical Society Quarterly* and the *NGS Magazine*. Members also have access to the "UpFront with NGS" blog.

- The **Members Only** section of the NGS site will give you access to:

    - Publication archives

    - National Genealogical Society Quarterly Index

    - NGS Magazine Online Recent issues (2005–current)

    - Database resources

    - NGS bible records

    - NGS Member Ancestry Charts (MACs)

    - Free research aids and forms

    - Research trips and discounts

---

titles are added almost daily. Nearly every book in this special collection is available for interlibrary loan to NGS members and nonmembers alike. Here you can find a link to the card catalog and instructions for getting a title through the interlibrary loan system.

This section also has a link to the requirements for the Boy Scouts of America Merit Badge in Genealogy (http://meritbadge.org/wiki/index.php/Genealogy).

Educational Courses

Free to NGS members, the online, self-paced, self-graded Family History Skills course is good for beginners or for those who need a refresher course. Other online courses cover population census records, special agricultural or mortality census schedules, deeds, and more, and range in price from free for members to $50 per course.

The famous NGS American Genealogy: Home Study Course is now on CD-ROM. Members and nonmembers can opt for the course to be self-graded or graded by a professional genealogist. You can buy the three-CD course one at a time for $85 or in bundles for as much as $565 (graded course, nonmember price).

Publications and Videos

Written and edited by leading experts in the genealogical field, NGS periodicals and books show you the best techniques to help you research and record your family history. The publications and videos cover the latest technology tools, case studies of how to solve a difficult research problem, and reference books on particular geographic areas. You can view for free the video "Paths to Your Past" in this section of the site (see Figure 18-2).

FIGURE 18-2.   *The 12-minute video "Paths to Your Past" is free on the NGS site.*

Conferences and Events

Many people first learn about the NGS as an organization at the conferences and events held around the country every year.

The NGS Family History Conference is the biggest event of the year for the society. Everyone from neophytes to those who want to become Certified Professional Genealogists will find something interesting at this conference. The location changes yearly, and fees range from $100 for one day to $275 for nonmembers for the whole conference. The 2011 NGS Family History Conference will be held in Charleston, South Carolina, May 11–14, 2011.

You can also sign up for a research trip where a professional genealogist leads a tour to help you research in the Family History Library in Salt Lake City. Two are held each year.

Family reunions and other genealogy groups also publicize their events on the NGS events calendar, so this is a place to bookmark for future reference.

Awards and Competitions

NGS awards are given each year at the annual conference. They are

- **Award of Honor** To recognize an individual or organization for dedicated and sustained service in support of an NGS Family History Conference.

- **Award of Merit** To recognize exceptional contributions to the field of genealogy by an individual or nonprofit genealogical or historical organization over a period of five years or more.

- **Certificate of Appreciation** To recognize an individual or organization for service during an NGS conference. A nominee need not be a member of NGS. This award may be presented to an individual or institution more than once.

- **Distinguished Service Award** To recognize outstanding contributions to the work of NGS. A nominee must have been a member of NGS for at least one year.

- **Fellow of the National Genealogical Society (FNGS)** To recognize outstanding work in the field of genealogy or the related fields of history, biography, or heraldry, in addition to outstanding service to the National Genealogical Society.

Several competitions such as the Family History Writing Contest and scholarships for students and adults are also outlined in this section.

About NGS and Become a Member

These two sections are self-explanatory. Here you can learn all about the benefits of membership, how to attend courses and events even if you are not a member, and sign up to join. You can also shop the store from these sections.

Members Only

This section is where you can actually research your genealogy on this site. As mentioned before, you can access the Family History Skills course from here to start your family history quest or brush up on genealogy basics, and get in-depth searches of the publication archives of National Genealogical Society Quarterly Online, as well as other publications.

This area also has some excellent databases not available anywhere else.

Database Resources

- ♦ **The National Intelligencer, 1800–1850**   Abstracts from *The National Intelligencer* (Washington, D.C.), 1800–1850, fully indexed marriage and death notices from this early newspaper. The name index is fully searchable, including assistance with name variations and misspelled names.

- ♦ **NGS Member Ancestry Charts (MACs)**   This massive collection of Family Group Sheets sent in by NGS members since the 1960s is being indexed and digitized. A full abstract of all (1,000,000+) names on every MAC, along with dates and places, has been completed for more than 66,000 MACs sent in before 1995. Work continues on MACs received since then.

- ♦ **NGS Bible Records**   The NGS Bible Records collection is currently being indexed and digitized. A large percentage of the Bibles, but not all, have an every-name index. The index to the database is fully searchable. Images of most of the Bible pages have been scanned and are available for download in PDF format.

- ♦ **Research Resources**   Research aids and forms, available free to members, include handy forms such as census and will abstract worksheets. They are from *The Organized Family Historian: How to File, Manage, and Protect Your Genealogical Research and Heirlooms*, by Ann Carter Fleming, CG, CGL, FNGS (Thomas Nelson, 2004).

- **Research Forums**   This includes topics on British Isles and Irish, Central European, German, Italian, Polish, and Scandinavian genealogy.

- **Partnership Discounts**   These include a 10 percent tuition discount for NGS members who enroll in the online Boston University Certificate in Genealogical Research Program. Members are also entitled to discounted pricing for conferences and events, research trips, the NGS online store, and the AMA deceased physician research database.

Glossary

This excellent glossary of genealogy terms is an important resource for members. From incomprehensible ancient abbreviations to what "third cousin" really means, you can learn a lot from this page.

My Account, My Orders, and My Downloadable Products

Whenever you order from the website, whether a member or not, the transactions are stored here. This is one reason to fill out the registration when you first visit the site so that you can trace your activity later.

Wrapping Up

- The NGS is a broad-based American institution for education and resources in genealogy.

- You can take online and at-home genealogy courses from NGS, take research trips, and attend NGS conferences to learn about genealogy.

- Certain databases can be searched online at the site by members; you can also pay a fee to have NGS staffers do the research for you.

Chapter 19

Ancestry.com and RootsWeb

The Ancestry.com family of sites and products is a collection of billions of historical records they have digitized, indexed, and put online over the past 12 years, available by subscription and through libraries around the world. The company developed their own systems for digitizing handwritten historical documents, and established relationships with national, state, and local government archives, historical societies, religious institutions, and private collectors of historical content around the world to build this collection. The records and documents, combined with their Web-based online search technologies and software, let subscribers research family history, build family trees, and use the Ancestry.com sites for social networking.

> ### Note
>
> *Follow Ancestry.com on Facebook at www.facebook.com/Ancestry .com?ref = ss and on Twitter at www.twitter.com/Ancestrydotcom.*

RootsWeb, the oldest online genealogy community, is part of the system. Ancestry.com at first had only one site and then merged with RootsWeb. Then it launched MyFamily.com and renamed itself after that service. Once the company absorbed Genealogy.com and Family Tree Maker genealogy software and expanded worldwide, the name was changed to The Generations Network, Inc. Then the company went public in 2009 and changed its name back to Ancestry.com. All the divisions together receive 10.4 million unique visitors worldwide and more than 450 million page views a month.

You can do some things for free, but fees apply for certain searches, some levels of disk space, and some other services.

Ancestry.com publishes books, magazines, and other genealogy materials, and has subscription-based research materials on their website, with mostly U.S. material. *Genealogical Computing* magazine covers technology issues and breakthroughs in genealogy; *Ancestry* magazine covers general topics, such as research techniques, success stories, and historical topics. *Ancestry's Red Book: American State, County, and Town Sources* by Alice Eichholz (Ancestry Publishing, 2004), *Finding Answers in U.S. Census Records* by Loretto Dennis Szucs and Matthew Wright (Ancestry Publishing, 2001), and *The Source: A Guidebook of American Genealogy* edited by Loretto Dennis Szucs and Sandra Hargreaves Luebking (Ancestry Publishing, 2006) are just three of the well-respected publications under the Ancestry.com imprint.

Ancestry.com

With sites around the world, you can research and build a family tree searching the databases at Ancestry.com and use the online tools to organize and share your story with other family members. Ancestry.com, MyFamily.com, and Genealogy.com are based in the United States. Ancestry.com.uk, Ancestry.com.ca, Ancestry.com.au, Ancestry.de, and Ancestry.it, the divisions in the UK, Canada, Australia, Germany, and Italy, respectively, all work basically the same as the one in the United States, and you can receive access to each part of the empire individually or, with a mega-membership, the whole enchilada!

Ancestry.com Family Tree Maker

Ancestry.com Family Tree Maker 2009 works with Ancestry.com to help you research and save data on your own computer, as well as upload it to the Ancestry.com site.

Ancestry.com DNA

Your DNA can tell you some surprising things about your heritage. You swab your cheek and mail it in. The resulting report from Ancestry.com DNA tells you about your ancient ancestry. Your DNA could also connect you with genetic cousins you never knew you had. Using this service, you can trace mother's heritage with MtDNA and your father's heritagewith YDNA. The maternal line of DNA can go back 50,000 years, but these results are not as useful for beginners. The paternal report can trace 33 markers on the DNA for $149 or 45 markers for $179. How many times the markers repeat will tell you who has the same number of repetitive sequences at the same location, meaning those who are more closely related to you.

RootsWeb

RootsWeb is the oldest and largest *free* online community dedicated to family history. You'll find millions of members communicating on thousands of message boards in this expansive environment for learning, collaborating, and sharing with others. The URL is http://Rootsweb .ancestry.com.

Blogs to Watch

Want to keep up with the latest in the Ancestry.com world? Check out these blogs:

♦ Ancestry.com Blog (http://blogs.ancestry.com)

♦ Ancestry.com DNA Blog (http://blogs.ancestry.com/ancestry/category/products/dna)

♦ MyCanvas Blog (http://blogs.ancestry.com/ancestry/category/products/mycanvas)

♦ MyFamily.com Blog (http://blog.myfamily.com)

♦ Ancestry.com Family Tree Maker Blog (http://blogs.ancestry.com/ancestry/category/products/ftm)

MyCanvas

MyCanvas.com lets you upload photos to share by creating books, posters, and more. It has helpful templates as well as online tools to create a project from scratch.

MyFamily.com

MyFamily.com is social networking with a family emphasis. Create your own family website and use it to share photos, news, recipes, calendars, and much more.

Ancestry.com

Ancestry.com has two parts. The research side has databases of transcribed and secondary material, much of which is accessible for a fee. The exchange side includes uploaded GEDCOMs, messages boards, and original articles on genealogy, all of which are accessible for free. Features include the following:

♦ **Name-indexed GEDCOM databases** are updated frequently, so future searches may turn up what today's search did not.

♦ **Regular genealogy columns** by writers such as George G. Morgan, Dick Eastman, Kip Sperry, Juliana Smith, Elizabeth Kelley Kerstens, and Drew Smith are available free of charge.

Anastasia Tyler, a genealogist at Ancestry.com, says getting started in genealogy on the site is easy.

"For beginners we suggest they start by beginning a tree on Ancestry.com," she said, "because it is free. You start with what you know, you invite family members to look at the tree, coordinate and corroborate, upload photos, stories and sources, all for free. With that information in the tree, you can search for the information in the paid databases. You can find military records, vital records, SSDI, newspaper articles and more. Also beginners can learn in the message boards, and connect to other people searching the same lines."

Social networking is very much a part of Ancestry.com's updated site (see Figure 19-1).

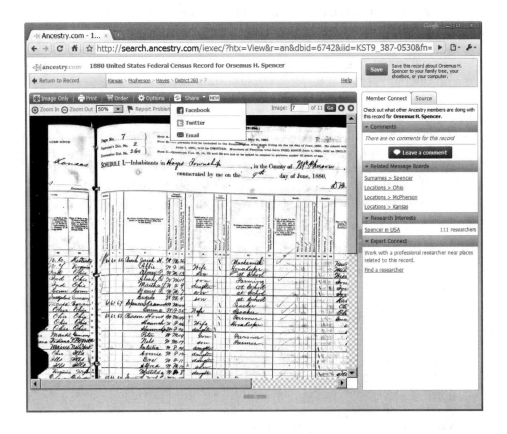

FIGURE 19-1. *Share Ancestry.com records via Facebook, Twitter, and e-mail from the content viewer by going to the Share tab and selecting Facebook, Twitter, or E-mail from the drop-down menu.*

"We have launched a new tool that people can use to share what [they] find with Facebook and other social networking sites," Anastasia said. "You and I look on the family tree, get a hit on another line and connect trees. You can share daily finds from the record page by clicking on the 'Share this record' link in the Page Tools section. Then select Facebook, Twitter or Email from the drop-down menu, login if needed, enter a personalized message and submit. Your friends do not need to be registered with or subscribed to Ancestry or RootsWeb to see the images that you share. You can try this by sharing a record, then logging out of Ancestry, and click through on the link to see what happens!"

Networking to help find records and people in the community is an important part of Ancestry.com in all countries because there are more than three million active users. Not all of the lines are completed, of course, but you can collaborate with others quickly and easily. In addition, Anastasia said, the community initiatives and structured index of names means every record will be indexed and searchable eventually. Ancestry.com has a partnership with the Society of Genealogy Alliance members to create indexes so that searching them is free (see the accompanying box).

New to Ancestry since the last edition of this book are the Family Tree, multiperson search, and the ability to search Ancestry.com for a specific ancestor. Siblings to parents options in the person view will triangulate records in the person search, which gives you some interesting results.

"We have several tools in the Learning Center," Anastasia said. "Look under Get Started. We have Webinars and online seminars that can help people get started. We have other websites about products and services, too."

You also want to make use of the Ancestry.com blogs. Here, new features are often discussed before launch, as is information on the latest articles in *Ancestry* magazine. You can pose questions to the Ancestry experts on how to best search the records and use them. See the accompanying box for a list of some of the indexes.

A large online genealogy library is searchable from the Web. The library includes such records as land, birth, marriage, death, census, and immigration records, as well as the Periodical Source Index (PERSI), Daughters of the American Revolution Lineage Books, the 1990 Census Collection, and the Early American Marriages Collection, to name just a few. Of note is the recent addition of the *London Times* (editions from 1986 to 1833) and the UK Census of 1891, with every name indexed for both.

Free Indexes

Indexes created through the Ancestry.com World Archives Project are free for all Ancestry.com users once complete. Here's a partial list of World Archives Project indexes:

- **England and Wales Criminal Registers** http://search.ancestry.com/iexec/?htx = List&dbid = 1590&offerid = 0%3a7858%3a0

- **Lubeck, Germany, Marriage Banns** http://search.ancestry.com/iexec/?htx = List&dbid = 1567&offerid = 0%3a7858%3a0

- **Ontario Marriage Registers** http://search.ancestry.com/iexec/?htx = List&dbid = 1584&offerid = 0%3a7858%3a0

Most foreign-language databases have index fields translated into English, as in the headings for Name, Date, and Location. However, the indexes are created in the language that the record was written in.

I think the card catalog is a great tool for beginners who are looking for international records. To get there, use the Search menu to get to the card catalog. You can drill down in the card catalog, for example, by selecting Marriage | Illinois | 1860s.

People who have the World Deluxe subscription can get records on all international sites. You can search England for emigration records, for example. Again, using the card catalog to see if the records exist can be a big help. However, remember that if record is in Italian, for example, it will not be translated into English; only the index fields such as date and location will be translated.

Tools to Use

The easiest way to use Ancestry is to just type a name in the search box. When you type a name in the search fields, some of the resulting links will be to the fee-based areas, as described earlier.

For example, when I put in my husband's grandfather, Thomas Wayne Crowe, with birth and death dates, the website quickly had a suggested historical record to attach to his entry, the Kentucky Death Records. Searching more brought up Thomas Wayne in the 1910 Census at age two.

> ## Note
>
> *You also might want to check out the software Ancestry Family Tree. You can load your GEDCOM into it, and it will search all the Ancestry.com databases (GEDCOMs) for matches.*

Ancestry.com also automatically searches for matches to each name in your database within other uploaded genealogies. You can add names, dates, and places as you find them; add sources and connect specific facts to them; and handle divorces and other records.

Other good links in the free area include articles on genealogy techniques, genealogy lessons, phone and address searches, Juliana's Links, a searchable database of websites, and maps and gazetteers. The site also features a chat area, bookstore, and sample articles from the print version of *Ancestry* magazine.

Member Connect is a feature that lets you contact people searching the same names, dates, and locations as you are. Used with the message boards and the member directory, this is a good way to find those distant cousins!

The Ancestry toolbar, an addition to your browser, helps you search Ancestry.com from other websites. For example, if you found an interesting bit of data on a RootsWeb personal page, you can search for the name and date in the Ancestry collection to find the original records for that data

You can also save and attach photos to people in your tree from any webpage; save text from the webpage to your tree as a story; save online links to keep a permanent record of where you got your data; access all of your Ancestry Quicklinks instantly; access your family tree on Ancestry instantly; and conduct an Ancestry-specific search powered by Google.

> ## Caution
>
> *Please note you are responsible for copyright permissions, not Ancestry.com.*

The Ancestry toolbar requires Windows XP/2000/Vista, Internet Explorer version 6 or 7, or Firefox 2 or higher. As of this writing, it does not work with Google Chrome.

You can use it while looking at your Ancestry family tree—while viewing a person in your tree, you'll notice a Search The Web link in the Web Links section. Clicking this will open a new window showing the results of a Google-powered online search for that person's name.

Or, if you are searching the Web for new information, the Ancestry toolbar appears at the top of your Internet browser and gives you the choice of two different searches from a drop-down menu. The default search allows a search on Ancestry only for a name using Google. To search the entire Internet, click the arrow to the right of the search field and select Search The Web (Google).

The OneWorldTree (www.ancestry.com/search/rectype/trees/owt) is a collection of GEDCOMS. Begin to type in the name of someone in your tree, and the Ancestry.com software will fill in the data you have on vital statistics, family members, etc. Then you will get a list of GEDCOM pages that match your input in whole or in part. You can e-mail the submitters to start swapping data!

OneWorldTree takes GEDCOMs submitted by Ancestry members from all over the world and connects them with family trees and historical records from other sources. OneWorldTree identifies probable name matches between these sources and displays consolidated results in a worldwide family tree that can help you with your family history research.

Remember, though, that this is all submitted material from volunteers. OneWorldTree can give you *hints* about your family history. Be careful about accepting what you find there as proven fact. Now and then, the computer algorithms in OneWorldTree can incorrectly link people with similar names. Furthermore, some submitted trees have errors; one that consistently comes up in my searches has my father's death date off by one day. Your family tree in OneWorldTree will always show the information you originally entered, and you can attach the data in other trees or not as you choose.

In addition to the community tree, OneWorldTree maintains the original family trees and source records as submitted. So when you look at the original source information for any person in a tree on the Edit Person page, you can use the Connection Service to anonymously contact the Ancestry member who submitted that family tree or record.

Certain information is never shared. OneWorldTree never shares information about living family members born after 1930. Any information in your family tree regarding living people born after 1930 will show up on your personal family tree but will remain hidden from other Ancestry members.

The Ancestry iPhone App lets you edit, add photos, and so forth from your iPhone. So if you discover a treasure trove of family heirlooms at your second cousin's house, you can take pictures and upload them to your tree with stories about each one. When you find a family member's headstone in a forgotten cemetery, you can add this new person and upload an image of the gravesite. Or you can take a picture of your great-great-grandfather's homestead and attach it to his file in your tree. Figure 19-2 shows how the app looks in your phone.

Costs

Ancestry.com's various levels of free and pay areas can be confusing. You can choose from several different levels of subscription to the site.

FIGURE 19-2. *Use Ancestry.com on the fly from your iPhone.*

Ancestry.com free services allow you to create an online family tree, upload family photos, create life timelines for each person in your tree, and share the tree with family members. In addition, those you invite to see your family tree on Ancestry.com will have full access to the family history records, photos, and more attached to that tree, much like having friends on MySpace or Facebook. The free services also provide access to the Ancestry.com message boards (which were RootsWeb message boards before the merger), where members can seek help, swap family stories, and receive answers to questions.

Free membership also includes the Ancestry Learning Center—virtual classrooms where you can learn about using the many resources on Ancestry.com. In fact, if you are new to genealogy, be sure to use the Learn tab in the navigation bar, where you will find links to beginner's guides on topics such as searching newspapers and periodicals and African-American family history. The guides are easy to understand and point you to specific Ancestry.com databases, saving you time and possibly money. Members can also sign up for the free weekly and monthly newsletters published by Ancestry.com, a good way to stay informed on the latest additions to the databases.

Family Trees & Connections Membership

This membership lets you search all the submitted genealogies (GEDCOMs) on Ancestry.com. At this level, you can communicate privately and anonymously with other members that have similar interests.

U.S. Deluxe

This membership adds access to all the U.S. records, which include census records; family and local histories; birth, marriage, and death records; member trees' immigration records; maps and photos; court, land, and probate records; directories; historical newspapers; and military records. You can test-drive the U.S. Deluxe package with a 14-day free trial, and find it at most public libraries.

World Deluxe

This membership offers unlimited access to everything in the U.S. Deluxe Membership and includes Ancestry.com's entire global collection. Historical documents, records, and newspapers from the United Kingdom, Canada, Ireland, and many other locations around the globe are available.

Is a membership worthwhile? If you only watched one movie a month, a premium movie channel would not be a good buy. If you have a 60-inch screen and your own popcorn machine because movies are your favorite thing to do, then a premium movie channel would save you money over going to the theater or buying individual pay-per-view movies. Ancestry is the same: If you have been seriously bitten by the genealogy bug, you will use it so much you will wonder how people ever found records without it. If you just wonder who your great-grandparents are, then don't get your own subscription. Use Ancestry at the local library or your local Family History Center on those rare occasions when you feel like doing some research.

Success Story: Smashing a Brick Wall

I smashed a brick wall recently using Ancestry.com. I have a basic subscription to Ancestry. There has been a story in my husband's family for as long as anyone can remember that the name Flynt isn't really the family surname, that it is really Damon. No one knew any more than that. Ancestry.com put an index to Maine court records online. I did a search for the great-great grandfather Daniel Flint/Flynt. I was rewarded with "Daniel Flint (Alias)." I copied down the book and page numbers, and contacted the State of Maine Archives for copies of the court records. The records showed a conviction for bigamy and included marriage records for the first marriage as Delafayette Damon to Esther Damon in Reading, Massachusetts, in 1805 and his second, unlawful marriage as Daniel Flint to Lydia Anne Williams in Farmington, Maine, in 1812. He appealed the conviction on the grounds that the first marriage took place in Massachusetts and Maine didn't have jurisdiction. He was granted a new trial, but the attorney general didn't pursue the matter, and Daniel Flint went home to Abbot, Maine, to raise his second family, from which my husband was descended. With this information, I was able to find his ancestors through his mother back to Thomas Flint, one of the early settlers of Reading, Massachusetts, and his first wife's family, as well as their three children. This has all been from secondary sources and not yet proved, but at least now I know where to look for proof.

—Alta Flynt

RootsWeb

How would you like a place where you can search dozens of databases of genealogical materials, look through hundreds of genealogical webpages, and subscribe to thousands of mailing lists? How about a place where you can publish your own page, upload your own data, and create your own mailing list? And all for free!

> ### Note
> *www.rootsweb.com and www.rootsweb.org take you to the same site: www.rootsweb.ancestry.com.*

Welcome to RootsWeb (www.rootsweb.org). Once upon a time, RootsWeb was a site for a group of people working at the research center RAND who dabbled in genealogy on the side and had a club for family history. They had a little mailing list, hosted by the University of Minnesota, and a little database on the RAND server for their club. That was 20 years ago. Today, RootsWeb is the largest all-volunteer genealogy site on the Web.

RootsWeb started and continues as a volunteer effort. But the costs of servers, disk space, and connections got so high that what was once a little club of genealogy enthusiasts that worked together merged with Ancestry.com. This means two things: First, people were no longer asked to contribute $25 a year to RootsWeb to help defray the costs the volunteers were incurring. Ancestry.com now subsidizes the hardware and software to keep RootsWeb up and running. Second, almost all of the secondary information is free, but some of the primary-source evidence is on Ancestry's site, and you have to subscribe to access it or use your local library's subscription. It's not a completely black-and-white situation; there are still plenty of transcribing projects that are free to access, such as ships' passenger lists, census transcriptions, and so on. And Ancestry.com hosts some of the free stuff, such as the message boards. For the RootsWeb user, little has really changed except the format.

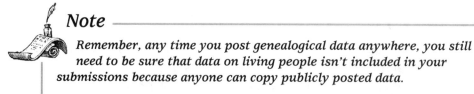

Note

Remember, any time you post genealogical data anywhere, you still need to be sure that data on living people isn't included in your submissions because anyone can copy publicly posted data.

The mission of RootsWeb is summed up in the following statement, published on its home page: "The RootsWeb project has two missions: To make large volumes of data available to the online genealogical community at minimal cost. To provide support services to online genealogical activities, such as Usenet newsgroup moderation, mailing list maintenance, surname list generation, and so forth."

A quick guided tour of RootsWeb only scratches the surface of all the helpful and informative services available on this site. The following story gives you an idea of the unique possibilities RootsWeb offers.

Success Story: RootsWeb Leads to a Reunion

About three years ago, I started searching for my Powell ancestors on my father's side, but about the only thing I knew how to do was search the surname and message boards. One night, after having done nothing in about two months, I decided to get online and read the [RootsWeb] surname message boards. On a whim, I went into the Hubbard message boards on my mother's side.

The first message I read was about someone searching for descendants of my grandmother's parents. When my grandmother was about three or four, her mother passed away and she went to live with an aunt and uncle. Eventually, my grandmother lost contact with her brothers. She did see her oldest brother once when she was about 15, but after that she never saw or heard from him again. That night, I found him—a person my grandmother had not seen in over 70 years. We flew to Washington State and met all kinds of new cousins, aunts, and uncles. Over the next two years, my grandmother spoke with her brother many times.

We figured out that the message I responded to had been posted for about a minute before I discovered it. The surname message boards are a wonderful tool in searching for the ancestors and relatives you never knew you had, or those you had but didn't know who they were.

—Jennifer Powell Lyons

Digging in RootsWeb

RootsWeb has more genealogical information than you can shake a stick at. Some of this is secondary-source information, such as the genealogy databases (GEDCOMs) members have submitted. Some of this information is close to primary-source information, though still derivative—for example, transcripts of wills, deeds, census forms, and vital records, with citations of where exactly the original information can be found. Some of it is primary information (for example, Ancestry.com's census images), and you have to pay a subscription fee to Ancestry.com to access that information.

At the top of all RootsWeb pages, you'll see a navigation bar with these categories: Home, Searches, Family Trees, Mailing Lists, Message Boards, Web Sites, Passwords, and Help. Home and Help are self-explanatory, and the following text explains Searches, Family Trees, Mailing Lists, Message Boards, and Web Sites.

The Passwords link displays a Help page for retrieving lost passwords to mailing lists and websites. When you look at the RootsWeb home page in your browser, you'll find two search templates to input a surname, first name, or any keywords. One searches RootsWeb's free information; the other searches Ancestry.com, and the results may be in the free area or in the subscription-only area. The search will look in all the RootsWeb pages or Ancestry.com databases and show you the results. It's a great way to get started on your genealogy!

Finding information on RootsWeb can be that simple. However, you can use many different tools on the site to get more targeted results.

Getting Started at RootsWeb

On the Home page index is a section called "Getting Started." The sections there—Getting Started at RootsWeb, Ancestry Tour, RootsWeb's Guide to Tracing Family Trees, RootsWeb Review Archives | Subscribe, and What's New—will give the beginner a good grounding in RootsWeb. Getting Started at RootsWeb is a short page on how to share, communicate, research, and volunteer with the site. Ancestry Tour is a multimedia overview of what the commercial side offers. RootsWeb's Guide to Tracing Family Trees is really a collection of guides sorted by general genealogy, sources, and countries. What's New lists the newest additions to the pages and databases on the volunteer side, and subscribing to RootsWeb Review will bring the same information to your e-mail inbox.

Available Files and Databases

ROOTS-L has tons of files and databases, which you can get access to by e-mailing the appropriate commands to the list server that runs ROOTS-L. You can search the ROOTS-L library for everything from a fabulous collection devoted to obtaining vital records, to useful tips for beginners, to book lists from the Library of Congress, and more. Some of the available files include

♦ **Surname Helper** (http://surhelp.rootsweb.com)   Looks at the RootsWeb message boards and personal websites.

♦ **U.S. Town/County Database** (http://resources.rootsweb.com/cgi-bin/townco.cgi)   Looks for locations. It's a sort of online gazetteer.

♦ **The WorldConnect Project** (http://worldconnect.rootsweb.com) Searches GEDCOMs of family trees submitted by RootsWeb members.

♦ **The USGenWeb Archives Search** (www.usgenweb.org)   Looks for pages posted across the United States in the GenWeb Project.

♦ **WorldGenWeb** (www.worldgenweb.org)   Searches for genealogy resources in nations outside the United States.

♦ **RootsWeb Surname List**   The RootsWeb Surname List (RSL), located at http://rsl.rootsweb.com, is a registry of who is searching for whom and in what times and places. The listings include contact information for each entry. When you find someone looking for the same name, in the same area, and in about the same time period, you might be able to help each other. That's the intent of the list. You don't have to pay to submit your own data or to search for data. To search the list, you can use the form on the search page or go to the page http://rsl.rootsweb.com.

♦ **WorldConnect Project**   The WorldConnect Project is one of several GEDCOMs databases on the web. When searching it from the RootsWeb home page, you can only input first and last names. The results page has another input form at the bottom, enabling you to fine-tune the search by adding places and dates. If you go to the WorldConnect page at http://worldconnect.rootsweb.com, you can find links to tips and hints for using the site. Remember, all the data here is uploaded by volunteers, so errors might exist!

- ◆ **Social Security Death Index** The Social Security Death Index (SSDI), located at http://ssdi.rootsweb.com, searches the federal records of deaths. Anyone who died before Social Security began in the 1930s won't be in this database. When searching from the RootsWeb home page, all you can input is the first and last name, but the results page will let you link to the Advanced Search page, where you can narrow the search by location and date. This is an excellent tool for researching 20th-century ancestors.

- ◆ **GenSeeker** GenSeeker looks for your search terms on the thousands of personal genealogy webpages at RootsWeb, plus any other registered documents, such as records transcriptions. You can also perform Boolean searches.

Other Search Engines

RootsWeb has several other ways for you to search both the site and the Web at large. Search Thingy (http://sitesearch.rootsweb.com/ cgi-bin/search) looks at all the databases and text files, and MetaSearch (http://resources.rootsweb.com/cgi-bin/metasearch) looks for names across RootsWeb. The Surnames search index, United States Counties/ States index, and the Countries index all search different subsets of RootsWeb information. All of these are worth looking at, and all can be accessed from http://searches.rootsweb.com.

These searches can be helpful in your research, but they assume you're a rank beginner with no more than a name or a place to launch your inquiries. Perhaps you know for sure that you're looking for a land record in Alabama or a cemetery in Iowa. RootsWeb has several searchable resources for items such as these. You'll find the search engines for the RSL and the other databases at http://searches.rootsweb.ancestry.com.

Research Templates

This collection of links from the home page index will lead you to lists of pages for different subjects. The surname list, for example, leads you first to an alphabetical list, then to all surnames under a certain letter, then to a page for a specific surname. Other research templates are for geographic locations, such as states in the United States or a whole country, such as France.

Message Boards and Mailing Lists

Among the best resources on RootsWeb are the mailing lists and message boards, now hosted on Ancestry.com. A message board is a place where messages are read, sent, and answered on the Web, using a browser. A mailing list is where messages are e-mailed to and from the members, using a mail client.

Click the bottom of any message board's page to read the frequently asked questions (FAQs), request a new board, read the rules, or get help. The mailing lists, located at http://lists.rootsweb.com, cover many topics, such as the RootsWeb newsletters, described later in this chapter. Lists exist for specific surnames, every state in the United States, other countries (from Aruba to Zimbabwe), and topics such as adoption, medical genealogy, prisons, and heraldry. From the Mailing Lists page, you can click a link to each one, and you'll get instructions on how to use the list, including subscribing, unsubscribing, sticking to the topic, and so on.

Besides ROOTS-L, which is the grandparent of genealogy mailing lists on the Internet, RootsWeb hosts literally thousands of mailing lists. As mentioned in Chapter 8, you can find lists for surnames and family names, regions, and topics being researched. The index, located at www.rootsweb.com/~maillist, has thousands of lists you can join, along with instructions explaining how to subscribe. It won't include all the mailing lists at RootsWeb, however, because it's a voluntary listing and not all list owners agree to be listed here.

A good rule of thumb: Be choosy in joining lists! Take on only a few at a time. Read the lists for a while, sign off if they don't prove useful, and then try some others. Some lists are extremely active—sometimes overwhelmingly so. One RootsWeb user who signed up for every possible mailing list for the United Kingdom had 9,000 e-mails in his inbox within 24 hours! Be careful what you wish for...

And remember, some lists are archived, so you needn't subscribe to see if that list is talking about subjects of interest to you. Just search the archive for your keywords, and save the important messages. You might even want to start a mailing list of your own someday, which contributors can do. You can learn more about what's required of a list owner by going to the Help page and clicking the Request A Mailing List link or by going to http://resources.rootsweb.com/adopt.

Gen-Newbie

Gen-Newbie located at www.rootsweb.ancestry.com/ ~ newbie, is a mailing list for people who are new to computers and/or genealogy. It is the place to ask questions, help others, and generally share information, research techniques, brick walls, and computer/genealogy woes. It began on October 31, 1996, as an offshoot of the renowned ROOTS-L. Subscribing is as simple as clicking one of the buttons at the bottom of the page at www.rootsweb.com/ ~ newbie. The Gen-Newbie archives include a six-part course in genealogy by Jean Legreid, a Certified Genealogical Records Specialist.

GENMTD-L

Genealogical methods and resources are the topics for GENMTD-L at www.rootsweb.ancestry.com/ ~ genmtd. This isn't a queries list. Instead, it's a list about the nuts and bolts of genealogy research. You can participate through e-mail or through Usenet news. The discussions are archived, searchable, and retrievable.

GENMTD-L is a moderated group intended for helpful discussions on the research methods, resources, and problems genealogists have in common, regardless of the different families or different cultural groups they study. The exception is methods relating to computing, databases, and online research. Often, a problem is presented to the group, which then discusses possible solutions. Also, useful research strategies and resources might be posted.

Newsletters

A newsletter, like a mailing list, comes straight to your e-mail inbox. Unlike the lists discussed previously, however, they are not for discussion; the communication is one-to-many. Like a print magazine, a newsletter will have news, notes, stories, and the occasional (text) advertisement. RootsWeb has several e-mail newsletters, all of which are worth reading. Here are some descriptions of them.

RootsWeb Review

RootsWeb is always growing, and you can't depend on luck to find out about the latest and greatest sites! *RootsWeb Review* is a free weekly newsletter sent to subscribers with news about RootsWeb. You'll find announcements of programs and services for RootsWeb users, new mailing lists, GenConnect boards, and websites, plus success stories from other online genealogists.

If you're interested in reading through previous issues, you can click the Archives link (http://rwr.rootsweb.ancestry.com).

Webpages at RootsWeb

RootsWeb hosts thousands of genealogy websites. Some, such as the USGenWeb Project's main site at www.usgenweb.com, you've already read about in this book. RootsWeb also hosts the WorldGenWeb Project at www.worldgenweb.org and a majority of the country sites.

RootsWeb-Sponsored Pages

Books We Own (www.rootsweb.ancestry.com/~bwo) is a list of resources owned and accessed by volunteers who are willing to look up genealogical information and then e-mail or snail mail it to others who request it. It works like a worldwide research library, where your shelf of genealogy books is one branch and you're one librarian of thousands. This is a volunteer service, and participants might ask for reimbursement of copies and postage if information is provided via snail mail. The project began in 1996 as a way for members of the ROOTS-L mailing list to share their resources with one another, and now some 1,500 people are involved.

FreeBMD (England and Wales), located at www.freebmd.org.uk, stands for Free Births, Marriages, and Deaths. The FreeBMD Project's objective is to provide free Internet access to the Civil Registration index information for England and Wales. The Civil Registration system for recording births, marriages, and deaths in England and Wales has been in place since 1837. This is one of the most significant single resources for genealogical research back to Victorian times.

Immigrant Ships Transcribers Guild (www.immigrantships.net) is a group of volunteers dedicated to making the search for our ancestors' immigration easier. The aim is to make as many ships' passenger lists as possible available online—and not just for U.S. ports. There are databases for Australia, Canada, Irish passengers to Argentina, and more. This group would also be happy to have your help!

Random Acts of Genealogical Kindness (www.raogk.org) is a cooperative effort. Once a month, the volunteers of this movement agree either to videotape cemeteries or to visit county courthouses in the county (or an area of a country) they live in to transcribe records. The cost to you would be reimbursement of costs incurred in granting your request (videotape, copying fees, and so forth).

State Resource Pages, one of the main areas of RootsWeb, is at www.rootsweb.ancestry.com/roots-l/usa.html. It offers a wealth of information to those researching in the United States.

Freepages are genealogy pages by volunteers. These pages must fit the RootsWeb mission; cannot contain copyrighted, commercial, or multimedia material; and cannot redirect to another site. If you meet these and all the other rules stated on http://accounts.rootsweb.ancestry .com, you can have free Web space at RootsWeb. The freepages include sites of major RootsWeb projects, such as USGenWeb and WorldGenWeb, as well as genealogical or historical organizations.

You can find kids' pages, lessons and help pages, memorials, and timelines among these pages. If you already have a genealogy-related website and want it linked from RootsWeb, you can register it as well.

The Help Desk

The Help Desk (http://helpdesk.rootsweb.com) maintains a page to help you find a FAQ file about RootsWeb and its services. If you have a question or problem, check here first. If you can't find an answer here, you can follow the links from this site to the message board, where you can post a question for the Help Desk team to answer. This quick tour is just enough to whet your appetite, but isn't even half of what's there. Spend some time getting to know RootsWeb.

MyFamily.com

MyFamily.com is a password-protected online community—a sort of MySpace for families. With a MyFamily site, you can post news, create albums and calendars, upload video and sound files, and allow your family members to access it all with a password. The site lets you save addresses and phone numbers in an online address book. Members use MyFamily to stay in contact and to keep track of birthdays, anniversaries, and other important dates in a shared calendar.

One of the most popular uses is to collaboratively work on the family tree with data input and GEDCOM uploads. Plus, you can use the disk space to upload images of your source documentation. In other words, this is a way to back up your work, which you should be doing at least monthly.

Genealogy.com

Genealogy.com has many of the features of Ancestry.com, just not quite so many records.

Go to Step 1, the First Steps Pages, at www.genealogy.com/fslanding .html, to get a good roadmap of the best way to traverse genealogy.com. You can

- **Start your first family tree**   Create and preserve your family legacy by entering a few simple facts about you and your family. The site will show you how to dig deeper into your family's past.

- **Search for more information**   This includes ancestors on the Internet and the site's data collections for data relevant to your family tree.

- **Create a personal home page**   This lets you safely store family trees, pictures, reports, and more for friends and family to view at their leisure. It's a great way to share your family story.

- **Add your voice to the message boards**   Join the largest online genealogy community. Scan the numerous topics being discussed, or post your own questions or comments. You're sure to find someone to lend their support and share their experiences.

- **Step-by-step instructions**   These make it easy for you to continue creating your family legacy.

- **Record your family's story**   Discover great tips for recording or documenting your family's personal story with Biography Assistant, which will take you through the process step by step.

- **Review the how-to guide**   This comprehensive overview of genealogy offers great advice on finding and organizing important family information, capturing oral histories, and much more.

- **Visit the library of articles**   From basics to advanced topics, you're sure to find something of interest to your research. Come in and roam the aisles to find out more.

- **Shop Genealogy.com**   Discover and organize your family history with the complete line of products. It has everything you need—from software to data resources.

- **Take an online genealogy class**   Enjoy self-paced tutorials on a variety of interesting topics as you learn from acknowledged genealogy professionals.

- **Explore the Helpful Web Sites list**   With more than 72,000 Internet destinations categorized by topic of interest, you're sure to find something engaging and helpful to your own family research.

- **Expert tips**   Check out the expert tips archives for helpful advice and to look at responses to questions from other family historians.

Note

Have you backed up this week? This month? This year? Uploading to a site such as this one is one way to do it!

Wrapping Up

- Ancestry.com has several different sites: RootsWeb, Genealogy.com, and Ancestry.com for research; MyFamily.com for interaction; and the message boards on all of them.

- Many Ancestry.com articles and helpful files are free, but the bulk of the data is only available to paying members.

- MyFamily.com allows you to create a family site with genealogy data, message boards, and so on. A small site is free, but over 5MB, charges begin.

- RootsWeb is the oldest gathering of volunteer pages, data, and programs in the world of online genealogy.

- Genealogy.com has a separate set of data in both the free and pay areas, as well as many similar features to Ancestry.com, MyFamily.com, and RootsWeb.

Chapter 20

Genealogical Publishing Houses and Their Sites

You will definitely want to read some books on genealogy (like this one!) as you pursue your family history. And someday, you may even want to publish your own book on your family history, or on the expertise you have gained in the process.

There are several ways to go about this. For a long time, your usual route to publishing a genealogy was to pay a book publisher anywhere from $5,000 to $10,000 to typeset, print, and bind your books. Sometimes you could find a short-run publisher, that is, a publisher who specialized in printing 1,000 or fewer copies of an old, out-of-print, and out-of-copyright book that someone wanted revived for libraries and archives. Again, this involved paying thousands of dollars up front.

Note

If you only want enough copies of your genealogy for your immediate family, consider using a genealogy program (Examples: Legacy Family, Family Origins, Family Tree Maker Deluxe, Personal Ancestral File, and others) that can output your data as a narrative. It will not be so professional in appearance, but will certainly be cheaper. This will, of course, entail much more effort on your part to create a nice "master copy"; indeed physically cutting and pasting may not be out of the question, but the result can be run off at your local office supply store. Binding can be as simple as having the store drill holes and then buying enough three-ring binders to hold your copies.

If your topic is more about how to do genealogy than the family history of one surname, sometimes a book publishing house will accept a genealogy methods book, pay an advance, foot the cost of the production, and pay royalties on the proceeds to an author, just as is the practice for novels and textbooks. Even more rarely, a particularly interesting genealogy will be printed in this way, as in *The Spencer Family* by Lady Diana's brother Charles Spencer (St. Martin's Press, 2000). (Note: Do not bet the farm on this happening to you, unless you prove a connection to a royal family!)

All of these options are still available and thriving.

The thing about the traditional self-publishing route, besides the obvious costs, is that you wind up with a basement full of books to sell (including collecting taxes, managing credit card sales, and so on), market, ship, and store. Lucky for us, in the 21st century we also have print-on-demand (POD) publishers. These hold an electronic version of your book, usually in PDF format, on their servers, and handle the sales, printing, and marketing for you, paying royalties, but as the name implies, usually printing copies only when someone has actually plunked down some money for them. If 100 copies are sold this week, then 100 copies will be printed. If none sell, none are printed. Sometimes the POD publisher can also sell and ship to traditional bookstores, as well as to individual buyers. Obviously, this makes the price for each book higher, but on the other hand, it makes life simpler.

POD publishers also handle things like payment by credit card or PayPal, taxes, and so forth. Furthermore, updates can be handled much more quickly, should more information on your ancestors be found after you complete your manuscript.

"Print-on-demand looks like a great service for genealogists," says *Eastman's Online Genealogy Newsletter* (EOGN) editor Dick Eastman. "The old-fashioned short-run printing services normally charge $5,000 or more (sometimes much more) to print the first run of a few hundred books. The author is saddled with the task of selling these books in order to recover expenses. A 'print-on-demand' publisher can be a much more cost-effective alternative."

Most of the time, a fee of some size is involved for the author, from $100 to more than $300, for publication design, cover art, binding, and the like. As you would imagine, the more of this you do yourself the less the POD publisher will charge.

And then there are e-books, which involve no materials at all except electrons and the machinery to zip them around between seller and buyer. When a book is published electronically, it can be for a specialized reader such as the Kindle or just as a large PDF file the buyer can read on the computer or print out as he chooses. Usually, e-books are much lower in cover price than a physical book, as no paper, shipping, or binding is involved for the producers of the book, only for the buyer. Therefore, often the author gets a larger percentage of the cover price for each sale.

For the reader, it is also not as permanent, a consideration if your genealogy work is meant for the ages. A computer crash or a Kindle in the pool, and the purchaser could be out of luck. Also, the buyer must have an expensive e-book reader or a computer to access his purchase. However, searching an e-book for surnames is incredibly fast and easy, and your references can link to websites as well as cite paper sources, a great convenience for the reader.

In this chapter we will look at the online presence of some typical publishers in the genealogy world. These are not the whole of the universe of publishers who have books on family history, but a representative sample. These publishers specialize in genealogy topics; other publishers like McGraw Hill and Booklocker have a broader scope, but will publish a genealogy book if it fits the market.

Avotaynu

Avotaynu, Inc. (www.avotaynu.com), is the leading publisher of products of interest to persons who are researching Jewish genealogy, Jewish family trees, or Jewish roots. The books include beginner guides and e-books about Jewish surnames. Avotaynu has an Internet newsletter for Jewish genealogy entitled *Nu? What's New?*

Genealogical Publishing Company

Genealogical Publishing Company and Clearfield Company, located on the Web at www.Genealogical.com or info@genealogical.com, publish genealogy books and CDs: in fact, more than 2,000 different genealogy books and compact discs featuring colonial genealogy, Irish genealogy, immigration, royal ancestry, family history, and genealogy methods and sources. Their genealogy books are found in every library in the country with a genealogy and family history collection, and are written by both amateur and professional genealogy authors.

Although the sister company, Gateway Press, is no longer in business, hundreds of Gateway Press publications, primarily self-published family histories, have been incorporated into the online catalog.

Their books and CDs cover the entire range of American genealogy, but one of the principal areas of strength is found in their collections of individual family histories. Typical of such collections, and among the best known in American genealogy, is Donald Lines Jacobus' *Families of Ancient New Haven*, a three-volume work that covers every family in pre-Revolutionary New Haven, Connecticut. Similarly, Robert Barnes' *British Roots of Maryland Families* (2010) establishes the origins of hundreds of pre-18th-century Maryland families, much like the comprehensive collection of magazine articles printed in the three volumes of *Genealogies of Pennsylvania Families* (1982).

GPC's 1973 publication of Val Greenwood's *Researcher's Guide to American Genealogy* set the standard for commercial book publishing in genealogy. I still have my mother's well-marked edition. Each year GPC publishes as many as 40 original works in genealogy, written or compiled by experts in the field; it also reprints dozens of genealogical classics. Typically, GPC's emphasis is on early American genealogy, especially the colonial and federal periods.

The company publishes many volumes of genealogy source records on CD-ROM, some going all the way back to the colonial period of American history. These books save you the trouble of traveling to search for materials on specialized topics such as immigration and royal and noble ancestry, while also supplying information on the more conventional records of birth, marriage, and death; will and probate records; land records; and census records. Transcribed and indexed by professionals, when published in book form and on CD, millions of records are conveniently available. Many of these publications are the pre-eminent works in their field.

For titles on the techniques of genealogy, check out the Genealogy Essentials page and the Genealogy for Beginners page, notably their guidebooks on German, English, Irish, Scottish, Italian, Polish, and Hispanic genealogy, as well as manuals and textbooks featuring both traditional instruction in genealogy methodology and contemporary instruction in the use of the Internet for genealogical research.

Print-on-Demand Comes to Genealogical.Com

Genealogical Publishing Company and its affiliate, Clearfield Company, started offering print-on-demand in 2008. They use print-on-demand to publish reprints of many old favorites for which there is a clear and evident demand as well as personal genealogies. Sample titles in this category include

+ *In Search of Your Canadian Roots, 3rd Edition*

+ *German-American Names, 3rd Edition*

+ *Black Genesis: A Resource Book for African-American Genealogy, 2nd Edition*

Family Roots Publishing

Both an online bookstore and a publishing house, the Family Roots Publishing Company (www.familyrootspublishing.com, Lmeitzler@gmail.com) provides a selected catalog of the genealogy research books and supplies at prices below retail. With new products nearly every day and a "Daily Special" on the home page, this site is worth a bookmark. They do not do print-on-demand at this time, and they specialize in how-to books, Leland Meitzler, the owner, told me.

"We publish genealogy guidebooks (how-to) only," he said. "Anyone interested in submitting a manuscript should contact me, Leland K. Meitzler, at Lmeitzler@gmail.com with an overview of the proposed book. If I like what I see and wish to publish the book, I'll most likely request a sample chapter prior to a contract being signed. We are presently seeking good manuscripts, with wide appeal within the family history community."

Among the outstanding publications from Family Roots Publishing is Bill Dollarhide's latest book, *Genealogical Resources of the Civil War Era* (2009).

Family Roots Publishing is also the exclusive distributor of limited numbers of new copies of back issues of *Heritage Quest Magazine*, as well as the *Genealogy Bulletin*. Thirty-three back issues of the "Bulletin" are now found on this website, while *Heritage Quest Magazine* back issues are now beginning to be posted. The co-owner of Family Roots Publishing is Patty S. Meitzler, former editor of *Heritage Quest Magazine* and wife of Leland K. Meitzler, former managing editor of *Heritage Quest Magazine* and the *Genealogical Helper Magazine*.

Martin Genealogy Publishing

William T. and Patricia Martin (mgp@wtmartin.com) specialize in Alabama and Florida resources for genealogical and historical research. Patricia's families are from Alabama, while William's are from Florida. Both family lines extend back through Georgia, the Carolinas, and up the eastern coast of the United States.

MGP (www.wtmartin.com) started publishing works for genealogical and historical research in 1990. The website now lists a collection of old books and will be adding collectibles as well that are available. Products include

♦ 1885 Florida State Census Index in one volume for the entire state or as individual counties

♦ The Gadsden Times (Etowah County, Alabama) Abstracts: Currently four volumes are available—Vol. I, 1867–1871; Vol. II, 1872–1875; Vol. III, 1876–1880; and Vol. IV, 1881–1885

♦ The Cubahatchee Baptist Church Book 1838–1850 (church minutes book) of Macon County, Alabama

The company's first publications were simple indexes created as finding tools. The 1885 Florida State Census Index was the first major publication. Other federal census indexes followed for a number of Florida counties, starting in 1910. Then opportunities arose to expand into Alabama resources, and that has been the focus for several years. The Gadsden Times Abstracts is now available in four volumes starting in 1867. The fifth volume, starting in 1886, is in production, the site says. Many libraries around the country have copies of the 1885 complete volumes, and several individuals have bought individual counties' volumes as needed.

"The Gadsden Times Abstracts has been well received by all who have used it," the site says. "It has proven to be an invaluable tool for researchers in northeast Alabama particularly although its reach goes far beyond that geographic area."

Heritage Books

For nearly 40 years, Heritage Books, Inc. (Info@HeritageBooks.com), has been a major publisher of titles in genealogy, history, military history, historical fiction, and memoirs. The company publishes 40 to 50 titles a month, some completely new compilations, others are historical reprints though often with added name indexes or other improvements. Heritage Books now has more than 3,900 titles under four publishing imprints. These cover the range of subject matter:

historical accounts, vital statistics of immigrants, and even fact-rich historical novels. The imprints are

- **Heritage Books**   Historical works and genealogical titles
- **Willow Bend Books**   Historical and genealogical titles now being imprinted under Heritage Books
- **Eagle Editions**   Memoirs
- **Fireside Fiction**   Historical fiction

Recent titles include *Missouri Genealogical Gleanings 1840 and Beyond, Vol. 7* by Sherida K. Eddlemon (2000), and *Rolls of Connecticut Men in French and Indian War, 1755–1762: Volume II, 1758–1762, Appendixes, 1755–1764* by Connecticut History Society (1994).

To submit your book, read the submissions requirements at www.heritagebooks.com/publishing.html.

Booklocker

BookLocker.com (http://booklocker.com) is a general publisher, but they have accepted genealogy titles. They specialize in print-on-demand and e-books. Costs run from about $300 for doing everything yourself to about $500 for using their cover design service for a black-and-white book.

Genealogy titles they have published include

- *The Genealogist's Guide to Digital Photography* (2009) by Danna Estridge
- *Find Your Roots Now!* (2005) by Joe Long
- *Roots Recovered! The How-To Guide for Tracing African-American and West Indian Roots Back to Africa and Going There for Free or on a Shoestring Budget* (2004) by James E. White and Jean-Gontran Quenum

The print books are listed on Amazon, Barnes and Noble, and other major online bookstores. Buyers can also special-order books from the local bookstores. BookLocker can provide an ISBN at no additional charge. The company's contract can be reviewed at www.BookLocker .com/contract/contract.txt, and submission guidelines are at http://publishing.BookLocker.com/submit.php.

Lulu.com

One of the largest self-publish, print-on-demand, and e-book houses, Lulu.com (www.lulu.com) has become quite popular with aspiring authors. They use a completely automated online system. A high-tech version of the traditional vanity press, Lulu.com offers both printing services and on-demand CD disks, DVD disks, e-publications, and more. Lulu.com's prices are low, but you can expect to do all the work, such as designing book covers, creating page layouts, and marketing. Lulu.com does some marketing work, but they do not publish catalogs or online websites for genealogists. (Pricing is covered at www.lulu.com/en/help/book_faqs). Like BookLocker, it does offer its books through major and smaller bookstores, online booksellers, and so forth. Among the authors using Lulu.com is Dick Eastman of *Eastman's Online Genealogy Newsletter*.

Using Lulu's publishing tools, authors format and upload digital content to the publisher, and then use Lulu's marketplace, social networking and author services, online storefronts, and retail listings on Amazon, Barnes and Noble, and so on. Lulu's has a good royalty rate of 80 percent for them/20 percent for authors to profit. The site says that according to R.R. Bowker's Books in Print database, some 276,489 books were published traditionally in the United States in 2008. Lulu alone published more than 400,000 titles last year.

In 2008, Lulu acquired weRead, a large social book discovery application on social networking sites such as Facebook, MySpace, Bebo, Orkut, and Hi5. Lulu also recently launched Lulu Poetry for poets who want to connect with peers for reviews and feedback on their poetry, not to mention publication.

iUniverse.com

At www.iUniverse.com, the company bills itself as "supported self publishing." In the ten years since its beginning, iUniverse grew to become a leader in the business and won a *PC Magazine* "Editors' Choice" Award as the best Web-oriented print-on-demand publishing service. Like the other sites, it can produce hard copy or electronic versions of your book. About 231 titles in their catalog match the keyword "genealogy."

The iUniverse.com service includes a custom cover and book design, an ISBN number, registration in the Ingram Books and Bowker's Books in Print databases, and listings on Amazon.com, Borders.com, and BN.com (Barnes and Noble's online site). The site says that the books are "available" through 5,000 bookstores (that is, available through special order to bookstores). iUniverse.com can be more expensive than other print-on-demand services, with prices starting at $599 in advance and going up to $2,099 in advance. More pricing information is available at www.iuniverse.com/Packages/PackageCompare.aspx. For more information about iUniverse.com, look at www.iuniverse.com.

Other Publishers to Consider

Creative Continuum (www.creativecontinuum.com, info@creativecontinuum.com) concentrates on family history books and other smaller publishing projects. A "vanity press" (the author pays the costs and uses the company's expertise and equipment), they provide a number of publishing services, including professional book design, layout and typesetting, and printing on archival paper. The company's website says they can assist an author with organizing a genealogy and family history, developing data into a publication-ready format, and publishing an heirloom.

This family history publisher provides the following publication services:

♦ Assist with interviewing and transcripting if needed

♦ Review your goals for the book and decide on a visual theme for the layout

♦ Proof your document for grammatical content

♦ Scan and digitally clean your photos and documents for placement in the book

♦ Provide a complete proof for approval

♦ Print the book on acid-free, archival paper

♦ Binding and stitching

♦ Press runs as small as 100 books

Family Heritage Publishers

E-mail: info@familyheritagepublishers.com

www.familyheritagepublishers.com

A traditional vanity press, this company is the binder for the Family History Library in Salt Lake City. They offer archival-quality printing for any size publishing job, from 1 copy to 1,000. Based in Bountiful, Utah, this publisher will print and bind books of all kinds—including family histories, town histories, biographies, and family reunion booklets. They can also help you prepare your manuscript for publishing. They do only physical books, not e-books or POD.

Modern Memoirs, Inc.

kitty@modernmemoirs.com

This is a vanity press with an emphasis on memoirs. Services include editing, printing, and binding. They specialize in memoirs and family histories, and can handle traditional printing and digital print-on-demand.

Shortrunbooks.com

This division of Dilley Manufacturing Company (www.shortrunbooks .com/) provides binding-only services for your self-printed family history. Print at home or your local copy shop, and then send the manuscripts to them for hard-cover binding.

Finding More

To find more options for self-publishing your genealogy work, try any of the following:

- ◆ Cyndi's List page (www.cyndislist.com/books.htm#Publishers).

- ◆ Search Google, Bing, or Yahoo! for "print on demand" +publisher.

- ◆ Talk to your local university or college to see if they have a press that prints local history and similar topics.

A Success Story:
A Gift of Biography

Jane Fraser of Pueblo, Colorado, has experience in publishing online for genealogy purposes and loved the experience, she said.

"My father, John M. Fraser, was born in Scotland, grew up in Brooklyn, and worked as an engineer on fascinating projects in the telephone industry at Bell Labs, Hughes Communication Satellites, and as a consultant," Jane said. "From his influence, I, too, am an engineer. After my sister died in 2004 (she was only 57), he was, of course, devastated, and I suggested he write his autobiography as a way to get his mind off her death. He agreed that 'it would keep him out of trouble.'

"The goal was to tell his life story. We knew from the start that mainly relatives would be interested, but he has been involved in some big projects (the first transatlantic telephone cable in the 1950s), so he was also writing for people who would care about the engineering history."

Choosing an online publisher seemed to Jane to be the way to go. It was simple, fast, and within her budget, she decided.

"I looked at a number of online publishers (Lulu, CreateSpace, and others). I thought the prices and services were best with CreateSpace (see Figure 20-1), although many of them looked good. I liked the facts that CreateSpace took care of getting an ISBN and that CreateSpace would put the book on Amazon (CreateSpace is owned by Amazon); neither of those options cost extra." Jane said.

So the process began.

"Dad was very computer literate and had his own computer. Because his eyesight was starting to fail, he bought Dragon NaturallySpeaking Speech Recognition software and a microphone headset so he could dictate rather than type. I think that approach was really good, because the book reads as he spoke. We talked often on the phone while he was writing and I reminded him of events to include. My stepmother did a lot of editing for him. As he was writing, I was also working on photos. We have always taken many family photos; sometimes I had to hunt through boxes of photos and slides to find exactly the one he was thinking of. I scanned the photos that he wanted to use in the book. I tried scanning slides, but found that very hard to do, so I projected each slide and took a photo of it with my digital camera."

FIGURE 20-1. *CreateSpace is an online publisher owned by Amazon.com.*

In Figure 20-2, you can see how the illustrations turned out.

"Dad e-mailed me the completed manuscript, *Muddling Through* (95,000 words), in September 2008," Jane said. "I was thrilled with it; I thought I knew all his stories, but there was so much new in the book. I really wanted to do a good job in publishing it. It took me a little over four months from when I received the manuscript to publication. I work full-time, so I worked on the book after work and on weekends."

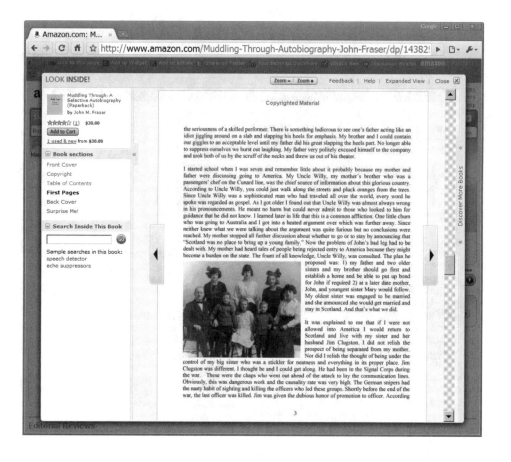

FIGURE 20-2. *Using a scanner and digital camera, Jane was able to illustrate the book with her father's old photographs and slides.*

This is an important point for the self-publishing genealogist: You are your own staff on this project. Editing, layout, and error control are all your responsibility and in your power!

"Proofreading, proofreading, and proofreading," Jane said. "I read the book extremely carefully three times, word by word, and I still found a few errors in the published version. I started to do some fact checking, but then decided not to. My father's memory was astounding. When he said that Miss Asti (one of his school teachers) had lived next door to his future brother-in-law (my father and this friend married sisters), the 1930 census confirmed that he was correct. I would have written some sentences differently, but I decided the book was my father's and it was his voice that should be heard. I did fix spelling and grammar. I picked a style (font for text, headings, and subheadings; layout of the first page of each chapter; etc.) and put [the entire] book in that format. I followed CreateSpace's advice and advice from CreateSpace user discussion boards for what to put on the copyright page."

You will learn quickly, as Jane did, that book design has certain parameters. The size of the book in finished form affects the choices you make in typesetting and layout.

"Laying out the photos was tricky. I had to learn how to insert and format photos in Microsoft Word. I put some of the photos on pages with text, but also made several other pages just containing photos. For a while, we contemplated publishing and assembling the book ourselves (through a copy chain such as Kinko's); thus, we were thinking about having some pages in black and white only and some pages in color only to reduce copying costs. With CreateSpace, the entire book is classified as either black and white or color, so keeping the photos separate didn't matter, but we liked the separate pages of photos so kept some of them."

Another technical consideration is that sometimes your equipment and software may not be entirely compatible with the online publisher's. There are always workarounds, but be prepared for some trial and error.

"I had trouble downloading a cover template from CreateSpace and using it in Photoshop," Jane said, "so I created my own cover in Photoshop. Dad wanted to keep the front cover simple, with title, his name, and subtitle; he selected the font for the title. I put a photo of my father on the back cover, with a brief description of the book. I had to figure out the dimensions to make sure the material on the back and front covers would be centered. CreateSpace tells you how to figure out the spine width and other dimensions, so the cover came out fine" (see Figure 20-3).

"From Photoshop and Word, I created PDF files for the cover and the interior and uploaded them to CreateSpace; those steps were easy. CreateSpace automatically reviewed both files for technical problems. For example, it told me a few photos were not of high enough resolution to print well, so I made them a little smaller. I got stuck for a while in converting the Word file to a PDF in the correct format. Page 1 should be on the right, but it kept coming out on the left. The margins are different on left and right pages (to allow for binding) so this point

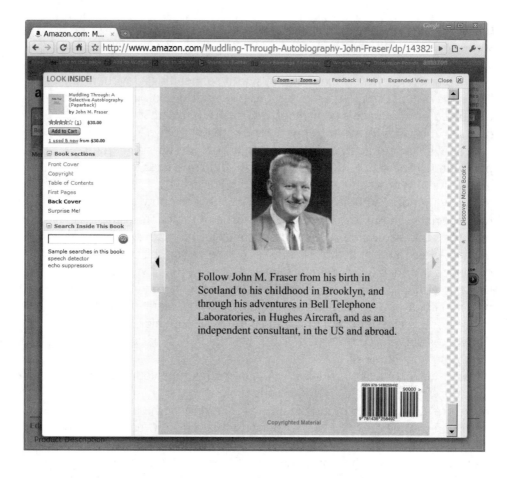

FIGURE 20-3. *Jane created her own covers with Photoshop, although most online publishers can provide predesigned ones.*

was very important. This was my moment (actually a month) of greatest frustration. I kept inserting a blank page, resubmitting the PDF file, and getting the same error. I finally figured it out, after finding detailed instructions on a CreateSpace discussion board (you have to tell Word in some obscure place that it should put the first page on the right). The users of CreateSpace are very helpful. I had to learn a lot of printing terms (for example, "full bleed"), but again the CreateSpace website and discussion boards helped. I had to read and reread some instructions several times," Jane said.

"Another difficulty arose because I wanted to include a very short article from the *New York Times*. My father had been mayor of our town in New Jersey and an amusing dispute (over licensing cats) actually got quite a bit of coverage in major papers. I requested permission from the *New York Times* to use it (the NYT website has an online form to do so), but their charge (over $300) was, we thought, crazy, so I took it out. I think they saw that the book would be on Amazon and thought there would be some money to be made."

But note that Jane was careful to follow that step of finding the copyright holder and asking for permission. This is very important if you are including photos, text, or other material in your publication.

CreateSpace required that Jane order (and pay for, at a reduced price) a proof copy, approve the proof, and then publish. Each proof copy cost her $19.47.

"I ended up having to do three proof copies due to my errors (and due to having to remove the *New York Times* piece) and I got a little frustrated then," Jane said. "When I finally figured out the right/left page stuff, I felt I could finish the book—but I did have doubts for a while. And Dad was getting very eager to have the book."

"I was very pleased with the quality of the product from CreateSpace. The interior paper is good quality, the soft cover is also good, the printing is clear, and the binding is sturdy. The book looks good and it feels nice to hold," Jane said.

Setting the price of the book at $30 gave Jane a return of $4.83 for each copy sold on Amazon and $10.83 for each copy sold through the CreateSpace storefront she set up.

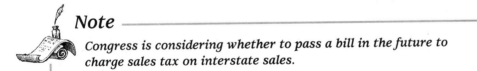

Note

Congress is considering whether to pass a bill in the future to charge sales tax on interstate sales.

"Two copies have been sold through the e-store and four on Amazon, so this has not been a money maker, but I didn't do it for that purpose," Jane said. "On sales through the e-store, the sales report tells me who bought it, but I don't get that information for Amazon sales. The book is currently #3,395,134 in Books on Amazon, which I find very amusing."

When the book first came out, Amazon listed it at a discounted price for promotion purposes ($24) but didn't cut the amount of the royalty. Now it is listed at the $30 price and can be found at www.createspace .com/3347370.

Amazon.com does some promotion on its sites, and Jane did a little publicizing of her own as well. "I sent copies to relatives and to friends of my father, in this country and in Scotland," Jane said. "I also sent five copies to museums and company archives related to my father's work. I got back nice thank you notes from everyone. I posted the URL (www.createspace.com/3347370) in a few online newsgroups about the telephone industry and history."

Overall, Jane said the process was not hard, but neither was it exactly easy. Learning to make Word and Photoshop do what she wanted took time and research, almost more than the book itself. Getting it looking right required a lot of attention to detail, but she wanted to do that for her father because this was a project of love.

"The best part was working with my father on the book. He had some health problems in the last year of his life, and I was traveling to his place often to visit and to help. Working on the book together was great. It was finally published in January 2009. Dad got to see a copy before he died early in March, at age 92. He was thrilled with it. I am so happy to have it as a legacy from him. The book has been a great comfort for me. I reread it often," Jane said.

Would she do it again?

"In a heartbeat," Jane said. "It was a remarkable gift that my father and I gave each other."

Wrapping Up

- ◆ Several publishing companies specialize in genealogy.

- ◆ Publishing your family's genealogy will likely involve a vanity press (self-publishing) outfit.

- ◆ Print-on-demand and e-books are economical ways to go about it.

- ◆ If you want to share your genealogy expertise, you may find a traditional publisher. Or, you could still go the self-publishing route.

Chapter 21

A Potpourri of Genealogy

As you've no doubt noticed while reading this book, genealogy websites come in all categories. You will find portals that aim to be your web home. You will find sites with images of original documents or transcribed records (perhaps both!) and sites with completed, annotated genealogies. You will find sites where folks have slapped up any data they found, regardless of accuracy or relevancy. You will find primary records, secondary records, family legends, and scams. It's truly an embarrassment of riches out there.

You must remember to judge each source you find critically and carefully. Compare it to what you have proven with your own research. Look for the original records cited in an online genealogy to see if they have been interpreted correctly (remember the lesson about census records in Chapter 1!). Most of all, look for application to *your* genealogy. How helpful is it?

This list of websites reflects what I've found to be valuable. Some of these sites are portals and will link you to sites I haven't found or that didn't exist at press time. Other links may be "dead" (as they say in web parlance) by the time you read this. Don't be discouraged by this. That's part of the fun of online genealogy: There's always something new!

Note

Most online genealogists have at least these five links bookmarked: Cyndi's List (www.cyndislist.com), DearMYRTLE (www.dearmyrtle .com), FamilySearch.com (www.familysearch.com), NARA (www.archives .gov), and RootsWeb (www.rootsweb.com).

Alexa.com Top 20 Genealogy Sites (Early 2010)

Alexa Internet is a site started in April 1996. The website not only has current trends in Web surfing, but also historical measures of the popularity of sites in thousands of categories. Among the top genealogy sites measured by Alexa for early 2010:

♦ **Ancestry.com** (www.ancestry.com), of course, tops the list with its subscription-based resource of worldwide census, marriage, newspaper, and various other records.

- **Legacy.com** (www.legacy.com) is a site where you can leave obituaries, photographs, and memories of those who have passed on. It collaborates with more than 750 newspapers in North America, Europe, and Australia to provide ways for you to express condolences and share remembrances of loved ones. You can also find articles and discussion boards on grief, and search a database of obituaries.

- **RootsWeb** (www.rootsweb.ancestry.com) is the still free, genealogical resource with searchable databases, family trees, mailing lists, and message boards. It's part of the Ancestry.com empire.

- **FamilySearch** (www.familysearch.org) is provided by the Church of Jesus Christ of Latter-day Saints with excellent online search tools of millions of names.

- **Genealogy.com** offers Family Tree Maker software, subscription-based access to searchable databases, and forums. It is now part of the Ancestry.com empire.

- **Geneanet.org** (www.geneanet.org) is a collection of submitted GEDCOMs, photographs, and social tools. You can also share your family pictures and old postcards, browse the collection, look at a geographical distribution of your ancestors, or find out if you have your famous relatives. It's a subscription site.

- **GenForum** (http://genforum.genealogy.com) has more than 14,000 online forums devoted to genealogy, including surnames, U.S. states, countries, and other countries as well. It is part of Genealogy.com.

- **Ancestry Message Boards** (http://boards.ancestry.com) hold the centralized collection of genealogical message boards hosted by Ancestry.com and RootsWeb. Forum categories number in the thousands, divided into localities (continents, countries, and subdivisions thereof) and topics (from adoption to volunteer projects). This is part of the free offerings of Ancestry.com.

- **Newspaper Archives** (http://newspaperarchive.com) provides registered members with access to databases of searchable and downloadable archived newspapers from the United States and around the world. The collection includes obituaries, birth announcements, sports articles, comics, and more. Share what you find in those stories with others through the community at OurNewspaperARCHIVE. All of the historical newspapers are full-page and fully searchable. This is a subscription service; some libraries may offer access to patrons.

♦ **About.com's Genealogy** page (http://genealogy.about.com) features Kimberly Powell's excellent blog and links for researching family history, including genealogical societies, ethnic sites, and more.

♦ **One Great Family** (www.onegreatfamily.com) is an online genealogy subscription service that provides a shared database giving users the ability to view, store, and collaborate. You can search more than 130,000,000 submitted ancestors in what the site claims is the largest Internet-based collaborative family tree. The site also offers automatic backup of your family tree data, merges two family trees when it finds the exact same person in both, and a software program called Genealogy Browser, a full-featured program for entering, storing, and surfing your family tree.

♦ **Family Tree DNA** (www.familytreedna.com) is the ultimate link in the family and social networking. Family Tree DNA claims to be the world leader in genetic genealogy. Founded in April 2000, they have developed methods that enable genealogists around the world to advance their family's research. Family Tree DNA works in association with a scientific advisory board and the University of Arizona Research Labs. The Arizona Research labs are led by Dr. Michael Hammer, a leader in the field of genetics.

♦ **Cyndi's List** (www.cyndislist.com) is a large, categorized, and cross-referenced directory of sites useful for genealogical research, which is profiled at the end of this chapter.

♦ **Ellis Island** (www.ellisisland.org) is the website of the American Family Immigration History Center on Ellis Island.

♦ **JewishGen** (www.jewishgen.org) provides a wide range of resources, including databases, Family Finder, articles, societies, projects you can volunteer to help with, and more. It is a free, cooperative site like RootsWeb, with an ethnic emphasis.

- **The Official Site of the British Monarchy** (www.royal.gov.uk) covers the monarch's role and the history of the monarchy; it gives biographies of the current royals and, of course, their genealogy (See "History of the Monarchy" at www.royal.gov.uk/HistoryoftheMonarchy/HistoryoftheMonarchy.aspx).

- **World Vital Records** (www.worldvitalrecords.com) offer users international record databases. It is a subscription site.

- **Tribal Pages** (www.tribalpages.com) is a service to build and store your family tree online. Upload photographs and organize your family tree. You can use it for free, or pay a monthly fee for more storage space.

- **The Peerage** (www.thepeerage.com) is a genealogy of the peerage of Great Britain and of the nobility and royalty of Europe.

- **Last Names Meanings Dictionary** (www.last-names.net) helps you find the ethnic origin and meaning of last names, including Irish, German, English, French, Latin, and Hebrew names.

Golden Needles in the World Wide Haystack

In the manner of websites everywhere, these sites will all lead you to other sites, where (I hope) you'll find the information you need. Note that this isn't even close to an exhaustive list. For that, see Cyndi's List and Genealogy Resources on the Internet. I have sorted these sites by topic.

Adoption

The following are places that concentrate on reuniting birth families:

- **Adoptee/Birth Family Connections** (www.birthfamily.com) This site's motto is, "You existed before you were adopted." The site has articles on topics such as activism and reform of adoption laws, birth family registry, and warnings about scams.

- **Adopting.org** (www.adopting.org)   Includes a birth-family search guide.

- **AdoptionForum.com** (www.adoptionforums.com/ adult-adoptees) This is a discussion board for adoptees, including birth mother searches.

- **American Adoption Congress** (www.americanadoptioncongress .org)   The American Adoption Congress (AAC) is an advocacy group for adoption reform. AAC members support those whose lives are touched by adoption or other loss of family continuity. AAC promotes honesty, openness, and respect for family connections in adoption, foster care, and assisted reproduction. The group educates members and professional communities about the lifelong process of adoption and advocates legislation that will grant every individual access to information about his or her family and heritage.

- **Bastard Nation** (www.bastards.org)   This organization fights to open all adoption records. It's a strident site, but has some good articles and book reviews. A sample from their "About Us" page: "We at Bastard Nation believe that there is NOTHING shameful about having been born out of wedlock or about being adopted. We selected our name because we will no longer be made to feel shamed by the odious state laws that permanently seal our original birth records. We do not fling the word 'bastard' at anyone. Rather, we wear it proudly as we work to achieve our goal of equal and unconditional access to original birth records for all adult adoptees."

- **Adoption and Genealogy Links** (http://skyatdawn.tripod.com/ index-2.html)   Provides good information for Canadian adoptees.

- **Facebook (www.facebook.com)** has several groups and pages for adoptees to network, many sorted by geography (states, countries, etc.). Some examples: International Adoptee Congress ("a self-organizing hub for people adopted internationally to connect with others, share successes, and post items of interest"); Adoptee/Birthparent Connections ("This group is for the purpose of helping all those in search or reunion ... adoptees, birthparents/family, or others looking for lost family members. Closed: Limited public content"); and Adoptee Search Rights ("[F]or those who have been adopted as a child and always have the question going through your mind. Always nice to have people to talk to who share the same thoughts and maybe also to do research on their 'actual' history.")

- **PeopleFinder UK Adoption Section** (www.peoplefinders.co.uk/ adoption.html) This site explains laws in the United Kingdom concerning finding birth mothers by adoptees.

- **RootsWeb Adoption Discussion Lists** (http://lists.rootsweb .ancestry.com/index/other/Adoptions) Four different lists for those researching adoptions in their genealogy: Adoption-Gen, Aus-Vic-Adoptions, Il-Rhbal, and Pre-1940_Adoption_Genealogy.

Beginners' "Classes," How-to Articles, Tips, and More

These sites feature articles, lessons, helpful hints, and columns:

- **About.com Genealogy** (http://genealogy.about.com) This site has tips, discussion groups, and weekly articles on genealogy.

- **Ancestors Series Teacher's Guide** (www.byub.org/Ancestors/ teachersguide) This site is a set of pages designed to help teachers and students in grades 7–12 use the ten-part Ancestors series to create their genealogies as a school project.

- **Family History, How Do I Begin?** (www.familysearch.org) Go to the Family Search site, and then click Research Helps | Guidance. In the bar at the left you will see a link to "How Do I Begin?" This is the Church of Jesus Christ of Latter-day Saints' basic tutorial.

- **Genealogy Dictionary** (http://freepages.genealogy.rootsweb .ancestry.com/~ randyj2222/gendict.html) This site gives you definitions for all those confusing terms such as "cordwainer" and "primogeniture."

- **Genealogical Glossary** (www.rootsweb.ancestry.com/~ nsdigby/ lists/glossary.htm) This site helps you decipher all those puzzling terms.

- **Genealogy Lesson Plan** (www.teachnet.com/lesson/misc/ familytrees040199.html) Located at TeachNet.com, this site has a lesson plan on family history for different curriculum areas.

- **Genealogy Today** (www.genealogytoday.com) This site announces and rates genealogy sites, has news updates and links to databases, lets readers vote for their favorite sites, and so forth.

- **Internet Tourbus** (www.internettourbus.com)   This is Patrick Douglas Crispen's e-mail course on how to use every part of the Internet. This site taught my mom everything she knows about the Net.

- **Kindred Trails** (www.kindredtrails.com)   This site has links, a kinship calculator, articles, message boards, and more.

- **Lineages, Inc**. (www.lineages.com)   This is the website for a group of professional genealogical researchers who, for a fee, will help you find your roots. Many of them hold professional certification. In addition, their site includes some free information, such as "First Steps for Beginners," a free genealogical queries page, and more.

- **Association of Personal Historians** (www.personalhistorians.org) Helps you find a professional to write your personal history.

- **StateGenSites** (www.stategensites.com)   This site has monthly and weekly columnists on all aspects of genealogy. Uncle Hiram's weekly column is especially good!

Blogging and Genealogy Blogs

Genealogy bloggers can help you with techniques, news, and more. Here are some to check out:

- Amy Coffin chronicles her own adventures in genealogy and works to inspire you to do the same in her blog **We Tree** at http://wetree.blogspot.com. Amy holds an MLIS, and writes on all aspects of genealogy, especially research strategy, the value of social networking, personal genealogy and society marketing opportunities, and advancing the value of family history to a wider audience. Follow her on Twitter at www.twitter.com/ACoffin.

- Anastasia Tyler blogs at the **Ancestry Insider** (http://blogs.ancestry .com/ancestry). Tyler is a genealogy research manager for different conferences and the PR team at Ancestry.com. She has worked in the publications department of Ancestry (associate editor of *Ancestry Magazine* and as an editor on newsletters and book projects, including the third edition of *The Source*).

- Arlene H. Eakle is a speaker, blogger, and president and founder of The Genealogical Institute, Inc. Arlene's blogs include **Arlene H. Eakle's Genealogy Blog** (www.arleneeakle.com/wordpress), **Tennessee Genealogy** (http://tnblog.arleneeakle.com), Virginia Genealogy (http://virginiagenealogyblog.com), and **Kentucky Genealogy** (http://kyblog.arleneeakle.com). She is on Twitter at http://twitter.com/arleneeakle.

- Cheryl Rothwell has three blogs: **Logan County Genealogy** (http://logancountygenealogy.blogspot.com) is about Logan County, Illinois, and the companion blog, **Graveyards of South Logan County** (http://southlogancounty.blogspot.com), focuses on the cemeteries there. **Ancestor Hunting** (http://genealogysleuth .blogspot.com) is more general. Her blogs are witty, informative, and fun.

- Gena Philibert Ortega writes the blogs at **Gena's Genealogy** (http://philibertfamily.blogspot.com) and at the **World Vital Records blog** (http://blog.worldvitalrecords.com). She is the Genealogy Community Communications Director for FamilyLink and Manager of GenealogyWise. Follow her on Twitter: @genaortega and @WVRNewsletter.

- **Geneabloggers** (www.geneabloggers.com) is Thomas McEntree's excellent blog about blogging … for genealogists, by genealogists, about genealogists, and so on! A good description is at www .geneabloggers.com/about. He is on Facebook at www.facebook .com/tmacentee and on Twitter at www.twitter.com/ tmacentee.

- Jean Wilcox Hibben blogs at **Circle Mending: Where music and genealogy meet** (www.circlemending.blogspot.com).

- Lee R. Drew writes **FamHist Blog** (http://famhist2.blogspot.com) and **Lineage Keeper Blog** (http://lineagekeeper.blogspot.com). His Twitter page is www.twitter.com/lineagekeeper.

- Lisa Alzo writes **The Accidental Genealogist** (http://theaccidentalgenealogist.blogspot.com) and is on Twitter at www.twitter.com/lisaalzo and Facebook at www.facebook .com/lisaalzo. Lisa has written seven books, including *Baba's Kitchen: Slovak & Rusyn Family Recipes and Traditions* (Gateway Press, 2005) and *Finding Your Slovak Ancestors* (Heritage Productions, 2005).

- Lisa Louise Cooke writes the blog for **Genealogy Gems News** at http://genealogygemspodcast.blogspot.com, hosts the Genealogy Gems Podcast and the Family History: Genealogy Made Easy podcast, audio and video genealogy shows, and The Family Tree Magazine Podcast. She is the author of *Genealogy Gems: Ultimate Research Strategies*, and has been featured in *Ancestry* and *Family Tree* magazines. You will find Lisa on Twitter at www.twitter.com/LisaCooke and on Facebook at http://www.facebook.com/LisaLouiseCooke.

- Renee Huskey blogs at the **Above the Trees** at http://photoloom.wordpress.com and on Twitter at www.twitter.com/PhotoLoom.

- Renee Zamora writes **Renee's Genealogy Blog** at http://rzamor1.blogspot.com and is on Twitter at www.twitter.com/rzamor1.

- DearMYRTLE (http://blog.dearmyrtle.com).

- Dick Eastman, **Eastman's Online Genealogy Newsletter** (http://blog.eogn.com).

- Maureen Taylor, **The Photo Detective** (www.photodetective.com).

- Randy Seaver, **Genea-musings** Blog (www.geneamusings.com).

- Colleen Fitzpatrick, **The Forensic Genealogist** (www.forensicgenealogy.info).

- Paula Hinkle, **Southern California Genealogy Jamboree** (www.scgsgenealogy.com/2010jam-home.htm).

- Stephen Danko PhD, genealogist and blogger (http://stephendanko.com/blog).

- The Carnival of Genealogy Blogs is often hosted at **Creative Gene** (http://creativegene.blogspot.com).

Birth, Death, Marriage, and Other Records

Here are just a few of the sites where volunteers are uploading data. Be sure you visit RootsWeb and Cyndi's List often for updates and new pages:

- **Cemetery Junction: The Cemetery Trail** (www.daddezio.com/cemetery/trail/index.html)   This site has transcriptions of tombstones found in cemeteries across the United States, collected and uploaded by volunteers and links to other sites focusing on cemeteries and some very interesting articles on the subject. Cemetery Junction launched in January 1999 with more than 250 pages of addresses and links to cemeteries across the United States. The database of cemeteries submitted by volunteers reached more than 10,000 just six months after the start of the project.

◆ **Census Bureau home page** (www.census.gov/genealogy/www) This site has a list of frequently occurring names in the United States for 1990, a Spanish surname list for 1990, an age search service, and a frequently asked questions (FAQ) file on genealogy.

◆ **Find A Grave** (www.findagrave.com/index.html) Find A Grave is a registration website for graves, a memorialization/ remembrance site, and a genealogical resource.

◆ **FreeBMD** (freebmd.rootsweb.com) FreeBMD stands for Free Births, Marriages, and Deaths. The FreeBMD Project is made up of volunteers transcribing the Civil Registration Index information for England and Wales from the years 1837 to 1898 onto the Internet. Progress is sporadic; volunteer if you can.

◆ **GENWED** (www.genwed.com) GENWED is a free genealogical research database for marriage records and a directory to other marriage records online for the United States, Canada, and the United Kingdom—some available for free; some require a subscription. Most of the more than 25,000 marriage records in the free database were submitted by visitors who added records found during a search for family history.

◆ **The Bureau of Land Management Land Patent Records** (www.glorecords.blm.gov) This is a searchable database. The information is invaluable, especially for the western states when they were territories and when local records were scarce.

DNA

DNA research is becoming part of online genealogy. These are sites you can explore for this topic:

◆ **Chris Pomeroy's DNA Portal** (www.dnaandfamilyhistory.com) What was a website of articles turned into a book, a free e-mail newsletter, and a set of articles on the cutting edge of DNA genealogy.

- **Family Tree DNA** (www.familytreedna.com)   You can pay this company to look for matches with people you suspect are relatives. In searching my mother's genealogy, we had long suspected that our Abraham Spencer was related to a certain Abner Spencer. Using this site, my uncle and another man submitted saliva samples. The other man (who wishes not to be named) was a proven descendant from that Abner. The results showed that he and my uncle have an ancestor in common. Many professional genealogists scoff at such proof (for example, the white descendants of Thomas Jefferson), but we feel this has finally solved our 30-year brick wall on Abraham's parents.

- **Genealogy DNA Mail List** (http://lists.rootsweb.ancestry.com/ index/other/DNA/GENEALOGY-DNA.html)   This is a discussion group about the topic of DNA, hosted by RootsWeb.

- **Oxford Ancestors** (www.oxfordancestors.com)   This is a company that does the same thing as Family Tree DNA, but in the UK.

- **Sorenson Molecular Genealogy Foundation** (www.smgf.org) Brigham Young University has a site explaining its DNA genealogy research. You can learn how this project is progressing and how you can participate in your area at the site. You can also read about how BYU hopes to use the data to further the Mormons' quest to have a family history for all mankind.

Ethnic/National

Here's a list of some important ethnic pages:

- **Australian National Library** (www.nla.gov.au/guides/#Genealogy_- _Australia)   The subject guides page has links to Australian genealogy resources, organizations, military service records, and so on, as well as an online card catalog.

- **Carpatho-Rusyn Genealogy Website** (www.rusyn.com)   This site is for those searching for Ruthenian—Carpatho-Rusyn— ancestry and those of the Byzantine Catholic/Orthodox faiths who came from the former Austro-Hungarian Empire.

- **Center for Basque Studies** (http://basque.unr.edu)   This site, at the University of Nevada, Reno, covers history, anthropology, and other aspects of Basque culture.

- **Center for Jewish History** (www.cjh.org)   This site has a special section on family history at www.cjh.org/collections/genealogy.

- **Christine's African American Genealogy Website** (www.ccharity .com)   This is an excellent site about African-American history and genealogy.

- **Federation of East European Family History Societies** (www.feefhs.org)   This site has databases, maps, and directories to help with genealogy in this region. The group is also on Facebook, http://www.facebook.com/#!/group.php?gid = 278430439787&ref = search&sid = 502976342.439862355..1.

- **History and Genealogy of South Texas and Northeast Mexico** (www.vsalgs.org/stnemgenealogy)   This is an interesting source if you're looking for relatives from the South Texas/Northeast Mexico area. The database has more than 11,000 names, all linked as lineages.

- **Hungarian Genealogy** (www.rootsweb.ancestry.com/ ~ wghungar) This is a good place to start if your research leads you to Hungary.

- **India Office Family History Search** (http://indiafamily.bl.uk/UI/ Home.aspx)   This site has data taken from a card index at the British Library. The card index was compiled by members of staff at the India Office Records from the mid-1970s onwards to meet the growing interest in genealogy. Although less than 10 percent of the biographical sources available in the India Office Records were incorporated into the index, the site notes that future additions are in the works.

- **New Zealand History Online** (www.nzhistory.net.nz/ handsonhistory/genealogy-links)   This site is a page of links to various sites with shipping lists, cemetery records, tribal history, archives, and so on in New Zealand.

- **ScotlandsPeople** (www.scotlandspeople.gov.uk)   This is one of the largest online sources of genealogical information with almost 80 million records. This is the official government source for genealogy data in Scotland.

♦ **National Hispanic Heritage Month** (www.hispanicheritagemonth
.gov)   Be sure to check this page out in September and October.
This Web portal is a collaborative project of the Library of
Congress and the National Endowment for the Humanities,
National Gallery of Art, National Park Service, Smithsonian
Institution, United States Holocaust Memorial Museum, and U.S.
National Archives and Records Administration.

♦ **Spanish Heritage Home Page** (www.shhar.net)   This is a great
site with articles, links, and networking opportunities for those
researching Hispanic family history in the Western Hemisphere.

♦ **The National Huguenot Society** (http://huguenot.netnation.com/
general)   This site is for the study and preservation of the history
of the sixteenth- and seventeenth-century Huguenots, especially
those who immigrated to the United States.

Historical Background

Certain historical events may have an impact on your genealogy. The
following sites can give you some information on the people in history:

♦ **The History DetectivesTV series** (www.pbs.org/opb/
historydetectives)   This is a favorite of genealogy junkies across
the United States. They take an object from a submission (click
the link on the home page) and trace its history, provenance,
and origins.

♦ **American Civil War Home Page** (http://sunsite.utk.edu/ civil-war)
This site has links to fantastic online documents from many
sources, including those of two academics who've made the Civil
War their career.

♦ **British Civil War, Commonwealth, and Protectorate**
(www.british-civil-wars.co.uk)   This site offers timelines,
biographies, and military history on the United Kingdom from
1638 to 1660.

♦ **Calendars Through the Ages** (www.webexhibits.org/calendars)
This site explores the fascinating history of how we have tried to
organize our lives in accordance with the sun and stars.

♦ **Glossary of Terms Used in Past Times** by John Owen Smith (www.johnowensmith.co.uk/histdate/terms.htm)   This is a page of definitions of assart, toft, and other terms you may come across in old records.

♦ **Dan Mabry's Historical Text Archive** (http://historicaltextarchive .com)   This is a compilation of articles and documents on various topics. Of special interest are the collections on African-American history and genealogy.

♦ **Daughters of the American Revolution** (www.dar.org)   This is the organization for those who can prove an ancestor fought in the American Revolution. A free lookup in the DAR Patriot Index is just one of the site's many features.

♦ **Directory of Royal Genealogical Data** (www3.dcs.hull.ac.uk/ genealogy/royal)   This is a database with the genealogy of the British Royal family and many other ruling families of the Western world—they all seem to be interrelated somehow. It contains more than 18,000 names.

♦ **Footnote.com** (www.footnote.com)   This is a site for original documents and photographs. The free membership allows you to create your own Footnote pages; search and browse all images; spotlight images and documents; upload images to your gallery; annotate member images; upload, annotate, and print your own images; and view and search member images.

♦ **Genealogy of the Royal Family of the Netherlands** (www.angelfire .com/in/heinbruins)   This is a detailed genealogical history of the House of Orange-Nassau. It covers the period from Heinrich the rich of Nassau (born 1180) to Juliana Guillermo (born 1981).

♦ **Hauser-Hooser-Hoosier Theory: The Truth about Hoosier** (www.geocities.com/Heartland/Flats/7822)   This site explains how genealogy solved the mystery of the term Hoosier in a white paper titled "Migration, Ministry, and a Moniker."

♦ **Immigration: The Living Mosaic of People, Culture & Hope** (http://library.thinkquest.org/20619/index.html)   This is a student project about immigration in the United States.

- **Mayflower Web Pages** (www.mayflowerhistory.com)   These pages contain the passenger lists of the *Mayflower*, the *Fortune*, and the *Anne*, plus many related documents.

- **Medal of Honor Citations** (www.history.army.mil/moh.html) This site contains the names and text of the citations for the more than 3,400 people who've been awarded the Congressional Medal of Honor since 1861.

- **Migrations** (www.migrations.org)   This site has two separate parts. First is a database of migration information submitted by volunteers (secondary source information, of course!), searchable by name and place. Second is a list of links to resources on migration.

- **The Olden Times** (http://theoldentimes.com/newsletterpage.html) This site has historic newspapers online, searchable and free.

- **Pitcairn Island Website** (www.lareau.org/genweb.html)   This is one place to go for information on the more than 7,500 descendants of the crew of the *H.M.S. Bounty*, of *Mutiny on the Bounty* fame. Another good site for history and to buy stamps and coins is the website of the island's government: www.government.pn.

- **Sons of the American Revolution** (www.sar.org)   This site has information on this organization's genealogical library, articles from its quarterly magazine, the history of the American Revolution, and more.

- **United States Civil War Center** (www.cwc.lsu.edu)   This site from LSU publishes book reviews, research tips, and articles about studying the War Between the States.

Libraries

Search the web catalogs (Yahoo!, Lycos, Google, and so on) for "library" plus "State" or "National" or the region you need. Some state libraries also have special genealogical collections, which you might find with a search such as "Michigan State library genealogy." These are some of the best library sites for genealogy:

- **Abrams Collection, Library of Michigan** (www.michigan.gov/
mde/0,1607,7-140-54504_18635—-,00.html)   The Library of
Michigan's genealogy collection is known as the Abrams
Foundation Historical Collection. The Abrams Collection provides
a variety of resources for researchers to explore their family history.
Materials are mostly for states east of the Mississippi River. This
includes the Great Lakes, New England, Mid-Atlantic, Southern
states, and the Canadian provinces of Ontario and Quebec. The
Abrams Collection Genealogy Highlights lists what researchers can
find at this wonderful library. From assistance on specific genealogy
topics to an online newsletter, this page lists resources at the
Library of Michigan and at other libraries and research centers.

- **Elmer's Genealogy Library**   Located in Madison, Florida, and
established by Elmer C. Spear, this collection merged with the
Huxford Genealogical Library in Homerville, Georgia, in 2010.
The merged library is in Homerville, Georgia, and the new
website is www.huxford.com/index.html.

- **Gateway to Northwestern Ontario History** (www.nextlibrary.com)
This site has more than 1,000 photographs and drawings as well as
the full text of several books.

- **Midwest Genealogy Center** (www.mcpl.lib.mo.us/genlh/
mgc.htm)   This is a branch of the Mid-Continent Public Library,
based in Independence, Missouri. The branch has its own page,
building, and card catalog, and participates in interlibrary loans.

- **Mobile Local History and Genealogy** (www.mplonline.org/
lhg.htm)   This site covers Pascagoula to Pensacola. The Local
History Collection includes works by local authors, Mobile histories,
periodicals, an extensive clippings file, Mobile newspapers on
microfilm (1819 to the present), city directories back to 1837,
and the federal census records for most of the southeastern
states. A recent addition to the collection is the Mobile Historic
Development Commission's survey of historic architecture in
Mobile with 10,000 images stored and indexed on CD-ROM.

- **Indiana State Library Genealogy Division** (www.in.gov/library/
genealogy.htm)   This site has searchable databases and an online
card catalog.

- **Virginia Memory** (www.virginiamemory.com)   A starting point where you can search Virginia colonial records, as well as Bible records, newspapers, court records, and state documents.

- **Repositories of Primary Sources** (http://uidaho.edu/special-collections/Other.Repositories.html)   This site is a listing of more than 5,000 websites describing holdings of manuscripts, archives, rare books, historical photographs, and other primary sources. Sorted by geographical region, this site is worth a look.

- **South Carolina State Library** (www.statelibrary.sc.gov)   This is the online card catalog for the South Carolina Library, which houses an extensive collection of genealogy holdings. Be sure to look at the pages under the menu choice "S. C. Information" for links to site with obituary records, histories of counties and towns, and libraries across the state.

- **Texas State Library and Archives** (www.tsl.state.tx.us/arc/genfirst .html)   This site lists available resources, including microfilm of the federal census schedules for all states through 1910, selected states from the 1920 and 1930 censuses, printed family and county histories, and a variety of Texas government records.

Maps, Geography, and More

"Where is that township?" is sometimes a hard question to answer. It can be even harder to find a community that no longer exists, or where county or state lines were moved. Searching for "Historical Maps" and the name of the county, state, province, or nation in question may turn up a hit in Google, Yahoo!, or other search sites. An excellent article on this topic can be found at www.joycetice.com/articles/place.htm. It's titled "You Gotta Know the Territory—The Links between Genealogy, Geography and Logic." Some other good sites to help with maps include

- **Deed Platter** (www.genealogytools.net/deeds)   If the deed with your ancestor has the metes and bounds, you can have this site draw a map. Learning to do this can sometimes help you see a connection you didn't see before.

◆ **The Hargrett Rare Book and Manuscript Library**, at the University of Georgia (www.libs.uga.edu/hargrett/maps/index.html)   This library has a collection of more than 800 historic maps spanning five centuries.

◆ **Global Gazetteer Version 2.2** (www.fallingrain.com/world/index.html)   This is a directory of over a quarter-million of the world's cities and towns, sorted by country and linked to a map for each town.

◆ **GEONET Name Server** (www.nima.mil/gns/html)   This site lets you search for foreign geographic feature names, and it responds with latitude and longitude coordinates. For names in the United States and Antarctica, visit the United States Geological Survey (www.usgs.gov) or Geographic Names Information System (www.geonames.usgs.gov) websites. The GNS contains 4 million geographic features with 5.5 million names.

◆ **U. S. Census Bureau Gazetteer** (www.census.gov/geo/www/gazetteer/gazette.html)   This is where you can search by entering the name and state abbreviation (optional), or the five-digit ZIP code.

◆ **A Vision of Britain** (www.visionofbritain.org.uk)   This project started in 1994, creating a major database of Britain's localities as they have changed over time. This website was created by the Great Britain Historical GIS Project (GIS stands for Geographical Information System), based in the Department of Geography of the University of Portsmouth.

◆ **Historical Maps of the United States,** from the University of Texas at Austin (www.lib.utexas.edu/maps/united_states.html) This site has dozens of maps under the headings "Early Inhabitants, Exploration and Settlement," "Territorial Growth, Military History, Later Historical Maps," and "Other Historical Map Sites."

◆ **Old Maps, UK** (www.old-maps.co.uk)   This site lets you search online and order hard copies.

Regional

If you need a regional resource, first go to Google, Yahoo!, Lycos, or another web catalog and search for "`archives`." For example, this search on Google brings you to the catalog page www.google.com/Top/ Reference/Archives, which has more than 100 links for government archives. The following links are good examples of what you can expect to find:

- **Alabama Department of Archives and History Genealogy Page** (www.archives.alabama.gov/research.html#) This is a collection of tutorials for how to search the Alabama Archives for family history, as well as links to various online records. Most state and province archives have something similar.

- **Canadian Heritage Information Network** (www.rcip-chin.gc.ca/ index-eng.jsp) This is a bilingual—French or English—guide to museums, galleries, and other heritage-oriented resources in Canada.

- **European Archival Network** (www.euan.org) This page lists national archive sites by alphabet and region.

- **GENUKI** (www.genuki.org.uk) This site is all about genealogy in the UK and Ireland.

- **Local Ireland: Genealogy** (www.local.ie/Ireland_Genealogy/ index.shtml) This is a portal with message boards, transcribed records, surname origins, and a newsletter.

- **New England Historic Genealogical Society** (www.newenglandancestors.org) This site is designed to be a center for family and local history research in New England. The society owns 200,000 genealogy books and documents. If you're a New England genealogist, you should check it out.

- **Surnames.com** (www.surnames.com) This site discusses general genealogy, with some focus on the Arizona area. It includes a surname search and a map of genealogical organizations in the United States. The site also has a useful beginner's section.

◆ **Utah State Archives** (www.archives.state.ut.us)   Here you can access the research center for the archives' public services. This site includes research, places where questions can be answered, and places where records can be ordered. Not everything here is free, but it's very convenient!

Starting Places

Here are some good places to begin your search for people, places, and pages:

◆ **Distant Cousin** (distantcousin.com)   This site has several online databases, including marriages, military rosters, tombstone transcriptions, and ships' passenger lists, which you can search for free, as well as a large human-edited directory of genealogical websites, organized by surname, ethnicity, and geographical location.

◆ **Genealogy Links.Net** (www.genealogylinks.net)   This site includes more than 9,000 links, most of them to online searchable databases, such as ships' passenger lists, church records, cemetery transcriptions, and censuses for England, Scotland, Wales, Ireland, Europe, United States, Canada, Australia, and New Zealand.

◆ **Genealogy Pages** (www.genealogypages.com)   This site provides a collection of links to free genealogical services, as well as to more than 29,000 online resources.

◆ **Genealogy Spot** (www.genealogyspot.com)   This is a free portal with links to online genealogy resources for beginners and experts alike. Sites featured here are hand-selected by an editorial team for quality, content, and utility.

◆ **GeneaNet** (www.geneanet.org)   Based in France, this is a genealogy database site you can search by name or geographic location. It is not based on GEDCOM, but rather has its own database format. Other resources are available, such as a list of genealogy books, genealogy news briefs, and more. Much of the emphasis is on French history, genealogy, and research, but there are other resources, too.

- **DMOZ Genealogy page** (www.dmoz.org/Society/Genealogy/ Directories) This is part of an edited catalog of the Web, so real people have gathered, verified, and edited the links here.

- **Marston Manor** (http://freepages.genealogy.rootsweb.ancestry.com/ ~dickmarston) This personal genealogy site offers numerous useful items for online genealogists, including a chart for calculating family relationships and a detailed discussion of the terms "proof" and "evidence" as they relate to genealogy.

- **The USGenWeb Project** (www.usgenweb.com) This is a noncommercial project with the goal of providing websites for genealogical research in every county and every state of the United States.

- **Yahoo! Genealogy Page** (http://dir.yahoo.com/Arts/Humanities/ history/Genealogy) A huge collection of links to guides, resources, and personal genealogies on websites. It also includes links to related resources.

Supplies, Books, Forms, and More

There are several good sources of free forms and supplies (see Chapter 1). Check out DearMYRTLE's page (www.dearmyrtle.com/bookshelf/ supplies.htm) for some downloadable ones. The Ancestors series Teacher's Guide has several PDF files of research forms for downloading, too. You can buy supplies from Ancestry.com (see Chapter 19) as well. Here are a few other sites:

- **Global: Everything for the Family Historian** (www.globalgenealogy.com) This is the Global Genealogy Supply website. Shop online for genealogy supplies—maps, forms, software, and so forth—and subscribe to the *Global Gazette*, a free e-mail newsletter covering Canadian genealogy and heritage.

♦ **Family Chronicle** (www.familychronicle.com)   The website for the *Family Chronicle* magazine, which is dedicated to families researching their roots. Check out their offerings and request a free sample of the magazine.

A Closer Look

Although one of the most exciting things about genealogy and web browsing is the joy of discovery, some sites deserve a guided tour. The sites featured here are particularly interesting or useful to online genealogists, and each one has something special to offer. If you want to discover everything yourself, however, you have more than enough information to spend years researching online. Just skip past the rest of this section and be on your way.

ProGenealogists.com

ProGenealogists is a consortium of professional genealogists who specialize in genealogical, forensic, and family history research. A private firm in business for more than 15 years, they have professional genealogists in several countries using a network of over 725 U.S. and international agents.

ProGenealogists is noted for its expert genealogical research and large and scholarly website. One review in *The Internet Scout Report* (funded in part by the Andrew W. Mellon Foundation and the National Science Foundation) stated, "ProGenealogists is an unparalleled resource in genealogical research," and "a fantastic starting point for anyone interested in conducting genealogical research." ProGenealogists's website was listed as one of the "Top Places to Start your Research," by *Internet Genealogy Magazine's* Janice Nickerson. The firm has worked as researchers for Ancestry.com, PBS's Ancestors Series, *African American Lives*, the BBC's *TimeWatch series*' episode entitled "The Iron Coffin," and Showtime's production *The Tudors*.

Many of their researchers belong to organizations such as the Utah Genealogical Association, the Association of Professional Genealogists, the National Genealogical Society, and the Utah Better Business Bureau. Several of the researchers are lecturers, instructors, and well-known authors.

"Our researchers seek truth in contemporary and historical records and we've a reputation for finding it!" the website says.

The site includes pages called "The Genealogy Sleuth." One is for the United States and one is for international genealogy. These are a mini-version of the idea behind Cyndi's List (see the next section) where links are grouped and categorized by topic for genealogists. The difference is that this list is highly selective, marked if a link is a for-fee site or if the ProGenealogists company can search and return results to you for a fee. Other sources and resources include a citation guide, free forms, and a free queries section.

Cyndi's List

Cyndi Howell's list of genealogy links is on everyone's list of top-five genealogy places on the World Wide Web. With more than 180,000 links, sorted into over 150 categories, it is the best place to start looking for genealogy sites. The links are categorized, alphabetized, and searchable, and the list has links to sites large and small, from national archives to personal genealogies.

The main index, available from the home page, lists each category in alphabetical order—from "Acadian, Cajun and Creole" to "Writing Your Family History." The topical index (www.cyndislist.com/topical .htm) rearranges those topics into about a dozen different groupings. The "no frills" index (www.cyndislist.com/ nofrills.htm) has every single category page, with no icons for the newest or latest update.

The main index page also has the FAQs about Cyndi's List, as in how she collects, verifies, and updates the links, and how to submit a link for her consideration. You will also find the newest links, sorted by month, and Cyndi's speaking schedule on the main page.

Cyndi's List is indispensable for finding pages on genealogy.

DearMYRTLE

For the beginning-to-intermediate genealogist, there's no better spot than DearMYRTLE's Place at www.dearmyrtle.com. DearMYRTLE has helped hundreds of genealogists with her daily columns, weekly chats, newsletters, and online courses. Her site will help you learn and grow as a genealogist. The first page of DearMYRTLE's site presents her list of favorite things to do on the Internet for family history.

The choices range from listening to her Internet radio talk show to her "step-by-step" guides.

Her "Best of the Internet for Genealogists" is a frequently updated list of helpful sites, especially for beginners. The Bookshelf is a collection of guided tours on genealogy. DearMYRTLE has book reviews, and the Events page is her schedule of speeches, workshops, and message boards hosted by RootsWeb and Ancestry, and you can subscribe to get her daily genealogy column delivered to your e-mail inbox.

Bookmark DearMYRTLE's site. You'll be coming back often!

Wrapping Up

◆ Thousands of websites exist to help with genealogy.

◆ Some of the most useful websites are collections of links to other sites, such as Cyndi's List and RootsWeb.

◆ A number of websites are more specific, with genealogies submitted from users (for example, GenServ).

◆ Several websites have data such as land records, family Bible entries, and transcribed census data (for example, AfriGeneas, The Library of Virginia, and the Bureau of Land Management).

◆ Other pages have good information on how to proceed with your research (for example, DearMYRTLE and the Adoptee Search Resource page).

Part **IV**

Appendixes

Appendix A

Genealogical Standards and Guidelines from the National Genealogical Society

These Genealogical Standards and Guidelines are recommended by the National Genealogical Society for the benefit of those who wish to improve their skills and performance in genealogical pursuits. NGS is neither an accrediting nor an enforcement agency and does not determine whether its recommendations are being followed in any particular case. These recommendations serve their purpose when an individual decides that the Standards and Guidelines have been applied appropriately in a matter of personal interest. NGS welcomes links to its Standards and Guidelines on other websites or their reproduction by others, as permitted by the copyright notice. However, such support from others does not assure that their websites or works conform to the recommended Standards or Guidelines.

Standards for Sound Genealogical Research

Recommended by the National Genealogical Society
   Remembering always that they are engaged in a quest for truth, family history researchers consistently:

♦ Record the source for each item of information they collect

♦ Test every hypothesis or theory against credible evidence, and reject those that are not supported by the evidence

♦ Seek original records, or reproduced images of them when there is reasonable assurance they have not been altered, as the basis for their research conclusions

♦ Use compilations, communications, and published works, whether paper or electronic, primarily for their value as guides to locating the original records, or as contributions to the critical analysis of the evidence discussed in them

♦ State something as a fact only when it is supported by convincing evidence, and identify the evidence when communicating the fact to others

- Limit with words like "probable" or "possible" any statement that is based on less than convincing evidence, and state the reasons for concluding that it is probable or possible

- Avoid misleading other researchers by either intentionally or carelessly distributing or publishing inaccurate information

- State carefully and honestly the results of their own research, and acknowledge all use of other researchers' work

- Recognize the collegial nature of genealogical research by making their work available to others through publication, or by placing copies in appropriate libraries or repositories, and by welcoming critical comment

- Consider with open minds new evidence or the comments of others on their work and the conclusions they have reached

© 1997, 2002 by National Genealogical Society. Permission is granted to copy or publish this material provided it is reproduced in its entirety, including this notice.

Guidelines for Using Records Repositories and Libraries

Recommended by the National Genealogical Society

Recognizing that how they use unique original records and fragile publications will affect other users, both current and future, family history researchers habitually:

- Are courteous to research facility personnel and other researchers, and respect the staff's other daily tasks, not expecting the records custodian to listen to their family histories nor provide constant or immediate attention

- Dress appropriately, converse with others in a low voice, and supervise children appropriately

- Do their homework in advance, know what is available and what they need, and avoid ever asking for "everything" on their ancestors

- Use only designated workspace areas and equipment, like readers and computers intended for patron use, respect off-limits areas, and ask for assistance if needed

- Treat original records at all times with great respect and work with only a few records at a time, recognizing that they are irreplaceable and that each user must help preserve them for future use

- Treat books with care, never forcing their spines, and handle photographs properly, preferably wearing archival gloves

- Never mark, mutilate, rearrange, relocate, or remove from the repository any original, printed, microform, or electronic document or artifact

- Use only procedures prescribed by the repository for noting corrections to any errors or omissions found in published works, never marking the work itself

- Keep note-taking paper or other objects from covering records or books, and avoid placing any pressure upon them, particularly with a pencil or pen

- Use only the method specifically designated for identifying records for duplication, avoiding use of paper clips, adhesive notes, or other means not approved by the facility

- Return volumes and files only to locations designated for that purpose

- Before departure, thank the records custodians for their courtesy in making the materials available

- Follow the rules of the records repository without protest, even if they have changed since a previous visit or differ from those of another facility

Standards for Use of Technology in Genealogical Research

Recommended by the National Genealogical Society

Mindful that computers are tools, genealogists take full responsibility for their work, and therefore they:

- ◆ Learn the capabilities and limits of their equipment and software, and use them only when they are the most appropriate tools for a purpose

- ◆ Do not accept uncritically the ability of software to format, number, import, modify, check, chart, or report their data, and therefore carefully evaluate any resulting product

- ◆ Treat compiled information from online sources or digital databases in the same way as other published sources—useful primarily as a guide to locating original records, but not as evidence for a conclusion or assertion

- ◆ Accept digital images or enhancements of an original record as a satisfactory substitute for the original only when there is reasonable assurance that the image accurately reproduces the unaltered original

- ◆ Cite sources for data obtained online or from digital media with the same care that is appropriate for sources on paper and other traditional media, and enter data into a digital database only when its source can remain associated with it

- ◆ Always cite the sources for information or data posted online or sent to others, naming the author of a digital file as its immediate source, while crediting original sources cited within the file

- ◆ Preserve the integrity of their own databases by evaluating the reliability of downloaded data before incorporating it into their own files

- ◆ Provide, whenever they alter data received in digital form, a description of the change that will accompany the altered data whenever it is shared with others

- Actively oppose the proliferation of error, rumor, and fraud by personally verifying or correcting information, or noting it as unverified, before passing it on to others

- Treat people online as courteously and civilly as they would treat them face-to-face, not separated by networks and anonymity

- Accept that technology has not changed the principles of genealogical research, only some of the procedures

© 2000, 2001, 2002 by National Genealogical Society. Permission is granted to copy or publish this material provided it is reproduced in its entirety, including this notice.

Standards for Sharing Information with Others

Recommended by the National Genealogical Society

Conscious of the fact that sharing information or data with others, whether through speech, documents, or electronic media, is essential to family history research and that it needs continuing support and encouragement, responsible family historians consistently:

- Respect the restrictions on sharing information that arise from the rights of another as an author, originator, or compiler; as a living private person; or as a party to a mutual agreement

- Observe meticulously the legal rights of copyright owners, copying or distributing any part of their works only with their permission, or to the limited extent specifically allowed under the law's "fair use" exceptions

- Identify the sources for all ideas, information, and data from others, and the form in which they were received, recognizing that the unattributed use of another's intellectual work is plagiarism

- Respect the authorship rights of senders of letters, electronic mail, and data files, forwarding or disseminating them further only with the sender's permission

♦ Inform people who provide information about their families as to the ways it may be used, observing any conditions they impose and respecting any reservations they may express regarding the use of particular items

♦ Require some evidence of consent before assuming that living people are agreeable to further sharing of information about themselves

♦ Convey personal identifying information about living people—like age, home address, occupation, or activities—only in ways that those concerned have expressly agreed to

♦ Recognize that legal rights of privacy may limit the extent to which information from publicly available sources may be further used, disseminated, or published

♦ Communicate no information to others that is known to be false, or without making reasonable efforts to determine its truth, particularly information that may be derogatory

♦ Are sensitive to the hurt that revelations of criminal, immoral, bizarre, or irresponsible behavior may bring to family members

Guidelines for Publishing Web Pages on the Internet

Recommended by the National Genealogical Society

Appreciating that publishing information through Internet websites and webpages shares many similarities with print publishing, considerate family historians:

♦ Apply a title identifying both the entire website and the particular group of related pages, similar to a book-and-chapter designation, placing it both at the top of each Web browser window using the < TITLE > HTML tag, and in the body of the document, on the opening home or title page, and on any index pages

- Explain the purposes and objectives of their websites, placing the explanation near the top of the title page or including a link from that page to a special page about the reason for the site

- Display a footer at the bottom of each webpage that contains the website title, page title, author's name, author's contact information, date of last revision, and a copyright statement

- Provide complete contact information, including at a minimum a name and e-mail address, and preferably some means for long-term contact, like a postal address

- Assist visitors by providing on each page navigational links that lead visitors to other important pages on the website or return them to the home page

- Adhere to the NGS "Standards for Sharing Information with Others" regarding copyright, attribution, privacy, and the sharing of sensitive information

- Include unambiguous source citations for the research data provided on the site, and if not complete descriptions, offering full citations upon request

- Label photographic and scanned images within the graphic itself, with fuller explanation if required in text adjacent to the graphic

- Identify transcribed, extracted, or abstracted data as such, and provide appropriate source citations

- Include identifying dates and locations when providing information about specific surnames or individuals

- Respect the rights of others who do not wish information about themselves to be published, referenced, or linked on a website

- Provide website access to all potential visitors by avoiding enhanced technical capabilities that may not be available to all users, remembering that not all computers are created equal

- Avoid using features that distract from the productive use of the website, like ones that reduce legibility, strain the eyes, dazzle the vision, or otherwise detract from the visitor's ability to easily read, study, comprehend, or print the online publication

- Maintain their online publications at frequent intervals, changing the content to keep the information current, the links valid, and the website in good working order

- Preserve and archive for future researchers their online publications and communications that have lasting value, using both electronic and paper duplication

Guidelines for Genealogical Self-Improvement and Growth

Recommended by the National Genealogical Society

Faced with ever-growing expectations for genealogical accuracy and reliability, family historians concerned with improving their abilities will, on a regular basis:

- Study comprehensive texts and narrower-focus articles and recordings covering genealogical methods in general and the historical background and sources available for areas of particular research interest, or to which their research findings have led them

- Interact with other genealogists and historians in person or electronically, mentoring or learning as appropriate to their relative experience levels, and through the shared experience contributing to the genealogical growth of all concerned

- Subscribe to and read regularly at least two genealogical journals that list a number of contributing or consulting editors, or editorial board or committee members, and that require their authors to respond to a critical review of each article before it is published

- Participate in workshops, discussion groups, institutes, conferences, and other structured learning opportunities whenever possible

- Recognize their limitations, undertaking research in new areas or using new technology only after they master any additional knowledge and skill needed, and understand how to apply it to the new subject matter or technology

- Analyze critically at least quarterly the reported research findings of another family historian for whatever lessons may be gleaned through the process

- Join and participate actively in genealogical societies covering countries, localities, and topics where they have research interests, as well as the localities where they reside, increasing the resources available both to themselves and to future researchers

- Review recently published basic texts to renew their understanding of genealogical fundamentals as currently expressed and applied

- Examine and revise their own earlier research in the light of what they have learned through self-improvement activities as a means for applying their newfound knowledge and for improving the quality of their work product

Appendix B

How to Find a
Professional
Genealogist

Most of the fun of genealogy, online and offline, is the solving of puzzles and learning about your family's place in history yourself, but sometimes you hit a brick wall.

You may need a consultant on a specific research problem or help finding a missing relative. Maybe you need a record translated from a foreign language or some handwriting deciphered. Maybe you need an experienced eye to look over what you have and help you develop a plan for what to do next. Maybe you want to surprise your mother with a genealogy for Christmas, or maybe there's just one whole branch of the tree you know you'll never find time for.

All of these are good reasons to use a professional genealogist. Professional genealogists can prove you are a descendant of someone for organizations such as the Daughters of the American Revolution. Professionals can help you with genealogy chores as simple as searching some records you cannot get to online or travel to physically, or they can take what information you have and trace the ancestry as far back as you are willing to pay for.

But hiring a professional genealogist is not as simple as a Google search. Genealogical research is a science requiring skillful analysis and intellectual concentration, as well as years of experience and education.

"I would not discount local history and genealogy experts in the areas where an ancestor once lived, but I find this is a touchy area," advised DearMYRTLE, the genealogy columnist and lecturer. "It is so difficult to evaluate the reliability of research when a person one might hire hasn't been certified or [is not an] accredited genealogist."

So, the solution, she said, is to look for someone certified as a researcher. First, there is the Certified Genealogist (CG) designation from the Board for Certification of Genealogists (www.bcgcertification.org). This organization tests and certifies researchers and teachers (the latter is a Certified Genealogical Lecturer, or CGL). A list of those certified is maintained on the website. The board has a code of ethics and genealogical proof standard that the members must adhere to. Another such certification body is The International Commission for the Accreditation of Professional Genealogists (ICAPGen), which certifies genealogists through comprehensive written and oral examinations.

The ICAPGen website is www.icapgen.org, which offers the following: The agreement between the Accredited Genealogist (AG) professional and ICAPGen outlines the responsibilities of each AG researcher to ICAPGen, to the researcher's clients, and to the genealogical community. Should a dispute or client complaint occur, the agreement outlines the arbitration process. Out of a desire to protect the consumer, ICAPGen tests the competence of genealogists and provides assurance to those who want to hire a professional in the field.

Again, you can find a list of ICAPGen members on the website. The Family History Library of the Church of Jesus Christ of Latter-day Saints (LDS) also has a staff of professional genealogists. The staff will test for AG status by the Genealogical Department of the LDS church. Examinations include specialized areas such as American Indian, Southern, United States, England, and Germany. These genealogists are not necessarily members of the LDS church, nor do they limit themselves to LDS clients. Accredited Genealogists sign an ethics agreement and agree to adhere to a code of conduct; they are required to renew their accreditation every five years. You can get a roster of these by sending a self-addressed stamped envelope (SASE) with the geographic or topical specialization needed to:

Family History Library
35 North West Temple Street
Salt Lake City, UT 84150-1003

Another organization to consult is the Association of Professional Genealogists (APG). Ethical conduct is extremely important to members of this association. Every member of APG signs a code of professional ethics, stating that the professional will:

- Promote a coherent, truthful approach to genealogy, family history, and local history

- Clearly present research results and opinions in a clear, well-organized manner, with accurately cited references

- Advertise services and credentials honestly

- Explain without concealment or misrepresentation all fees, charges, and payment structures

- Abide by agreements regarding project scope, number of hours, and deadlines or reporting schedules

- Refrain from knowingly violating or encouraging others to violate laws and regulations concerning copyright and right to privacy

- Give proper credit to those who supply information and provide assistance

These are good things to ask any professional genealogist to provide. Various certification boards in other countries may be of help, examples of which are included in the following sections.

Australia

Australian Association of Genealogists and Record Agents
P.O. Box 268
Oakleigh, Victoria 3166, Australia

Send five international reply coupons for a roster. Tests and certifications in Australian and New Zealand records.

Canada

Genealogical Institute of the Maritimes
Universite de Moncton, Moncton
New Brunswick, E1A 3E9, Canada

Send SASE (with Canadian postage or two international reply coupons) for a roster. Tests and certifications for specialized research areas in Canada.

England

Association of Genealogists and Researchers in Archives
Hon. Secretary
31 Alexandra Grove
London N12 8HE, England

Send five international reply coupons for a roster. Peers recommend those listed as competent by long experience.

France

Chambre Syndicale des Genealogistes—Heraldistes de France
74, Rue des Saints-Peres
75005 Paris, France

Send five international reply coupons for a roster.

Ireland

Association of Professional Genealogists in Ireland
c/o The Genealogical Office
30 Harlech Crescent
Clonskeagh, Dublin 14

Send two international reply coupons for a roster. Membership is based on independent assessment and experience.

New Zealand

Genealogical Research Institute of New Zealand
P.O. Box 36-107 Moera
Lower Hutt 6330, New Zealand

Send a large envelope and two international reply coupons for a roster. Members sign a code of ethics.

Scotland

Association of Scottish Genealogists and Record Agents
51/3 Mortonhall Road
Edinburgh EH9 2HN, Scotland

Send two international reply coupons for a roster. Members sign a code of practice.

Set Terms

Hiring a genealogist is a bit like hiring a contractor: You must have a clearly defined project and budget in mind before you sign a contract. You need to ask the genealogist for a letter of agreement that lists:

- ♦ The scope of work to be performed

- ♦ How many hours they will work for you, with some provision for time extensions under specified circumstances

- ♦ A schedule of fees for various actions

◆ Definition of what the retainer covers and how it will be applied toward final payment

◆ How you will agree on more research activities after the original work is finished

It is also a good idea to define who holds the copyright to the written research reports. Often, the professional genealogist wants to retain those rights, which means you cannot publish the report without the researcher's permission. If your researcher is a member of the Association of Professional Genealogists and you believe he or she has not worked within the code of ethics, you can file a grievance with the organization. APG will work with you and the professional to mediate the disagreement.

I know several people who ask at genealogy societies and clubs for the names of good professional genealogists before contacting one. Once you find one to talk to, it never hurts to ask for and check references. If the professional is reluctant to provide such a name, use your best judgment in deciding whether you want to hire this person. It's also a good idea to begin with a short, simple assignment, such as a research chore in a city you just cannot travel to. See how quickly and accurately the candidate can work and how important your business is. Then you can judge whether you have the confidence to agree on a larger project.

Most genealogists charge by the hour, but the fees can range from $10 to $95 per hour. An average is $30 to $50 per hour for the professional in the United States. However, you may find a researcher who prefers to charge a flat daily fee, such as $150 to $500 per day for their services. Indeed, several professionals prefer a minimum retainer, (usually $350 to $500) for a research project. This gives the researcher a good block of time and some working capital for transportation, copies, and so on. It also gives the genealogist some time to do a careful and thorough job on your project.

Once you have a specific list of research needs, a list of professional genealogists who meet your criteria in price and expertise, and you have checked their references, you can determine who to hire and sign an agreement. Then you give the researcher the information you have and the fees to begin.

Glossary

A

a.   About (or circa, in Latin), often used in front of uncertain dates.

Accredited Genealogist (AG)   A designation conferred by the Church of Jesus Christ of Latter-day Saints (LDS). In 1964, the Genealogical Department of the Church of Jesus Christ of Latter-day Saints established the accreditation program for genealogists to credential genealogy researchers through comprehensive written and oral examinations that require the use of the highest professional genealogy standards and ethics. In 2000, administration of the program was transferred to an independent testing organization, the International Commission for the Accreditation of Professional Genealogists (ICAPGen).

aggregator (also called feed reader, news reader, RSS reader)   Software or a web application that collects syndicated web content, such as news headlines, blogs, podcasts, and vlogs, in a single location for easy viewing.

ahnentafel   The word means "ancestor table" in German, and the format is more than a century old. The ahnentafel lists all known ancestors of an individual and includes the full name of each ancestor, as well as dates and places of birth, marriage, and death. It organizes this information along a numbering scheme. Any individual's father is twice that individual's number in the table; any individual's mother is twice plus one that individual's number in the table. Therefore, all males in the table are even numbers and all females are odd numbers. If you are #1 in the table, your father is #2 and your mother is #3. Your father's father is #4, your father's mother #5, and so on.

Ancestral File (AF)   A searchable collection of genealogical data submitted to the LDS archives in GEDCOM format to help genealogists coordinate their research.

anonymous File Transfer Protocol (FTP)   The process of connecting to a remote computer, either as an anonymous or guest user, to transfer public files back to your local computer. (*See also* File Transfer Protocol (FTP) and protocol.) Anonymous FTP is usually read-only access; you often cannot contribute files by anonymous FTP.

Atom A syndication format written in eXtensible Markup Language (XML) used for web feeds and as a publishing protocol (APP is the acronym, but it is referred to as "AtomPub" for short) for creating and updating web resources. It is a form of "push" technology that allows the user to retrieve information without the problems of e-mail and web browsing.

B

backbone A set of connections that make up the main channels of communication across a network.

BCG Board for Certification of Genealogists.

blog A "web log," or journal, is a website where someone posts regular articles and information for public use and reading. The articles may contain commentary, descriptions of events, or other material such as graphics or video. "To blog" is to write and maintain such a site.

browser An Internet client for viewing the World Wide Web.

bulletin board A way of referring to online message systems where you must log onto the site or Internet service provider (ISP) to read and post messages. Also called a message board, forum, or discussion board.

C

cadastre A survey, map, or some other public record showing ownership and value of land for tax purposes.

catalog A search page for the Web within an edited list, not the whole Internet.

CG Designates a Certified Genealogist by BCG.

CGI Designates a Certified Genealogical Instructor by BCG.

CGL Designates a Certified Genealogical Lecturer by BCG.

CGRS Designates a Certified Genealogical Record Specialist by BCG.

chat When people type messages to each other across a host or network, live and in real time. On some commercial online services, this is called a conference.

client A program that provides an interface to remote Internet services, such as mail, RSS feeds, Telnet, and so on. In general, the clients act on behalf of a human user (perhaps indirectly).

cloud computing Internet-based development and use of computer technology.

cloud (the) An often used metaphor for the Internet because of how it is shown in computer network diagrams of cloud computing and because it is a way to express the complex infrastructure the Internet conceals.

collateral line A family that is not in your direct line of ancestry but of the same genealogical line. For example, if you are descended from Patrick Henry's sister, his direct descendants are your collateral line.

compression A method of making a file, whether text or code, smaller by various methods. This is so the file will take up less disk space and/or less time to transmit. Sometimes, the compression is completed by the modem; sometimes, the file is stored that way. The various methods to do this go by names (followed by the system that used it), such as PKZIP (DOS), ARC (DOS), tar (UNIX), STUFFIT (Macintosh), and so forth.

D

database A set of information organized for computer storage, search, retrieval, and insertion.

default In computer terms, the "normal" or "basic" settings of a program.

directory 1. A level in a hierarchical filing system. Other directories branch down from the root directory. Also called a "folder." 2. A type of search site where editors choose the websites and services in the catalog instead of a robot collecting them indiscriminately. One example is www.dmoz.org.

domain name   The Internet naming scheme. A computer on the Internet is identified by a series of words, from more specific to more general (left to right), separated by dots: www.microsoft.com is an example. (*See also* IP address.)

domain name server (DNS)   A computer with software to translate a domain name into the corresponding numbers of the IP address. "No DNS entry" from your browser means a name such as www.first.last.org wasn't in the domain name server's list of valid IP addresses.

downloading   To get information from another computer to yours.

E

e-mail   An electronic message, text, or data sent from one computer or person to another computer or person.

F

Family Group Sheet   A one-page collection of facts about one family unit: husband, wife, and children, with birth and death dates and places.

FHC   Family History Center; a branch of the Family History Library in Salt Lake City, found in a local LDS parish.

File Transfer Protocol (FTP)   Enables an Internet user to transfer files electronically between remote computers and the user's computer.

Firefox   A popular web browser. Originally called "Netscape."

firewall   Electronic protection against hackers and other unauthorized access to your files while you're connected to a network or the Internet.

flame   A message or series of messages containing an argument or insults. Not allowed on most systems. If you receive a flame, ignore that message and all other messages from that person in the future.

folksonomy   Categorizing things by common use, social networking, or another informal process.

forum   A set of messages on a subject, usually with a corresponding set of files.

French Revolutionary Calendar   The French Revolutionary Calendar (or Republican Calendar) was introduced in France on November 24, 1793, and abolished on January 1, 1806. It was used again briefly during the Paris Commune in 1871.

G

gateway   Used in different senses (for example, mail gateway, IP gateway) but, most generally, a computer that forwards and routes data between two or more networks of any size or origin. A gateway is never, however, as straightforward as going through a gate. It's more like a labyrinth to get the proper addresses in the proper sequence.

GEDCOM   The standard for computerized genealogical information, which is a combination of tags for data and pointers to related data.

Gregorian calendar   Introduced by Pope Gregory XIII in 1582, adopted by England and the colonies in 1752, by which time it was 11 days behind the solar year, causing an adjustment in September 1752.

H

hacker   Originally, someone who messed about with computer systems to see how much could be accomplished. Most recently, a computer vandal.

hash tag   A form of folksonomy where you use a pound sign (#) before one word to designate the topic of your MMS, tweet, or status entry.

host computer   In the context of networks, a computer that directly provides service to a user. In contrast to a network server, which provides services to a user through an intermediary host computer.

hub   A computer that collects e-mail regionally and distributes it up the next level. It collects the e-mail from that level to distribute it back down the chain.

HyperText Markup Language (HTML)   A coding system to format and link documents on the World Wide Web and intranets.

I

IGI   The International Genealogical Index; a database of names submitted to the LDS Church.

instant message (IM)   A type of text communication that requires users to register with a server. Users build "buddy lists" of others using the same program and are notified when people on their buddy list are available for chat and messages.

Internet protocol (IP)   The Internet-standard protocol that provides a common layer over dissimilar networks, used to move packets among host computers and through gateways, if necessary.

Internet service provider (ISP)   A company that has a continuous, fast, and reliable connection to the Internet and sells subscriptions to the public to use that connection. The connections may use TCP/IP, shell accounts, or other methods.

intranet   A local network set up to look like the World Wide Web, with clients such as browsers, but self-contained and not necessarily connected to the Internet.

IP address   The alpha or numeric address of a computer connected to the Internet. Also called "Internet address." Usually, the format is usersomeplace.domain, but it can also be seen as ###.##.##.##.

J

Julian calendar   The calendar replaced by the Gregorian calendar, which had also fallen behind the solar year.

L

LDS   Accepted abbreviation for the Church of Jesus Christ of Latter-day Saints, also known as the Mormons.

list (Internet)   Also called "mail list" or "mailing list." Listserv lists (or listservers) are electronically transmitted discussions of technical and nontechnical issues. They come to you by electronic mail over the Internet using LISTSERV commands. Participants subscribe via a central service, and lists often have a moderator who supervises the information flow and content.

lurk   To read a list without posting messages yourself. It's sort of like sitting in the corner at a party without introducing yourself, except it's not considered rude online. In fact, in some places, you're expected to lurk until you get the feel of the place.

M

mail list   Same as *list*.

metadata   Data about data. When you add keywords to your webpage, or a hash tag to a post, that is metadata about the page or post.

Microcom Networking Protocol (MNP)   Data compression standard for modems.

MMS   A protocol for sending instant messages to a smart phone; "texting" is the most common synonym.

modem   A device to modulate computer data into sound signals and to demodulate those signals to computer data.

moderator   The person who takes care of a message list, newsgroup, or forum. This person takes out messages that are off topic, chastises flamers, maintains a database of old messages, and handles the mechanics of distributing the messages.

Mozilla   A nickname for Netscape or "Firefox" in its latest form. In the early days, Netscape's mascot was a little dragon-like creature called Mozilla.

N

navigation bar   A set of words and/or images that appears on every page of a website, with links to other sections or pages of the same website.

NEHGS   New England Historic Genealogical Society, founded in 1845. The website is www.newenglandancestors.org. Published quarterly since 1847, *The New England Historical and Genealogical Register* is the oldest and most respected journal of American genealogy.

Network Information Center (NIC)   An NIC provides administrative support, user support, and information services for a network.

NGS   National Genealogical Society, United States.

O

offline   The state of not being connected to a remote host.

online   The state of being connected to a remote host.

OPAC   Acronym for online public access catalog, a term used to describe any type of computerized library catalog.

P

Pedigree Chart   The traditional way to display a genealogy; the familiar "family tree," where one person's ancestors are outlined. Other formats are the fan chart, decadency chart (starts with the ancestor and comes down to the present), and timeline.

Pedigree Resource File (PRF)   Genealogical information submitted by users of FamilySearch.com.

Personal Ancestral File (PAF)   A free genealogy program for use by members of the LDS Church for submittal to the Temple in Salt Lake City.

plat   (v.) To draw a map of a piece of land by the description of a deed. (n.) The map of a piece of land as defined by the deed.

podcast   A media file (sound, perhaps video) that is distributed to users though a "push" system such as syndication (Really Simple Syndication, or RSS) or downloaded from a site. Like "radio," this can mean either the content or the medium. A podcast is played with a program such as Windows Media Player, iTunes, or RealAudio.

Point-to-Point Protocol (PPP)   A type of Internet connection.

Portable Document Format (PDF)   An Adobe-copyrighted format that allows a document to be saved to look a certain way, no matter what computer is used to display it. The computer, however, must use Adobe's Acrobat Reader (a free program) to display the file.

post   (n.) An entry in one's blog ("My post is on the use of Endnote for genealogy.") (v.) To display an entry to one's blog, status line or website. ("He didn't post that yet.")

protocol   A mutually determined set of formats and procedures governing the exchange of information between systems.

push   A communication protocol where the request for a given transaction originates with the creator of content and the user receives it with a special client. (*See also* Atom and RSS.) E-mail is a "pull" technology; RSS readers receive "push."

Q

query   A request for genealogical information. To be effective, it must have at least one name, one date, one geographical location, and your contact information.

R

register style   A format for a genealogy created for the NEHGS publication. It is a narrative style that assigns each ancestor a superscript number representing a generation. The first ancestor (the "primary") is 1, and each descendant of the primary individual is assigned a consecutive number; children are assigned lowercase roman numerals as well as Arabic numbers. The result looks much like an outline, as we were taught to do when learning how to write a research paper.

RSS   Really Simple Syndication is a family of web feed formats used to publish frequently updated content, such as blog entries, news headlines, or podcasts. Atom is a similar format. They allow the user to retrieve content without the problems of spam and pop-ups that often accompany e-mail and web browsing.

S

search engine   A program on the World Wide Web that searches parts of the Internet for text strings. A search engine might search for programs, webpages, or other items. Many claim to cover "the whole Internet," but that's a physical impossibility. Getting more than 40 percent of the Internet is a good luck.

seminar   An educational event highlighting the interaction and exchange of information, typically among a small number of participants. Genealogy seminars (sometimes called workshops) are often held by local organizations.

server   A computer that allows other computers to log on and use its resources. A client program is often used for this. (*See also* client.)

shareware   The try-before-you-buy concept in microcomputer software, where the program is distributed through public domain channels and the author expects to receive compensation after a trial period. Brother's Keeper, for example, is shareware.

signature   A stored text file with your name and some information, such as names you're searching or your mailing address, to be appended to the end of your messages. Your signature should contain only ASCII (text-only) characters, no graphics.

social bookmarking   A way to share, organize, search, and manage bookmarks for website resources.

social networking   A rather redundant term for the interaction of users of services such as Facebook, Twitter, and others where people connect as "friends" or "followers" to share links, thoughts, messages, and files.

Social Security Death Index (SSDI)   A searchable database of records of deaths of Americans with Social Security numbers, if that death was reported to the Social Security Administration. It runs from the 1960s to the present, although a few deaths prior to the 1960s are in it. The records give full name, place and date of death, where the card was issued, and birth date. Many websites have online searches of the SSDI, some with Soundex (see the following definition).

Soundex   An indexing system based on sound, rather than on the spelling of a surname.

spider   A program that gathers information on webpages for a database, usually for a search engine.

T

tag   A notation of keywords to associate with a resource, page, message, tweet, blog post, or status. Often preceded by a pound sign, but not always.

tag cloud   Also called a word cloud, this is a weighted list shown in a visual representation of user-generated tags, or simply the word content of a site. The more often a tag appears in the resource, the larger the word appears in the visual depiction.

tagline   A short, pithy statement tagged on to the end of an e-mail message. Example: "It's only a hobby, only a hobby, only a …" Taglines are rarely seen on commercial networks, such as AOL, MSN, and CompuServe.

taxonomy   The science of finding, describing, classifying, and naming things, especially organisms, in a hierarchical system.

Telnet   An Internet client that connects to other computers, making yours a virtual terminal of the remote computer. Among other functions, it enables a user to log in to a remote computer from the user's local computer.

terminal server   A computer that connects terminals to a network by providing host Telnet service.

thread (message thread)   A discussion made up of a set of messages in answer to a certain message and to each other. Sometimes, worthwhile threads are saved in a text file, especially on Yahoo! groups.

tiny tafel (TT)   A TT provides a standard way of describing a family database so the information can be scanned visually or by computer. All data fields are of fixed length, with the obvious exceptions of surnames and optional places. Many TTs are extracted from GEDCOMs.

Transmission Control Protocol/Internet Protocol (TCP/IP)
A combined set of protocols that performs the transfer of data between two computers. TCP monitors and ensures correct transfer of data. IP receives the data from TCP, breaks it up into packets, and ships it off to a network within the Internet. TCP/IP is also used as a name for a protocol suite that incorporates these functions and others.

Trojan horse   A type of malicious code. This is usually a program that seems to be useful and harmless. In the background, however, it might be destroying data or breaking security on your system. It differs from a virus in that it rarely propagates itself as a virus does.

U

Universal Serial Bus (USB)   A connection to a computer. Unlike a parallel port (where your printer probably plugs in) or a serial port (where your modem probably plugs in), a USB port enables you to "daisy chain" peripherals. If you have a USB printer, modem, and CD-ROM drive, you could plug only one into the USB port, and the rest connect by USB cables in a chain (in theory, say, computer to modem to printer to CD-ROM). In practice, however, sometimes it's a little tricky to get them in an order that makes all the peripherals happy.

upload   To send a file or message from your computer to another. (*See also* downloading.)

V

virus   A program that installs itself secretly on a computer by attaching itself to another program or e-mail and then duplicates itself when that program is executed or e-mail is opened. Some viruses are harmless, but most of them intend to do damage, such as erasing important files on your system.

vital records   The official records of birth, death, marriage, and other events of a person's life.

vlog   A blog that uses videos for posts instead of text and/or still pictures.

W

web feed (or news feed)   A data format used for providing users with frequently updated content, usually in RSS form.

wiki   Website or other online resource that allows users to add and edit content collectively.

workshop   *See* seminar.

worm   A computer program that makes copies of itself and spreads through connected systems, using up resources in affected computers or causing other damage.

X

XML   eXtensible Markup Language, or XML, is a specification developed by the World Wide Web Consortium (W3C). It is designed especially for web documents. It allows designers to create their own customized tags, enabling the definition, transmission, validation, and interpretation of data between applications and between organizations. Most "push" technology on the Internet is written in XML.

Index

H

N

S